The Court vs. Congress
Prayer, Busing and Abortion

D0076451

The Court vs. Congress

....

Prayer, Busing, and Abortion

Edward Keynes with Randall K. Miller

Duke University Press   Durham and London 1989

For Christine

Contents

....

Acknowledgments

....

As an author, I am indebted to those friends, colleagues, and students who have contributed to this book. Although I cannot acknowledge everyone who has contributed to this book, I would like to thank several individuals whose advice and assistance were indispensable. I am grateful to my colleague Robert S. Friedman for his encouragement, careful reading, and thoughtful criticism of the manuscript. I am indebted to my friend Robert S. Kish, M.D., who took time from his practice to read and criticize chapter 9 from a physician's perspective.

I am particularly grateful to my friend and former student Randall K. Miller, who participated as a colleague in every phase of this book's development. Randall Miller is the author of chapter 8, "School Desegregation and Court-Ordered Busing," which he first wrote as a senior honor's thesis. He also participated in the research, preparation of the manuscript, and copyediting of the book. Four other students—Alan P. Garubba, Kenneth MacKunis, Warren R. Mowery, and David L. Tubbs—contributed to the research and completion of the manuscript, for which they deserve recognition. A fifth student, Richard M. Kerns, prepared the index.

I thank my colleagues Diane Garner, Head of the Documents and Maps Section, Helen Sheehy, Diane H. Smith, and Jack Sulzer, in the Documents Section, and Ruth Senior, in the Interlibrary Loan Department, of the Pennsylvania State University Libraries, for their professional assistance and patience in completing the research for this book. Dr. John Kaminski, Director of the Archive of the Documentary History of the Ratification of the Constitution at the University of Wisconsin, deserves special recognition for his generous assistance in researching the Ratifiers' views on the federal judiciary. Dr. Kaminski provided access to the archive, assisted in locating and verifying documents, and gave permission to publish materials from the archive. The University of Wisconsin also merits recognition for creating and supporting the archive, which is a treasure to constitutional scholars.

My two computer genies, Mrs. Barbara A. Ayala and Ms. Melanie S. Romig, performed feats of wizardry in producing the manuscript for publication. Claire A. and Glen D. Kreider, in the Center for Computing Assistance, College of the Liberal Arts, also provided invaluable assistance in preparing the manuscript. I am also indebted to my colleagues Trond Gilberg, Chairman, Department of Political Science, and Joseph W. Michels, Associate Dean for Research and Graduate Studies, College of the Liberal Arts, for their support in providing the time and resources necessary to complete this book. Finally, I thank my editor, Mr. Richard C. Rowson, Director of Duke University Press, for his advice and assistance in shepherding this book to publication. Of course, I assume responsibility for any errors that appear in this book.

Edward Keynes
University Park, Pennsylvania
June 1989

Introduction

....

Although this book addresses the Supreme Court's power of judicial review in a constitutional democracy, its primary concern is the authority of Congress to curb the federal courts' jurisdiction. If the federal judiciary's constitutional judgments about the rights of individuals vis-à-vis the states and the national government are "mistaken," does Congress have plenary power to curb the Supreme Court's appellate jurisdiction and the lower federal courts' jurisdiction to decide specific constitutional questions? Aside from amending the Constitution, can the people's elected representatives reverse the Court's decisions in cases that involve fundamental rights? If Congress disagrees with the Supreme Court's decisions banning prayer from the nation's public schools, requiring school busing to end de jure racial segregation in public education, and limiting the states' power to interfere with a woman's decision to have an abortion, can the nation's lawmakers with a simple majority vote simply strip the federal courts' jurisdiction to decide future prayer, busing, and abortion controversies?

Since 1954 academicians, jurists, and members of Congress have debated the scope of authority under the Judiciary Article's ordain and establish and exceptions and regulations clauses (Article III, sections 1 and 2), as well as under the enforcement clause (section 5) of the Fourteenth Amendment, for Congress to curb the Supreme Court's constitutional decision making and reverse its judgments. Senators and representatives have introduced numerous bills to restrict the federal courts' jurisdiction and remedial powers as well as constitutional amendments and substantive proposals to reverse the Supreme Court's judgments in cases involving state and national loyalty-security programs, the investigatory powers of Congress and the states, desegregation of the

public schools, the rights of criminal defendants, congressional districting and state legislative reapportionment, and, more recently, school
prayer, school busing, and state antiabortion laws. These jurisdiction-
stripping proposals imply that Congress has plenary power over the
federal courts' jurisdiction.

Even in cases involving fundamental rights, the Court's critics argue,
Congress can close the federal courthouse door to persons seeking to
vindicate their rights in the district courts, the courts of appeals, and
the Supreme Court. If Congress enacts legislation depriving the federal
courts of jurisdiction over school prayer, school busing, and state abortion cases, aggrieved individuals would have no recourse beyond their
own states' courts. Regardless of whether state judges will be less
hospitable to the protection of fundamental liberties than their brethren
on the federal bench, does the Constitution authorize Congress to
selectively deny individuals access to a federal forum in which they
can vindicate their rights?

The thesis of this book is that, despite the Judiciary Article's "plain
language," neither the Framers nor Ratifiers of the Constitution empowered Congress to undermine the Supreme Court's authority to enforce constitutional supremacy, provide a uniform interpretation of
national law, and protect the individual's fundamental liberties under
the guise of regulating the federal courts' jurisdiction. The Framers
implicitly granted the Court authority to enforce constitutional supremacy over the states under the supremacy clause of Article VI. By
conferring this power on the Supreme Court, the Framers and Ratifiers
corrected a basic defect of the Articles of Confederation, which failed
to provide for national supremacy and a final constitutional arbiter.

Ever since Congress enacted the Judiciary Act of 1789, it has assured
individuals access to some federal forum in which they could vindicate
their constitutional rights against state and national infringement. Congress has never completely closed the federal courts to persons who
allege that the states or national government have diminished their
constitutional rights. In fact, since 1875 Congress has greatly expanded
the federal courts' jurisdiction. Congressional policy regarding the federal courts' jurisdiction over constitutional claims is not merely a matter of legislative grace. Congress has acknowledged the Framers' and
Ratifiers' intent to grant the Supreme Court an important constitutional role in maintaining constitutional supremacy, providing a uniform interpretation of national law, and protecting the individual's
fundamental rights. Even in the tumultuous years following the Civil
War, Congress did not completely abolish the Supreme Court's habeas

corpus jurisdiction, although a seditious southern newspaper editor's petition for the Great Writ threatened the entire congressional program of military reconstruction.

Contrary to conventional interpretations of Supreme Court and lower federal court decisions, the federal judiciary has never clearly recognized congressional power to abolish its jurisdiction to entertain and decide cases involving constitutional claims. Many of the so-called 'precedents' involve statutory rather than constitutional questions. In other cases, the precedents are really dicta, nonbinding statements that go beyond the *ratio decidendi*, or point of decision. These opinions demonstrate judicial deference toward congressional authority over the federal courts, but they do not acknowledge plenary legislative power to gerrymander the Supreme Court's appellate jurisdiction. Indeed, several decisions suggest that in cases involving constitutional rights, Congress lacks authority to deny individuals access to some federal forum. However, the Supreme Court has never authoritatively determined the scope of congressional power to abolish federal jurisdiction selectively, that is, regarding particular constitutional rights.

Congressional attempts to curb the federal courts' jurisdiction over school prayer, school busing, and state antiabortion cases indicate that the remedial objective, that is, the purpose and primary effect of such legislation, is to burden the vindication of judicially determined constitutional rights. The language, legislative histories, and juxtaposition of jurisdiction-stripping proposals to constitutional amendments and substantive legislation demonstrate that jurisdictional restrictions are designed to reverse or limit the effect of the Supreme Court's decisions in *Engel* v. *Vitale* (1962)[1] and *Abington* v. *Schempp* (1963),[2] the school prayer cases; *Swann* v. *Charlotte-Mecklenburg* (1971),[3] the school busing case; and *Roe* v. *Wade* (1973)[4] and *Doe* v. *Bolton* (1973),[5] the abortion cases. Unable to secure the necessary two-thirds majority to propose a constitutional amendment, various senators and representatives who oppose these Supreme Court decisions have attempted to limit the federal courts' jurisdiction over future prayer, busing, and abortion controversies. However, jurisdictional gerrymandering is a constitutionally questionable methodology that alters the Framers' plan of government, undermines the Supreme Court's status as a coequal partner in the national political system, changes the relationship between the states and the national government, burdens the individual's judicially protected constitutional rights, and circumvents the constitutional-amendment process.

Not since *Brown* v. *Board of Education* (1954)[6] have the Supreme

Court's decisions generated such intense and widespread opposition as the school prayer, school busing, and abortion cases. The Court's decisions in the reapportionment, loyalty-security, and defendant's rights cases angered state politicians and members of Congress, but they did not engender the prolonged and acrimonious public controversy that the prayer, busing, and abortion cases have provoked. *Engel*, *Abington*, *Swann*, *Roe*, and *Doe* have instigated a national debate over the Supreme Court's authority to decide fundamental social questions that face the nation. Although the prayer, busing, and abortion cases present questions of fundamental constitutional rights, both the public and politicians perceive the Court's decisions as interfering with policy choices, which, in a representative democracy, Congress and the states have constitutional authority to decide. There is a widely held belief that the Supreme Court has exceeded its constitutional function, that it has interfered in the "politics of the people," and that it has created new, extraconstitutional rights reflecting little more than the justices' own social, moral, and philosophical values.

Since the Court has usurped legislative power, the critics continue, Congress can legitimately curb the federal judiciary's authority and prevent the federal courts from deciding political controversies that should be resolved through the democratic process. When the Supreme Court acts as the nation's school board or its national medical board, it is evaluating evidence, making decisions, and determining values that are beyond judicial expertise and competence. Some critics argue that the Court is interfering with functions that the Constitution explicitly assigns to Congress and the states. Therefore, the Supreme Court's intrusion into the democratic process justifies extraordinary measures to curb its jurisdiction and remedial powers in order to restrain the judiciary and preserve democratic self-government, which is the core value of the U.S. Constitution.

However, in the United States, the nation's fundamental law places certain values beyond the reach of ordinary majorities. In the U.S. constitutional system, the Supreme Court has the unique function of protecting fundamental, constitutional liberties against the onslaughts of temporary and, at times, impassioned legislative and popular majorities. Periodically, opposition to the Court's decisions may undermine its legitimacy, authority, and power to enforce the rights of unpopular individuals and minorities. If the Supreme Court is "wrong," it deserves the intelligent criticism of jurists, scholars, and public officials. Such criticism is essential to maintaining a healthy and robust dialogue among Congress, the Court, and the American people, a dialogue that promotes the articulation and continuing evolution of constitutional values.

If the Supreme Court's decisions are "wrong," there are opportunities to correct its "mistaken" constitutional judgments. Amending the Constitution, appointing new justices to fill vacancies on the High Bench, and, in rare instances, impeaching and removing errant justices are legitimate checks on a Court that has lost its reason, perverted traditional American values, or lost touch with the people's consensus on basic national problems. Despite intense popular and congressional dissatisfaction with the Court's decisions, constitutional shortcuts that threaten the Framers' plan of government, alter the basic structures of federalism and the separation of powers, or vitiate the individual's fundamental rights compromise constitutional government. Constitutional government or the rule of law requires that the people's representatives act according to the prescribed methodology in changing the basic charter when they disagree with the Supreme Court's constitutional judgments.

This book addresses constitutional limitations on congressional power by examining the scope of legislative authority to restrict the Supreme Court's appellate jurisdiction and the lower federal courts' jurisdiction and remedial powers in cases that present constitutional claims. First, the book examines the major theoretical justifications for congressional power over the federal courts' jurisdiction. Second, it explores the Framers' and Ratifiers' perceptions of legislative power over the courts in relation to the role they anticipated that the federal judiciary would play vis-à-vis Congress and the states. Third, it describes and analyzes the Supreme Court's views on the scope and limits of congressional power over the federal judiciary's jurisdiction. Fourth, it traces the history of congressional legislation regulating the federal courts' jurisdiction and examines congressional perceptions of legislative power to curb federal jurisdiction. Finally, the book analyzes recent attempts to limit the Supreme Court's appellate jurisdiction and the lower federal courts' jurisdiction and remedial powers in the school prayer, school busing, and antiabortion cases.

Chapter one asserts that Congress has broad but limited power over the federal courts' jurisdiction. Despite the "plain language" of the Judiciary Article's ordain and establish and exceptions and regulations clauses, neither the ambiguous language of Article III nor the basic constitutional framework of government suggests that Congress has plenary power to restrict the Supreme Court's appellate jurisdiction and thereby undermine the Court's performance of its constitutional functions. This chapter also rejects the argument that Congress has an affirmative duty to vest the entire federal jurisdiction in some federal forum. However, Congress does not have authority to withdraw jurisdiction selectively in a way that burdens the vindication of specific constitutional rights.

Chapter two contends that the Framers intended the national judiciary to enforce constitutional supremacy in relation to Congress, the president, and the states. Despite their failure to provide specifically for judicial review, the Framers' acceptance of the concept pervades the language and framing of the Judiciary Article and the supremacy clause of Article VI. Therefore, any explanation of the ordain and establish and exceptions and regulations clauses must account for the judiciary's function of judicial review within a framework of federalism, balanced government, and the separation of powers. While the plenary view of legislative power would give Congress authority to interfere with the courts' performance of their constitutional functions, the mandatory view would leave Congress virtually powerless to regulate federal jurisdiction. Indeed, the Framers specifically rejected a proposal giving Congress plenary power over federal jurisdiction.

Chapter three argues that, although some Anti-Federalists feared that the federal judiciary would become a dynamo of national power, others anticipated that the federal courts would limit the national government's exercise of power vis-à-vis the states and would protect the individual's liberties. The Federalists anticipated that the Supreme Court and the lower federal courts would enforce constitutional supremacy over the states and provide a uniform interpretation of national law. In the ratification debates on federal jurisdiction and the scope of congressional authority to regulate the Supreme Court's appellate jurisdiction, only a few Ratifiers conceded plenary legislative power to prevent the federal courts from deciding cases involving constitutional claims.

Chapters four and five contend that the Supreme Court has never ruled authoritatively on the question of congressional power to limit its appellate jurisdiction and to prevent the High Court from deciding cases concerning constitutionally protected rights. However, both chapters concede congressional authority to abolish the federal courts' jurisdiction in cases that involve statutory questions. The Supreme Court's decisions imply that various constitutional provisions, including the supremacy clause, the habeas corpus provision, the prohibition on bills of attainder, and the Bill of Rights impose constitutional limitations on the exercise of congressional power under Article III, sections 1 and 2 (the ordain and establish and exceptions and regulations clauses).

Chapter six demonstrates that Congress has never denied access to the Supreme Court to petitioners who seek to appeal the adverse decisions of state courts in cases raising federal constitutional claims. Despite congressional ire with specific judicial decisions, Congress has expanded rather than contracted the jurisdiction of the federal courts. Unlike contemporary attempts to restrict federal jurisdiction in cases that present specific constitutional claims, until the 1950s Congress imposed limits on the federal courts' jurisdiction over statutory questions. Congress has often expressed irritation with the Supreme Court's decisions, but has exercised restraint regarding the federal courts' jurisdiction and remedial powers. Congress has acknowledged the Supreme Court's pivotal role in promoting constitutional supremacy, national authority, and protecting the individual's constitutional rights.

Chapters seven, eight, and nine examine the Supreme Court's definition, under the due process and equal protection clauses of the Fourteenth Amendment and the due process clause of the Fifth Amendment, of the rights to be free from an establishment of religion, de jure segregation in the public schools, and governmental interference with a woman's right to privacy in choosing abortion over childbirth. These chapters conclude that, despite legitimate arguments with the Supreme Court's rationales and decisions in prayer, busing, and abortion cases, Congress cannot employ its authority under Article III or the enforcement clause (section 5) of the Fourteenth Amendment to burden the individual's rights to due process and equal protection. Chapters seven through nine conclude that Congress lacks power to reverse or limit the effect of the Supreme Court's prayer, busing, and abortion decisions through jurisdictional restrictions or other statutory measures that circumvent the constitutional-amendment process.

In a constitutional system that limits the exercise of governmental power, the rule of law also requires that the people's representatives adhere to the fundamental charter of government whether or not it favors their immediate interests and objectives. In his play "A Man For All Seasons," Robert Bolt expressed this idea eloquently in an exchange between Sir Thomas More and Will Roper:

Roper: So now you'd give the Devil benefit of law!
More: Yes. What would you do? Cut a great road through the law to get after the Devil?

Roper: I'd cut down every law in England to do that!

More: Oh? And when the last law was down, and the Devil turned round on you—where would you hide, Roper, the laws all being flat? This country's planted thick with laws from coast to coast—man's laws, not God's—and if you cut them down—and you're just the man to do it—d'you really think you could stand upright in the winds that would blow then? Yes, I'd give the Devil benefit of law, for my own safety's sake.[7]

By taking a shortcut, proponents of jurisdictional gerrymandering eventually will discover that others can employ the same constitutionally questionable methods to burden rights they deem fundamental.

Commenting on Goethe's
Faust, Dr. Julius Goebel wrote:
"Like all the really great
productions of literature this
world-poem possesses the magic
power of appealing in a different
way to every new generation;
and like the fathomless crystal
lake of the high Sierras it reflects
only the picture of the be-
holder."—Dr. Julius Goebel,
Faust, at vi.

Congress, the Courts, and Federal Jurisdiction: Theoretical Perspectives

....

Congressional Power To Limit Federal Jurisdiction

Since 1955 members of Congress have introduced numerous bills to curb the federal courts' jurisdiction over selected areas of judicial decision making. Piqued by the Supreme Court's decisions on state and federal loyalty-security programs, public school segregation, defendants' rights and the administration of criminal justice, congressional districting, state legislative reapportionment, school busing as a tool of desegregation, prayer in the nation's public schools, and state antiabortion laws, the Court's congressional opponents have attempted to limit federal-court jurisdiction in these areas.[1] Although there are many differences among the hundreds of bills that have been introduced, essentially they all leave the future definition and protection of federal constitutional rights or interests to the solicitude of the states' courts.

Sometimes referred to as court curbing, jurisdiction stripping, or jurisdictional gerrymandering, proposed limitations on federal jurisdiction reflect substantial congressional and, perhaps, public dissatisfaction with the Warren and Burger courts' definition and protection of the individual's rights against state and federal interference.[2] Jurisdictional limitations also have constitutional consequences that reach beyond dissatisfaction with particular judicial decisions. Attempts to curb federal jurisdiction raise serious questions about congressional authority over the federal courts, the legitimate scope of judicial review in a democracy, and the Supreme Court's role as an arbiter of congressional, presidential, and state power within an institutional framework of federalism and the separation of powers.[3]

In their attempts to curb "extraconstitutional" judicial policy making, the Court's congressional foes have zeroed in on the Court's controversial decisions on school prayer, *Engel* v. *Vitale* (1961)[4] and *Abington* v. *Schempp* (1963);[5] school busing, *Swann* v. *Charlotte-Mecklenburg* (1971);[6] and state antiabortion laws, *Roe* v. *Wade* (1973).[7] At times intense, the struggle over prayer, busing, and abortion reflects the fact that once again the Supreme Court is at the center of the political storm. This struggle raises basic questions about congressional authority to limit the Supreme Court's appellate jurisdiction as well as the lower federal courts' jurisdiction.[8] A seemingly dry and technical subject, the debate engenders passionate discourse over congressional power on questions such as the Framers' and Ratifiers' original understanding of the Court's relationship to Congress. It is a high stakes debate about the Supreme Court's future role as a constitutional policymaker in a society that is theoretically committed to political democracy (popular sovereignty, majority rule, and responsible and responsive government) as well as a debate about constitutional limitations on the exercise of governmental power vis-à-vis individuals and minorities.[9]

This perennial but unresolved debate includes at least three major positions on the scope of congressional authority to regulate and limit federal jurisdiction. The conventional view is that under Article III of the Constitution, congressional power to regulate federal jurisdiction is plenary.[10] A second argument, the mandatory view, often associated with Justice Joseph Story, is that Article III imposes an affirmative duty on Congress to vest the entire constitutional jurisdiction in some federal court.[11] A third view of more recent parentage is that, while Article III may impose few or no restrictions on Congress, other constitutional limitations external to Article III do impose specific limits on the exercise of congressional power over federal jurisdiction.[12]

According to the plenary view, the language of the exceptions and regulations clause (Article III, section 2) imposes no limit on congressional power to regulate and make exceptions to the Supreme Court's appellate jurisdiction. Similarly, under the ordain and establish clause (Article III, section 1), Congress has plenary power to create and abolish lower federal courts and to define and limit their jurisdiction. These two clauses are legitimate checks on judicial usurpation of congressional and state legislative authority.[13] Therefore, Congress can leave the final determination of federal constitutional questions to the states' courts without recourse to the federal judiciary. There may be a right to judicial process, but there is no guarantee of a federal forum in which individuals can vindicate their constitutional claims. Furthermore, under the supremacy clause (Article VI, section 2), state courts have an obligation to enforce the individual's rights against infringements by the states and the national government.[14]

As the mandatory view implies, Article III imposes a constitutional obligation on Congress to create federal courts and to vest the maximum constitutional jurisdiction in the federal judiciary. The exceptions and regulations clause merely grants Congress authority to distribute federal jurisdiction between the Supreme Court and inferior federal courts. It is neither a grant of power to restrict access to the federal courts nor a legitimate check on the exercise of judicial power. If the federal judiciary is to act as a coequal partner to Congress and the president, its jurisdiction must extend to the limits of Article III and must be coterminous with the legislative power of Congress.[15] Otherwise, Congress and the president could shield themselves from constitutional scrutiny and emasculate the federal judiciary's power of judicial review. From the mandatory perspective, Article III simply confers on Congress housekeeping power to promote the efficiency and effectiveness of the federal judiciary.[16]

In response to recent attempts to curb federal jurisdiction on a selective basis, some scholars argue that congressional power under Article III may be broad, but it is not unlimited. Taken in context, the language of Article III does not warrant a complete closure of the federal courts to litigants presenting constitutional claims. Indeed, various constitutional provisions, including the supremacy clause (Article VI, section 2), the habeas corpus clause (Article I, section 9, clause 2), and the due process clause of the Fifth Amendment establish a right to a hearing before a federal judge on a constitutional claim.[17] Access to a federal forum is necessary to promote the rule of law, a uniform construction of fundamental national rights, and federal constitutional supremacy. Inasmuch as state courts are state instrumentalities, they cannot provide a fair and neutral forum to persons who allege state violations of constitutional rights.[18]

Each of these three views embodies different assumptions about the language and logic of Article III, the basic plan of government in the United States, the Framers' and Ratifiers' intentions, the relationship between Congress and the federal courts, and the relationship between the federal and state judiciaries and governments. Each view leads to different consequences for the Supreme Court's authority to define and protect constitutional rights and liberties. Each view incorporates subtle and complex arguments that require explanation and analysis before an informed reader can pass judgment on the adequacy and consequences of accepting a particular perspective. Each embodies a different vision of the nation's constitutional future as well as its constitutional heritage.

The Plenary View of Congressional Power

Proponents of the plenary view argue that the language of Article III is clear and unambiguous. Article III provides that:

> The judicial power of the United States, shall be vested in one Supreme Court, and in such inferior courts as the Congress may from time to time ordain and establish. (section 1)
>
> In all cases affecting ambassadors, other public ministers and consuls, and those in which a State shall be a party, the Supreme Court shall have original jurisdiction. In all other cases before mentioned, the Supreme Court shall have appellate jurisdiction, both as to law and fact, with such exceptions, and under such regulations as the Congress shall make. (section 2, clause 2)[19]

Except for the Supreme Court's original jurisdiction, which the Constitution mandates, its appellate jurisdiction is subject to congressional discretion. Unless Congress enacts jurisdictional legislation, the Supreme Court cannot exercise its appellate jurisdiction. Once Congress has acted, as John Marshall observed, the Court cannot exercise jurisdiction that Congress has not specifically conferred. As Chief Justice Salmon Chase noted in *Ex parte McCardle*, Congress can withdraw subjects from the Court's appellate jurisdiction, even in a pending case.[20] Article III establishes the maximum appellate jurisdiction that Congress can confer, but it does not require Congress to grant any portion of that jurisdiction to the Supreme Court. Not unlike the Biblical potter, Congress shapes the vessel in which the Supreme Court exercises its judicial power.

Similarly, Article III authorizes but does not mandate Congress to create a lower federal judiciary. If Congress has the power to create federal tribunals to exercise the judicial power of the United States, it can abolish such courts. The power to create courts also comprehends the lesser power to regulate and restrict their jurisdiction.[21] In fact, until the Judiciary Act of 1875, Congress severely restricted the lower courts' jurisdiction over federal questions. The state courts determined most federal questions with limited appeal to the U.S. Supreme Court.[22]

"Nominally," Eugene Rostow once wrote, "the courts exist on sufferance. . . . They are taught to believe they should be 'lions under the throne,' in Coke's phrase."[23]

The plenary view is consistent with democratic theory, which emphasizes the primacy of congressional policy making and presidential discretion in the faithful execution of the law. Unlike the federal judiciary, whose members are appointed with lifetime tenure, Congress and the president are responsible to the people through regular and periodic elections. Despite such nondemocratic features as the electoral college, the equal representation of the states in the U.S. Senate, and legislative rules and organization that sometimes tend toward oligarchy, Congress and the president are representative institutions.[24] Therefore, when scrutinizing the constitutionality of congressional legislation and presidential conduct, the federal judiciary should act with humility and self-restraint toward the people's representatives. Only when Congress has made a clear mistake about the scope and limits of legislative authority should the courts intervene.[25]

The plenary view is also consistent with the basic plan of government, which provides for the separation of powers and balanced government (checks and balances). By vesting legislative, executive, and judicial power in three separate national institutions, the Framers and Ratifiers created separate but overlapping zones of authority. While the Supreme Court sometimes polices the boundaries between Congress and the president, the separation of powers strongly suggests that the judiciary should not interfere in those areas of national decision making constitutionally (i.e., textually) committed to another branch of government.[26] Not only is such intervention imprudent and probably ineffective, it violates the separation-of-powers doctrine. Accordingly, each branch of the national government should avoid impairing the ability of other branches to perform their essential or core functions. The federal judiciary should only intervene when there is resolute conflict between the legislature and the executive that threatens the balance or harmony of the national government.[27]

Should the federal courts stray too far from their constitutional function, proponents of plenary congressional power continue, the Framers equipped Congress with a check on judicial policy making. The Framers intended the exceptions and regulations clause and the ordain and establish clause of Article III as democratic checks on judicial usurpation of legislative and executive power. In other words, these clauses are the price for judicial review in a democratic polity.[28] As an empirical observation, several scholars note that when the federal courts stray too far from popular or governmental consensus, Congress employs its plenary power over federal jurisdiction to discipline the judiciary and to mold future judicial decision making in accordance with popular preferences.[29] According to Judge J. Skelly Wright, "if the Justices are not themselves sufficiently attuned to the times, Congress can bring reality home through its power over the Court's appellate jurisdiction."[30]

Another variant of this argument involves the interpretivist-noninterpretivist controversy that continues to rage in the nation's law journals. Interpretivists contend that the judiciary is bound by the Framers' and Ratifiers' original intent or understanding of the Constitution and its amendments, insofar as their intent is manifest in or can be inferred from the Constitution's language, framing, and ratification and contemporaneous debates. In deciding constitutional questions, the judiciary may fill in the "interstices" of the basic law, but cannot substitute its own or contemporary values for those of the Framers and Ratifiers.[31] If due process means the process due in judicial proceedings, the Warren Court is no more justified in embodying its own substantive values of equality and individual freedom and autonomy than the Fuller Court was in discovering substantive property rights in the Fifth and Fourteenth amendments. When the Court amends the Constitution in derogation of the regular amendment process (Article V), Congress has the authority and responsibility to remind the federal courts of their judicial function. Although Michael Perry favors noninterpretivist review in human rights cases, he concedes that one cannot reconcile noninterpretivist judicial review with the democratic principle of "electorally accountable policymaking."[32]

By incorporating the Bill of Rights into the due process clause of the Fourteenth Amendment and adopting a broad construction of equal protection that the Framers never intended, interpretivists continue, the Supreme Court has trenched on powers reserved for the states under the Tenth Amendment.[33] In defining due process and equal protection to include the rights to be free from prayer and racial segregation in public schools and to privacy in deciding whether to seek and obtain an abortion, the Court has arrogated powers that the amendment's Framers conferred on Congress.[34] As a remedy to judicial aggrandizement, some of the Court's critics suggest that Congress employ its powers under Article III and section 5 of the Fourteenth Amendment to restore the authority of the states and their judiciaries to define the individual's constitutional rights. The substantive effects of this proposal notwithstanding, Congress rather than the Supreme Court would become the primary arbiter of American federalism.[35]

In its pure form, the plenary view of Article III, sections 1 and 2, would have fundamental consequences for the basic plan of government. Congress could use its authority to emasculate the federal courts' power of judicial review. By eradicating federal jurisdiction over constitutional rights, Congress could upset the delicate balance of power between the legislative and judicial branches. If Congress were to employ this technique on a wide range of constitutional issues, it could impair the separation of powers, which the Framers apparently believed essential in maintaining limited, constitutional government.[36] Moreover, from the Framers' perspective, the maintenance of equilibrium is essential in preserving political liberty against government tyranny.

Of course, one can argue that the federal courts are also capable of threatening the individual's liberties. However, Congress and the president have ample disciplinary powers over the federal judiciary, including the power to nominate, confirm, and appoint federal judges, impeach and remove judges, revise legislation to circumvent constitutional infirmities and disfavored statutory constructions, and amend the Constitution to correct the courts' mistaken views. Given the difficulties of constructing congressional majorities, the Supreme Court sometimes frustrates majority rule, as in the child labor case (*Hammer* v. *Dagenhart*).[37] Nevertheless, the American political system represents a careful balance between democratic norms and constitutional limitations on majoritarian impulses. Rather than existing as an aberrant institution, the federal courts are an essential element in a liberal democracy. Even if due process does not guarantee access to a federal court in order to vindicate constitutional claims, legislation that alters or threatens the delicate balance of governmental power is constitutionally suspect.[38]

Such legislation also could fundamentally alter the federal system. In addition to making the states final arbiters of federally protected rights, such proposals would undermine the Supreme Court's authority to enforce the supremacy clause of Article VI and police the boundaries between state and national power.[39] While Jesse Choper argues that Congress, as a popular institution, is better suited to arbitrate national-state relationships,[40] the states' interests are already well represented in Congress. The federal courts provide another forum in which state, national, and individual interests can be balanced and adjusted, somewhat removed from the daily clash of partisan and parochial forces.

Oliver Wendell Holmes, who discounted the importance of judicial review of congressional acts, recognized the profound effects of losing federal judicial power to review the constitutionality of state acts.[41]

Despite Holmes's and Choper's deference to Congress in policing the federal system, there remains considerable conflict over the scope of legislative and judicial power to delineate the constitutional boundaries between the nation and its states. Whether the controversy concerns the application of the Bill of Rights to the states; the substantive meaning of equal protection, due process, and the privileges and immunities of national citizenship; or the scope of interstate commerce, the question is whether Congress or the Supreme Court should determine the degree of diversity or uniformity that is permissible and desirable in the American federal system. Attempts to curb or expand federal jurisdiction make transparent the nexus between federalism and the separation of powers.[42]

The Mandatory Obligation To Create a Federal Court System

Proponents of the mandatory view argue that the language of Article III is clear and unambiguous. Article III begins, "The judicial power of the United States, shall be vested in one Supreme Court, and in such inferior courts as the Congress may from time to time ordain and establish." Taken in its natural, eighteenth-century sense, the vesting clause's "shall" is an imperative rather than a permissive construction. The argument is strengthened by comparing the vesting clause with the permissive, conditional, or contingent "may" in the same sentence conferring power on Congress to create lower federal courts. As Story observed in *Martin* v. *Hunter's Lessee* (1816), the parallel construction of all three vesting clauses in articles I, II, and III strengthens the mandatory view.[43] The mandatory language of the vesting clause, as Story and subsequent commentators emphasize, suggests that the Framers intended to create a national judiciary coequal to Congress and the president, with authority to enforce national constitutional supremacy against state and national abuses of power.[44]

Admittedly, the exceptions and regulations clause confers some power on Congress, but it does not permit the legislature to destroy the basic structure of government or vitiate the Framers' remedial purpose. According to Story, Chancellor Kent, William Crosskey, and such recent commentators as Leland Beck, Robert Clinton, and Wilfred Caron, the Framers intended to establish a national judiciary with power to assure the national government's supremacy over the states in those areas of national policy making conferred on the new government.[45] In the field of external sovereignty, for example, the Framers recognized the indispensability of national courts to assure the states' compliance with treaty obligations and abstention from the conduct of diplomatic and military policy. Within the spheres of authority that the Constitution vests in the national government, the mandatory language of Article III as well as the language of Article VI ensures that the federal courts will play an essential, coequal role in enforcing national supremacy and in providing a uniform construction of national law.[46]

If the mandatory construction does not render the exceptions and regulations clause meaningless or superfluous, what is its function in the context of Article III? Here, the parsimonious language of the Judiciary Article requires proponents of the mandatory view to examine its recesses with Talmudical skill and to explore the debates of the Federal Convention, the records of the state ratifying conventions, and other contemporaneous sources. Several possible explanations emerge from these excursions. First, the clause merely distributes subjects between the Supreme Court's original and appellate jurisdiction. Second, the clause clarifies congressional power to distribute cases between the Court's appellate jurisdiction and the lower federal courts' jurisdiction. Third, inasmuch as the Supreme Court's original jurisdiction is not entirely exclusive, Congress has the power to assign some cases concurrently to the inferior federal courts. None of these views pose serious problems to the argument that Congress must confer all of the judicial power of Article III on some federal court.[47]

A fourth position is that the exceptions and regulations clause permits Congress to assign federal jurisdiction either concurrently or exclusively to the states' judiciaries. If jurisdiction is concurrent, with appeal on a writ of error to the U.S. Supreme Court, both national constitutional supremacy and a uniform rule of national law remain intact. However, if Congress assigns exclusive jurisdiction over federal constitutional questions to the states' judiciaries, such a statute would imperil constitutional supremacy, a national rule of law, and the Framers' plan for a federal government. Article III does not oblige Congress to create inferior tribunals; however, if Congress assigns their jurisdiction to the states' courts, it must provide a mode of appeal to the Supreme Court. Similarly, if Congress removes cases from the Court's appellate jurisdiction, it must provide some inferior tribunal to hear constitutional claims in order to preserve a measure of federal supremacy. In sum, the basic equilibrium of the federal system requires the existence of some federal forum for the resolution of constitutional claims.[48]

Even more arcane than the previous explanations is the argument that some Framers were concerned that the federal courts could use their judicial power to revise the decisions of local juries in civil and criminal cases that involve federal questions. Some Framers and Ratifiers feared that federal judges would act like Star Chamber jurists, striking down juries' findings and thereby undermining both democratic government and the citizen's ancient rights and liberties.[49] Other Framers, notably James Wilson, who was instrumental in drafting the Judiciary Article, were suspicious of local juries' decisions in admiralty and maritime cases.[50] Unable to reconcile their differences on the scope of federal judicial review of juries' findings in cases raising federal questions, the Framers granted Congress the power to make exceptions as to both law and fact, which, despite the plain language of this clause, does not confer legislative power to divest federal courts of their jurisdiction selectively over constitutional questions.[51]

The mandatory view is anchored in the belief that the federal judiciary, especially the Supreme Court, performs essential functions for the American political system. In a constitutional government that incorporates both liberal and democratic values, the Court functions as a legitimate restraint on popular majorities that threaten unpopular causes, individuals, and minorities. Removed from the political thicket, armed with legal expertise, and committed to stare decisis, the Supreme Court is a more appropriate forum than Congress to enforce constitutional norms, limitations, and boundaries. A constitutional system that fragments power through federalism and the separation of powers requires a final judicial arbiter in the event that the political process falters and fails to resolve basic conflict.[52] When democracy fails, an impartial judiciary stands ready to enforce the rules of the political game and restore equilibrium to the political system, a herculean task for the least dangerous branch of government.

Critics of the mandatory view argue that without authority to limit federal jurisdiction, there is little effective check on an imperial judiciary. The federal courts have become the most dangerous, rather than the least dangerous, branch of government. Casting aside the Framers' and Ratifiers' manifest purpose, the federal judiciary has created new rights and remedies that have little or no textual foundation.[53] *Roe* v. *Wade*[54] exemplifies judicial legerdemain, a sleight of hand unsupported by the text or legislative history of the Fourteenth Amendment. Even more damning, the Supreme Court cannot reasonably infer the right to an abortion from the amendment's due process clause. Wholly without warrant, the Court has invaded areas of public policy making conferred on Congress, the president, and the states.[55]

Although the Grim Reaper ultimately purges the federal courts of errant judges and justices, in the interim the courts continue to frustrate legislative majorities and the popular will. Ironically, congressional inertia, legislative organization, and institutional deference to the judiciary impede efforts to circumvent the Supreme Court's adventuresome policy making. The extraordinary majorities that the constitutional amendment process requires frustrates efforts to surmount judicial invasion of the national government's discretionary authority and the states' sovereignty.[56] However, if the national political process were genuinely democratic, it should not impede efforts to translate popular preferences into public policy. Yet if the Supreme Court's decisions frustrate intense national majorities, there is little danger that its policies will secure the voluntary compliance necessary to enforce judicial decisions. Indeed, the quest for judicial supremacy may lead to judicial impotence.[57] The fact that neither has occurred is a testimony to both congressional and judicial caution concerning the regulation and exercise of federal jurisdiction.

Congressional Power as Broad but Limited

If both the plenary and mandatory views of congressional power over federal jurisdiction stress the textual clarity of Article III, the broad but limited approach emphasizes the Judiciary Article's ambiguity. Relying on the article's parsimony, contemporary scholars have begun a search for intrinsic as well as extrinsic constitutional limitations. Advocates of this third approach are attempting to accommodate judicial review and democracy within an institutional framework of the separation of powers and federalism. Since the broad view incorporates elements of both the plenary and mandatory approaches, the terrain may seem familiar. But the development of a workable, coherent accommodation of judicial power to protect constitutional interests and congressional power over federal jurisdiction requires a carefully drawn road map through a war zone that has been sown with land mines for more than three decades.

As the language of the Constitution and the records of the Federal Convention and state ratifying conventions reveal, the Framers and Ratifiers paid less attention to the federal judiciary than to Congress, the presidency, and the national government's relationship to the states. Indeed, their discussions of the new federal judiciary focused on the relationship between the state and national courts. While the federal judiciary's critics harbored suspicions that these courts would swallow up the existing state courts, the advocates of national judicial power emphasized that the federal courts would not endanger the states' sovereignty. The Anti-Federalists perceived the federal courts as an instrument of national sovereignty and a potential source of tyranny over the states and the people.[58] The Federalists countered by arguing that the new courts would have little power to enforce their decisions and that most judicial business would remain with the state courts.[59]

The parsimonious language of Article III left many of these disputes unresolved. The Judiciary Article is shorter than either the legislative or executive articles. Its scant 369 words provide a general sketch for an unprecedented federal judiciary rather than a detailed blueprint for a federal court system. In drafting the Judiciary Article as well as other constitutional provisions conferring power on the national government, the Framers were more interested in stating broad principles of government than in drafting a prolix legal code.[60] They were practical men who left much for the future clash of political forces to resolve. Unable or unwilling to resolve their conflicts, the Framers employed deliberate ambiguity to patch over differences of interest and principle. As Gouverneur Morris, a member of the Committee of Style, remarked in 1814, "it became necessary to select phrases which, expressing my own notions, would not alarm others."[61]

Although Article III contains no specific language restricting congressional power over federal jurisdiction, as Telford Taylor writes, conceding plenary power simply defies the Framers' logic in creating a balanced, tripartite system of government. Echoing Henry Hart's dialectical exercise, Taylor stresses that Congress cannot employ the exceptions and regulations clause to swallow entirely the Supreme Court's power of judicial review. Logically, any exception to the Court's appellate jurisdiction cannot wipe out a power that the Constitution vests directly. At least, in all cases arising under the Constitution, Congress must leave some residue of federal jurisdiction.[62]

Not unlike Leonard Ratner and Theodore Eisenberg, Taylor concludes that Congress cannot invade the Court's essential role or function.[63] Nevertheless, Taylor and other proponents of an essential-functions test fail to answer satisfactorily several fundamental questions. What are the Supreme Court's essential functions? Who defines the Court's essential functions: the Framers and Ratifiers, Congress, the Supreme Court, or a bevy of scholarly oracles? Despite the difficulty of answering these questions, Taylor is correct in observing that it makes little sense to create a Supreme Court, imply powers of judicial review, and then, through the exceptions and regulations clause, give Congress the power to destroy the institution and alter the basic structure of government.

The real issue is the scope of judicial review. If there is virtually no limit on congressional authority to curb jurisdiction, the scope of judicial review is potentially rather restricted and subject to legislative whim. Conversely, if the Supreme Court's appellate jurisdiction is inherent and self-executing, there are few limits to the Court's reach, save the justices' sense of self-restraint and the constitutional amendment process. In attempting to reconcile judicial review and popular government, advocates of broad but limited legislative power once again turn to exegetical analysis of the language, grammar, and punctuation of Article III.

Resurrecting the law/fact distinction as a means of preserving the right to trial by jury in civil and criminal cases, Henry Merry asserts that the "exceptions" provision applies only to questions of fact, which would authorize Congress to limit federal judicial power to revise juries' verdicts. The "regulations" provision applies to questions of law and fact, giving Congress the power to regulate the mode of appeal, but not the power to deny appeals on federal constitutional questions.[64] Admittedly, eighteenth-century rules of punctuation were not as clear or fixed as later nineteenth-century rules. The Framers sometimes used a dash rather than a period to denote a full stop. Their placement of commas in sentences was not always consistent. Thus a twentieth-century rendering of Article III, section 2, might read as follows:

> In all the other cases before mentioned, the Supreme Court shall have appellate jurisdiction as to law, under such regulations, and as to fact, with such exceptions and under such regulations, as the Congress shall make.

If the Framers' punctuation of the Constitution reflected rhetorical concerns (i.e., the public reading of an important state paper to a mass audience), rather than precision and regularity, the previous reconstruction becomes plausible. But there is little warrant for imposing twentieth-century rules of construction on an eighteenth-century document. Moreover, the very lack of regularity in punctuation renders such an enterprise highly debatable.

Since the language and drafting of Article III do not lay to rest competing claims of legislative and judicial competence, does subsequent judicial and congressional construction answer the conundrum? Proponents of the broad but limited approach deny that later judicial decisions and congressional legislation resolve the debate. Despite the fact that the Judiciary Act of 1789 leaves most judicial business to state courts, section 25 clearly provides for appeal by a writ of error from the decisions of state courts that would jeopardize federal constitutional supremacy.[65] Section 25 fulfills the promise of Article VI, section 2, of the Constitution, the supremacy clause, which corrected a major defect in the Articles of Confederation. The first Judiciary Act recognizes the necessity for access to the Supreme Court to protect the structure of federalism and provide a uniform national construction of some constitutional questions.[66] While limiting access to the lower federal courts on federal questions, Congress has assured access to a federal forum since 1789 to protect the basic plan of government. Is this merely a matter of congressional grace and wisdom or a necessary concomitant of constitutional integrity?

Even though Congress has not vested the full jurisdiction of Article III in the lower federal courts, is congressional silence equivalent to selective divestment of federal jurisdiction to the state courts? Critics of the plenary-powers school argue that one cannot equate inaction with affirmative action to withdraw jurisdiction selectively on questions of constitutional right. Failure to provide jurisdiction (inaction) is motivated by legitimate concerns of federalism, consideration of state authority, the smooth interaction of state and federal courts, and the effective and efficient operation of the federal judiciary. Selective withdrawal of jurisdiction singles out and attempts to burden the vindication of specific constitutional rights. Of course, one must assume that the states' courts will be less hospitable to those rights than the federal judiciary.[67]

Whatever assumptions one makes, prior to the 1950s members of Congress rarely attempted to use the exceptions and regulations clause as an instrument of judicial discipline, despite extreme pique toward the Supreme Court and the federal judiciary.[68] Although proponents of jurisdictional limitations cite the Norris-La Guardia Act (1932), the Johnson Act (1934), the Tax Injunction Act (1937), the Emergency Price Control Act (1942), and the Portal-to-Portal Act (1947) as legitimate exercises of congressional power (under the ordain and establish and exceptions and regulations clauses), these measures did not completely close the federal courts to litigants seeking to vindicate a constitutional right.[69] These acts either limited the remedies available, regulated the mode of appeal or, as in the Portal-to-Portal Act, denied federal and state courts jurisdiction over statutorily defined rights. If the Portal-to-Portal Act had involved a question of constitutional right, the Second Circuit Court of Appeals intimated in *Battaglia* v. *General Motors Corp.* (1948), the act would have been constitutionally suspect.[70]

Although the Supreme Court has been deferential toward Congress, the Court has never clearly acknowledged plenary power to selectively divest all federal jurisdiction on a constitutional issue (under the exceptions and regulations clause). In some cases the issue was one of statutory, not constitutional, right. In other cases the issue was the mode or timing of judicial review; that is, a regulation of, rather than an exception to, federal jurisdiction. In *United States* v. *Klein* (1872), the Court indicated that Congress cannot exercise its power under the exceptions and regulations clause as a means to an unconstitutional end. In *Klein*, the Court rejected a jurisdictional limitation that interfered with judicial power to enforce presidential pardons.[71] Therefore, critics of plenary power stress, there is no binding precedent on the power of Congress to bolt the federal courthouse door to litigants raising a federal constitutional question. The Court's pronouncements on this issue are dicta, without binding effect.[72]

The one glaring exception, answer advocates of plenary power, is the Supreme Court's decision in *Ex parte McCardle* (1869),[73] a post–Civil War case brought by a southern newspaper editor who had been tried for seditious libel by a military commission. After a circuit court had denied McCardle's petition for a writ of habeas corpus under the Habeas Corpus Act of 1867, on March 27, 1868, Congress repealed the previous measure, which had been enacted to protect freed slaves from their former masters. The conventional interpretation of *McCardle* is that the Court recognized the plenary power of Congress to withdraw jurisdiction, even in a case pending before the High Court. Chief Justice Chase's opinion for the Court certainly provides evidence for the plenary view.[74] Nevertheless, the repeal of the Habeas Corpus Act of 1867, which applied to persons in a state's custody, did not repeal the habeas corpus provision, section 14, of the Judiciary Act of 1789, which applies to persons in federal custody.[75] Thus McCardle still had access to a federal court under the act of 1789 since he was a prisoner in federal military custody.[76]

Speaking for the Court on October 25, 1869, in *Ex parte Yerger*, Chief Justice Chase acknowledged that the act of 1868 had not repealed the habeas corpus provision of the act of 1789.[77] In a clear reference to *McCardle*, Chase implied but did not state unequivocally that, since the habeas corpus jurisdiction is derived directly from the Constitution,

Congress could not limit access to the Great Writ, except in conformity with the provisions of Article I, section 9,[78] which states, "The privilege of the writ of habeas corpus shall not be suspended, unless when in cases of rebellion or invasion the public safety may require it."[79] By the time the Court decided *McCardle* and *Yerger*, the rebellion had ended. In any event, the act of 1867 did not completely eradicate the Supreme Court's appellate jurisdiction in habeas corpus cases. It merely changed the mode of appeal from the lower courts, which implies that Congress may regulate but not eliminate access to the federal judiciary on a question of fundamental constitutional right. The Great Writ is so fundamental to human liberty, as Chase recognized, that attempts to limit access to the writ of habeas corpus require careful judicial scrutiny.

The Search for External Limits on Congressional Power

Neither the language, framing, and ratification of the Constitution nor subsequent judicial and legislative history have disposed of the continuing controversy over congressional power to limit federal jurisdiction. Since Henry Hart's seminal article appeared in the *Harvard Law Review* (1953), two fundamental approaches have developed in an attempt to reconcile congressional power and judicial review (i.e., popular government and constitutional limitations on the exercise of governmental power). Alluded to earlier, the functional and structural approaches deserve more systematic treatment, explanation, evaluation, and informed criticism. Neither approach has much or any textual, constitutional basis. Both approaches are derived from inferences based on the Framers' and Ratifiers' basic purposes as well as general theoretical assumptions about constitutional democracy. The "essential-functions" approach assumes that Congress cannot employ its jurisdictional power to destroy the courts' core powers. In a constitutional democracy, the courts must have judicial power to protect the rule of law, fundamental constitutional rights of individuals, and the rights of insular minorities. The "structural" approach emphasizes the federal judiciary's role in maintaining the basic structure of government, that is, the distribution of power among the branches of the national government as well as equilibrium between the nation and the states.[80] While these two approaches differ somewhat, both emphasize the basic values that each scholar believes indispensable to the American constitutional system.

The Essential Functions of the Federal Courts

Elaborating on Henry Hart's dialectical exercise, Leonard Ratner and Theodore Eisenberg argue that the exceptions and regulations clause cannot be understood in isolation. Because its meaning is less than transparent, this clause can be understood only within the context of Article III and the Framers' plan for the federal judiciary, a perfectly sensible rule of constitutional interpretation.[81] Thus Ratner notes that only those exceptions and regulations consistent with the judiciary's essential functions are permissible.[82] Relying on the *Records of the Federal Convention*,[83] Ratner infers that congressional power may be broad, but it is not plenary. Congress can restrain but not negate the Court's judicial powers. Congress can promote the Supreme Court's efficiency, but cannot vitiate its power to act as a final judicial arbiter, without whose guidance the lower federal and state judiciaries would be lost at sea on federal constitutional questions.[84]

Eisenberg goes even further than Ratner, asserting that Madison's compromise, giving Congress the power to create lower federal courts and define their jurisdiction, is not central to the Framers' plan for the federal judiciary. The Framers intended the federal judiciary, with the Supreme Court at its apex, to function as a check on congressional and presidential power. They also intended the federal judiciary to promote uniformity of decision, to assure national supremacy, to implement national law, to provide a neutral forum for out-of-state and foreign suitors, and to preserve the citizens' constitutional rights against popular oppression. In 1787, the lower courts were not indispensable to the Supreme Court's performance of these essential functions. Therefore, the Framers left their creation to congressional discretion. Given the small volume of judicial business, the Supreme Court had ample time to review the constitutional decisions of the states' courts of last resort.[85]

Today, however, the lower federal courts have become indispensable to the High Court's effective operation inasmuch as the volume of judicial business has grown exponentially, albeit as a result of congressional expansion of federal jurisdiction. If Congress were to abolish the lower federal courts or curtail their jurisdiction, there would be no effective way to screen the Supreme Court's case load, articulate and apply its decisions, and ensure the enforcement of federally protected rights. Attempts to curb the lower courts' jurisdiction in ways that would impair the Supreme Court's performance of its core functions, according to Eisenberg, are at war with the Framers' plan for the federal judiciary.[86] If the federal courts go beyond their judicial function, invading congressional, presidential, or the states' authority, then legislative restrictions become permissible restraints on judicial excess. Undoubtedly, the definition of each institution's essential functions is indispensable to Ratner's and Eisenberg's theses. However, since jurists cannot agree on the scope and boundaries of judicial, legislative, and executive power, they cannot define the essential functions of each institution with precision.

Undaunted by such difficulties, William Crosskey wrote in 1953 that the Framers' basic purpose was to create a national judiciary that would establish justice. Since the 1760s, Crosskey states, American lawyers have attempted to promote "a great judicial reform," which included establishing " 'a supreme court of appeal and equity'."[87] Confronted with inchoate diversity, Crosskey notes, the architects of the Judiciary Article sought to create a great national court with the essential function of establishing a uniform rule of law on questions of national concern. Absent a national court with jurisdiction over questions of constitutional right, the rule of law—the uniform application of constitutional principle—cannot exist. If Congress limits the Supreme Court's appellate jurisdiction, it must expand the lower federal courts' jurisdiction in order to provide access to a neutral forum capable of rendering uniform and impartial justice. Access to a federal forum on questions of constitutional right, Crosskey might conclude, is a constitutional norm, if not explicitly provided in Article III or elsewhere in the text.

The text to the contrary notwithstanding, fundamental fairness and protection of the individual's constitutional rights are the principal concerns of a federal judiciary rather than of Congress, the president, or the states. In cases of state deprivations of national right, Crosskey and advocates of the essential-functions test assume that the states' judiciaries are either unable or unwilling to shield individuals and minorities against state and local deprivations. In cases of national threats to individual freedom and minority rights, the states' courts lack power to issue a writ of habeas corpus for the release of persons in federal custody or otherwise restrain federal officials from abridging an individual's constitutional rights.[88] The protection of national rights of individuals and minorities, as Charles Black also suggests, is primarily a national function. Black concludes that the vindication of national rights "is the highest function of any government."[89]

To promote individual and minority rights, the Framers and Ratifiers of the original Constitution and the Bill of Rights recognized the need to limit majority rule. Since popular majorities influence government through presidential and congressional elections, the representative process cannot safeguard unpopular individuals, minorities, and causes. The judicial function, Ratner concludes, is to enforce constitutional limitations on transient and hostile majorities. Legislation restricting federal jurisdiction or denying access to effective remedies, in cases that raise questions of constitutional right, impairs the federal judiciary's essential function.[90] The argument is plausible if one assumes that only the federal courts can protect individuals and minorities from an intense and determined majority's wrath. However, the Supreme Court's decisions in the Japanese curfew and detention cases, *Hirabayshi* v. *United States* (1943)[91] and *Korematsu* v. *United States* (1944),[92] raise serious doubts about the Court's ability to withstand intense popular pressure and racial bigotry, particularly in times of emergency.

As the essential-functions test implies, if there is a federal constitutional right, there is a concomitant guarantee of a federal forum. Although the supremacy clause obliges state judges to enforce constitutional norms, Robert Sedler notes, Article III does not confer the judicial power of the United States on the states' judiciaries. Nor do most state judges have the same constitutional protections of life tenure and guaranteed compensation that shield the federal judiciary and promote judicial neutrality and independence.[93] Without assuming that state judges are craven figures or, even worse, political hacks, "[i]t is too much to expect wholly impartial justice," writes Osmond Fraenkel, "when one state official sits in judgment on another."[94] Only a federal court can provide a neutral forum to challenge alleged state deprivations of constitutional rights.

Considerations of federalism aside, those who claim that access to a federal forum is indispensable to protecting constitutional rights assume that Congress is attempting to shield its legislative acts from federal courts that are hostile to congressional policy, or that jurisdictional restrictions invite the states to ignore the Supreme Court's decisions on issues such as school prayer, school busing, and abortion. As several critics of court-curbing legislation write, proponents of judicial gerrymandering intend to give the states a knowing, "illicit" wink.[95] They are indicating that the states can ignore the Supreme Court's decisions with impunity. In fact, congressional proponents of selective divestment may have all or none of these motives, but scholars have an obligation to document their charges before concluding that the legislative intent is illicit. The normal assumption is, or should be, that Congress and the states have acted with reasonable intent.

The Federal Courts and the Structure
of Government

Structuralists argue that neither Congress nor the Supreme Court can legally alter the basic structure of government. The Constitution does not authorize either branch to change the balance of power between the national government and the states or upset the equilibrium among Congress, the president, and the federal judiciary.[96] By inference, the vesting clauses of the first three articles prohibit each branch of the national government from interfering with one another's powers and institutional integrity. The nation's preconstitutional history, the framing and ratification of the Constitution, and virtually every constitutional provision presume the states' existence and continuing structural integrity. One of the Framers' and Ratifiers' basic purposes was to prevent each institution from changing the basic structure of government, except according to the process of constitutional amendment (in Article V).[97]

Structuralists presume that Congress and the president will exercise self-restraint before trenching on one another's powers, since there is no provision for an ultimate arbiter to police the boundaries. Structuralism is similar to the departmental theory of constitutional interpretation that Thomas Jefferson articulated and that Pennsylvania Supreme Court Justice Gibson elaborated in *Eakin* v. *Raub* (1825),[98] a response to John Marshall's case for judicial review in *Marbury* v. *Madison* (1803).[99] In the performance of its constitutional functions, Gibson reasoned, each branch is the ultimate arbiter of the scope and boundaries of its own constitutional authority.[100] In the absence of a final constitutional arbiter, both structuralism and the departmental theory of constitutional review are little more than appeals for mutual restraint and adherence to the principle of comity. In a system of federalism and the separation of powers, however, there is a need for a final constitutional arbiter when mutual courtesy and civility fail to resolve institutional conflict.[101] Of course, when mutual restraint gives way to resolute conflict there is probably little that the Supreme Court can do to avoid systemic crisis. The trick is to reconcile conflicts before they become resolute. But structuralism simply fails to answer the metaquestion of who shall decide who is to determine the scope and boundaries of institutional authority.

Extrinsic, Constitutional Limits on
Congressional Power

Neither structuralism nor any of the preceding theories based on interpretations of Article III adequately define the scope of congressional power to limit federal jurisdiction. Therefore, some contemporary scholars have turned to other constitutional provisions, so-called external restraints, in a search for limits on legislative power.[102] What limits, if any, do other constitutional provisions impose on congressional power to curb the Supreme Court's appellate jurisdiction and the lower federal courts' jurisdiction? If Congress were to enact a Bill of Attainder, establish a national church, deny trial by jury in U.S. criminal cases, or deny a person the right to vote on the basis of race, such statutes would clearly violate specific constitutional prohibitions. These are easy cases that hardly merit debate. However, Daan Braveman, Lea Brilmayer, Ronald Rotunda, and Lawrence Sager, among others, assert that Congress cannot use its jurisdictional powers to effectively deprive parties of their constitutional rights.[103] What Congress cannot do directly, it also cannot do indirectly, no matter how clever the subterfuge. Referring to the lower federal courts' jurisdiction, Rotunda notes:

> Although article III does give Congress power to affect the jurisdiction of the lower federal courts, other provisions of the Constitution limit the reach of that power. Specifically, Congress may not exercise its article III power over the jurisdiction of the courts in order to deprive a party of a right created by the Constitution. For example, since the equal protection aspect of the due process clause of the fifth amendment guarantees equal access to the courts, Congress could not enact a statute totally denying original or appellate jurisdiction over actions brought by members of a particular racial group.[104]

Jurisdictional statutes based on race, nationality, gender, and other personal characteristics would be highly suspect classifications having little, if any, relation to a compelling or even a permissible governmental interest.[105]

Thus far, Rotunda's argument poses no insurmountable problems. However, he continues, "a survey of congressional limitations on the jurisdiction of the lower federal courts indicates that the Supreme Court has never upheld a statutory infringement of constitutional rights under the guise of a jurisdictional statute."[106] Although Rotunda's argument applies to the lower federal courts, it can be applied with equal vigor to the Supreme Court. However, are classifications based on categories of "rights" equivalent to those based on individual characteristics?[107] One branch of equal-protection analysis, according to William Van Alstyne, suggests that classifications burdening fundamental rights are highly suspect and can be justified only by a compelling governmental interest. Therefore, Van Alstyne concludes:

> The use by Congress of the exceptions power to single out a class of cases involving fundamental rights, withdrawn from the Supreme Court's appellate jurisdiction only from dissatisfaction with the Court's exercise of its power of substantive constitutional review in respect to such cases, may, ironically, today be subject to fifth amendment challenge.[108]

Despite the attractiveness of Van Alstyne's position, Martin Redish doubts that equal-protection analysis is applicable to categories of rights. While "discrete and insular minorities" have a right to equal treatment, Redish concludes, there is no constitutional guarantee that all rights must have equal access to a federal forum. Congress has discretionary power to determine that some rights should be heard with finality in a state forum, but other rights should be within the Supreme Court's appellate jurisdiction.[109] In other words, Congress has final authority to decide how much uniformity or diversity is permissible in the American constitutional system with regard to fundamental rights.

Redish's criticism of fundamental-rights equal-protection analysis is less persuasive than it initially appears. If a right is fundamental, that is, constitutionally protected, can Congress burden the vindication of that right by transferring the level of decision making from a federal to a state forum?[110] Of course, one must demonstrate that targeting a particular right for differential treatment represents a constitutionally unacceptable burden. In some cases the discriminatory intent may be transparent; in others, an exhaustive examination of a jurisdictional statute's legislative history and effects may reveal a constitutionally unacceptable intent. Even a facially neutral statute may have been enacted under circumstances that reveal a discriminatory purpose.[111]

A careful analysis may also reveal that some proposed jurisdictional measures actually burden a class of persons rather than a category of rights. A statute that excludes state antiabortion laws from federal jurisdiction places a heavy, if not an exclusive, burden on women. A statute restricting jurisdiction over school busing, where the remedy is indispensable to the right to be free from racial segregation in public education, would burden blacks and, potentially, other racial and ethnic minorities.[112] In each case, however, one must prove that the legislative intent, the purpose and effect, is to burden an identifiable class of persons or a category of fundamental rights. Recent developments in equal-protection analysis are worth exploring further in the search for external limits on congressional power over federal jurisdiction.[113]

Constitutional Interpretation and Congressional Power Under Article III

Thus far, the various theories advanced to reconcile congressional power over the federal courts, and judicial authority to protect constitutional interests, fail to accommodate judicial review and democratic government. Some theories are partisan statements; they are briefs for either legislative or judicial supremacy and omniscience. But a fair reading of the Constitution indicates that its Framers and Ratifiers were suspicious of all governmental power. As eighteenth-century liberals, the Constitution's authors apparently believed that by limiting and fragmenting governmental power they could "establish justice, insure domestic tranquility, provide for the common defense, [and] promote the general welfare" without sacrificing "the blessings of liberty."[114] Would they have conferred power on any governmental institution to destroy the integrity of any other institution and to upset the delicate balance essential to liberty?

Although the Framers believed they were writing "the fundamental and paramount law of the nation," as John Marshall observed in *Marbury* v. *Madison*,[115] they drafted many key provisions in broad and ambiguous terms, without providing a Rosetta stone to decipher their meaning.[116] Theories of congressional power over federal jurisdiction that stress the textual clarity of Article III are unlikely to illuminate the subject. In fact, both the plenary and mandatory theories of congressional power have spawned endless debate. Nevertheless, in a system of limited constitutional government, neither jurists nor scholars are free to ignore the Framers' and Ratifiers' intent insofar as it is discernible.

A nation committed to limited government and the rule of law is bound to observe its constitution's commands. By its very terms (Article VI, section 2), the U.S. Constitution is a binding, organic law that only the people can amend according to the provisions of Article V. However, there is no consensus on the scope of congressional power to limit the Supreme Court's appellate jurisdiction and the jurisdiction of the lower federal courts. While the language of the ordain and establish and exceptions and regulations clauses is ostensibly clear and specific, it is set in the context of the Judiciary Article's broad, spare, and ambiguous language. And the debates of the Federal Convention and the state ratifying conventions reveal a plethora of interpretations rather than a pellucid original intent. What is the answer to this dilemma?

What is the question? as Gertrude Stein reputedly replied on her deathbed to a vexing question. What canons of constitutional interpretation should apply in determining the scope of congressional power to regulate the federal courts' jurisdiction? First, scholars should remember that the Constitution is a general charter of government whose broad provisions distributing governmental power lack the precision of a municipal building code or a life insurance contract. Careful analysis of contemporaneous sources is required to understand its Framers' and Ratifiers' broad purposes. Since the Federal Convention only had the power to recommend a constitution to the states, while the people acting through the states had the binding authority to accept or reject the Framers' handiwork, it is equally important to ascertain both the Framers' *and* the Ratifiers' understandings of the document. Because the records of the federal and state conventions are fragmentary, it is necessary to examine the debate out of doors as well as the debate on the floor. The members' diaries, letters, newspaper articles, and other published works are relevant but, obviously, of less weight than their statements on the floor. Nevertheless, these materials may illuminate the meaning of the exceptions and regulations clause, the ordain and establish clause, and other related provisions.

Second, the constitutional scholar should evaluate the evidence in a manner that gives positive effect to the Constitution's broad purposes and does not nullify any of its provisions. An interpretation of the exceptions and regulations clause that is inconsistent with the purposes of Article III or the general framework of government is unacceptable. An explanation of this clause that is inconsistent with federalism, the separation of powers, and balanced government would undermine the charter's norms and the government's institutional integrity. In other words, if neither the specific language nor the contemporaneous debate provides satisfactory answers, inferences based on the general purposes and the structure of government are admissible.

Other constitutional provisions, for example, the supremacy clause, the habeas corpus clause, the due process clause of the Fifth Amendment, and the Fourteenth Amendment's due process and equal-protection clauses, are relevant in determining the scope and limits of congressional power. However, the same canons of interpretation apply in determining the meaning and relevance of external restraints on legislative power under Article III. If contemporary equal-protection analyses are not compatible with the purposes of the Fourteenth Amendment, such analyses are of doubtful value in determining the limits of congressional power under Article III or any other constitutional provision. Thus the external-restraint argument is subject to the same searching standards as internal analyses of Article III.

Third, both judicial and congressional understandings of their respective powers are germane to the problem. How has Congress exercised its power under the exceptions and regulations clause? How has the Supreme Court interpreted the scope and limits of congressional power over the federal courts' jurisdiction? Are current attempts to curb federal jurisdiction over busing, prayer, and abortion consistent with judicial precedent and the historic exercise of congressional power? Do current proposals directly or indirectly violate any previously recognized constitutional rights? Is there some textual or inferential basis for the assertion of these substantive rights? None of these questions is answered easily, but scholars must continue to address these questions, lest partisan advocates convert legitimate constitutional questions into party platforms and querulous briefs!

Fourth, after a searching inquiry, the scholar should be prepared to admit that the answer to the question is uncertain. If the language, original understanding, judicial precedent, and legislative record do not support a single, comprehensive explanation of the exceptions and regulations and ordain and establish clauses, constitutional scholars should not convert empirical doubt into logical certainty in order to win academic debates, impress their colleagues, or influence Congress and the courts! After all, many constitutional provisions are an invitation to political dialogue and struggle, which the Framers apparently believed would restrain government, prevent the abuse of power, and preserve liberty.[117]

Balanced government and the separation of powers, for example, encourage dialogue between Congress and the Supreme Court regarding the definition, scope, and boundaries of their respective powers. For two centuries, that struggle and dialogue have promoted equilibrium, self-restraint, occasionally mutual restraint, and the continuing adjustment of legislative and judicial power. The contemporary conflict between Congress and the Court over busing, prayer, and abortion represents another important attempt to adjust the balance of power, redefine substantive constitutional rights and interests, and chart the future course of the nation's constitutional development. The struggle over busing, prayer, and abortion furnishes an opportunity for reexamining the power of Congress and the federal courts in order to define constitutional values in a liberal democracy.

2

Jurisdiction and Judicial Review:
The Framers' Perspective

....

The Framers' Remedial Intent

Writing to Timothy Pickering in 1814, Gouverneur Morris, the Committee of Style's draftsman for the Constitution, commented on the deliberate ambiguity of the Judiciary Article. Although Morris emphasized the importance of clarity and precision in drafting the Constitution, he also stressed the necessity of interpreting its "plain" words in light of the Framers' general objectives. He alluded to the conflicts among the Convention's lawyers over the scope of judicial power, the structure of the federal judiciary, the relationship between the state and federal judiciaries, the enforcement of federal constitutional supremacy, and the scope of congressional power to control the federal courts' jurisdiction.[1] Indeed, Gouverneur Morris's felicitous phrasing of the Judiciary Article obscured the conflicts that had occurred on the Convention floor and in the Committee of Detail, and avoided captious debate in the closing days of the Constitutional Convention.

The spare, parsimonious language of Article III and the paucity of debate further illuminate the difficulties of interpreting the "plain meaning" of the article's provisions and its Framers' specific intentions. Examined in isolation, the ordain and establish and exceptions and regulations clauses ostensibly confer plenary power on Congress to create and abolish lower federal courts, define their jurisdiction, and control the Supreme Court's appellate jurisdiction. The plain language of Article III apparently creates a federal judiciary that exists and exercises its power at congressional sufferance. However, advocates of plenary congressional power err because they analyze the ordain and establish and exceptions and regulations clauses out of context. They ignore the Framers' remedial purposes; the relationship of the judiciary to Congress, the president, and the states; and the developmental process of debating and drafting various constitutional provisions.

The Constitutional Convention, which deliberated almost continuously between May 25 and September 17, 1787, confronted three major problems. First, how could the delegates create a national government with requisite power and not imperil the states' existence? Their solution involved a delicate transfer of power from the states to the national government over national, international, and transstate questions while leaving broad, unspecified domestic powers to the states. Second, how could the delegates restrain the national government's exercise of power so that it would not threaten either the individual's liberty or the states' sovereignty? The delegates' solution involved well-known constitutional limitations on all governmental power, the separation of powers among national governmental institutions, and balanced government (checks and balances). Third, how could the delegates maintain equilibrium between Congress and the president, balance state and national interests, and assure constitutional supremacy? Their solution involved creating a new institution, a partially autonomous federal judiciary with power to entertain constitutional and statutory disputes within the limits of Article III.

Under the Articles of Confederation, Congress was the final judge of boundary, jurisdictional, and all other disputes among the states. Congress also had authority to decide private disputes over conflicting land grants from two or more states. The Articles authorized Congress to establish courts for the trial of piracy and felonies committed on the high seas as well as prize courts, "provided that no member of Congress shall be appointed a judge of any of the said courts."[2] While Article IX contained the germ of an independent judiciary, it left the existence of federal courts of admiralty and maritime jurisdiction entirely to congressional discretion. The Articles assumed that the states' courts would retain jurisdiction over all other civil and criminal cases, including treason, and that state courts would honor one another's judicial proceedings and decisions.[3] There was no provision for a federal judiciary, other than prize, admiralty, and maritime courts. Nor was there a glimmer of judicial enforcement of federal constitutional supremacy, a concept antithetical to the tenor of the Articles of Confederation.

Nevertheless, the Framers were familiar with the concept of judicial review.[4] They accepted judicial review of state and national acts as a legitimate restraint on democratic impulses, popular sovereignty, and governmental power.[5] Despite their commitment to constitutionalism, the Framers did not explicitly provide for constitutional review. However, approximately 26 delegates assumed that the federal judiciary would exercise the power to enforce constitutional supremacy over congressional and state legislative acts.[6] Elbridge Gerry, Alexander Hamilton, Rufus King, Luther Martin, George Mason, Gouverneur Morris, John Francis Mercer, and James Wilson acknowledged the federal judiciary's power to enforce constitutional supremacy over congressional acts that violated the Constitution's command. Arguing against creating a Council of Revision that included the judiciary, with the power to veto legislative acts, Luther Martin commented, "as to the Constitutionality of laws, that point will come before the Judges in their proper official character. In this character they have a negative on the laws."[7] Mason urged the inclusion of the judiciary in a Council of Revision with the power to veto unjust, oppressive, or pernicious laws, but he, too, agreed that the federal judiciary "could declare an unconstitutional law void."[8] On July 23, 1787, Madison noted that under a written constitution, "[a] law violating a constitution established by the people themselves, would be considered by the Judges as null & void."[9] In a political system based on a hierarchy of laws and constitutional supremacy, in the event of a conflict judges have a binding obligation to enforce the organic law over mere legislative acts in cases within their jurisdiction.

Despite the fact that neither the Constitution's text nor the records of the Federal Convention demonstrate conclusively that the Framers intended the federal judiciary to exercise the power of judicial review,[10] "[i]n the debate on the judiciary article itself, the power of judicial review was taken for granted."[11] Today, as in 1787, the issue is not the legitimacy of judicial review, but the legitimate scope of judicial power. Did the Framers perceive judicial review merely as a defensive mechanism against legislative encroachments on the normal judicial function, rather than as a positive restraint on the exercise of legislative power, as Leonard Levy claims?[12] Did they conceive of judicial review exclusively, if at all, as a means of enforcing national constitutional supremacy over the states, as William Crosskey and John Schmidhauser argue?[13] Or, as Raoul Berger and Henry Abraham observe, did the Framers intend the federal courts to exercise the review power over both state and national actions in conflict with the federal Constitution?[14] If the debate over congressional power to limit the federal courts' jurisdiction is, in reality, a debate over the legitimate exercise of judicial power, one must understand the jurisdictional question within the scope of the federal judiciary's power of judicial review.[15]

Creation of a Federal Judiciary

Structure and Power

On May 29, 1787, shortly after the Constitutional Convention concluded its preliminary business, Edmund Randolph proceeded to the main business with a long speech that "pointed out the various defects of the federal system, the necessity of transforming it into a national efficient Government, and the extreme danger of delaying this great work."[16] Among the Articles' major defects Randolph enumerated the supremacy of state constitutions over the Articles, the lack of authority to reconcile conflicts among the states, and the Confederation's inability to prevent the states from encroaching on the federal government.[17] As a remedy, Randolph proposed the Virginia Plan, which dominated the first two weeks of the Committee of the Whole's deliberations. In part, the Virginia Plan provided for a national judiciary to remedy the defects of the Articles of Confederation. Randolph's ninth resolution,[18] the germ of Article III, proposed an independent national judiciary with limited jurisdiction over national and international questions. Although Congress had discretion over judicial organization, there was little doubt about the existence of national trial and appellate courts. There was no indication of congressional power to limit either the original or appellate jurisdiction of the new national courts.[19] The Virginia Plan introduced the concept of national courts with authority to enforce national sovereignty over questions within the federal government's constitutional competence as well as authority to reconcile interstate conflicts that might threaten political stability.

After Governor Randolph presented his proposals, Charles Pinckney of South Carolina offered his plan for a federal government.[20] Pinckney's plan called for a federal judiciary, including a supreme court of error, with power to try U.S. officials for their official misconduct and to hear appeals from state courts in all cases involving treaties, questions of international law, and matters of trade and revenue, and cases in which the U.S. government is a party. Unlike the Randolph plan, Pinckney's original draft did not create lower federal courts. Instead, it empowered Congress to create an admiralty court in each state with jurisdiction over maritime cases.[21] Both Pinckney's proposals and his subsequently published "Observations on the Plan of Government" reflect his intention to create an independent supreme court with appellate jurisdiction over a limited number of national and international questions.[22] His provision for appellate jurisdiction over cases in which the U.S. government is a party reflects the suspicion that a national court of error would be more likely to protect national sovereignty than state courts, which are state instrumentalities. His provision for admiralty courts echoes James Wilson's belief that the national government should have exclusive jurisdiction over admiralty questions since these cases involve potential conflicts with foreigners.[23] Although Pinckney's original draft provides for a supreme court and federal admiralty courts, both the structure and power of the federal judiciary are more limited than in Randolph's proposal.

On June 15, William Paterson of New Jersey offered a series of amendments to the Articles, which emphasized the government's federal character, but recognized "that the central government needed more power."[24] Paterson's amendments mirrored the concerns of the small states, which feared a loss of sovereignty in a highly centralized government dominated by the large states.[25] Accordingly, Paterson's plan called for a supreme court with authority to try cases of impeachment of national officers and to hear appeals from state courts in cases involving ambassadors, captures and prizes, and piracies and felonies on the high seas; in all cases involving foreigners; and in cases concerning the interpretation of treaties and national trade and revenue acts.[26] Paterson's plan did not provide for any lower federal courts. Instead, it vested federal-question jurisdiction in the states' judiciaries with appeal to a national judiciary "for the correction of all errors [in trade and commerce cases], both in law & fact in rendering Judgments."[27] The New Jersey Plan limited the Supreme Court's original and appellate jurisdiction and placed the primary responsibility for enforcing national laws on the states' courts.[28] The plan acknowledged a need for central governmental authority, but it rendered the federal judiciary virtually harmless by severely restricting its structure and function. Under these conditions, there was little need to grant Congress discretionary power to curb the federal courts' jurisdiction.

Although Roger Sherman never presented his proposals to the Convention, Farrand argues, he probably used his document in developing the New Jersey Plan. Like Paterson's proposals, Sherman's recommendations emphasize the states' sovereignty.[29] Sherman's plan contemplates judicial review and constitutional supremacy, but places the primary responsibility for enforcing the Constitution on the states' courts. It does not create a federal judiciary. Rather, Sherman recommended "[t]hat the legislature of the United States be authorised to institute one supreme tribunal, and such other tribunals as they may judge necessary for the purpose aforesaid, and ascertain their respective powers and jurisdictions."[30] Sherman's proposals protect the states' internal sovereignty, restrict federal judicial power, and give Congress discretion over the federal courts' power, structure, function, and jurisdiction. Thus Sherman rendered the federal judiciary harmless to the states.

On June 18, Alexander Hamilton sketched his plan of government before the Committee of the Whole. While there are considerable differences among the various reports of Hamilton's speech, essentially he proposed a supreme judicial authority (court) with original jurisdiction in prize cases, and appellate jurisdiction from the states' courts in revenue cases and cases involving foreign citizens. Hamilton's initial proposal also incorporated the idea of constitutional supremacy, but conferred on the governors of the states (appointed by the national government) the power to negate unconstitutional laws.[31] In a document that Hamilton sent to James Madison near the end of the Convention, Hamilton expressed his personal views in greater detail. In Article V of his draft constitution, Hamilton proposed a supreme court with original jurisdiction in cases in which the United States is a party, in cases involving controversies among the states, and in all cases involving foreign diplomats. He also provided for appellate jurisdiction, on questions of law and fact, in cases concerning foreign citizens and citizens of different states as well as "in all others [cases] in which the fundamental rights of this Constitution are involved, subject to such exceptions as are herein contained and to such regulations as the Legislature shall provide."[32] Similar to the Convention's final draft, Hamilton's proposal left the creation of lower federal courts to congressional discretion. However, he provided specifically for congressional power to abolish such courts.[33]

Clearly, Hamilton's views on the federal judiciary matured between the beginning and end of the Convention. He accepted the need for federal constitutional supremacy, a strong central government, and a judiciary with the power to vindicate national authority. By the Convention's end, he advocated broad judicial power, which is reflected in his draft of the exceptions and regulations clause. While admitting only those exceptions contained in the Constitution's language, Hamilton conceded legislative power to regulate the Supreme Court's appellate jurisdiction. He also recognized plenary congressional power over the lower courts. Hamilton anticipated a powerful federal judiciary as a corrective to the weakness of the Articles of Confederation. However, his draft also provided for constitutional and congressional limits on the structure and function of the federal judiciary.

All five proposals—the Randolph, Pinckney, Paterson, Sherman, and Hamilton recommendations—contemplated the existence of a supreme court of error empowered to enforce constitutional supremacy and vindicate the national government's power within its zone of constitutional authority. These proposals differ regarding the scope of the court's appellate jurisdiction, ranging from the narrow definition in Paterson's and Sherman's recommendations to the broad definition of jurisdiction in Hamilton's draft constitution.[34] None of the five proposals contemplates congressional power to make exceptions to the Supreme Court's appellate jurisdiction.[35] Three of the five—the Randolph, Sherman, and Hamilton proposals—anticipate the existence of lower courts, but Sherman and Hamilton leave their creation to congressional discretion. Three of the plans—Pinckney's, Paterson's and Sherman's—rely on state courts to enforce constitutional supremacy. Obviously, the scope of congressional authority over the federal courts as well as judicial authority vis-à-vis the states varies according to each author's understanding of the general plan of government (i.e., the structure of federalism and the function of courts in a constitutional democracy). Each plan includes various elements that the Convention incorporated into a working draft of the Constitution.

On Monday, June 4, the Committee of the Whole first considered Randolph's resolution (No. 9) proposing a federal judiciary. That day and the next, Wilson, Pinckney, Madison, Sherman, Rutledge, Franklin, Dickinson, Butler, and King expressed their views on the establishment of federal courts and the appointment of judges. Predictably, Rutledge and Sherman advocated relying on the states' courts to decide federal questions, with an appeal to the Supreme Court to assure justice and a uniform interpretation of law. Madison opposed Rutledge's motion, arguing for the establishment of a supreme court and inferior tribunals, without which the high court could not effectively perform its appellate function of promoting uniformity and constitutional supremacy.[36] Madison also observed that it was imperative to create a federal judiciary to correct "improper Verdicts in State tribunals obtained under the biassed [sic] directions of a dependent Judge, or the local prejudices of an undirected jury."[37] He concluded that "an effective Judiciary establishment commensurate to the legislative authority, was essential."[38] Wilson supported Madison, insisting on the necessity of creating admiralty courts with exclusive maritime jurisdiction. Neither Madison nor Wilson trusted state courts to enforce the Constitution or vindicate national authority, while their opponents feared that a national judiciary would vitiate state sovereignty.[39]

After a brief debate, Rutledge's motion deleting the provision for lower courts passed (5/4/2 divided).[40] Madison and Wilson then offered a key compromise granting Congress discretionary authority to create lower federal courts. Butler and King debated the cost and political expediency of creating such courts. Butler argued that the states would regard such an innovation as an encroachment on their power. The committee accepted Madison's compromise without further debate (8/2/1 divided).[41] At no point in the discussion did any of the delegates even imply that Congress would have discretionary power to limit the lower federal courts' jurisdiction. However, at this early stage in the Convention, the debate focused on the federal courts' role as an instrument of national supremacy rather than the scope of congressional authority over federal jurisdiction.

The Committee of the Whole did not return to the organization of the federal judiciary until Wednesday, June 13, when it debated Randolph's resolution establishing a national supreme court and authorizing Congress to create lower federal courts with jurisdiction over cases involving national revenues, the impeachment of national officers, and "the national peace and harmony."[42] Randolph argued that the federal courts should also have jurisdiction over cases involving "the security of foreigners where treaties are in their favor," but he confessed the difficulty of establishing the judiciary's powers.[43] Having established federal jurisdiction in principle, Randolph proposed that the Convention refer the drafting of specific language to a Committee of Detail. Apparently, at no time on June 13 did the delegates consider giving Congress discretionary power to limit the federal courts' jurisdiction. The delegates then concluded their deliberations by accepting Madison's amendment conferring the power to appoint federal judges on the Senate rather than on Congress, as Pinckney had proposed.[44]

Jurisdiction

Six days later, on June 19, Madison returned to the subject of the federal judiciary in a lengthy speech on the relative merits of Paterson's and Randolph's proposals. Arguing that Paterson's plan did not remedy the alleged defects of the Articles of Confederation, Madison stressed the lack of federal authority to meet the nation's international obligations, protect domestic peace and stability, enforce the national government's constitutional authority, and protect the individual's rights against infringements by the states.[45] Criticizing Paterson's proposals, Madison argued once again that the plan failed to provide for adequate federal jurisdiction to protect the individual's rights against state infringements.[46] Wilson, Hamilton, and King supported Madison's criticisms, while Luther Martin of Maryland defended the states' sovereignty.[47] The records of Madison, Yates, and King clearly place the discussion of the federal judiciary in the context of a debate on the structure of the federal system. As a major critic of the New Jersey Plan, Madison viewed the federal judiciary as an instrument of constitutional supremacy, national sovereignty, and individual liberty.

A month later, on July 18, the Committee of the Whole returned to three resolutions (Nos. 11, 12, and 13) providing for the organization and jurisdiction of the federal judiciary as well as the mode of judicial selection.[48] The delegates agreed to establish a national judiciary consisting of a supreme court, and they conferred discretionary authority on Congress to create lower federal courts. This time, in defining the national judiciary's jurisdiction, the committee agreed unanimously "[t]hat the jurisdiction of the national Judiciary shall extend to cases arising under laws passed by the general Legislature, and to such other questions as involve the National peace and harmony."[49]

Following a long debate on the comparative merits of presidential versus senatorial appointment, with delegates unable to agree on the mode of appointment, the committee turned to the courts' organization and jurisdiction.[50] As before, Butler and Martin opposed creating lower courts, arguing that federal tribunals would interfere with the jurisdiction of the states' courts.[51] Just as predictably, Randolph and Gouverneur Morris opined that national courts were necessary. As Randolph commented, "the Courts of the States can not be trusted with the administration of the National laws. The objects of jurisdiction are such as will often place the General & local policy at variance."[52] Sherman equivocated, conceding power to Congress but hoping that the government would confer federal-question jurisdiction on state tribunals.[53]

The July 18 debate on the federal judiciary ended with the delegates agreeing to Madison's general formulation of federal jurisdiction. Despite the shift from a specific to a general formulation, the delegates had not yet considered granting Congress the power to limit either the jurisdiction of the Supreme Court or lower federal tribunals over federal questions and matters of national peace and harmony. Some delegates

perceived the federal courts as instruments of constitutional supremacy, national power, and the vindication of individual liberties against
state intervention. If some delegates also perceived the judiciary as
having power to enforce constitutional supremacy over Congress and
the president, they did not articulate their views in the debate on the
organization of the federal courts. On Tuesday, July 24, the delegates
referred Randolph's revised resolutions and Paterson's propositions to
a Committee of Detail, composed of Rutledge, Randolph, Gorham,
Ellsworth, and Wilson. Two days later, the delegates referred Pinckney's propositions to the same committee and adjourned until
August 6.

Genesis of the Exceptions and Regulations
Clause: The Achilles Heel?

As Julius Goebel notes, the Committee of Detail's surviving records
"reveal virtually nothing" about the drafting process.[54] However, by
comparing various working documents with the proposals submitted
to the committee, one can infer the committee's intent concerning the
judiciary, judicial power, and federal jurisdiction. As a starting point,
Randolph's draft, with Rutledge's emendations, provides for a supreme
tribunal and such inferior tribunals as the legislature may establish.[55]
The draft then enumerates the general subjects of the supreme tribunal's jurisdiction, including all cases arising under national law, impeachments of national officers, and "*such* other cases, as the national
legislature may assign, as involving the national peace and harmony, in
the collection of the revenue[,] in disputes between citizens of different
states[,] in disputes between different states; and in disputes, in which
subjects or citizens of other countries are concerned."[56] For the first
time in the Convention's proceedings, as Goebel stresses, congressional
discretion over the Supreme Court's jurisdiction appears in the
records.[57]

The Exceptions and Regulations Clause as a
Distributing Clause

The Randolph draft included one other remarkable feature. Until this
time the Convention's records refer to the national judiciary's jurisdiction. Now, suddenly, Randolph's draft refers to a supreme tribunal's
jurisdiction, which shall be appellate only, except in cases of impeachment, and in cases in which the legislature shall provide for original

jurisdiction.[58] Thus Randolph's draft divides the high court's jurisdiction into an original and an appellate jurisdiction, and grants Congress the power to organize the court's jurisdiction. Furthermore, "[t]he whole or a part of the jurisdiction aforesaid according to the discretion of the legislature may be assigned to the inferior tribunals, as original tribunals."[59] It is tempting to speculate that Randolph's language is a precursor of the exceptions and regulations clause, in which case Article III, section 2, would be no more than a distributing clause.[60] As such, it probably confers power on Congress to distribute a portion of the Supreme Court's appellate jurisdiction to the lower federal courts in order to promote the efficiency and effectiveness of the judicial system. However, there is considerable ambiguity in the language of Randolph's "arrangement" of the committee draft.

Another version of the committee's resolutions, in Wilson's handwriting with Rutledge's emendations, clarifies the structure, jurisdiction, and mode of appointment of the federal judiciary. In Wilson's arrangement, the judicial power of the United States is vested in a supreme court and such inferior courts as Congress shall, from time to time, create. Resolution fourteen defines the Supreme Court's jurisdiction as follows:

> The Jurisdiction of the Supreme (National) Court shall extend to all Cases arising under Laws passed by the Legislature of the United States; to all Cases affecting Ambassadors (and other) <other> public Ministers <& Consuls>, to the Trial of Impeachments of Officers of the United States; to all Cases of Admiralty and Maritime Jurisdiction; to Controversies between <States,—except those wh. regard Jurisdn or Territory,—betwn> a State and a Citizen or Citizens of another State, between Citizens of different States and between <a State or the> Citizens (of any of the States) <thereof> and foreign States, Citizens or Subjects. In Cases of Impeachment, (those) <Cases> affecting Ambassadors (and) other public Ministers <& Counsels>, and those in which a State shall be (one of the) Part(ies)<y>, this Jurisdiction shall be original.[61]

After specifying the Supreme Court's original jurisdiction, the resolution then defines the court's appellate jurisdiction:

> In all the other Cases beforementioned, it shall be appellate, with such Exceptions and under such Regulations as the Legislature shall make. The Legislature may (distribute) <assign any part of> th(is)e Jurisdiction <above mentd.,—except the Trial of the Execu-

tive—>, in the Manner and under the Limitations which it shall think proper (among) <to> such (other) <inferior> Courts as it shall constitute from Time to Time.[62]

As in Randolph's transcription, Wilson's record of the resolutions divides the Supreme Court's jurisdiction into an original and appellate jurisdiction. However, Wilson's version is stated with some clarity and precision. Whether the differences between the two transcripts reflect Wilson's more precise, lawyerly mind or merely a later stage in the drafting process, only a clairvoyant can answer with certainty. Nevertheless, in both drafts the exceptions and regulations provision is followed immediately by a sentence granting Congress the power to distribute a portion of the Supreme Court's jurisdiction to the lower federal courts, with the exception of trying the president. The juxtaposition of these two provisions in two separate documents strongly suggests that the Committee of Detail incorporated the exceptions and regulations clause into the Constitution as a distributing clause rather than as a democratic check on the exercise of judicial review.[63]

On Monday, August 6, the Committee of Detail reported a draft of the Constitution to the Convention. The draft resembles Wilson's transcription concerning judicial appointments and the vesting of judicial power in a supreme court and such lower courts as Congress may create. The committee's draft makes it clear that congressional power over the lower courts is more extensive than over the Supreme Court. Once more, the exceptions and regulations clause is followed immediately by a sentence granting Congress the power to distribute jurisdiction between the Supreme Court and whatever lower tribunals it establishes.[64] For the third time, the close juxtaposition of the two provisions raises serious questions about the scope of congressional power to limit the Supreme Court's appellate jurisdiction.[65] Is the exceptions and regulations clause no more than a distributing clause? Does it confer plenary power on Congress to curb the Supreme Court's appellate jurisdiction? If Congress abolishes appellate jurisdiction over a subject, must it confer equivalent jurisdiction on a lower federal court? Would such an interpretation require Congress to create lower federal courts capable of exercising any jurisdiction carved out of the Supreme Court's appellate jurisdiction? If so, does Article III mandate the existence of lower federal courts, despite its plain language to the contrary? The temptation to answer these questions with an emphatic "yes" is great, but, thus far, the evidence is ambiguous!

Between August 7 and 25 the Committee of the Whole considered several issues related to the judiciary, including the supremacy clause,[66] which the delegates adopted without further debate, and the Supreme Court's participation in a Council of Revision that would have power to veto congressional legislation, which the Convention eventually rejected.[67] However, aside from adopting a revision of the supremacy clause on August 25, the Convention did not discuss the judiciary until Monday, August 27. After revising the judicial compensation provision, the delegates turned to Article XI, section 3, of the draft, on federal jurisdiction. At this point they adopted Madison's and Gouverneur Morris's amendment including controversies to which the United States is a party, William Johnson's amendment including cases arising under the Constitution, and Rutledge's amendment including past as well as future treaties.[68] Although Madison thought that it might be "going too far to extend the jurisdiction of the Court generally to cases arising Under the Constitution, & whether it ought not to be limited to cases of a Judiciary nature," Dr. Johnson answered that "the jurisdiction given was constructively limited to cases of a Judiciary nature."[69] Madison then dropped his objection to Johnson's amendment. The Committee of the Whole turned immediately to the exceptions and regulations provision.

The Law/Fact Distinction

At this time a crucial exchange occurred regarding congressional power over federal jurisdiction:

> Mr. Govr. Morris wished to know what was meant by the words "In all the cases before mentioned it (jurisdiction) shall be appellate with such exceptions&c," whether it extended to matters of fact as well as law—and to cases of Common law as well as to Civil law.
>
> Mr. Wilson. The Committee he believed meant facts as well as law & Common as well as Civil law. The jurisdiction of the federal Court of Appeals had he said been so construed.
>
> Mr. Dickinson moved to add after the word "appellate" the words "both as to law & fact which was agreed to nem: con:
>
> Mr. Madison & Mr. Govr. Morris moved to strike out the beginning of the 3d sect. "The jurisdiction of the supreme Court" & to insert the words "the Judicial power" which was agreed to nem: con:
>
> The following motion was disagreed to, to wit to insert "In

all the other cases before mentioned the Judicial power shall be exercised in such manner as the Legislature shall direct"

<Del. Virga ay

N.H Con. P. M. S. C. G no> [Ayes—2; noes—6.]

On a question for striking out the last sentence of sect. 3. "The Legislature may assign &c—"

N.H. ay—Ct ay. Pa ay. Del—ay—Md ay—Va ay—S—C. ay—Geo. ay [Ayes—8; noes—o.][70]

Perhaps the most plausible interpretation of the August 27 debate is that the Framers could not resolve conflicting practices among the states regarding the reviewability of a jury's verdict. Henry Merry, for example, asserts that the Framers simply could not formulate a uniform rule concerning appeals from jury trials in civil, equity, criminal, common law, and admiralty and maritime cases.[71] Therefore, they granted Congress discretionary authority to resolve the problem in the future. According to Merry, the exceptions and regulations clause grants Congress the power to limit the Supreme Court's appellate jurisdiction over a jury's verdict, but not a lower court's determination of legal (e.g., federal constitutional) questions.[72] However, Robert Clinton rejects Merry's interpretation, on the grounds that the Framers inserted the exceptions and regulations clause long before Dickinson moved the "law and fact" amendment. Clinton adheres to the argument that the Framers intended the exceptions and regulations clause as a distributing clause.[73] But Clinton overlooks the important fact that William Paterson's plan specifically provided for appeals to the U.S. judiciary from the states' judiciaries "for the correction of all errors [in trade and commerce cases], both in law & fact in rendering Judgments."[74] Paterson made his proposal on June 15, more than two months before the August 27 debate. Whether Merry or Clinton is correct, the debate suggests that congressional power is less than plenary. Despite the lack of clarity, some commentators argue with certainty that the debate indicates the Framers' intent to give Congress plenary power over the Supreme Court's appellate jurisdiction, while others assert with equal certainty that the debate denies any such intention.[75] In reality, the debate does not clarify the scope of congressional power to limit the Court's appellate jurisdiction.[76] The exchange between Morris and Wilson suggests that appellate jurisdiction extends to questions of law and fact in common and civil law cases, but the language of the amendment also permits Congress to limit and regulate that jurisdiction. Finally, the Framers struck out the last sentence of Article XI, section 3, which reads:

> The Legislature may assign any part of the jurisdiction above mentioned (except the trial of the President of the United States) in the manner, and under the limitations which it shall think proper, to such Inferior Courts, as it shall constitute from time to time."[77]

The deletion of the previous sentence casts doubt on the interpretation that the Framers intended the exceptions and regulations clause exclusively as a distributing clause.

Neither the debate nor the language that the Convention adopted on August 27 clarifies the Framers' intent. As George Mason commented earlier on the Committee of Detail's draft of the exceptions and regulations provision, "a more explicit Definition seems necessary." In another document written between August 6 and 27, Mason records the provision as reading: "And in all the other Cases before mentioned the Supreme Courts shall have appellate Jurisdiction as to Law only— except in Cases of Equity & Admiralty & Maritime Jurisdiction in which last mentioned Cases the Supreme Court shall have appellate Jurisdiction, both as to Law & Fact."[78] If Mason's record is correct, the clause clarifies the Supreme Court's function as a high court of error without power to revise the verdicts or factual determinations of common law juries. In equity, maritime, and admiralty cases, which do not arise under the common law, the Court would have power to revise both the legal interpretations and factual determinations of lower courts.[79] However, in several paragraphs Mason's record goes beyond the committee's report of Article XI. Furthermore, there is no way to determine exactly when Mason wrote the document, what his purpose was, and whether his fellow delegates had access to the document.[80] Thus the meaning of the exceptions and regulations clause remains ambiguous.

A Model of Ambiguity

From the August 27 debate, several interpretations of the exceptions and regulations clause remain plausible, but both the plenary and mandatory approaches are less credible than the other interpretations of the Framers' intent. First, the language of the clause plainly gives Congress plenary power over the Supreme Court's appellate jurisdiction. Second, despite the plain language, congressional power is broad, but not plenary, since the Framers specifically rejected a proposal giving the legislature such authority. Third, although the Framers struck the last sentence from section 3, the provision is a distributing clause, which permits Congress to assign a portion of the Supreme Court's jurisdiction to *either the lower federal courts or the states' judiciaries.* Fourth, Congress has authority to limit the Court's appellate jurisdiction to revise a common law jury's verdict, but lacks power to limit such jurisdiction over questions of law. Fifth, there must be some federal forum to decide constitutional issues. Admittedly, the last interpretation presumes judicial review and federal constitutional supremacy. Before analyzing the plausibility of these five interpretations, one should follow the drafting process to its conclusion. As the drafting process indicates, it is essential to relate the Judiciary Article to the implicit concept of judicial review and the explicit provision for constitutional supremacy.

On Tuesday, August 28, the Convention turned briefly to the Judiciary Article. The delegates accepted an amendment to Article XI, section 3, clarifying the distinction between the Supreme Court's appellate jurisdiction and the judicial power of the United States, which the Constitution vests directly in the federal judiciary.[81] However, there is no indication that the delegates intended this change to authorize Congress to limit the Supreme Court's appellate jurisdiction, as distinguished from the judicial power of the federal courts. In addition to this change, the Convention accepted an important substantive amendment to section 4, providing for trial by jury in criminal cases outside a state's jurisdiction.[82] The amendment obviously answered charges that the proposed constitution did not safeguard the right to trial by jury in U.S. criminal cases.

In another important move designed to secure individual liberty, the Convention inserted a habeas corpus provision in the Judiciary Article. While Pinckney argued that the privilege could be suspended in grave emergencies for no more than twelve months, Rutledge believed that it should be declared an inviolable right. As Gouverneur Morris phrased the amendment, "[t]he privilege of the writ of Habeas Corpus shall not be suspended; unless where in cases of rebellion or invasion the public safety may require it."[83] The constitutional guarantee of the Great Writ and its original placement in the Judiciary Article suggest that, although Congress has authority to suspend the privilege, there is a constitutional guarantee of access to a federal court to determine whether the writ is sustainable. The ancient writ of habeas corpus may be a fundamental guarantee against arbitrary government, but the record is silent regarding access to a federal court to vindicate that privilege.

Between August 28 and September 8, two other debates touched on the federal judiciary. On August 30 the delegates debated but rejected Luther Martin's amendment specifically conferring jurisdiction on the

Supreme Court to decide U.S. territorial claims involving the western territories that Great Britain had ceded in the treaty of peace (1783). Both Wilson and Madison opposed the motion. After Gouverneur Morris pointed out that Article XI already conferred jurisdiction in cases in which the United States is a party, seven states defeated the amendment.[84] The amendment is interesting because it indicates Martin's reliance on the Supreme Court to decide territorial controversies between the U.S. government and the states. Obviously, Martin had greater confidence in the Court than in Congress as an arbiter between the national government and the states.

Finally, on September 4, the Convention conferred power on the Senate rather than on the Supreme Court to try impeachments.[85] Four days later, on September 8, the delegates appointed a Committee of Style, consisting of Johnson, Hamilton, Gouverneur Morris, Madison, and King, to which they referred their resolutions "to revise the style of and arrange the articles agreed to by the House."[86] The delegates did not authorize the committee to make further substantive changes. As referred to the committee, the relevant sections of the Judiciary Article read as follows:

> Sect. 1. The Judicial Power of the United States both in law and equity shall be vested in one Supreme Court, and in such Inferior Courts as shall, when necessary, from time to time, be constituted by the Legislature of the United States.
>
> Sect. 2. The Judges of the Supreme Court, and of the Inferior courts, shall hold their offices during good behaviour. They shall, at stated times, receive for their services, a compensation, which shall not be diminished during their continuance in office.
>
> Sect. 3. The Judicial Power shall extend to all cases both in law and equity arising under this Constitution and the laws of the United States, and treaties made or which shall be made under their authority; to all cases affecting Ambassadors, other Public Ministers and Consuls; to all cases of Admiralty and Maritime Jurisdiction; to Controversies to which the United States shall be a party, to controversies between two or more States (except such as shall regard Territory and Jurisdiction) between a State and citizens of another State, between citizens of different States, between citizens of the same State claiming lands under grants of different States, and between a State or the citizens thereof and foreign States, citizens or subjects. In cases affecting Ambassadors, other Public Ministers and Consuls, and those in which a State

shall be party, the Supreme Court shall have original jurisdiction. In all other cases beforementioned the Supreme Court shall have appellate jurisdiction both as to law and fact with such exceptions and under such regulations as the Legislature shall make.

Sect. 4. The trial of all crimes (except in cases of impeachments) shall be by jury and such trial shall be held in the State where the said crimes shall have been committed; but when not committed within any State then the trial shall be at such place or places as the Legislature may direct.

The privilege of the writ of Habeas Corpus shall not be suspended; unless where in cases of rebellion or invasion the public safety may require it.[87]

In a comparison of the Committee of Detail's report of August 6 with the Convention's journal and Madison's notes between August 7 and September 8, both stylistic and substantive changes in the Judiciary Article become apparent.[88] The delegates distinguished judicial power from jurisdiction, and extended the federal judiciary's power to cases both in law and equity arising under the Constitution as well as past and future international treaties. They also included cases in which the U.S. is a party and certain land claims cases. They extended the Supreme Court's appellate jurisdiction, in the cases enumerated in Article XI, to questions of law and fact, and retained the exceptions and regulations provision. The Framers deleted the provision giving Congress discretion to distribute a portion of the appellate jurisdiction to the lower courts. They attempted to clarify the right to trial by jury in criminal cases, and they inserted a habeas corpus provision in the Judiciary Article.

The Committee of Style reported to the Convention on September 12. As Merrill Jensen observed, "The Committee of Style reduced the twenty-three articles and forty sections . . . to seven articles and twenty-one sections, and rearranged some clauses. The Committee made only a few substantive changes."[89] The Judiciary Article (now Article III) included several changes in style and arrangement. The first two sections were reduced to one section vesting judicial power directly in the federal courts and providing for the selection of judges.[90] In section 2, defining the jurisdiction of the federal courts, the committee made one important change in the exceptions and regulations clause by adding a series of commas that had not appeared in the Convention's draft: "In all the other cases before mentioned, the supreme court shall have appellate jurisdiction, both as to law and fact, with such exceptions, and under such regulations as the Congress shall make."[91] The placement or misplacement of the comma after "exceptions" has spawned endless debate about the Framers' intentions. Was the placement deliberate? Does it indicate an intention to grant Congress the power to make exceptions with regard to questions of "fact" and not questions of "law?" Is it merely a rhetorical device indicating a pause to a public orator reading a great state paper to an eagerly awaiting assembly of the new nation's citizens? Or does the sentence simply mean that Congress has power to make exceptions to the Supreme Court's appellate jurisdiction? Again, the record is silent!

As Julius Goebel noted regarding the Committee of Detail's draft,[92] the Constitution that the Convention eventually adopted is ambiguous regarding the Supreme Court's appellate jurisdiction. Despite the enumeration of specific cases that fall within the judicial power of the United States, Article III does not fix the Supreme Court's appellate jurisdiction. It establishes constitutional limits on that jurisdiction, but it does not define the scope of congressional power to regulate and make exceptions to the Court's appellate jurisdiction. Thus far, neither the language nor the drafting process reveals the Framers' precise intentions. Given these ambiguities, one cannot conclude with certainty that Congress has either plenary power over the Supreme Court or an affirmative duty to provide some federal forum for the vindication of constitutional rights. Before commenting on the scope of congressional power, however, one should examine the judiciary's function in the plan of government, that is, its authority to enforce constitutional supremacy within a framework of federalism and the separation of powers.

Judicial Review and Federal Jurisdiction

Madison and other delegates to the Philadelphia Convention were familiar with the concept of judicial review. In the seventeenth and eighteenth centuries the "ancient doctrine of natural law gave birth to a conception of natural rights,"[93] which American revolutionaries incorporated into a developing higher-law tradition in the new nation. Along with this new tradition, British constitutionalism, state constitutional developments in the 1780s, and the decisions of several state appellate courts fostered judicial review as a restraint on the arbitrary exercise of legislative power.[94] As Edward Corwin once wrote, between 1780 and 1787 there was a constitutional reaction against legislative supremacy. During this period, several states incorporated the separation of powers, balanced government, and judicial review into their constitutions.[95] If judicial review is a product of the times and historic developments in the 1780s rather than the explicit language of the Constitution or the Framers' explicit intentions, as Leonard Levy asserts, it is a widely shared assumption that pervades the Framers' deliberations as well as their explicit rejection of legislative and executive supremacy.[96]

In a letter to Governor Edmund Randolph (April 8, 1787), James Madison lamented the Confederation's impotence vis-à-vis the states. He urged the creation of a national government having sovereign power to negate state laws in conflict with the fundamental charter. "Without such a defensive power," Madison wrote, "every positive power that can be given on paper [to the national government] will be unvailing."[97] On April 16, Madison penned a similar letter to George Washington, criticizing the states' invasion of national authority, recommending an expansion of national power in areas requiring uniformity, and calling for a national judiciary to expound the law and defend national sovereignty.[98] Shortly before the Philadelphia Convention assembled, Madison clearly linked constitutional supremacy and national sovereignty to the creation of an independent judiciary having power to veto state actions in conflict with the national charter. Among others, Madison favored establishing a federal judiciary to enforce national sovereignty and the uniformity of law.

The Randolph, Paterson, Pinckney, Sherman, and Hamilton proposals assume the existence of a supreme court of appeals with authority to enforce constitutional supremacy and vindicate national power in areas delegated to the national government. While none of these plans includes an explicit reference to judicial review, the concept is implicit in all five proposals. Although judicial review is implicit rather than explicit, only the most ardent literalist would deny that the Framers assumed judicial review. The question is the legitimate scope of judicial review vis-à-vis Congress, the president, and the states. The delegates did not explicitly debate the concept of judicial review; however, they did explore three important issues that relate to the subject. The rejection of a Council of Revision, the deletion of congressional power to veto state legislation, and the drafting of the supremacy clause all illuminate the Framers' intentions on the legitimate scope of judicial review, congressional power over the federal courts' jurisdiction, and the constitutional relationship between Congress and the federal judiciary.

The Council of Revision

On four separate occasions, the Convention considered and rejected motions to create a Council of Revision, including the judiciary and the executive, with power to veto unjust, unwise, or unreasonable national laws.[99] In their debates, the delegates disputed the need to strengthen the executive in relation to the legislature, the dangers inherent in giving the president virtually monarchical power over Congress, the problem of fusing judicial and executive power, the wisdom of granting the judiciary a double veto over legislation, and the potential bias of including the judiciary in a Council of Revision. Eventually, the Framers deleted the council, substituting instead a conditional executive veto for judicial participation in the policy-making process. Throughout the debates on the Council of Revision and the executive veto, the delegates' assumption of judicial review of congressional legislation is patently evident.

In the opening debate on Randolph's resolution (No. 8), providing "that the Executive and a convenient number of the National Judiciary, ought to compose a Council of revision with authority to examine every act of the National Legislature before it shall operate,"[100] Gerry expressed serious reservations about including the judiciary in a council, since:

> [T]hey will have sufficient check agst. encroachments on their own department by their exposition of the laws, which involved a power of deciding on their Constitutionality. In some States the Judges had <actually> set aside laws as being agst. the Constitution. This was done too with general approbation. It was quite foreign from the nature of ye. office to make them judges of the policy of public measures.[101]

King supported Gerry, "observing that the Judges ought to be able to expound the law as it should come before them, free from the bias of having participated in its formation."[102] As the record indicates, both King and Gerry clearly believed that the judiciary would exercise judicial review over congressional acts in derogation of the Constitution. Although Dickinson opposed conferring extrajudicial (i.e., legislative and executive) functions on the judiciary, he too implied that the courts would have the power of judicial review. After considerable dispute, the delegates postponed further consideration of Randolph's resolution (No. 8) to debate Gerry's motion granting the executive a conditional veto over legislation.[103]

On Wednesday, June 6, Wilson moved to "reconsider the vote excluding the Judiciary from a share in the revision of the laws."[104] Madison seconded the motion, arguing that the inclusion of the judiciary in a council would strengthen both the president and the judiciary against legislative encroachments. He recognized that judicial participation might bias the courts in cases that would subsequently come before the judiciary, but argued that only "a small proportion of the laws coming in question before a Judge wd. be such wherein he had been consulted."[105] Rather than threatening the separation of powers, Madison believed that judicial participation in a Council of Revision would save the people from laws that were "unwise in their principle, or incorrect in their form," and would prevent "the Legislature from encroaching on the other co-ordinate Departments, or on the rights of the people at large."[106] In any event, Madison's statement implies that the judiciary would have authority to judge the constitutionality of congressional legislation.

Twice defeated, but still determined, Wilson moved on July 21 to include the judiciary along with the executive in a Council of Revision. In defending the concept, Wilson explicitly recognized the power of judicial review:

> The Judiciary ought to have an opportunity of remonstrating agst projected encroachments on the people as well as on themselves. It had been said that the Judges, as expositors of the Laws would have an opportunity of defending their constitutional rights. There was weight in this observation; but this power of the Judges did not go far enough. Laws may be unjust, may be unwise, may be dangerous, may be destructive; and yet not be so unconstitutional as to justify the Judges in refusing to give them effect. Let them have a share in the Revisionary power, and they will have an opportunity of taking notice of these characters of a law, and of counteracting, by the weight of their opinions the improper views of the Legislature.[107]

Although Wilson accepted the principle of judicial review, he apparently believed that the courts should exercise the power only when the legislature has made a clear mistake concerning its constitutional authority. In other words, Wilson accepted the principle of judicial self-restraint.

Once again, Gerry objected to including the judiciary, which would convert judges into lawmakers or, even worse, statesmen. In Gerry's judgment, the motion would involve the courts in extrajudicial functions.[108] While supporting Gerry, Luther Martin conceded that the judges would possess the power of judicial review:

> [A]s to the Constitutionality of laws, that point will come before the Judges in their proper official character. In this character they

have a negative on the laws. Join them with the Executive in the Revision and they will have a double negative. It is necessary that the Supreme Judiciary should have the confidence of the people. This will soon be lost, if they are employed in the task of remonstrating agst. popular measures of the Legislature.[109]

Not unlike Wilson, Luther Martin conceded judicial review, but insisted that inclusion of the judiciary in a Council of Revision would vitiate the public's perception of judges as neutral oracles of the Constitution. As the debate continued, George Mason, who favored including the judiciary, admitted that the courts would possess the power of constitutional review.[110] Toward the end of the debate Rutledge, an opponent of including the judiciary, concluded, "Judges of all men [are] the most unfit to be concerned in the revisionary Council. The Judges ought never to give their opinion on a law till it comes before them."[111] Thus proponents and opponents alike conceded that the federal judiciary would have authority to determine the constitutionality of congressional acts.

During the debate on the Committee of Detail's report on August 15, Madison offered an amendment to Article VI, section 13, of the draft, providing "that all acts before they become laws should be submitted both to the Executive and Supreme Judiciary Departments, that if either of these should object 2/3 of each House, if both should object, 3/4 of each House, should be necessary to overrule the objections and give to the acts the force of law."[112] Wilson seconded the motion, again underscoring the need to strengthen the executive and judiciary against legislative tyranny.[113] Mercer "heartily approved the motion," but he "disapproved of the Doctrine that the Judges as expositors of the Constitution should have authority to declare a law void. He thought laws ought to be well and cautiously made, and then to be uncontroulable."[114] Apparently, Mercer opposed but conceded the power of constitutional review to the federal judiciary.

Charles Pinckney, Gerry, Dickinson, Sherman, and Williamson adamantly opposed Madison's amendment. Agreeing with Mercer on the dangers of judicial review, Dickinson "was strongly impressed with the remark . . . as to the power of the Judges to set aside the law. He thought no such power ought to exist. He was at the same time at a loss what expedient to substitute. The Justiciary of Aragon he observed became by degrees the lawgiver."[115] Despite his opposition to judicial review, Dickinson nevertheless acknowledged that the power existed. After a heated and confusing debate, the delegates dropped the proposal for a

Council of Revision and moved toward acceptance of a conditional executive veto. The next day, August 16, they agreed to a new section, virtually identical to the final language of the presentation clause (Article I, section 7, cl. 3) of the Constitution, granting the president a conditional veto over congressional acts.[116] As the Convention's debates on the Council of Revision indicate, most of the delegates who addressed the issue either tacitly or explicitly assumed that the federal judiciary would have authority to determine the constitutionality of congressional acts. Whether they favored or opposed judicial review and/or a Council of Revision, Dickinson, Gerry, King, Madison, Martin, Mason, Mercer, Randolph, Rutledge, and Wilson recognized that the judiciary would possess such power under the new constitution.[117] If the debates on the Council of Revision indicate the Framers' assumption of judicial review, the struggle over authorizing Congress to veto state legislation in conflict with the Constitution reflects a similar acquiescence.

The Congressional Veto over State Legislation

Toward the end of his life, James Madison reflected on the greatest problem that the Federal Convention had faced, namely, establishing the national government's supremacy over the states. Writing to N.P. Trist in December 1831, Madison summarized the delegates' central problem concisely:

> The obvious necessity of a controul on the laws of the States, so far as they might violate the Constn. & laws of the U.S. left no option but as to the mode. The modes presenting themselves, were 1. a Veto on the passage of the State laws. 2. a Congressional repeal of them, 3 a Judicial annulment of them. The first tho extensively favord, at the outset, was found on discussion, liable to insuperable objections, arising from the extent of Country, and the multiplicity of State laws. The second was not free from such as gave a preference to the *third* as now provided by the Constitution.[118]

In 1833 Madison wrote two other letters, to John Tyler and W.C. Rives, in which he described the three modes of assuring national supremacy that the Framers had considered. Madison's correspondence clearly establishes national judicial review of state laws as the method the Framers finally selected to enforce the supremacy clause.[119] After the Convention rejected both a congressional veto and a repealer of state legislation in conflict with the Constitution, Madison recalled, "the only remaining safeguard to the Constitution and laws of the Union, agst. the encroachment of its members and anarchy among themselves, is that which was adopted, in the Declaration that the Constitution laws & Treaties of the U.S. should be the supreme law of the Land, and as such be obligatory on the Authorities of the States as well as those of the U.S. [sic]"[120]

Both the Randolph and Pinckney plans include provisions for a congressional veto of state legislation. Randolph's sixth resolution granted Congress the power "to negative all laws passed by the several States, contravening in the opinion of the National Legislature the articles of Union."[121] The legislative veto clause was followed immediately by a provision authorizing the use of force against any state that failed to meet its constitutional obligations.[122] In Pinckney's plan, each state retained the power not specifically delegated to the national government, a concept later included in the Tenth Amendment, "[b]ut no Bill of the Legislature of any State shall become a law till it shall have been laid before S. & H.D. in C. [Senate and House of Delegates in Congress] assembled and received their approbation."[123]

The three other plans offered to the Convention provided for the supremacy of national law but did not authorize either a congressional veto or repealer of state legislation. In his speech of June 18, Hamilton proposed granting the national government a veto over state legislation, but conferred the power on the governors of the states who were to be appointed by the central government.[124] Hamilton's later draft is similar to the supremacy clause, but it obliges the states' judiciaries to enforce constitutional supremacy. Paterson's plan also provided for the supremacy of national law. However, like Hamilton's later draft, Paterson left enforcement of constitutional supremacy to the states' courts. As in Randolph's proposal, Paterson's resolution authorized the national executive to use armed force to compel obedience to congressional acts and U.S treaties.[125] Sherman, too, proposed the supremacy of national law, but he simply obliged the executive and judiciary in each state to execute the law. Sherman's conception of national supremacy is hortatory rather than binding, organic law. Despite his proposal "[t]o make laws binding on the people of the United States, and on the courts of law, and other magistrates and officers, civil and military, within the several states," Sherman simply did not provide for any effective national enforcement mechanism.[126]

As Madison's later correspondence recalled, the delegates apparently agreed that some method of enforcing constitutional supremacy was necessary, but they could not assent to a particular mode. Between

May 31 and July 17 they accepted, reconsidered, and defeated (3/7) Randolph's proposal conferring a congressional veto over state legislation.[127] On July 10 Randolph offered a compromise to assuage the small states' fears that a congressional veto would operate to their disadvantage. Randolph suggested, "[t]hat altho' every negative given to the law of a particular State shall prevent its operation, any State may appeal to the national Judiciary against a negative; and that such negative if adjudged to be contrary to the power granted by the articles of the Union, shall be void."[128] Randolph's compromise is the first proposal directly linking the national judiciary to the enforcement of constitutional supremacy over state authority.

After rejecting Randolph's original resolution granting Congress a veto, on July 17 the delegates adopted Luther Martin's resolution, similar to the language of the Constitution's supremacy clause:

> [T]hat the Legislative acts of the U.S. made by virtue & in pursuance of the articles of Union, and all treaties made & ratified under the authority of the U.S. shall be the supreme law of the respective States, as far as those acts or treaties shall relate to the said States, or their Citizens and inhabitants—& that the Judiciaries of the several States shall be bound thereby in their decisions, any thing in the respective laws of the individual States to the contrary notwithstanding.[129]

During the debates, Gouverneur Morris indicated his growing opposition to the congressional veto. "The proposal of it [the veto]," he opined, "would disgust all the States. A law that ought to be negatived will be set aside in the Judiciary departmt. and if that security should fail; may be repealed by a Nationl. law."[130] Sherman also opposed the congressional veto, indicating his confidence in the states' judiciaries to invalidate state legislation in conflict with the Constitution.[131] Although Madison favored the veto, he too admitted that the national courts would have power to set aside state laws in conflict with national authority. Madison revealed his distrust of state judiciaries to enforce national supremacy. "In all the States," Madison noted, "these [courts] are more or less dependant on the Legislatures."[132] In the end, Luther Martin's resolution carried the day, but the proponents of a congressional veto remained undaunted.

Despite the devotion of Pinckney, Wilson, and Madison to the congressional veto as a remedy for the impotence of the Confederation vis-à-vis the states, on August 23 the delegates narrowly defeated Pinckney's motion (5/6) to include such a provision.[133] Through the political process of debate, negotiation, and compromise, between July 10 and August 23 the Framers shifted the primary responsibility for enforcing constitutional supremacy and national power over the states from the Congress to the judiciary. While the language of Article VI, section 2, does not specify the national judiciary as a guardian of constitutional supremacy and national authority, the debates on the evolution of the supremacy clause indicate that both the proponents and opponents of the congressional veto anticipated that the courts would perform this function.

Drafting the Supremacy Clause

The delegates modified the supremacy clause several times between July 24 and September 12. However, the proposal that the Convention submitted to the Committee of Detail (July 24) contains the substance of Article VI, section 2. It establishes a strict legal hierarchy that includes the Constitution, national laws, and international treaties. The resolution implies constitutional limitations on congressional lawmaking. It also requires that state judges enforce the legal hierarchy in the event of conflict between state and national laws.[134] The draft that the Committee of Detail referred back to the Convention (August 6) clarifies the congressional obligation to legislate pursuant to the Constitution, but it does not include any substantive changes.[135] Neither the resolutions submitted to the Committee of Style (September 10) nor the committee's draft (September 12) indicate any major substantive changes.[136] The committee did include future as well as past treaties within the meaning of the law of the land. Otherwise, the September 12 draft contains the language that the Convention finally adopted:

> This Constitution, and the Laws of the United States which shall be made in Pursuance thereof; and all Treaties made, or which shall be made, under the Authority of the United States, shall be the supreme Law of the Land; and the Judges in every State shall be bound thereby, any Thing in the Constitution or Laws of any State to the Contrary notwithstanding.[137]

Although the final language of Article VI does not elucidate the national judiciary's role in enforcing constitutional supremacy, the transformation of the congressional veto into the supremacy clause reveals, as Arthur Prescott once wrote, "the unique vindication of the supreme law by the judiciary. No specific provision confers this power, but the logic of developments in convention is axiomatic."[138] Article VI also does not confer power to enforce the Constitution on the national judiciary in preference to the various states' judiciaries. However, it is inconceivable that the Framers would have entrusted the latter with the function of enforcing national supremacy. From the Framers' perspective, this would have been analogous to placing the proverbial fox in the hen house to guard the chicks. Furthermore, the development of the clause (in Article VI, section 2) that requires state judges to enforce constitutional supremacy was born out of some Framers' deep suspicions that state judges would uphold their own states' policies rather than the national Constitution, laws, and treaties.

The third section of Article VI, prescribing an official oath, reveals similar fears about state judges and executives. As early as June 5, Madison expressed support for Randolph's fourteenth proposition requiring state officials, including judges, to take an official oath to support the Constitution. Without this provision, Madison believed, state judges would decide in favor of state authority.[139] On June 11, the delegates agreed unanimously to the resolution, which read, "that the legislative, executive, and judiciary powers within the several States ought to be bound by oath to support the articles of union."[140] While Gerry and Luther Martin opposed the oath, Randolph supported his proposition, saying:

> The Natl. authority needs every support we can give it. The Executive & Judiciary of the States, notwithstanding their nominal independence on the State Legislatures are in fact, so dependent on them, that unless they be brought under some tie <to> the Natl. system, they will always lean too much to the State systems, whenever a contest arises between the two. [sic][141]

Luther Martin then offered a motion to strike the provision, which was defeated (4/7).[142]

The official oath was debated only once more, on July 23, when the Convention accepted Gerry's motion to include national as well as state officials. Not unlike the debates on the legislative veto and the Council of Revision, the discussions of the official oath reflect a suspicion that state officials would not enforce the federal Constitution in the event of a conflict between state and national authority. The oath, per se, does not define the scope of national judicial authority, but it is one of several integral components of Article VI that imply a key role for the national judiciary in enforcing constitutional supremacy over the states.

In the closing days of the Convention, on September 12, Madison reiterated his understanding that the Supreme Court would have authority to enforce constitutional supremacy. During a discussion of state tax policies that might interfere with trade and commerce, Madison noted:

> There will be the same security as in other cases—The jurisdiction of the supreme Court must be the source of redress. So far only had provision been made by the plan agst. injurious acts of the States. His own opinion was, that this was insufficient,—A negative on the State laws alone. could meet all the shapes which these could assume. But this had been overruled. [sic][143]

If Madison doubted the Supreme Court's authority to protect constitutional supremacy or vindicate national authority, his closing remarks do not reflect uncertainty. However, his remarks do establish a vital link between the Court's appellate jurisdiction and national judicial enforcement of the supremacy clause.

Congress and the Federal Courts

By focusing on the exceptions and regulations and ordain and establish clauses of Article III, judicial scholars have obscured the central role that the Framers expected the national judiciary to play in maintaining the plan of government. They anticipated that the national judiciary would enforce constitutional supremacy in relation to Congress, the president, and the states. While the Framers did not explicitly provide for judicial review, their acceptance of the concept pervades the debates on articles III and VI, the rejection of a Council of Revision and the congressional veto over state legislation, and the inclusion of explicit limitations on legislative power in Article I, section 9. The records of the Federal Convention support Raoul Berger's thesis that judicial review is implicit throughout the Convention's proceedings.[144] Therefore, any explanation of the exceptions and regulations and ordain and establish clauses must account for the central role of judicial review within the framework of federalism, balanced government, and the separation of powers.

The delegates came to Philadelphia to remedy the perceived defects of the Articles of Confederation, namely, the want of a central government possessing sovereign power over national, international, and transstate problems. At the same time, they recognized the need to restrain the central government's power over individuals and the states. As eighteenth-century liberals, the Framers believed in the efficacy of constitutional limitations on the exercise of all governmental power—legislative, executive, and judicial. Twentieth-century mass democracy notwithstanding, they did not accept legislative supremacy and unrestrained, majority-rule democracy. In solving the conundrum of granting the national government adequate power to provide for the national defense and secure domestic stability without tyrannizing the people, the Framers established a quasi-autonomous national judiciary to enforce constitutional limitations on government and police the boundaries between state and national authority. During the Convention's debates, advocates of national power stressed the judiciary's authority to enforce constitutional supremacy over the states, while advocates of state sovereignty emphasized the judiciary's responsibility to protect the people and the states against a voracious Congress. Nevertheless, both stressed judicial authority to maintain the political system's equilibrium.

Within this context, the relationship between the Judiciary Article and the supremacy clause becomes patently clear. Article III defines the subject matter over which the judiciary has jurisdiction in enforcing the hierarchy of law that the supremacy clause establishes. The supremacy clause does not explicitly confer this enforcement role on the national judiciary, but the Framers' intent is transparent in their deliberations on the congressional veto, the Council of Revision, and the official oath. Their distrust of the states' judiciaries to enforce constitutional supremacy is equally transparent in the debates on the clause that specifically binds state judges to uphold the federal Constitution in the event of a conflict between state and national laws.

The drafting of Article III also affirms the Framers' understanding that the national judiciary would employ its power of judicial review to maintain the federal structure of government, police the boundaries among governmental institutions, and restrain the arbitrary exercise of power. No plan submitted to the Convention provided for congressional control over the federal judiciary's jurisdiction. All five plans (Randolph's, Paterson's, Pinckney's, Hamilton's, and Sherman's) included a supreme court of error on federal questions. The principal functions of the supreme court of error were to (1) promote the new Constitution's supremacy, (2) vindicate the national government's authority over the states, (3) provide a uniform interpretation of national law, especially the Constitution, and (4) protect individuals against state and national infringements of constitutionally (i.e, textually) protected rights.

The drafting of articles III and VI as well as the sifting and winnowing of constitutional chaff suggests that the Framers did not confer plenary power on Congress to limit the Supreme Court's appellate jurisdiction, despite the "plain language" of the exceptions and regulations clause. Indeed, the Framers considered and rejected a proposal granting Congress plenary power over federal jurisdiction. The plenary view would grant Congress authority to interfere with the Supreme Court's power to protect the national political system's equilibrium, the structure of federalism, and the individual's constitutionally protected rights. Rejection of the plenary view concedes to the Supreme Court the role of final constitutional arbiter, but does not leave Congress powerless to limit the Court's function of statutory construction. Furthermore, the president and the Senate can alter the judiciary's constitutional interpretation through the process of nominating, confirming, and appointing judges and justices who share their constitutional values. If the Court frustrates a determined majority, the people can and have altered the Supreme Court's constitutional interpretations through the amendment process. While this view may offend majoritarian democrats, the Framers did not entrust the protection of constitutional values and structure to majority rule.

The development of Article III does not support Theodore Eisenberg's thesis that Congress has an affirmative duty to create lower federal courts, however indispensable they have become to the Supreme Court's performance of its essential functions.[145] The Framers believed that the states' judiciaries would decide most federal questions, with an appeal to the Supreme Court on federal constitutional questions, a belief that Congress has sustained for almost two centuries. If Congress should limit the Supreme Court's role as a high court of error, the Framers' deliberations suggest that Congress would have an obligation to provide some other federal forum to decide constitutional questions. While some authorities rest this claim on theories of individual right, from the Framers' perspective the issue is the national judiciary's power to protect national authority and constitutional supremacy. Other than this single important limitation on congressional power, legislative authority over the structure and jurisdiction of the lower federal courts is plenary. The debates on Madison's compromise leave little doubt that Congress can create and abolish lower courts and regulate their jurisdiction. Thus modified, the mandatory view has only limited credence.

Within these perimeters, the debates on the exceptions and regulations clause do not define the precise scope of congressional power to limit the Supreme Court's appellate jurisdiction. There is some evidence to suggest that the Framers intended the clause to operate either exclusively or primarily as a distributing clause. As such, the clause confers power to distribute a portion of the Court's appellate jurisdiction to the lower federal courts. Although several drafts of the Constitution contain explicit language to this effect, the Framers eventually eliminated the explicit language permitting Congress to distribute the Court's appellate jurisdiction to the inferior courts. Some authorities suggest that, despite the deletion of the provision, the power is implicit. Indeed, Congress does have authority to distribute the Court's appellate jurisdiction, but there is no evidence to suggest that, as adopted by the Convention, the exceptions and regulations clause is exclusively a distributing clause.

The Convention's records also support the argument that the Framers intended the exceptions and regulations clause to give Congress authority to limit the Supreme Court's power to revise juries' verdicts in civil and criminal cases. However, this argument defies the plain language that the Framers adopted. As the debates indicate, the Framers had considerable difficulty in reconciling the states' diverse practices regarding jury trials in equity, civil law, common law, and admiralty and maritime law. Both the early drafts and Gouverneur Morris's stylistic alterations are less than models of clarity. Indeed, Morris later indicated that he drafted various provisions of the Judiciary Article ambiguously to promote the article's acceptance without further cavil. Morris's felicitous style may have promoted consensus, but the language does not clarify the scope of and/or limitations on congressional power to control the Supreme Court's appellate jurisdiction.

Nor did the language assuage some delegates' fears that the national courts would become star chambers, setting aside juries' verdicts. The issue arose again in the state ratifying conventions, where the Constitution's critics called for amendments to safeguard the right to trial by jury in criminal cases and civil cases at common law. The debates on the Sixth and Seventh amendments, in the First Congress, also testify to the fear that the Federal Convention had not secured the people's right to trial by jury.

A critical reading of the Convention's debates, comparison of successive drafts of the Judiciary Article and other relevant constitutional provisions, and an analysis of the Framers' remedial intent and broad constitutional objectives indicate that Congress has broad but not unlimited authority to control the Supreme Court's appellate jurisdiction and the jurisdiction of the lower federal courts. However important the Framers' objectives, the Ratifiers' understanding is no less significant and, perhaps, more binding on future generations.

Since the states authorized delegates to attend the Federal Convention and, subsequently, ratified the new Constitution, the Ratifiers' understanding of the Judiciary Article and the exceptions and regulations and ordain and establish clauses bears close scrutiny.

3

The Judicial Function, Jurisdiction, and
Congressional Power: The Ratifiers' Intent

....

On September 15, two days before the delegates to the Federal Convention signed the Constitution, Edmund Randolph, Elbridge Gerry, and George Mason criticized the new federal judiciary. Gerry characterized the judiciary as a Star Chamber in civil cases.[1] Mason argued that "the Judiciary of the United States is so constructed and extended, as to absorb and destroy the judiciaries of the several States; thereby rendering law as tedious, intricate and expensive, and justice as unattainable, by a great part of the community, as in England, and enabling the rich to oppress and ruin the poor."[2] On September 17 Randolph, Mason, and Gerry became the only members present who refused to sign the Constitution. The struggle for ratification had begun, even before the Convention adjourned sine die and the printer prepared copies of the Constitution.

Both Gerry's and Mason's comments reveal that the Constitution's critics viewed the federal judiciary as a dynamo of national power, a threat to individual liberty, and a menace to state sovereignty. They also believed that the Convention's failure to safeguard trial by jury, especially in civil cases, would reduce the ordinary citizen to ruin. In civil and criminal cases, the critics asserted, the Supreme Court could employ its appellate jurisdiction to overturn the verdicts of juries, which they portrayed as a democratic safeguard against an appointed judiciary beholden to the national government. Apparently, the Anti-Federalists perceived the Supreme Court and a swarm of federal judges as a reincarnation of the British judiciary, which was an agent of the Crown.[3]

The continuing debate on the federal courts was an integral part of the struggle for ratification, which formally opened with the reading of the Constitution to the Pennsylvania legislature on Tuesday, September 18, and finally ended when Rhode Island ratified the Constitution on May 29, 1790. In this great national debate the Ratifiers, other state politicians, prominent statesmen, newspaper editors, and foreign observers disputed the federal courts' powers and functions, the scope of judicial review of state and national legislative acts, the supremacy of national laws and treaties over state laws, the extent of the federal courts' jurisdiction, the breadth of congressional power to limit the Supreme Court's appellate jurisdiction, the necessity for lower federal tribunals, the state courts' authority to decide federal questions, and the sanctity of jury trials and the ancient writ of habeas corpus. Whereas the delegates to the Federal Convention had debated these issues with civility and decorum, the Ratifiers were sometimes uncivil, argued ad hominem, and accused one another of illicit motives. The debate in the public press was so vile that public figures wrote under pseudonyms to avoid facing personal threats and vilification. By contemporary standards, the ratification debates were scurrilous.

Despite the vituperative nature of the debate, the ratifying process amplifies an original understanding of the Judiciary Article, the federal judiciary's authority to enforce constitutional supremacy and national authority, and congressional power over the federal courts' jurisdiction. Furthermore, under the Articles of Confederation only the states had authority to alter the basic law. The delegates to the Federal Convention could recommend changes in the Articles, but only the states had sovereign power to accept or reject proposed changes. Since the states had the last word, the Ratifiers' intent is fundamental to an original understanding of the Constitution as a binding, organic national law.[4]

An examination of Elliot's *Debates in the Several State Conventions* reveals that the delegates to nine state conventions discussed the new federal judicial establishment. In the Virginia, Maryland, and Pennsylvania conventions, Federalists and Anti-Federalists paid considerable attention to the Judiciary Article. Three other state conventions (North Carolina, New York, and South Carolina) were fairly attentive to the federal judiciary. In Connecticut, Massachusetts, and New Hampshire, extant records indicate that the delegates paid the judiciary only modest concern. Out of doors, in New York, Virginia, Pennsylvania, and Maryland, Article III engendered some passionate debate in the public press and private correspondence before, during, and after the state conventions met. Both in Massachusetts and Connecticut public interest appears to have been moderate. In North Carolina, South Carolina, and New Hampshire there is little evidence of either public or private discussion of the federal judiciary. In the remaining states, apparently neither the public nor the conventions focused on the federal judiciary during the ratification campaign.[5]

Throughout the struggle for ratification, delegates to the state conventions focused on five major questions concerning the federal judiciary. First, how extensive are the power and functions of the federal judiciary in relation to Congress and the states? Second, how broad is the power of judicial review vis-à-vis the state and national governments? Third, what is the scope of the federal courts' jurisdiction? Fourth, how extensive is congressional power to regulate the federal courts' jurisdiction? Fifth, does the Constitution safeguard the right to a jury trial by granting Congress power to regulate the federal courts' jurisdiction? The ratification debates reveal that the Ratifiers as well as the Framers perceived the question of congressional power over the courts within the broader framework of the legitimacy of judicial review in a constitutional democracy.

Judicial Power and Function

In various state conventions Federalists and Anti-Federalists contested the courts' powers and functions. They debated the scope of the federal judiciary's authority to enforce constitutional supremacy in relation to the states and the national government. The Constitution's friends and foes crossed swords over the judiciary's power to enforce national authority over the states in those areas that the Constitution vests in the national government. Spokesmen for both sides disagreed about the judiciary's right to provide a uniform construction of national law—the Constitution, congressional acts, and international treaties. They debated the need for a neutral forum in cases involving foreigners, citizens of different states, and the United States government. Federalists and Anti-Federalists disagreed about the new judiciary's essential functions and powers in the plan of government.

On November 26, 1787, several days after the Pennsylvania Convention convened, James Wilson, who had attended the Federal Convention and had played a key role in the Committee of Detail, addressed his fellow delegates. In his address, Wilson described the federal judiciary's principal functions. The courts, Wilson asserted, have the authority to enforce the Constitution over the legislature as the highest expression of the popular will. Wilson linked constitutional supremacy, judicial review, and popular sovereignty. In defending the judiciary's role of maintaining constitutional supremacy, Wilson characterized the judiciary as an instrument of democratic government.[6]

Of equal importance, Wilson observed, is the federal judiciary's obligation to enforce national supremacy with regard to treaties, the protection of diplomats, and the interpretation and enforcement of the international law of the sea. The national courts, he concluded, have a major function in promoting the national government's international obligations and preserving peace between the United States and other sovereign powers.[7] In the domestic arena, Wilson believed that the courts had a similar obligation to enforce national sovereignty in cases in which the U.S. government is a party. Finally, he argued that the U.S. courts had authority to mediate interstate conflicts, that is, to provide a neutral forum for conflicts among the states. Throughout his remarks, Wilson assumed that the states' courts would be biased against the national government as well as foreign and out-of-state suitors.[8]

In addition to these functions, the federal courts would provide a uniform construction of national law, especially in cases affecting foreign citizens, wrote Timothy Pickering, a delegate to the Pennsylvania Convention.[9] More than six months later, on July 10, 1788, Tench Coxe (a leading Federalist propagandist and Pennsylvania's representative to the ill-fated Annapolis Convention) echoed Pickering's belief that the new Constitution would promote the uniform administration of justice throughout the United States, a prerequisite for securing foreign trade and credit.[10] As the remarks of Wilson, Pickering, and Coxe indicate, the uniform construction of national law was perceived as essential to both domestic stability and international confidence. All three viewed the federal courts as instruments of constitutional supremacy and national authority in foreign and domestic affairs.

On December 3, 1787, a month before the Connecticut Convention convened, the *Connecticut Courant* of Hartford published one of several "Letters of a Landholder," probably written by Oliver Ellsworth.[11] The Landholder argued that the federal judiciary was necessary to assure a uniform interpretation of national law, enforce the national government's acts and decisions, and guarantee constitutional supremacy.[12] Evidently, the Landholder distrusted the state's judiciary to perform these important functions:

> Judges who owe their appointment and support to one state will be unduly influenced and not reverence the laws of the Union. It will at any time be in the power of the smallest state, by interdict-

ing their own judiciary, to defeat the measures, defraud the revenue, and annul the most sacred laws of the whole empire. A legislative power without a judicial and executive under their own control
is in the nature of things a nullity.[13]

In one of two surviving speeches that he delivered to the Connecticut
Convention, Ellsworth again stressed the judiciary's responsibility to
enforce constitutional supremacy and vindicate national authority.[14]
Although the Connecticut debates did not focus on the judiciary, Ellsworth's speech and the two newspaper commentaries parallel Wilson's
remarks in Pennsylvania. In both states, the Constitution's friends
argued that the federal judiciary would enforce constitutional supremacy over an errant Congress, vindicate national authority over state
encroachments, and preserve domestic peace and stability among the
states.

In Massachusetts the debate focused on the relative competence
of the state and national judiciaries to decide federal questions. The
Constitution's critics denied the need to create a potentially oppressive
judicial establishment.[15] In a letter to the *Independent Chronicle* (December 6, 1787), Candidus (either Samuel Adams or Benjamin Austin)
denied that the state's judiciary was biased against out-of-state suitors.
"The equity of our State Judicial Courts," Candidus wrote, "has never
been a subject of complaint. Why then should we give up these State
trials, and suffer ourselves to be harassed by a long and expensive appeal
to a Continental Supreme Judicial Court?"[16] On January 9, the day
that the Massachusetts Convention convened, a spirited defense of the
federal judiciary appeared in the *Hampshire Gazette*. Responding to
criticism of the judiciary, the author argued that the federal courts'
powers were limited to "cases of national and general concern." The
unknown author described the judicial function in terms of enforcing
the Constitution, international treaties, and congressional acts as well
as resolving transstate conflicts.[17] Finally, he noted that "controversies
between citizens of different states, may no doubt, be decided with
greater impartiality by a federal court, than by a court in either of the
states of which the parties are citizens."[18] Despite the lively exchange
in the public press, there is no evidence that the Convention explicitly
debated these questions of judicial structure and function.

While the Massachusetts Convention was in session, the South Carolina legislature (January 16–19, 1788) debated calling a state convention
to ratify the Constitution. On January 16 Charles Pinckney, who had
attended the Federal Convention, defended the Constitution. Pinckney

described the federal judiciary as a keystone to the new government. The federal courts were necessary to preserve legal uniformity, decide national questions, and keep the states' judiciaries within appropriate limits.[19] Apparently referring to the Supreme Court, Pinckney concluded that the Court's function "would be not only to decide all national questions which should arise within the Union, but to control and keep the state judicials within their proper limits whenever they shall attempt to interfere with its [the national government's] power."[20]

On June 2, ten days after the South Carolina Convention ratified the Constitution, the Virginia delegates gathered in Richmond. Beginning on June 18, several delegates addressed the questions of judicial power, structure, and jurisdiction. Referring to the Supreme Court's appellate jurisdiction, Edmund Pendleton (the convention's president) asserted that such jurisdiction was necessary "in order to prevent injustice by correcting the erroneous decisions of local subordinate tribunals, and introduce uniformity in decision."[21] Since he favored granting state courts concurrent jurisdiction over federal questions,[22] Pendleton believed that the Supreme Court's function as a high court of error was essential in maintaining both constitutional supremacy and national authority. Pendleton also argued that national judicial power should be coterminous with congressional power, that the judiciary should have authority "to arrest the executive arm," and that national judicial authority should reach "all parts of society intended to be governed."[23]

Two days later, urging a liberal construction of the Constitution, Madison echoed Pendleton's observation that the judicial power is coterminous with the legislative power of Congress. Madison believed that the Supreme Court's appellate jurisdiction was essential to a uniform interpretation of treaties and other international subjects, including the rights of diplomats, admiralty and maritime law, and foreign commerce. In these areas, Madison reasoned, the Supreme Court and the lower federal courts had an indispensable function concomitant with the nation's international responsibilities as a sovereign power.[24] "Controversies affecting the interest of the United States," Madison stressed, "ought to be determined by their own judiciary, and not be left to partial, local tribunals."[25] In a specific reference to debtor-creditor relations, Madison ventured the opinion that the Supreme Court had a responsibility to establish uniform and universal justice throughout America.[26] The next day, Saturday, June 21, Governor Randolph echoed Madison's views.[27] As Randolph perceived the judicial function, the federal courts, with the Supreme Court at the apex of the judicial establishment, have authority to enforce constitutional supremacy and protect national authority.

Only a month after the Federal Convention adjourned, the New York *Daily Advertiser* announced the publication of Charles Pinckney's "Observations on the Plan of Government, etc." The publication of Pinckney's pamphlet marked the beginning of a hotly contested struggle for ratification in New York. Pinckney commented on the need for a federal judiciary to decide questions arising under congressional acts, international law, and admiralty and maritime law, subjects requiring a uniform interpretation. The performance of these functions, Pinckney concluded, requires an independent national judiciary.[28]

Alexander Hamilton reiterated Pinckney's call for a national judiciary in the twenty-second *Federalist*, which appeared on December 14, 1787. Hamilton argued that the absence of a national judiciary had been one of the Articles' principal defects. Without a supreme court there could be no uniform interpretation of national law.[29] Both in domestic and international cases, he concluded, "all nations have found it necessary to establish one court paramount to the rest—possessing a general superintendence, and authorised to settle and declare in the last resort, an [sic] uniform rule of civil justice."[30] He also argued for a high court to enforce national authority and to correct the "bias of local views and prejudices."[31] Hamilton distrusted state and local judges to enforce congressional acts and international treaties because "nothing is more natural to men in office, than to look with peculiar deference towards that authority to which they owe their official existence."[32] The absence of a final judicial arbiter, Hamilton concluded, could only produce confusion at home and a loss of confidence in the new nation abroad.

In the *Federalist* No. 39, which appeared on January 16, 1788, Madison emphasized the Supreme Court's function as an arbiter between the states and the national government. As an arbiter, the Supreme Court was responsible for maintaining constitutional supremacy. "Some such tribunal is clearly essential to prevent an appeal to the sword, and a dissolution of the compact," Madison wrote.[33] Having failed to secure a Council of Revision and a congressional veto over state legislation, apparently Madison was now prepared to trust in the Supreme Court to preserve domestic peace and stability. The only alternative, as he remarked, is an appeal to heaven or to the sword, neither of which appeared sufficiently persuasive or desirable.

On May 28, in *Federalist* No. 80, Hamilton returned to the function of the federal judiciary. First, he stressed the importance of a uniform interpretation of national law, without which there would be a hydra of thirteen final arbiters, resulting in contradiction and confusion. Second, national peace and harmony could not be left to state tribunals to protect. Hamilton was particularly concerned about conflicting interpretations in foreign affairs. He saw a special need for national courts with exclusive jurisdiction over admiralty and maritime law. Third, a federal system, he noted, requires a neutral arbiter among the states, a role that state tribunals simply could not perform. Fourth, the states should not judge disputes with their own citizens regarding federally protected rights.[34] In the last weeks before the New York Convention assembled, Hamilton emphasized the federal judiciary's functions of promoting constitutional supremacy, national authority, legal uniformity, and constitutionally protected rights. Implicit in his writings is a distrust of the states' judiciaries to enforce these values or interests.

During the New York Convention, which assembled on June 17, 1788, the delegates did not debate the federal judiciary's functions. However, they did discuss the courts' role as an arbiter between the states and the national government. Within the context of an extended debate on the concurrent power to tax citizens and property, Melancton Smith, Alexander Hamilton, and John Lansing agreed that the federal courts would have authority to resolve such jurisdictional disputes. Smith, a leading Anti-Federalist, argued that the national government would have a natural advantage since "all disputes relative to jurisdiction must be decided in a federal court."[35] He concluded, "there will be no possibility of preventing the clashing of jurisdictions, unless some system of accommodation is formed."[36] Another ardent Anti-Federalist, John Lansing, assumed that the federal judiciary would have extensive jurisdiction to resolve disputes over the taxing power.[37] Like Smith, Lansing recognized that the federal courts would defer to national authority in disputes with the states. "There is no doubt," concluded Lansing, "that they [the national government] must prevail in every controversy; and every thing which has a tendency to obstruct the force of the general government must give way."[38] Both Federalists and Anti-Federalists anticipated the judiciary's function as an arbiter of the federal system.

On July 21, 1788, the first of two North Carolina conventions to consider ratification convened in Hillsborough. When the Hillsborough Convention failed to agree to the Constitution, the legislature convened a second convention, which, on November 23, 1789, ratified the document. The Hillsborough Convention paid little attention to the federal judiciary's powers and functions. However, on July 29, William Davie, a delegate to both the federal and state conventions, addressed the federal judiciary's principal functions. The courts' first obligation, according to Davie, is to enforce the Constitution and national laws vis-à-vis the states. Second, the federal courts would provide a neutral forum to resolve conflicts among the states and among citizens in diversity cases. Third, Davie cited the need for the uniform administration of justice and a uniform construction of the Constitution and national laws. Fourth, he stressed the federal judiciary's authority to preserve peace with other nations by providing a neutral forum to enforce treaties, protect the rights of foreign citizens, and decide admiralty and maritime cases. In these areas of external sovereignty, a uniform construction is essential to prevent confusion and conflict with other nations.[39] Davie portrayed the federal judiciary as indispensable to the Constitution's survival.[40]

Although fragmentary, the evidence suggests that both Federalists and Anti-Federalists anticipated that the federal judiciary would perform several important, if not essential, functions for the political system. First, the courts would promote constitutional supremacy vis-à-vis Congress, the president, and the states. Second, the courts would have power to vindicate national authority (however, the Anti-Federalists feared the danger of national judicial tyranny). Third, the federal judiciary would have power to assure domestic stability by promoting "justice," resolving transstate conflicts, and fostering legal uniformity. Fourth, the federal judiciary would have the power to protect the national government's authority in external affairs from state encroachments. The evidence is not conclusive, but it supports the argument that the Ratifiers anticipated that the federal courts would preserve the structure of government that the Framers had proposed.

Federal Jurisdiction and the Judicial Function

If the Ratifiers expected the federal courts to play a key role in maintaining the structure of government, what was their understanding of federal jurisdiction and the scope of congressional power to limit the Supreme Court's appellate jurisdiction, as well as the jurisdiction of the lower courts? As on other issues related to Article III, the Constitution's friends and foes quarrelled over the scope of the federal judiciary's jurisdiction. The Federalists defended the federal courts' jurisdiction vis-à-vis state courts and conceded little regarding congressional power to limit federal jurisdiction.[41] The Anti-Federalists also assumed that

Article III vested broad federal jurisdiction over the states' judiciaries, but claimed that this all-embracing national jurisdiction would destroy the states and advance consolidated government.[42] As Robert Clinton has written, both the Federalists and Anti-Federalists apparently assumed "that the Constitution itself invested [the federal] courts with the jurisdiction prescribed in the first paragraph of section 2 of Article III."[43]

In Pennsylvania, as elsewhere, the Constitution's friends focused on the indictment that the federal courts would use their jurisdiction to "swallow" the states. On December 3, 1788, James Wilson proclaimed to the Pennsylvania Convention, "I do not recollect any instance where a case can come before the judiciary of the United States, that could possibly be determined by a particular state, except one."[44] Here, Wilson was referring to certain land claims, which citizens of one state could bring against a second state in a federal court.[45] As Wilson commented, the Constitution confines the federal judiciary's jurisdiction to subjects that concern the national government and are beyond the competence of a single state. On February 20, 1788, an anonymous writer, Conciliator, reiterated Wilson's views. Conciliator argued that the jurisdiction of both the Supreme Court and the lower federal tribunals was limited to federal questions. The Constitution, Conciliator stressed, does not impair the state judiciary's jurisdiction.[46]

Apparently the Massachusetts Convention did not confront the scope of federal jurisdiction, but several newspaper articles appeared on the subject. On December 11, 1787, Agrippa (probably James Winthrop) objected to the federal courts' extensive jurisdiction, which in his judgment would emasculate the state's judiciary. Along with the state judiciary's oath to protect the Constitution and its obligation to enforce the supremacy clause, as well as broad congressional power under the necessary and proper clause (Article I, section 8, cl. 18), the federal courts would employ their extensive jurisdiction to consolidate governmental power.[47] On New Year's Day, 1788, Agrippa again protested the consolidation of governmental power that he feared implicit in Article III.[48] Two weeks later, A Farmer wrote "To the Town of Boston" that the federal judiciary would employ its jurisdiction to "swallow up every other Court, or bring them under its power," which will lead to a consolidated government. Obviously, Agrippa and A Farmer believed that Congress and the federal judiciary would join forces to subvert the states.[49]

In a speech delivered to the Maryland House of Representatives, Luther Martin objected to the scope of federal jurisdiction. He criticized the withdrawal of state jurisdiction over revenue cases, the federal courts' exclusive jurisdiction over admiralty and maritime cases, and the Supreme Court's appellate jurisdiction, which, he claimed, included the power to revise a state jury's verdict in a criminal case. Martin argued that Congress could use its legislative powers to enact odious and repressive laws, and then confer jurisdiction on the federal courts to enforce these repressive measures.[50] Like the Massachusetts Anti-Federalists, Luther Martin assumed that Congress and the federal courts would act jointly to undermine the states and usurp their authority.

On April 1, 1788, three weeks before the Maryland Convention opened, A Farmer (probably John Francis Mercer) wrote in the *Maryland Gazette* that the ill-defined and overlapping jurisdictions of the state and federal courts would undermine the states' judiciaries. Despite the potential for concurrent jurisdiction on most federal questions, Mercer objected, the federal courts will have the last word. If decided in a state court, a case involving a federal question could be appealed to the Supreme Court. If decided in a federal court, no state court would have an opportunity to hear the federal question. Mercer either ignored the ordain and establish and exceptions and regulations clauses or minimized their significance in limiting the federal courts' jurisdiction vis-à-vis the states.[51]

Samuel Chase (a delegate to the Maryland Convention) also claimed that the federal judiciary would absorb the states' courts.[52] In fact, Chase endorsed a series of amendments that William Paca (another delegate and constitutional critic) introduced. Paca's constitutional amendments would have narrowed the federal courts' jurisdiction and guaranteed the state courts concurrent jurisdiction over various federal questions. His proposals included amendments limiting federal jurisdiction over trespass actions, civil cases involving property and contractual disputes, and jury verdicts in criminal cases. Paca also attempted to establish a *de minimis* dollar requirement in revenue cases. Finally, he proposed "that the federal courts shall not be entitled to jurisdiction by fictions or collusion."[53] The proposed amendments revealed a profound distrust of the federal judiciary.

In contrast to the Maryland Anti-Federalists' fears of national judicial power, South Carolinians scarcely discussed the scope of the federal courts' jurisdiction. Charles Pinckney (a member of the South Carolina legislature, the state ratifying convention, and the Federal Convention) delivered a major speech to the legislature in which he argued the necessity of conferring the entire appellate jurisdiction that Article III vests in the Supreme Court.[54] However, his statement is somewhat ambiguous. Pinckney did not clarify whether Congress has an affirmative duty to confer the entire appellate jurisdiction or merely a prudential responsibility to do so. His argument that the Supreme Court's jurisdiction is indispensable to maintaining the structure of federalism, honoring the nation's international treaty commitments, limiting the states to their constitutional sphere, and promoting a uniform standard of justice strongly suggests that Congress does have an affirmative duty. While Pinckney concedes congressional authority to regulate the Court's appellate jurisdiction, he does not indicate that the power to organize and regulate the Supreme Court's jurisdiction comprehends the power to make exceptions. His statement intimates that Congress has the power to advance the Court's effectiveness and efficiency rather than prevent it from deciding constitutional questions. Pinckney's remarks clearly relate the Court's jurisdiction to its power and function as well as the structure of federalism. Evidently, Charles Pinckney envisioned the Supreme Court as a keystone in the constitutional system.[55]

During the Virginia Convention George Mason, who had refused to endorse the Constitution in the Federal Convention, criticized the federal judiciary's extensive jurisdiction. Mason claimed that the Judiciary Article granted the Supreme Court virtually unlimited appellate jurisdiction. Article III, he observed, gave the Court "appellate jurisdiction in all the other cases mentioned, both as to law and fact, indiscriminately, and without limitation."[56] Although Mason did not object to federal jurisdiction over treaties, foreign affairs, foreign commerce, and maritime and equity cases, he criticized federal intervention in diversity cases and controversies between a state and its citizens.[57] He also feared that foreign creditors would sue the states in federal courts, to the states' detriment. Mason was particularly critical of the Supreme Court's appellate jurisdiction in common-law controversies, which, he argued, would allow the Court to set aside a jury's verdict and thereby vitiate the ancient right of trial by jury. Throughout his remarks, Mason argued that the Supreme Court had unlimited appellate jurisdiction and that the federal courts would employ their jurisdiction to undermine the states' authority and the citizens' liberties.[58]

In New York the Anti-Federalists opened their attack on the federal courts shortly after the Federal Convention adjourned. On October 18 Brutus (possibly Robert Yates or Thomas Tredwell) published the first in a series of newspaper broadsides attacking the proposed Constitution. Brutus criticized the federal courts' jurisdiction as vague and all-encompassing.[59] Indeed, Brutus predicted that the federal courts would "eclipse the dignity, and take away from the respectability, of the state courts. . . . and in the course of human events it is to be expected, that they will swallow up all the powers of the courts in the respective states."[60]

Writing under a pseudonym (as the Federal Farmer), Richard Henry Lee of Virginia published a series of letters in New York.[61] In Letter No. 18, Lee claimed that the federal courts, operating from a safe haven in the Federal District, would have jurisdiction in cases throughout the nation. The Federal Farmer was particularly suspicious of the federal bankruptcy jurisdiction, which, he claimed, the courts would manipulate to expand their powers.[62] Comparing the federal courts to the British courts of the King's Bench and the Exchequer, Lee claimed that the new federal courts would employ their jurisdiction to undermine the states' authority and the individual's liberty, which he linked closely to the integrity of the states.[63]

On February 14, 1788, Brutus renewed his attack on the federal judiciary. This time, Brutus asserted that the federal diversity jurisdiction would give the lower courts jurisdiction over all civil cases. Although he admitted the need for a neutral federal forum in diversity cases, Brutus claimed that some suitors would engage in legal fictions to circumvent their own states' courts.[64] In addition to an expansive diversity jurisdiction, Brutus claimed that federal jurisdiction over state cases involving federal questions would strengthen national political authority. On this point, both the Federalists and Anti-Federalists agreed. Even where the state and national courts have concurrent jurisdiction, Brutus concluded, "the laws of the United States must prevail, because they are the supreme law. . . . From these remarks it is easy to see, that in proportion as the general government acquires power and jurisdiction, by the liberal construction which the judges may give the constitution, will those of the states lose its rights, until they become so trifling and unimportant, as not to be worth having."[65]

A week later, on February 21, Brutus returned to the subjects of judicial power and jurisdiction. He admitted that the federal courts would have power to explain and enforce congressional acts, but denied judicial power to determine or construe the powers of Congress.[66] With reference to federal jurisdiction over the states, Brutus thought it improper, pernicious, and destructive to authorize the courts to hear controversies between a state and citizens of another state. While Brutus recognized broad congressional authority to regulate the federal courts' jurisdiction, nowhere in his letter does he intimate that Congress can employ its regulatory power to prevent the federal courts from deciding constitutional questions.[67]

During the New York Convention, the Anti-Federalists introduced various amendments to the Constitution imposing limits on the federal courts' jurisdiction. They sought to severely restrict the lower courts' jurisdiction to admiralty, maritime, and piracy cases. In common-law cases involving federal questions, they attempted to limit appeals from state courts to the U.S. Supreme Court exclusively by a writ of error.[68] By restricting the mode of appeal, the Anti-Federalists hoped to limit the Supreme Court's appellate jurisdiction to questions of law. Both in 1787 and today, a writ of error authorizes an appeal only on questions of law. Through this device, the Constitution's critics attempted to clarify the meaning of the exceptions and regulations clause of Article III and protect the right to a jury trial.

Toward the end of the convention, Governor George Clinton characterized the extensive jurisdiction of the federal courts as a threat to the states. The powers vested in the federal judiciary, he concluded, would totally annihilate the states. Clinton believed that the federal courts' power and jurisdiction were even more comprehensive than congressional authority, which would allow the national courts "to collect into the sphere of their jurisdiction every judicial power which the States now possess."[69] Governor Clinton reflected the New York Anti-Federalists' fears that the federal courts would destroy the states' judiciaries.

In North Carolina, as elsewhere, the debate on the scope of the federal courts' jurisdiction focused on national authority vis-à-vis the states. Samuel Spencer, a critic of the Constitution, claimed that the federal judiciary's extensive jurisdiction was potentially oppressive to the states. Spencer asserted that the Supreme Court would interfere in cases that state courts were competent to decide.[70] Richard Spaight, who advocated ratification, responded by contending that the Judiciary Article limited the federal courts' jurisdiction to national questions.[71] Neither Spencer nor Spaight alluded to congressional power to limit the jurisdiction of the Supreme Court or the lower federal courts over federal constitutional questions.

As the debates in and out of doors indicate, the Anti-Federalists took the initiative in condemning the "expansive" jurisdiction of the federal courts as destructive to the states, their judiciaries, and the people's liberties. The Anti-Federalists focused their attack on the lower federal courts, attempting to further limit the jurisdiction of these courts to questions of national and international law. Some of the critics conceded the necessity for a supreme court, but they argued that it should have jurisdiction to review state courts' decisions on questions of law rather than questions of fact. The New York Anti-Federalists' amendments of July 5, 1788, indicate that they either did not expect Congress to prevent the Court from reviewing the verdicts of common-law juries or did not believe the exceptions and regulations clause to be an adequate safeguard. Therefore, they proposed a clear and precise limitation on the Supreme Court's appellate jurisdiction.

While the Anti-Federalists dominated the debate on the federal courts' jurisdiction, the Federalists parried the attack and ultimately defeated proposed constitutional amendments. The Constitution's friends defended the federal courts' jurisdiction as limited to and commensurate with the authority of the national government. In defending their position, the Federalists argued that the federal courts' jurisdiction was necessary to enforce the national government's authority in foreign affairs and in domestic affairs that affected the national peace, welfare, and stability. They also characterized the courts' jurisdiction as essential in providing a neutral forum for citizens and to resolving conflicts among the states. Some Federalists described the federal courts' jurisdiction as the keystone to the Constitution, as an essential means to vindicate the Framers' plan of government. In the debate over federal jurisdiction, neither side conceded congressional power to prevent the Supreme Court from deciding constitutional questions.

Congressional Power Under the Exceptions and Regulations Clause

If the Ratifiers anticipated that the Supreme Court would perform the important functions of promoting constitutional supremacy, providing a uniform interpretation of national law, vindicating the national government's authority, resolving conflicts among the states, protecting the citizens' constitutional rights, and maintaining the equilibrium of the federal system, how broadly did they conceive congressional authority to restrict the Court's appellate jurisdiction? Did they believe that Congress had plenary power to restrict the Court's appellate jurisdiction, an affirmative duty to fully vest such jurisdiction, or broad but limited power to regulate the Court's exercise of its appellate jurisdiction? While the Ratifiers did not discuss the exceptions and regulations clause in these terms, they did debate the Framers' purpose in terms of: (1) the right to trial by jury in common-law, civil-law, equity, and

admiralty and maritime cases; (2) the distribution of jurisdiction between the Supreme Court and the lower courts; and (3) the Court's
effective and efficient operation. The ratifying process suggests that the
Ratifiers understood congressional power over the Supreme Court's
appellate jurisdiction to be broad, but not unlimited.

The Exceptions and Regulations Clause as a Distributing Clause

Only in four states—Pennsylvania, Maryland, New York, and Connecticut—is there any evidence to indicate that any of the Ratifiers and
other public figures perceived the exceptions and regulations clause as
a distributing clause. In Pennsylvania, Noah Webster defended congressional power to create inferior federal courts. He countered the Anti-
Federalists' argument that such courts would "absorb the judiciaries of
the federal states" by noting that:

> The truth is, the creation of all inferior courts is in the power of
> Congress; and the constitution provides that Congress may make
> such exceptions from the right of appeals as they shall judge proper.
> When these courts are erected, their jurisdictions will be ascer-
> tained, and in small actions, Congress will doubtless direct that a
> sentence in a subordinate court shall, to a certain amount, be
> definite and final.[72]

In addition to indicating that Congress would have plenary power to
create lower courts and regulate their jurisdiction, Webster implied
that one purpose of the exceptions and regulations clause is to distribute
federal jurisdiction between the Supreme Court and lower tribunals.
Thus Congress could prevent vexatious, frivolous, or trivial appeals.
However, Webster did not argue that this is the exclusive purpose of
the clause.

Similarly, in *Federalist* No. 81, Alexander Hamilton referred to
the exceptions and regulations clause as a distributing clause. He
observed:

> Let us now examine in what manner the judicial authority is to be
> distributed between the supreme and the inferior courts of the
> union . . . we have seen that the original jurisdiction of the supreme
> court would be confined to two classes of cases, and those of a
> nature rarely to occur. In all other causes of federal cognizance, the
> original jurisdiction would appertain to the inferior tribunals, and

the supreme court would have nothing more than an appellate jurisdiction, "with such *exceptions*, and under such *regulations* as the congress shall make."[73]

The major thrust of Hamilton's argument, however, is that the exceptions and regulations clause permits Congress to limit the Court's appellate jurisdiction to revise a jury's verdict. Hamilton also intimates that the clause may serve other congressional objectives, which he does not define.

During the Maryland Convention, A. Contee Hanson noted that the exceptions and regulations clause had "caused much private debate and perplexity," but he was:

> fully persuaded, that, as the article speaks of an original and appellate jurisdiction, of a supreme court, and inferior courts; and, as there is no intimation of appeals from the several (22) state tribunals, the inferior federal courts are intended to have original jurisdiction in all cases, wherein the supreme court has appellate jurisdiction.[74]

Although several observers, including Hanson, perceived that the Framers intended the exceptions and regulations clause as a distributing clause, there is no evidence to demonstrate that the delegates to the state ratifying conventions shared these views.

In December 1787, Roger Sherman gave the exceptions and regulations clause a somewhat different, but related, gloss. In his essay "Observations on The New Federal Constitution," Sherman claimed that the Framers intended to give Congress the power to limit appeals from state courts to the Supreme Court. Thus Congress could not expand the Court's jurisdiction beyond the scope of the national government's powers, but it could limit the appellate jurisdiction to "such cases of importance & magnitude as cannot Safely be trusted to the final decision of the courts of the particular States."[75] While Sherman's "Observations" suggests that Congress has authority to distribute the appellate jurisdiction between the Supreme Court and the states' judiciaries, his remarks indicate a distrust of the latter. At the very least, Sherman implies a need for Supreme Court review of important constitutional questions. Furthermore, since Article III limits the Supreme Court's appellate jurisdiction to federal questions, Sherman denied any threat to the states, their judiciaries, or trial by jury, the very concerns that preoccupied the Constitution's Anti-Federalist critics.

The Right to Trial by Jury and the
Fact/Law Distinction

Although the Ratifiers did not focus on the exceptions and regulations clause as a distributing clause, they thoroughly examined its implications for preserving the right to trial by jury. In nine states, the Ratifiers and various commentators disputed whether the clause adequately protected the common-law right to a jury trial. Once again, Federalists clashed with Anti-Federalists, the latter raising the specter of the Star Chamber. The Anti-Federalists depicted the Court's appellate jurisdiction as a threat to liberty and an instrument of centralized power. The Federalists denied any such intention, claiming that variations in states' practices concerning jury trials necessitated granting Congress discretionary authority to regulate appeals in common-law, civil-law, equity, and admiralty and maritime cases. As the contemporaneous debates and commentaries suggest, many Ratifiers understood the exceptions and regulations clause as conferring discretion to regulate the mode of appeal on questions of fact rather than limiting the Supreme Court's authority to decide constitutional questions.

On October 5, 1787, Centinel (either Judge George Bryan or his son, Samuel) opened the Pennsylvania Anti-Federalists' barrage on the Supreme Court's appellate jurisdiction. Centinel asserted that Article III, section 2, would allow the Court to dismiss the verdicts of juries in civil cases, although he admitted that the Constitution expressly provided for jury trials in criminal cases.[76] In a second article, Centinel denied James Wilson's explanation "that it would have been impracticable to have made a general rule for jury trial in the civil cases assigned to the federal judiciary, because of the want of uniformity in the mode of jury trial, as practised in the several states."[77] The real motive, implied Centinel, was to vitiate popular sovereignty, since juries constitute a restraining force on appointed magistrates who owe their positions to the national government.[78]

Writing under the pseudonym of the Democratic Federalist, Richard Henry Lee on October 17 continued the attack on the Court's appellate jurisdiction, asserting that *"trial by jury in civil cases, is, by the proposed constitution entirely done away, and effectually abolished."*[79] Lee stressed that by permitting appeals on questions of fact, the Framers had done away with a fundamental common-law right, since, under the common-law writ of error, only a lower court's interpretation of law could be appealed to a higher court. Even in chancery or equity, he asserted, the states' chancery courts referred cases to common-law juries for a trial on the facts. If the Framers had wished, they could have excepted admiralty and maritime cases from jury trials while protecting that right in equity and common-law cases.[80] Obviously, Lee did not believe that Article III, section 2, protected the citizens' property and other fundamental rights.

On Saturday, October 6, the day after Centinel opened the attack on the Judiciary Article, James Wilson delivered a speech in Philadelphia's State House Yard in which he justified the exceptions and regulations clause. In his speech, Wilson clearly linked the provision to the difficulty of providing for appeals in equity, civil-law, and admiralty and maritime proceedings. Given these difficulties, he observed:

> When, therefore, this subject was in discussion, we were involved in difficulties which pressed on all sides, and no precedent could be discovered to direct our course. The cases open to a trial by jury differed in the different states, it was therefore impracticable on that ground to have made a general rule. The want of uniformity would have rendered any reference to the practice of the states idle and useless; and it could not, with any propriety, be said that "the trial by jury shall be as heretofore," since there has never existed any federal system of jurisprudence to which the declaration could relate. Besides, it is not in all cases that the trial by jury is adopted in civil questions, for causes depending in courts of admiralty, such as relate to maritime captures, and such as are agitated in courts of equity, do not require the intervention of that tribunal. How then, was the line of discrimination to be drawn? The Convention found the task too difficult for them, and they left the business as it stands, in the fullest confidence that no danger could possibly ensue, since the proceedings of the Supreme Court are to be regulated by the Congress, which is a faithful representation of the people; and the oppression of government is effectually barred, by declaring that in all criminal cases the trial by jury shall be preserved.[81]

On two occasions during the Pennsylvania Convention, Wilson reiterated his earlier position that the exceptions and regulations clause is a congressional check on the Supreme Court's power to set aside the decisions of juries in civil cases.[82] Following Wilson's remarks, Thomas McKean restated the Federalists' position that the exceptions and regulations clause confers discretionary authority on Congress to reconcile conflicting state practices concerning jury trials in civil cases.[83]

Evidently, neither Wilson's nor McKean's explanations satisfied the

Constitution's opponents, who continued to object to Article III, section 2, as an assault on the jury system and the people's liberties. In the "Report of the Dissenting Minority" of the state convention, published in the *Pennsylvania Packet* on December 18, the minority charged that *"trial by jury* and the liberty of the people went out together," under the Judiciary Article.[84] Several months after the Pennsylvania Convention adjourned, two anonymous writers, An Honest American and Algernon Sidney, continued the refrain that the Supreme Court would use its appellate jurisdiction to vitiate the right to a jury trial, which the exceptions and regulations clause did not protect.[85]

As in Pennsylvania, in Massachusetts the debate over the Supreme Court's appellate jurisdiction focused on the threat to trial by jury. Writing to Henry Knox, John Peirce (of Virginia) complained that appeals "from Law and Fact to the Supreme bench will not only deprive them [the citizens] of the benefit of a Jury from their vicinage but also oblige them to submit to an unnecessary expence in forwarding their evidence for the tryal [sic]."[86] Candidus (an anonymous writer) echoed these criticisms in the Boston *Independent Chronicle* (December 6, 1787), claiming that appeals to the Supreme Court would threaten jury trials in state courts, result in long and expensive litigation, and favor the wealthy. In a letter to Peter Osgood (a delegate to the state convention and a state legislator), delegate William Symmes denied that the exceptions and regulations clause would protect the right to a jury trial.[87]

William Cushing, responding to these criticisms in a speech to the Massachusetts Convention (February 4, 1788), remarked that the term "regulations" in Article III, section 2, plainly referred to juries and jury trials.[88] Rufus King and Nathaniel Gorham (both delegates to the state and federal conventions) also denied that the appellate jurisdiction would be oppressive. Specifically answering Elbridge Gerry's criticisms of the Constitution, King and Gorham noted that Congress had power to distribute the Court's appellate jurisdiction to the lower federal courts. "Or in other words," they emphasized, "Congress may determine what causes shall be finally tried in the inferior [federal] Courts."[89] Although King and Gorham addressed the distributive nature of the clause, they directed their remarks toward the criticism that the Court would employ its appellate jurisdiction to undermine the right to a jury trial. In Massachusetts, neither the Constitution's friends nor foes depicted the clause as granting Congress broad authority to prevent the Supreme Court from deciding constitutional questions.

In neighboring New Hampshire, the Anti-Federalists attacked the

Judiciary Article in terms similar to those used by their Massachusetts brethren. On February 8, 1788, a few days before the first session of the state convention convened, the *Freeman's Oracle* published a letter from A Friend (possibly Thomas Cogswell) who claimed that the exceptions and regulations clause was ambiguous. At the time, he could not forecast what exceptions or regulations Congress would eventually enact. Therefore, he predicted, ordinary citizens would confront appeals in a remote federal supreme court, at great expense and potential ruin.[90] During the Convention's second session, A Farmer criticized the Constitution's failure to protect the right to trial by jury. Trial by jury, the Farmer noted, is a democratic check on the judicial system. The day after the Farmer's essay appeared in the *Freeman's Oracle*, Alfredus (possibly Samuel Tenney) responded with a spirited defense of the Constitution. Alfredus observed that the Framers had specifically provided for jury trials in criminal cases. Obviously referring to the exceptions and regulations clause, he noted that "Congress may extend it [trial by jury] as much further as they please," with respect to civil cases.[91] In New Hampshire, as in Massachusetts, the debate on the Supreme Court's appellate jurisdiction focused on the adequacy of the exceptions and regulations clause as a safeguard to the ancient right of trial by jury.

Although there is virtually no extant record of the Maryland Convention, in the state legislature and out of doors public figures debated the meaning of Article III, section 2. A. Contee Hanson argued that, while the Judiciary Article permits appeals on questions of law and fact, Congress has authority to regulate all appeals.[92] Hanson was one of the few Federalists who argued that Congress had plenary power over the Supreme Court's appellate jurisdiction. Unlike Hanson, James McHenry, who had represented Maryland in the Federal Convention, stated to the House of Delegates that "the right of tryal by Jury was left open and undefined from the difficulty attending any limitation to so valuable a priviledge, and from the persuasion that Congress might hereafter make provision more suitable to each respective State [sic]."[93] In a speech to the Maryland Convention, an unidentified delegate reiterated McHenry's view, and added that the clause also gave Congress the power to limit trifling appeals and prevent vexatious delays. The delegate's remarks suggest that he believed the Framers intended to confer a housekeeping function on Congress so that it could promote the Court's efficient operation.[94]

In the public press, A Friend to Order (anonymous) denied that the Framers intended to abolish trial by jury in civil cases. After responding to the charge, the anonymous author elaborated on the Framers' intent:

> The 2d sect. 3d art. expressly stipulates "that the *appellate jurisdiction* of the supreme court, both as to law and fact, shall be exercised with such *exceptions* and under such *regulations as the Congress shall make.*" If Congress enact no exceptions and regulations, the supreme court can exercise no appellate jurisdiction; and if Congress enact exceptions and regulations, these, to be valid, must accord with the Constitution. But further, it must occur to every unprejudiced person, that exceptions and regulations respecting the trial by jury in cases of appeals, could not make a part of the Constitution without rendering it ridiculous by a detail proper only to appear in an act or statute. Such regulations, therefore, have been wisely left to be framed by the representatives of the people, who, it cannot be presumed, will dare to *abolish* what they are *thus enjoined to preserve.*[95]

Aside from forecasting John Marshall's negative-pregnant doctrine,[96] the Friend to Order stated that Congress cannot make any exceptions and regulations that conflict with other constitutional provisions. It is tempting to speculate whether the anonymous author would include the subsequent provisions of the Bill of Rights and other constitutional amendments. If his answer were "yes," it would be intriguing to know the identity and the authority of A Friend to Order!

Other than Pennsylvanians and New Yorkers, perhaps the Virginians debated the scope of the Supreme Court's appellate jurisdiction and the meaning of the exceptions and regulations clause the most extensively. The state legislature's "Instructions to Delegates to the State Ratifying Convention" contains an important clue to an original understanding of Article III, section 2. According to the delegates' instructions, "[t]he appellate court should not revise facts but be confined to the record—The trial by jury should be secured in civil as well as criminal cases."[97] Evidently, the state legislature did not believe that the Framers had protected jury trials in civil cases.

Between October 1787 and June 1788, when the Virginia Convention opened, Richard Henry Lee, James Monroe, Joseph Jones,[98] and other public figures communicated their objections to the Judiciary Article. Lee's letters to Governor Randolph, George Mason, and Edmund Pendleton epitomize the critics' objections to Article III. In all three letters, Lee urged amending the Constitution to guarantee the right to a jury trial in civil cases. Lee recommended that the Supreme Court's appellate jurisdiction be confined to questions of law, excluding questions of fact from the Court's competence.[99] In a pamphlet (ca. May 25), James Monroe also urged limiting the Court's appellate jurisdiction to questions of law.[100] Monroe considered the Court's jurisdiction over questions of fact extraordinary, exceptionable, and dangerous to the rights of the people. Well before the Virginia Convention convened, James Monroe, among other leading public figures, questioned whether the exceptions and regulations clause secured the right to a jury trial in civil cases.

After the Virginia Convention assembled, several delegates, including Governor Randolph, Edmund Pendleton, George Mason, James Madison, Patrick Henry, John Marshall, and William Grayson,[101] commented on the clause in reference to preserving the right to trial by jury. On five separate occasions, Governor Randolph addressed the issue. His remarks tend to confirm James Wilson's explanation that variations in state practice recommended leaving Congress the discretion to reconcile these differences.[102] Randolph did perceive an evil in the Supreme Court's appellate jurisdiction, but he never specified the threat.[103] At a later date, he denied that the clause posed a threat to jury trials or that Congress would exercise its discretion to jeopardize the right.[104] On June 21, Randolph conceded that the meaning of the clause was ambiguous and that it authorized Congress to make exceptions with regard to law and fact. However, he asserted that Congress would regulate appeals properly.[105]

On June 18 George Mason also objected to the Framers' formulation of the exceptions and regulations clause. Although he recognized the need to accommodate differences between common-law trials and courts of equity and admiralty, Mason thought that granting Congress discretion to limit appeals on questions of fact was dangerous. Therefore, he proposed an amendment that "would confine the appellate jurisdiction to matters of law only, in common-law controversies."[106]

James Madison immediately responded to Mason's objections, stating that:

Where it [the Constitution] speaks of appellate jurisdiction, it expressly provides that such regulations will be made as will accommodate every citizen, so far as practicable in any government. The principle criticism which has been made, was against the appellate cognizance as well of fact as law. I am happy that the honorable member who presides, and who is familiarly acquainted with the subject, does not think it involves any thing unnecessarily danger-

> ous. I think that the distinction of fact, as well as law, may be satisfied by the discrimination of the civil and common law. But if gentlemen should contend that appeals, as to fact, can be extended to jury cases, I contend that, by the word *regulations*, it is in the power of Congress to prevent it, or prescribe such a mode as will secure the privilege of jury trial. They may make a regulation to prevent such appeals entirely; or they may remand the fact, or send it to an inferior contiguous court, to be tried; or otherwise preserve that ancient and important trial.[107]

Unlike Mason, Madison trusted that Congress would employ its discretion to adopt regulations securing the ancient privilege to trial by jury. Madison emphasized the fact that the Framers intended the term "regulations" to permit Congress to reconcile conflicting state practices and to avoid inconvenience in the Supreme Court's exercise of its appellate jurisdiction. He denied any diabolical plot to deprive citizens of their rights, but he conceded broad congressional power to make both exceptions and regulations.

Despite Madison's assurances, Patrick Henry objected to the Supreme Court's jurisdiction to review the verdicts of common-law juries. Henry objected because he doubted congressional authority to limit the Court's appellate jurisdiction. Although he admitted that Congress had the power to regulate, he denied that it had power to abolish the Court's appellate jurisdiction.[108] Henry assumed that the Constitution vested the appellate jurisdiction directly in the Supreme Court. Therefore, the Court would be compelled to declare any legislative alteration of its appellate jurisdiction null and void.

On the same day, John Marshall made a statement almost as equivocal as James Madison's regarding the scope of congressional power to regulate the Supreme Court's appellate jurisdiction. Denying that the exceptions and regulations clause posed a threat to jury trials, he emphasized the need to grant Congress discretion to reconcile state practices regarding appeals in chancery, admiralty, and common law.[109] He disavowed any intention to vitiate the people's rights. However, Marshall asserted that Congress had authority to make any exceptions and regulations to the Supreme Court's appellate jurisdiction. Marshall's statement clearly reflects his later view that congressional power over the Court's appellate jurisdiction is plenary:

> The Honorable Gentleman says, that no law of Congress can make any exception to the Federal appellate jurisdiction of fact as well as law. He has frequently spoken of technical terms, and the mean-

ing of them. What is the meaning of the term *exception*? Does it not mean an alteration and diminution? Congress is empowered to make exceptions to the appellate jurisdiction, as to law and fact, of the Supreme Court.—These exceptions certainly go as far as the Legislature may think proper, for the interest and liberty of the people.—Who can understand this word, *exception*, to extend to one case as well as the other? I am persuaded, that a reconsideration of this case will convince the Gentleman, that he was mistaken.[110]

Although Virginians continued to debate the meaning of Article III after their convention adjourned, Patrick Henry, James Madison, Governor Randolph, and John Marshall had staked out the basic lines of the controversy. Henry argued that Congress lacked the power to limit the Supreme Court's appellate jurisdiction, despite the specific language of the exceptions and regulations clause. While Congress has the power to regulate the mode of appeal, Henry might argue, it has an affirmative duty to confer the appellate jurisdiction that the Constitution vests in the Court. Both Madison and Randolph argued that Congress has broad authority to regulate the Court's appellate jurisdiction, but neither elucidated the scope of congressional authority to prevent the High Court from deciding constitutional claims. Evidently, John Marshall accepted the plenary approach, a viewpoint to which he adhered as chief justice. In the absence of consensus, should later generations accept the views of Henry and Marshall, neither of whom attended the Federal Convention, or the views of Mason and Randolph, both of whom attended the state and Federal conventions and took an active part in shaping and explaining the Constitution of 1787?

Two South Carolinians who attended the Federal Convention, Charles Pinckney and Charles Cotesworth Pinckney, agreed that the Framers intended to grant Congress contingent authority to reconcile conflicting state practices regarding jury trials in civil-law, equity, admiralty, and common law. In his address to the South Carolina Legislature (January 16, 1788), Charles Pinckney declared:

On the subject of juries, in civil cases, the Convention were anxious to make some declaration; but when they reflected that all courts of admiralty and appeals, being governed in their propriety by the civil law and the laws of nations, never had, or ought to have, juries, they found it impossible to make any precise declaration upon the subject; they therefore left it as it was.[111]

Two days later, on January 18, Charles Cotesworth Pinckney seconded these views, stating that the Framers simply could not draft a general rule to meet all contingencies. Since a constitution should not descend into minutiae, he concluded, the Framers left the regulation of appeals on questions of fact to congressional discretion.[112] Both Charles Pinckney and Charles Cotesworth Pinckney related the drafting of the exceptions and regulations clause to the difficulty of stating a uniform rule to govern appeals from the verdicts of juries.

Although the delegates to the New York Convention did not debate the scope of congressional power to limit the Supreme Court's appellate jurisdiction, Federalists and Anti-Federalists engaged in a lively exchange on the issue. As a leading Federalist spokesman, Alexander Hamilton stated the need for a uniform and final interpretation of national laws and treaties. The states' judiciaries, he wrote in *Federalist* No. 22 (December 14, 1787), will construe national laws according to local prejudices and will interfere with the execution of international treaties.[113] Therefore, as in all nations, it is necessary "to establish one court paramount to the rest—possessing a general superintendence, and authorized to settle and declare in the last resort, an uniform rule of civil justice."[114]

Consistent with his commitment to the Supreme Court as a final constitutional arbiter vis-à-vis the states, Hamilton proposed in his draft constitution that the Court's appellate jurisdiction, "in all others [cases] in which the fundamental rights of this Constitution are involved, [should be] subject to such exceptions as are herein contained, and to such regulations as the legislature shall provide."[115] In other words, Hamilton proposed that congressional power to make exceptions should be subject to the internal limitations of the Judiciary Article as well as the external restraints of other constitutional provisions.

While Hamilton conceded that Congress could authorize state courts to exercise concurrent jurisdiction over federal questions, in *Federalist* No. 82 he argued that the Framers' plan of government requires that the national courts have either appellate or original jurisdiction to determine such questions. "The evident aim of the plan of the convention is that all the causes of the specified classes shall for weighty public reasons receive their original or final determination in the courts of the union," Hamilton observed.[116] Hamilton believed that there must be some federal forum to decide constitutional issues. Indeed, he posited an integral relationship between the jurisdictions of the Supreme Court and the lower federal courts. By expanding the jurisdiction of the lower federal courts, Congress could contract the Supreme Court's appellate jurisdiction, or vice versa, without sacrificing the federal judiciary's function of maintaining constitutional supremacy and vindicating national authority.[117] Hamilton admitted that Congress has ample authority to make exceptions and regulations to the appellate jurisdiction, but he described the exceptions and regulations clause as a means to promote the Supreme Court's efficiency rather than as a political lever that Congress could employ to prevent the Court from deciding constitutional claims.[118]

As in the other states, the ratifying convention in North Carolina debated the scope of congressional authority to regulate and restrict the Supreme Court's appellate jurisdiction. As elsewhere, the delegates focused on the Court's authority to set aside the verdicts of common-law juries. While Richard Spaight, William MacLane, and James Iredell argued for the necessity of granting Congress discretion to reconcile conflicting state practices, Samuel Spencer, James Bloodworth, and Matthew Locke perceived a threat to the right of trial by jury in the exceptions and regulations clause.[119] The opposition argued the need for effective constitutional limitations on the Court's appellate jurisdiction, which, in its judgment, the clause did not provide. Indeed, on July 1, 1788, the Anti-Federalists proposed an amendment that would have limited the Supreme Court's review of factual determinations to equity, admiralty, and maritime law. In all other cases, the amendment would have limited the appellate jurisdiction to questions of law.[120] Following the defeat of the Anti-Federalists' amendments, the Hillsborough Convention adjourned without ratifying the Constitution.

Throughout the ratification process, in doors and out of doors, the delegates to the various state conventions and other public figures debated the scope of congressional authority to regulate and restrict the Supreme Court's appellate jurisdiction. They also debated the breadth of congressional authority to organize lower federal courts and regulate their jurisdiction. Undoubtedly, the Ratifiers who addressed the issue believed that Congress has plenary power to create and abolish lower courts, which comprehends the power to expand and contract their jurisdiction as convenience and necessity dictate. With reference to the Supreme Court's appellate jurisdiction, all three views—the plenary, the mandatory, and the broad but limited approaches—appeared in the debates, in the press, and in private correspondence.

A few delegates (most notably John Marshall) argued that congressional power is plenary. Evidently, Marshall believed that Congress could prevent the Supreme Court from hearing appeals on questions of law and fact arising in state and federal courts. Without affirmative legislative action, the Court simply could not exercise its appellate jurisdiction. Once Congress had acted, the Supreme Court could exercise only the jurisdiction that the legislature had explicitly conferred. Apparently, only John Marshall (in the Virginia Convention) and A. Contee Hanson (in Maryland) clearly articulated the plenary view.

One delegate, Patrick Henry (in the Virginia Convention), argued the mandatory position, which Associate Justice Joseph Story later articulated in *Martin* v. *Hunter's Lessee* (1816).[121] Henry assumed that the Judiciary Article vests the appellate jurisdiction directly in the Supreme Court. If the Court's appellate jurisdiction is inherent, Congress cannot restrict such jurisdiction without altering the vesting clause of Article III. Should Congress attempt to prevent the Court from deciding constitutional issues, an independent judiciary would be compelled to declare such legislation unconstitutional.

In contrast to Marshall and Henry, most of the Ratifiers who debated the issue focused on the breadth of congressional authority to regulate the Supreme Court's appellate jurisdiction. These delegates disputed the adequacy of the exceptions and regulations clause in protecting the common-law right to trial by jury. The Anti-Federalists feared that, with congressional complicity, the Court would manipulate its appellate jurisdiction to undermine the ancient right by reversing a jury's verdict in cases involving federal questions. Therefore, they called for various constitutional amendments to explicitly preserve this right in civil as well as criminal cases. The Anti-Federalists finally succeeded, in 1791, with the adoption of the Seventh Amendment, which provides: "In suits at common law, where the value in controversy shall exceed twenty dollars, the right of trial by jury shall be preserved, and no fact tried by jury shall be otherwise re-examined in any Court of the United States, than according to the rules of the common law."[122] The Federalists attempted to answer their critics' charges by arguing that the Framers could not reconcile various states' practices regarding the mode of trial in common-law, civil-law, equity, and admiralty and maritime cases. Unable to draft satisfactory general language, the Framers conferred discretionary authority on Congress to resolve the problem in the future. Despite their disagreements on the ambiguity and adequacy of the exceptions and regulations clause, neither the Federalists nor the Anti-Federalists expressed the view that the clause granted Congress the power to prevent the Supreme Court from deciding constitutional claims. There is no evidence that the Ratifiers believed Congress could use its authority to deny litigants access to a federal forum in which they could vindicate their constitutional rights. In fact, Alexander Hamilton specifically argued that the Framers' plan of government requires a federal forum to decide constitutional issues. Since Hamilton (in the *Federalist*) was attempting to win support for the Constitution rather than alarm the opposition, his strong defense of judicial nationalism assumes added significance. Within the context of a written constitution and a federal system, Hamilton argued, the availability of a federal forum is essential to establishing constitutional supremacy and vindicating national political authority. Therefore, Hamilton admitted congressional authority to make exceptions and regulations that promote the Supreme Court's effectiveness and efficiency, but he did not concede legislative power to curb the Court's jurisdiction over constitutional issues. However broad congressional authority may be, it does not encompass the power to impair the Supreme Court's performance of its core functions.

The Judicial Function, Jurisdiction, and Congressional Power

The Ratifiers as well as the Framers conceived of the federal courts' jurisdiction, and the scope of congressional authority to control such jurisdiction, in relation to the judiciary's functions within a framework of federalism. While several Ratifiers argued that congressional authority over the Supreme Court's appellate jurisdiction is plenary, at least one Ratifier, Patrick Henry, reasoned that the Court's jurisdiction is mandatory. Most of the Ratifiers anticipated that, under the Constitution of 1787, the Supreme Court's appellate jurisdiction would be commensurate with the political and constitutional responsibilities of the national government.

Despite intense disagreements between Federalists and Anti-Federalists concerning the Supreme Court's core functions, at a minimum a majority of the Ratifiers who addressed the Judiciary Article agreed that the Court would have authority to enforce constitutional supremacy and national authority vis-à-vis the states. While the Federalists stressed judicial review of state acts that might encroach on the national government's powers in foreign and domestic affairs, the Anti-Federalists emphasized judicial review of congressional and presidential actions that would jeopardize the states' integrity and authority to regulate their internal affairs and protect their citizens' rights. The Ratifiers disagreed about the scope of national judicial review because they also disagreed about the relative powers of the states and the national government under the new constitution.

Some Ratifiers expected the Supreme Court and the lower federal courts to perform important functions in addition to promoting constitutional supremacy and national authority. First, with the Supreme Court at its apex, the federal judiciary would provide a uniform construction of national law—the Constitution, congressional acts, and international treaties—as the supremacy clause implies. Second, the national courts would afford foreign and out-of-state suitors a neutral forum in which to decide federal questions. Third, the federal judiciary would protect the citizens' constitutional rights against state and national interference. Fourth, the Supreme Court would offer the states a neutral forum for the resolution of interstate conflicts. The Federalists either distrusted the states' judiciaries or doubted that state courts would perform these functions satisfactorily. The Anti-Federalists suspected that national courts would favor the national government's interests, vitiate the authority of the states' judiciaries, and absorb their functions.

Just as Federalists and Anti-Federalists disagreed about the federal judiciary's functions, they contested the scope of the federal courts' jurisdiction. Condemning that jurisdiction as expansive and dangerous, Anti-Federalists introduced resolutions and constitutional amendments in various state ratifying conventions to restrict federal jurisdiction exclusively to questions of national and international law. Fearing that the Supreme Court would employ its appellate jurisdiction to undermine the common-law right to a jury trial, the Anti-Federalists attempted to limit the appellate jurisdiction to questions of law. This fear explains the Anti-Federalists' attempts to confine the mode of appeal in common-law cases exclusively to a writ of error.

Despite the intensity of the Anti-Federalists' barrage, the Federalists ultimately won the campaign. They defended the federal courts' jurisdiction as no more than commensurate with the national government's authority in foreign and domestic affairs. Therefore, the federal courts could not pose a threat to the states, their judiciaries, or the citizens' rights, as the opposition claimed. Inasmuch as federal jurisdiction was limited to national objects, the new federal courts could not undermine either popular sovereignty or individual liberty.

In the debates on federal jurisdiction and the scope of congressional authority to limit and regulate the Supreme Court's appellate jurisdiction, only a few Ratifiers conceded plenary power to Congress. The debate focused on congressional authority to (1) distribute a measure of the Court's appellate jurisdiction to the lower federal courts and the states' courts, (2) promote the Supreme Court's effective administration and supervision of the federal judiciary, and (3) limit appeals to questions of law and/or fact. Although the preponderance of evidence suggests that many Ratifiers believed that Congress could restrict appeals on questions of fact, a majority of those Ratifiers who expressed themselves questioned legislative power to restrict appeals on questions of law. No evidence implies legislative power to gerrymander the Supreme Court's appellate jurisdiction to prevent the Court from deciding constitutional claims. However, both Federalists and Anti-Federalists opined that the exceptions and regulations clause was ambiguous despite its ostensible clarity. Given this unresolved ambiguity, both the Framers and Ratifiers effectively left the adjustment of legislative and judicial authority to the political process.

4

Judicial Power, the Judicial Function, and Jurisdiction: The Formative Period (1789–1835)

....

A careful analysis of the Federal Convention and the state ratifying conventions indicates that both the Framers and the Ratifiers perceived the exceptions and regulations clause as ambiguous, despite the ostensible clarity of its language. In effect, the Judiciary Article established a broad constitutional framework within which Congress and the federal courts could accommodate one another's authority and adjust federal-state relationships in response to changing conditions. During the nation's first four decades, Congress and the Supreme Court articulated their respective views of judicial power, the judicial function, legislative authority to regulate and limit the federal courts' jurisdiction, and an appropriate relationship between the state and federal judiciaries.

Debates in the First Congress on the Bill of Rights, the president's implied power to remove executive officers, and the Judiciary Act of 1789 support the view that Congress need not confer the entire appellate jurisdiction. However, these debates do not support the argument that legislative power to curb the Court's appellate jurisdiction is plenary. The same evidence indicates that congressional power to create and abolish lower federal courts as well as regulate their jurisdiction is plenary. Since 1789, however, Congress has left the Supreme Court's door open to review the decisions of state courts raising federal questions in cases that might jeopardize constitutional supremacy and national authority. Whether prudential or constitutional considerations have motivated Congress remains a fundamental question.

During the nation's first decade, the Supreme Court advanced tentatively from a defensive toward an expansive theory of judicial power and function. After more than a decade of self-restraint, John Marshall asserted the Court's authority to review and, simultaneously, declare a congressional act unconstitutional. During the next sixteen years Marshall and Joseph Story extended the doctrine of constitutional review to state legislative acts and judicial decisions. Both Marshall and Story emphasized the Supreme Court's power to promote constitutional supremacy, protect national authority, provide a uniform interpretation of national law, correct state judicial prejudice and parochialism, and protect the citizen's constitutional rights.

Despite their agreement on the Court's core functions, Marshall and Story differed over the nature of the Supreme Court's appellate jurisdiction. While Marshall viewed the appellate jurisdiction as constitutionally vested, he denied that it was self-executing. Story conceded that the Court's appellate jurisdiction was not self-executing, but argued that Congress had an affirmative duty to confer the entire judicial power and jurisdiction on some federal court.[1] However, Story's view has never prevailed. And Marshall's opinions do not imply that Congress has plenary power to withdraw questions of constitutional right from the Supreme Court's appellate jurisdiction. In light of the Court's and Congress's early views of judicial power and function, how have both institutions defined the scope of legislative power to curb the Supreme Court's appellate jurisdiction? Do either the Court's decisions or legislative enactments lend credence to the argument that congressional power is plenary?

Congressional Perceptions of Judicial Power and Function

When the First Congress convened on March 4, 1789, the members turned to the problems that the Framers and Ratifiers had not resolved. "During the first session," wrote Charlene Bickford and Helen Veit, "the Senate and House focused their attention on organizing the legislative, executive, and judicial branches of the government, on establishing a revenue system . . . on regulating commerce, and on amending the Constitution."[2] On June 12, four days after Madison proposed a series of constitutional amendments,[3] Richard Henry Lee introduced S. 1, the Judiciary Act of 1789, which organized the federal judiciary and defined its jurisdiction within the broad framework of Article III.[4] Since Madison, Lee, Ellsworth, Paterson, and other important Framers and Ratifiers were well represented in the First Congress,[5] the language and drafting of the Judiciary Act of 1789 provide important insight into a congressional understanding of the federal judiciary's functions and the scope of legislative authority to limit and regulate the jurisdiction of the federal courts. Without ascribing either oracular wisdom or organic authority to the First Congress, it provided the basic framework within which the federal judiciary would operate and it defined the judiciary's constitutional role.

While Madison's statement on the proposed Bill of Rights supports judicial review of congressional and presidential acts,[6] the language of the Judiciary Act of 1789 explicitly confers power on the Supreme Court to enforce constitutional supremacy and national authority over the states. Section 25 of the act provides for Supreme Court review, by a writ of error, of state court decisions that question the validity of congressional acts and international treaties, that declare state acts unconstitutional or in conflict with national laws and treaties, and that deny a litigant's claim to protection under the federal Constitution, laws, and treaties.[7] Sections 9 and 11 curtail the lower federal courts' jurisdiction,[8] leaving the decision of most federal questions to state courts. Section 25 confers appellate jurisdiction on the Supreme Court to promote a uniform interpretation of national law and to vindicate the individual's rights against state interference. The states' judiciaries retained jurisdiction to curb potential abuses of congressional power, while the Supreme Court could employ its appellate jurisdiction to prevent state encroachments on national political authority.[9]

Even William Crosskey, who denies that Congress implied judicial review of its own acts, admits that section 25 confirms the Supreme Court's power to enforce national authority over the states.[10] However, the close juxtaposition of the debates on the Bill of Rights and the president's implied power to remove executive appointees, as well as the debate on the Judiciary Act, cast doubt on Crosskey's argument. As Raoul Berger emphasizes, these debates reflect the congressional expectation that the Supreme Court would enforce constitutional supremacy vis-à-vis the states and the national government.[11] Since the members of Congress had already fully aired the issue of judicial review, there was little cause to continue the debate when considering the Judiciary Act.[12]

Although the language and legislative history of the Judiciary Act imply judicial review, they do not support either the plenary or the mandatory view of the Supreme Court's appellate jurisdiction. Obviously, Congress assumed that Article III is not self-executing.[13] Otherwise, Congress would have left the regulation of the appellate jurisdiction to the Supreme Court. In regulating the review of state court decisions involving questions of individual rights, the validity of the national government's conduct, and the constitutionality of state actions, Congress did not provide for review of decisions that favored the national government's authority or the individual's claim. Nor did Congress provide for review of state court decisions that denied the states' claims. If the language of section 25 fails to support the view that Congress has an affirmative duty to confer the entire appellate jurisdiction, it does not support the argument that congressional power is plenary. Congress was careful to leave the Supreme Court's door open to decide constitutional questions in cases arising in state courts. Whether the members of the First Congress believed they had a constitutional obligation or merely a prudential responsibility to provide for some federal forum to vindicate constitutional rights and national authority, the Judiciary Act of 1789 established a basic pattern that has survived the vicissitudes of judicial-legislative conflict.

With regard to the relationships among the Supreme Court, the lower federal courts, and state courts, the Judiciary Act conforms to some Framers' and Ratifiers' expectations that the exceptions and regulations clause is a distributing clause, which Congress can employ to adjust the relationship between the state and federal judiciaries, minimize friction between the two judicial systems, and promote the federal judiciary's efficiency and effectiveness. Some observers claim that the Judiciary Act of 1789 failed to accomplish these objectives, but others believe that it represents a necessary concession to the states in the nation's formative period.[14] Whether Congress can employ its distributive powers to deny access to some federal forum regarding constitutional rights remains debatable.

Despite Theodore Eisenberg's claim that the lower federal courts have since become indispensable to the Supreme Court's performance of its essential functions,[15] the framing and language of the Judiciary Act of 1789 do not support this "essential-functions" test. The members of the First Congress believed that the Constitution confers plenary power to create lower courts, fix their structure, and curtail their jurisdiction. Although Article I (section 8, cl. 9) grants Congress the power "[t]o constitute federal tribunals inferior to the Supreme Court," the ordain and establish clause (Article III, section 1) is permissive rather than mandatory. According to the latter clause, Congress "*may* from time to time ordain and establish" lower courts.[16] Under the Judiciary Act and subsequent legislation, until 1875 Congress did not vest broad federal-question jurisdiction in the lower courts. Federal court decisions adhere to the Framers' premise that congressional authority over the existence and jurisdiction of the lower courts is plenary.[17] Eisenberg to the contrary, Congress has discretionary authority to create and abolish as well as expand and contract the lower courts' jurisdiction.[18] However, does Congress have plenary authority to completely close all federal courts, including the Supreme Court, to persons seeking to protect their constitutional rights? Neither Eisenberg nor his critics answer this question satisfactorily.

As the debates in the First Congress indicate, the scope of legislative power over the Supreme Court's jurisdiction is closely related to the scope of the Court's power of judicial review. Both Charles Haines and Raoul Berger contend that the First Congress accepted judicial review of state and congressional acts.[19] During early congresses (1789–1800), Berger writes, with relatively few exceptions the members and other political leaders accepted judicial review as a concomitant of limited, constitutional government. James Wilson's "Lectures on Law" (1790–1791), the debates on chartering the First Bank of the United States, numerous statements by Federalist and Anti-Federalist members, the congressional response to the Court's decision in *Hayburn's Case* (1792), and the debates on the Sedition Act of 1798 reflect the fact that Federalists and Anti-Federalists alike assumed that the Supreme Court would enforce constitutional supremacy over Congress and the states.[20] Only after the Supreme Court failed to declare the Alien and Sedition Act unconstitutional did the Anti-Federalists focus their attack on the Court.

Early Judicial Perceptions of the Courts' Powers and Functions

In the early formative period, the Supreme Court moved cautiously toward a theory of judicial review that, under John Marshall's forceful leadership, encompassed the Framers', Ratifiers', and Congress's expectations that the federal judiciary would enforce constitutional supremacy, national authority, and a uniform interpretation of national law. In four cases, several justices and federal judges articulated an incipient theory of judicial review. Although the Court never pronounced judgment in *Hayburn's Case* (1792), the decision of the Circuit Court for the District of New York (consisting of Chief Justice Jay, Justice Cushing, and District Judge Duane) cast doubt on the constitutionality of the congressional pension law, which, in effect, assigned nonjudicial duties to the courts. While expressing deference toward Congress, the judges rejected the proposition that Congress could assign nonjudicial duties to the federal courts.[21] The justices' opinions suggest a defensive theory of judicial review. Namely, when Congress enacts legislation that encroaches on the Supreme Court's functions or requires the Court to perform nonjudicial functions, the Court has authority and a responsibility to protect the structure of government by declaring the act null and void.

In a second case, *Hylton* v. *United States* (1796), involving a constitutional challenge to an annual tax on carriages, Justice Chase observed:

> As I do not think the tax on carriages is a direct tax, it is unnecessary, at this time, for me to determine, whether this court, constitutionally possesses the power to declare an act of congress void, on the ground of its being made contrary to, and in violation of, the constitution; but if the court have such power, I am free to declare, that I will never exercise it, but in a very clear case.[22]

The Court did not void the statute, but it clearly made a judgment regarding its constitutionality, despite Chase's disclaimer. Without challenging congressional authority, the justices extended the concept of judicial review, albeit cautiously, beyond *Hayburn's Case*, to subjects (congressional taxation) far removed from judicial autonomy, independence, and inherent power. However, Chase denied that the Court should exercise its power unless Congress has made a clear mistake regarding the scope of its constitutional authority. Justice Chase thus anticipated James Bradley Thayer's argument for judicial self-restraint by a century.[23]

Justice Chase further articulated his views of judicial power, constitutional supremacy, and national authority during the February 1796 term of the Court. In *Ware* v. *Hylton* (1796), the Court sustained the constitutionality of the Treaty of Peace with Great Britain, in preference to Virginia's confiscation law. Sustaining the rights of British creditors under the treaty's terms, Chase noted, "If the court possess a power to declare treaties void, I shall never exercise it, but in a very clear case indeed."[24]

Ignoring the states' preconstitutional antecedents and the Tenth Amendment's limitations on national power, Chase restated the Framers' view that treaties are the supreme law (under Article 6, section 2), that valid treaties supersede state laws, that treaties are binding domestic law, and that both state and federal judges have a duty to enforce constitutional supremacy. Implicit in Chase's seriatim opinion is that, should state judges fail to enforce the supreme law, federal judges are bound by their oath and their judicial duty to defend the Constitution and national authority. Once again, Chase carefully avoided a dangerous confrontation with Congress by finding the treaty valid; nevertheless, he exercised the power of judicial review. Both in *Hylton* and *Ware* he exhibited self-restraint, disclaiming judicial authority to declare federal laws and treaties null and void unless Congress has made a clear mistake.

Chase issued his most forceful statement on judicial power in the infamous trial of James Callender for seditious libel against the president of the United States.[25] Denying the jury's right to determine the constitutionality of the Sedition Act of 1798, Chase claimed exclusive power for the judiciary as a coequal branch of the national government. The right to determine a statute's constitutionality, he argued, "is expressly granted to the judicial power of the United States."[26] Although Chase conceded that the Court should not exercise its power in "doubtful cases," he reminded Congress and the president that "the judicial power of the United States is co-existent, co-extensive, and co-ordinate with, and altogether independent of, the federal legislature, or the executive."[27]

After asserting judicial power (under Article III) to enforce constitutional supremacy (under Article VI, section 2), Chase concluded "that the judicial power of the United States is the only proper and competent authority to decide whether any statute made by congress (or any of the state legislatures) is contrary to, or in violation of, the federal constitution."[28] Despite his intemperate management of the jury, Chase's statement is the most comprehensive exposition of judicial power and the judicial function prior to John Marshall's opinions in *Marbury* v. *Madison* (1803), *McCulloch* v. *Maryland* (1819), and *Cohens* v. *Virginia* (1821), and Joseph Story's opinion in *Martin* v. *Hunter's Lessee* (1816). Chase clearly asserted judicial power to maintain constitutional supremacy vis-à-vis Congress and the states as well as national authority over the states, a claim that he attributed to the Framers, the First Congress, and George Washington.[29]

Casting Chase's judicial caution to the winds, John Marshall in *Marbury* v. *Madison*[30] claimed the power of judicial review and declared section 13 of the Judiciary Act of 1789 unconstitutional.[31] According to Marshall's view, when Congress and the president exceed their respective constitutional powers, the Court must entertain and decide cases that meet its jurisdictional and procedural requirements.[32] Since the Constitution is a binding and enforceable organic law, the Court cannot abstain from deciding legal controversies within its jurisdiction. Marshall recognized that Article III, section 2, is a distributing clause, but he denied that Congress had authority to redistribute or add to the Court's original jurisdiction.[33] Although Marshall could have read Article III and section 13 of the Judiciary Act in an alternative manner that would have rendered the latter valid, he chose instead to assert judicial power while avoiding a direct confrontation with President Jefferson or the Jeffersonian Republican majority in Congress.

One plausible interpretation of Article III, section 2, is that the Framers stated the Supreme Court's minimum original jurisdiction, which Congress could expand statutorily by carving out subjects from the Court's appellate jurisdiction. Since the language of Article III specifies both the subjects of the Court's original and appellate jurisdiction, Marshall rejected this contention.[34] He could have read section 13 of the act in its natural sense, as regulating the Supreme Court's power to issue writs of mandamus in appeals from lower courts.[35] Obviously, neither alternative interpretation would have served Marshall's political objectives of promoting constitutional supremacy and judicial independence without presenting a palpable threat to Congress and the president.

Having decided that section 13 of the Judiciary Act was unconstitutional, Marshall had little reason to determine whether Marbury had a legal right to his commission as justice of the peace or whether he had a remedy in some other federal court. Although Marshall's opinion regarding Marbury's legal rights and remedies is merely dictum, he restates the common-law principle that where there is a legal right, there must also be a remedy, lest the right become a hollow promise.[36] Marshall's opinion addresses statutory rights and remedies, but he also commented on the judiciary's obligation to protect the individual's constitutional rights. With reference to bills of attainder, ex post facto laws, and the limitations of the treason clause (Article III, section 3, cl. 1), Marshall asserted the federal judiciary's responsibility to enforce constitutional supremacy against congressional encroachments.[37] His theory of judicial review in *Marbury* encompasses judicial power to enforce individual rights vis-à-vis Congress. Marshall's opinion also affirms a right to a judicial remedy, perhaps in a federal forum.

In *McCulloch* v. *Maryland* (1819) and *Cohens* v. *Virginia* (1821) Marshall further articulated his views on judicial power, the judicial function, and the Supreme Court's appellate jurisdiction to enforce constitutional supremacy and national authority over the states. Sustaining congressional power to charter the Second Bank of the United States as an appropriate exercise of various delegated and implied powers (under Article I, section 8), in *McCulloch* Marshall described the Court's function in promoting constitutional supremacy. First, under the supremacy clause, the states cannot interfere with the national government's exercise of its constitutionally delegated and implied powers.[38] Second, if a state law were to take precedence over a valid national law, the national government would lay prostrate "at the foot of the states," which would violate the express terms of the supremacy clause.[39] Third, Marshall clearly stated that the Supreme Court had authority to declare the Maryland law, "imposing a tax on the Bank of the United States . . . unconstitutional and void."[40] Since Marshall had already justified the exercise of judicial review in relation to Congress, he hardly needed to vindicate its exercise over the states.

Two years later, in *Cohens* v. *Virginia* (1821), Marshall asserted the Supreme Court's appellate jurisdiction, under section 25 of the Judiciary Act of 1789, to review a decision of Virginia's highest appellate court drawing into question the validity of a federal treaty or statute. Although he claimed jurisdiction under the Judiciary Act, Marshall addressed the constitutional bases and functions of the Court's appellate jurisdiction, arguing that the Constitution vests subject-matter jurisdiction directly in the Supreme Court. If the Court's jurisdiction over cases in law and equity arising under the Constitution, congressional acts, and treaties is inherent, as Marshall reasoned, any exceptions must "be implied, against the express words of the article."[41] Or, as he stated the argument:

> The jurisdiction of the court, then, being extended by the letter of the constitution to all cases arising under it, or under the laws of the United States, it follows, that those who would withdraw any case of this description from that jurisdiction, must sustain the exemption they claim, on the spirit and true meaning of the constitution, which spirit and true meaning must be so apparent as to overrule the words which its framers have employed.[42]

Despite his conviction that the Court's subject-matter jurisdiction is inherent, Marshall also argued that it is not self-executing. If Congress had not regulated the Supreme Court's appellate jurisdiction under the Judiciary Act, it would have been free to exercise the full jurisdiction that Article III confers. Since Congress had acted, the Court must exercise its jurisdiction within the framework that Congress has established. However, congressional legislation must be consistent with the Constitution, over which the Supreme Court has the last word, a cautionary note that Marshall omitted from his opinion.

In addition to examining the constitutional bases of the Court's appellate jurisdiction, Marshall explored the Framers' underlying objectives in creating a high court of error. First, in cases involving claims of state interference with an individual's constitutionally protected rights, according to Marshall, the Framers believed that "justice" demands access to a supreme court to correct the errors of state courts.[43] Second, in a federal system, the United States government requires a national court to enforce its constitutional authority and protect its citizens' rights.[44] Third, there should be a national forum to provide a uniform interpretation of national law, inasmuch as "[d]ifferent states may entertain different opinions on the true construction of the constitutional powers of congress."[45] Fourth, Marshall argued that a supreme tribunal is necessary to correct local judicial bias. Marshall implied, but did not declare, that the Framers intended to mandate access to an independent, impartial Article III tribunal to decide constitutional claims.[46]

In his analysis of Article III, section 2, as a distributing clause, Marshall stressed the importance of the Court's appellate jurisdiction in protecting the national government's domestic authority and the nation's international sovereignty.[47] Indeed, he argued that the appellate jurisdiction is indispensable to enforcing the Constitution and laws throughout United States territory. As Marshall noted, "[t]he exercise of the appellate power over those judgments of the state tribunals which may contravene the constitution or laws of the United States, is, we believe, essential to the attainment of those objects,"[48] that is, the supremacy of the national government in its sphere of constitutional authority. Marshall's opinion in *Cohens* implies that the Supreme Court's appellate jurisdiction to review the decisions of state courts concerning the federal constitution, laws, and treaties is constitutionally vested.[49] Furthermore, he denied that Congress could withdraw subject matter from this appellate jurisdiction. Evidently, John Marshall related his views on judicial review and the Court's appellate jurisdiction to the Supreme Court's function of maintaining constitutional supremacy, protecting national authority, and vindicating the individual's constitutional rights against state infringement.

Unlike Marshall, Justice Joseph Story believed that Congress has an affirmative duty to confer the entire judicial power on some federal court. Five years before *Cohens*, in *Martin v. Hunter's Lessee* (1816),[50] Story sustained the Supreme Court's authority, under section 25 of the Judiciary Act, to review a decision of the Virginia Court of Appeals questioning the validity of the Treaty of 1794 with Great Britain. In upholding section 25 of the Judiciary Act, which provoked intense reaction in Virginia, Story explained his views on judicial power, the judicial function, and federal jurisdiction. Emphasizing that the language of the Judiciary Article is general, Story began his inquiry by examining the Framers' broad intentions. He argued that Article III is mandatory, imposing an affirmative duty on Congress to confer the entire judicial power and constitutional jurisdiction on the federal judiciary, since the Framers intended to create three coequal branches of government. Without the judiciary, Story noted, "it would be impossible to carry into effect some of the express provisions of the constitution."[51] Comparing the vesting clauses of the legislative, executive, and judiciary articles, he argued that the parallel construction of all three clauses is imperative rather than discretionary. Otherwise, "congress might successively refuse to vest the jurisdiction in any one class of cases enumerated in the constitution, and thereby defeat the jurisdiction as to all."[52] Story thus anticipated a congressional strategy of jurisdictional gerrymandering, which could impair the Supreme Court's coequal status and vitiate the Framers' plan of government.

Despite the discretionary language of the ordain and establish clause, Story insisted that Congress also has a responsibility to establish lower federal courts. Inasmuch as he assumed that Congress could not vest the judicial power of the United States in the states' courts, he reasoned that the failure to create lower federal courts would defeat the Supreme Court's appellate jurisdiction. As Story wrote:

> If congress may lawfully omit to establish inferior courts, it might follow, that in some of the enumerated cases, the judicial power could nowhere exist . . . and if in any of the cases enumerated in the constitution, the state courts did not then possess jurisdiction, the appellate jurisdiction of the supreme court . . . could not reach those cases, and consequently, the injunction of the constitution, that the judicial power "shall be vested," would be disobeyed. It would seem, therefore, to follow, that congress are bound to create some inferior courts, in which to vest all that jurisdiction which, under the constitution, is exclusively vested in the United States.[53]

He concluded, "the whole judicial power of the United States should be, at all times, vested, either in an original or appellate form, in some courts created under its authority."[54]

Story's analysis rests on the explicit assumption that the Framers intended the exceptions and regulations clause exclusively as a distributive clause, permitting Congress to apportion various classes of cases among the Supreme Court, the lower federal courts, and the states' courts. The first class includes cases that arise under the Constitution, national laws, and treaties; cases involving foreign diplomatic personnel; and admiralty and maritime cases. In this class, the Constitution's language is mandatory, requiring Congress to extend either appellate or original jurisdiction to some federal court. These cases involve questions of national power, policy, rights, and sovereignty.[55] In a second class, involving cases in which the United States is a party, Story admitted congressional power to withdraw jurisdiction. Congress has authority to prevent suits against the United States, which, in the legislature's judgment, might impair or compromise national sovereignty.[56] Here the Constitution's language gives Congress discretion to determine the wisdom of permitting, prohibiting, and regulating such cases. Other than the Supreme Court's exclusive, original jurisdiction, Story conceded that Congress could distribute the appellate jurisdiction between the Supreme Court and lower federal courts. Since no other constitutional provision restricts legislative authority, Congress can employ the exceptions and regulations clause to distribute the appellate jurisdiction among those Article III courts that the legislature creates.[57]

In a third class of cases, Story recognized that "cases within the judicial cognisance of the United States, not only might, but would, arise in the state courts, in the exercise of their ordinary jurisdiction."[58] Acknowledging that state judges would decide federal questions in such cases, Story wrote, the Framers explicitly imposed a judicial duty to enforce the supremacy of the federal constitution, laws, and treaties in preference to the laws and constitutions of the various states. Without a mandatory appellate jurisdiction, the national government would lay prostrate at the foot of the states, to paraphrase John Marshall.[59] Admitting that state judges are as learned, honorable, and wise as federal judges, Story nevertheless stated that the Constitution presumes "that state attachments, state prejudices, state jealousies, and state interests, might sometimes obstruct, or control, or be supposed to obstruct or control, the regular administration of justice."[60] Therefore, in various enumerated controversies, "reasons of a higher and more extensive nature, touching the safety, peace and sovereignty of the nation, might well justify a grant of exclusive [appellate] jurisdiction."[61] In addition to this raison d'état, Story argued that in a federal system there must be a final judicial arbiter to provide a uniform interpretation of national law.[62] From Story's perspective, the requirement of a uniform construction of national law is not merely sound policy; it is essential to the Framers' plan of government.

In a concurring opinion, Justice Johnson sustained the constitutionality of section 25 of the Judiciary Act. However, he disagreed with Story's mandatory construction of Article III. Attempting to reconcile state and national judicial authority, he denied that the language of the judicial vesting clause is imperative.[63] If the language of Article III is discretionary rather than imperative, Story's entire analysis collapses, as Johnson evidently understood. Furthermore, Congress would have discretionary authority to apportion cases among state and federal courts as national policy, prudence, wisdom, and federalism require. However, Johnson did not suggest that congressional authority, under the exceptions and regulations clause, is plenary.

Judicial Perceptions of Congressional Power Under the Exceptions and Regulations Clause

The Pre-Marshall Era: Oliver Ellsworth v. James Wilson

"Despite indications at the time of the adoption of the Constitution that the Court possessed a power of appellate jurisdiction totally independent of Congressional action," writes Jerome Levy, "the Court has held that Congressional authority is necessary to any exercise of jurisdiction."[64] Even if Levy's observation is correct, has the Supreme Court ever sustained congressional authority to gerrymander or withdraw constitutional issues selectively from the Court's appellate jurisdiction? Has Congress denied litigants access to some federal forum in which to vindicate their constitutionally protected rights? It is one thing to recognize legislative authority to regulate the mode of appeal, but quite another to concede congressional authority to interfere with the Court's power and functions.

In one early case, *Wiscart* v. *D'Auchy* (1796), Chief Justice Oliver Ellsworth conceded that the Supreme Court's appellate jurisdiction flows directly from the Constitution, but argued that the Court exercises its jurisdiction only in conformity with the rules that Congress prescribes.[65] Speaking for a majority in *Wiscart*, Ellsworth commented:

> In all other cases, only an appellate jurisdiction is given to the court; and even the appellate jurisdiction is, likewise, qualified; inasmuch as it is given "with such exceptions, and under such regulations, as the congress shall make." Here, then, is the ground, and the only ground, on which we can sustain an appeal. If congress has provided no rule to regulate our proceedings, we cannot exercise an appellate jurisdiction; and if the rule is provided, we cannot

depart from it. The question, therefore, on the constitutional point of an appellate jurisdiction, is simply, whether congress has established any rule for regulating its exercise?[66]

Several observations are worth noting about Ellsworth's opinion in *Wiscart*. First, he addressed congressional power to *regulate* the mode of appeal in equity and civil-law cases rather than congressional authority to *exclude* these cases from the Court's jurisdiction. Second, Ellsworth's opinion rests on a statutory construction of sections 21 and 22 of the Judiciary Act of 1789, regulating the mode of appeal in civil cases. Inasmuch as Ellsworth claimed that Congress had included appeals in admiralty and maritime cases under sections 21 and 22, there was no reason to address the constitutional issue. Hence, Ellsworth's observations on congressional authority to regulate the appellate jurisdiction are dicta.

In a dissenting opinion, Justice Wilson, who had drafted the relevant constitutional provisions in the Federal Convention's Committee of Detail, denied that the Judiciary Act comprehended appeals from the circuit courts in admiralty and maritime cases.[67] Although Wilson conceded legislative authority to make both exceptions and regulations, unlike Ellsworth he claimed inherent judicial power to exercise the appellate jurisdiction, absent statutory exceptions and regulations.[68] If the Court's appellate jurisdiction is inherent, how far can Congress go in enacting exceptions and regulations before it trenches on the Supreme Court's inherent power? Wilson did not answer this intriguing hypothetical question. However interesting his response might have been, it would not have been binding since his was a minority opinion.[69]

The Marshall Era

Following Ellsworth's dictum in *Wiscart*, in 1803 the Marshall Court ruled that it could not issue a writ of error to review a decision of the general court of the Northwest Territory, since Congress had not regulated appeals in such cases.[70] The attorney for the plaintiff in *Clarke v. Bazadone* (1803) argued that the Supreme Court would have appellate jurisdiction to superintend the lower courts and correct manifest errors in the record, even without a statutory or a constitutional grant of authority. Apparently rejecting counsel's reasoning, the Court adhered to the view that it could not exercise appellate jurisdiction without legislation regulating the mode of appeal from a lower court. Nevertheless, the Court's decision rests on statutory rather than constitutional interpretation. In the absence of a statute regulating appeals from the territorial court, the Supreme Court simply refused to entertain the case. Therefore, *Clarke* is of no precedential value in determining the scope of congressional power to exclude subjects from the Supreme Court's appellate jurisdiction.

On February 23, 1803, one day before John Marshall delivered the Court's opinion in *Marbury* v. *Madison*, the chief announced a unanimous decision in *United States* v. *Simms*.[71] Although the statutes did not specifically authorize criminal appeals to the Supreme Court (on a writ of error), the Court accepted jurisdiction, *sub silentio*, on appeal from the Circuit Court for the District of Columbia. To some commentators, the Court's acceptance of jurisdiction implies that Marshall viewed the appellate jurisdiction as inherent. However, Marshall subsequently rejected *Simms* as a binding precedent. The conventional interpretation of *Simms* is that it has no precedential value regarding the inherent nature of the Court's appellate jurisdiction or the scope of congressional power to curb such jurisdiction. Nevertheless, the proximate juxtaposition of *Marbury* and *Simms*, and Marshall's subsequent opinion in *United States* v. *More*,[72] invite speculation about John Marshall's views on the scope of congressional and judicial authority. Given his conception of jurisdiction, judicial power, and the judicial function (in *Marbury*), the Court's acceptance of jurisdiction, *sub silentio* (in *Simms*), and Marshall's subsequent opinion in *More*, the *Simms* decision is not compatible with either a plenary approach to congressional power or a mandatory view of the Supreme Court's appellate jurisdiction.

In *United States* v. *More* (1805), Marshall articulated the "negative-pregnant" doctrine, which expanded on Ellsworth's opinion in *Wiscart* v. *D'Auchy* (1796). Marshall dismissed the writ of error to the Circuit Court for the District of Columbia, noting that the statutes did not provide expressly for appeals in such cases.[73] He rejected *Simms* explicitly as precedent, commenting during oral argument that "[n]o question was made, in that case, as to the jurisdiction. It passed *sub silentio*, and the court does not consider itself as bound by that case."[74] Since the decision turned on an interpretation of the Judiciary Act of 1789 and the law concerning the District of Columbia,[75] once again there was little need to discuss the constitutional basis of the Court's appellate jurisdiction. Nevertheless, Marshall noted that the Court cannot infer appellate jurisdiction from congressional silence. Absent any legislation on the subject, the Supreme Court could conceivably exercise the full appellate jurisdiction that Article III vests.[76] Once Congress has acted, however, the Court can only exercise jurisdiction according to the specific regulations that the legislature has authorized. Since Congress has never been entirely silent on the subject, as James Lenoir wrote, Marshall's remark remains purely speculative.[77]

Aside from an apparent theoretical difference between Marshall and Ellsworth, much of Marshall's opinion is dictum. First, Congress had regulated the Court's appellate jurisdiction in this case. Therefore, his observations on the inherent nature of the appellate jurisdiction in the absence of legislative regulation are neither binding nor relevant. Second, Marshall did not clearly distinguish between "exceptions" and "regulations." At one point, he used both terms interchangeably. When discussing the relevant provisions of the Judiciary Act, however, he employed the term "regulation." In either event, Marshall's opinion does not offer explicit support for judicial gerrymandering, a practice that would be inconsistent with his previously expressed views in *Marbury*. Nor does his opinion suggest that Congress can make exceptions without regard to constitutional limitations external to the Judiciary Article.

In *Durousseau* v. *United States* (1810) the Supreme Court returned to the question of congressional power to make exceptions to its appellate jurisdiction.[78] Speaking for the Court, Marshall addressed the broad constitutional question, but the decision actually rests on a statutory construction of an act establishing the territorial government of Louisiana. Does section 8 of the act of March 26, 1804, permit the Supreme Court to review the decisions of the district court for the territory of Louisiana?[79] By comparing the act of 1804 with section 10 of the Judiciary Act of 1789, Marshall concluded that Congress had not intended to make the decision of the district court final in the present case. As he interpreted the act of 1804, the "true" intent of Congress was "to place those courts precisely on the footing of the court of Kentucky, in every respect, and to subject their judgments, in the same manner, to the revision of the supreme court."[80]

Acknowledging congressional power to make exceptions to the Court's appellate jurisdiction, Marshall noted that the statute did not expressly restrict the Supreme Court's power to review, on a writ of error, the district court's decision. Furthermore, he observed, the statute's affirmative grant of power to the district court did not imply any exception to the Supreme Court's appellate jurisdiction. Therefore, "[i]t would be repugnant to every principle of sound construction, to imply an exception against the intent."[81] Urging a liberal construction of the statutes establishing courts in the western territories, Marshall asked whether it could "have been the intention of the legislature, to except from the appellate jurisdiction of the supreme court, all the causes decided in the western country, except those decided in Kentucky."[82] Obviously, Marshall concluded that Congress could not have intended such an absurd and inequitable result.

Although *Durousseau* turned on a question of statutory construction, Marshall took the opportunity to reaffirm the negative-pregnant doctrine that he had expressed in *United States* v. *More*.[83] Admitting that the Constitution vests appellate powers directly in the Court, Marshall nevertheless affirmed congressional authority to limit the exercise of these powers. Even though the Judiciary Act of 1789 did not expressly limit the Supreme Court's appellate jurisdiction, Marshall inferred such exceptions from the limited grant of appellate power:

> They [Congress] have not, indeed, made these exceptions in express terms. They have not declared, that the appellate power of the court shall not extend to certain cases; but they have described affirmatively its jurisdiction, and this affirmative description has been understood to imply a negative on the exercise of such appellate power as is not comprehended within it.[84]

As in *More*, Marshall rendered his argument concerning the inherent nature of the Court's appellate jurisdiction meaningless or without any practical significance.[85] Since Congress had not conferred the entire appellate jurisdiction in 1789, Marshall's view is identical with Ellsworth's in *Wiscart*; that is, unless Congress affirmatively grants appellate jurisdiction, the Court cannot exercise its inherent power. In addition to this logical flaw, the entire discussion of congressional power under the exceptions and regulations clause is beyond the point in *Durousseau*. Inasmuch as Marshall concluded that Congress had not limited the Supreme Court's appellate jurisdiction in the act of 1804, his comments are dicta. While they may be interesting to advocates of plenary power, jurists and commentators should not read *Durousseau* as settling the question of congressional authority to curb the Supreme Court's appellate jurisdiction.

Almost two years after *Durousseau*, on March 10, 1812, the Supreme Court dismissed a writ of error to the Circuit Court for the District of Pennsylvania in *United States* v. *Goodwin*, for want of jurisdiction.[86] Speaking for the Court, Justice Bushrod Washington denied that the jurisdictional statutes provided for a writ of error "to reverse the judgment of a circuit court in a civil action, which has been carried up to the circuit court from the district court, by writ of error."[87] Inasmuch as the present case arose on a writ of error from the district and circuit courts, Washington concluded, the statutes did not confer appellate jurisdiction to review the circuit court's decision.[88] Although Washington's opinion is consistent with Ellsworth's view that the Court can exercise its appellate jurisdiction only according to the statutes regulating appeals, there is no reference to either the constitutional basis of the Supreme Court's jurisdiction or the scope of congressional power to curb the appellate jurisdiction. The binding rule in *Goodwin* is that Congress intended only one reexamination of a district court's decision in a civil case tried by a common-law jury. *United States* v. *Goodwin* simply does not address the issue of congressional power to prevent the Supreme Court from reviewing cases that present constitutional claims.

If John Marshall's opinion in *Marbury* v. *Madison* raised serious questions about the Supreme Court's power to declare congressional acts unconstitutional, his opinions in *McCulloch* v. *Maryland* (1819), *Cohens* v. *Virginia* (1821), and *Osborn* v. *Bank of the United States* (1824)[89] created a political storm. In these decisions, the Court sustained the supremacy of national laws and treaties over state laws and judicial decisions. Prior to the Court's decision in *McCulloch*, which upheld congressional power to incorporate the Bank of the United States and declared the Maryland tax on the bank's operations unconstitutional, Ohio had enacted a law taxing each branch of the bank in the state $50,000 per year. Despite *McCulloch*, Ohio attempted to collect the tax, which eventually resulted in *Osborn*.[90]

In determining the constitutionality of Ohio's tax, Marshall raised a series of questions relevant to the jurisdiction of the United States courts. First, does the act incorporating the Bank of the United States authorize it to sue in the United States courts? Second, can Congress confer such jurisdiction on the circuit courts through the act of incorporation? Third, can Congress confer original jurisdiction on the circuit courts in cases that fall within the Supreme Court's appellate jurisdiction? Fourth, does the Eleventh Amendment bar this suit against the state of Ohio?[91] If the answer to the last question is "yes," there is no need to examine the previous questions.[92]

Marshall disposed of the sovereign immunity issue (posed by the Eleventh Amendment) by arguing that this was not a suit against the state. Both on the face of the record and in fact, Ohio was not a party to the suit, despite the state's claim that Osborn and others were acting as its agent.[93] Since Osborn was personally responsible for taking money from the bank, he could be sued as an individual who had a substantial interest in the outcome of the decision. As Marshall observed, the Eleventh Amendment did not pose a constitutional bar because Osborn had "a real interest in the case, since [his] personal responsibility is acknowledged, and, if denied, could be demonstrated."[94]

If the Eleventh Amendment does not pose a constitutional bar, does the statute incorporating the bank authorize this suit? Marshall disposed of the question by noting that the language of the act explicitly provided that:

> the bank shall be 'made able and capable in law,'—'to sue and be sued, plead and be impleaded, answer and be answered, defend and be defended, in all state courts having competent jurisdiction, and in any circuit court in the United States.' These words seem to the court to admit of but one interpretation; they cannot be made plainer by explanation.[95]

Marshall then declared that Congress could authorize the federal courts to enforce national laws; Article III, section 2, cl. 1:

> enables the judicial department to receive jurisdiction to the full extent of the constitution, laws and treaties of the United States, when any question respecting them shall assume such a form that the judicial power is capable of acting on it. That power is capable of acting only when the subject is submitted to it, by a party who asserts his rights in the form prescribed by law. It then becomes a case, and the constitution declares, that the judicial power shall extend to all cases arising under the constitution, laws and treaties of the United States.[96]

While Marshall's statement is consistent with the view that the Supreme Court exercises its appellate jurisdiction according to the statutes, an equally plausible interpretation is that the Court can exercise its judicial power only in cases or controversies that are within its jurisdiction.

After determining that the original suit, *Bank of the United States* v. *Osborn*,[97] arose under the laws of the United States, despite the fact that some issues did not present federal questions, Marshall examined the scope of congressional power to apportion the Supreme Court's appellate jurisdiction among the circuit courts. Simply stated, Marshall argued that Congress can employ the exceptions and regulations clause as a distributive clause to promote constitutional supremacy and national authority through the Supreme Court or the lower federal courts, as prudence and wisdom dictate.[98] Aside from promoting national authority, Marshall's statement reveals a distrust of the states' judiciaries to enforce national policy.

Although Marshall explicitly acknowledged the constitutional limitation that the Eleventh Amendment imposes on the federal courts' jurisdiction, he deftly circumvented the problem of the state's sovereign immunity by denying that *Osborn* was a suit against the state. Thus he was free to assert the federal courts' authority to vindicate the powers of the national government. Marshall's only explicit reference to the exceptions and regulations clause treats the provision as a distributive clause, which Congress can employ to assure access to some judicial forum for the vindication of federal claims. At no point does Marshall suggest that Congress has authority to gerrymander the appellate jurisdiction to prevent litigants from raising federal questions in the Supreme Court.

The Supreme Court decided *Osborn, Cohens, McCulloch*, and *Martin* during the zenith of John Marshall's prestige and authority (1815–1825). By 1826, however, the Court's influence began to decline.[99] "It was apparent before the election of Andrew Jackson," Charles Grove Haines wrote, "that the Court was giving some consideration to what Mr. Dooley called 'election returns.' "[100] Between 1826 and 1831 the Supreme Court faced a series of conflicts with Congress, the president, and the states. During the last five years of Marshall's stewardship, the Court was so internally divided that it lost credibility and influence.[101] However, despite external conflict and internal division, in *Craig* v. *Missouri* (1830)[102] Marshall asserted the Court's appellate jurisdiction under section 25 of the Judiciary Act of 1789.[103] Although Marshall's opinion did not raise any constitutional issues regarding the Supreme Court's appellate jurisdiction, it reflected his broad construction of the Judiciary Act as a means to promote national political and constitutional authority.[104] His interpretation of section 25 of the act also prompted congressional attempts to repeal the provision.[105]

Craig raised two important issues. First, under section 25, did the Court have jurisdiction to review the decision of the Missouri Supreme Court? Second, did a state statute requiring Missouri treasury officials to issue interest-bearing certificates violate Article I, section 10 (cl. 1) of the U.S. Constitution, which prohibits the states from emitting bills of credit?[106] Although it was not clear from the trial record that Craig had challenged the constitutionality of the Missouri law, as the Judiciary Act required, Marshall argued that this was the only real question raised and decided by the state's courts.[107] Since the Missouri Supreme Court had sustained the constitutionality of the state statute, Marshall concluded that the case was "within the 25th section of the judiciary act, and consequently, within the jurisdiction of this court."[108] Marshall devoted the remainder of his opinion to demonstrating that the Missouri law violated the U.S. Constitution.[109]

Marshall's opinion fragmented the Court and provoked congressional ire. Justices Johnson, Thompson, and McLean dissented from various sections of Marshall's opinion. While Johnson agreed that the Court had jurisdiction, he disagreed on the constitutional question.[110] Justice Thompson acknowledged that precedent supported Marshall's interpretation of the Judiciary Act, but questioned the applicability of precedent since Craig had not raised the constitutional issue directly in the state court. Thompson also disagreed with Marshall on the constitutional issue.[111] McLean concurred with Thompson on the jurisdictional question and disagreed with Marshall on the merits, arguing that Missouri's certificates were not bills of credit prohibited under Article I.[112]

On January 24, 1831, the Judiciary Committee of the House of Representatives issued a report "favoring the repeal of the twenty-fifth section of the Judiciary Act under which the Supreme Court had annulled some of the most important laws of the states."[113] As Haines noted, the committee's majority report claimed that the Framers had not intended "to provide for appeals from the state courts to the Supreme Court."[114] Therefore, the majority concluded that section 25 was unconstitutional and should be repealed. Despite congressional pique with the Supreme Court, the House exercised self-restraint, defeating the bill 138/51.[115]

Judicial Power, Function, and the Supreme Court's Appellate Jurisdiction: The Early Years

In the nation's formative years (1789–1835), both Congress and the Supreme Court assumed that the Court would play a central role in promoting constitutional supremacy, national authority, and a uniform interpretation of national law. The debates in the First Congress on the Judiciary Act of 1789, the president's power to remove executive officers, and the Bill of Rights all support the argument that the nation's leading politicians and statesmen, many of whom had attended the Federal or state conventions, expected the Supreme Court to enforce constitutional supremacy vis-à-vis Congress and the president. During the 1790s both the Federalists and Anti-Federalists anticipated that the Court would enforce the supremacy clause against state and national abuses of constitutional authority.

Even before Marshall's landmark opinion in *Marbury* v. *Madison*, the Court had moved, tentatively, toward a theory of judicial review. In *Marbury*, Marshall articulated the theory to include judicial enforcement of constitutional supremacy vis-à-vis Congress. In subsequent decisions, both Marshall and Story expanded the theory of judicial review to enforce constitutional supremacy and national authority over the states. As ardent nationalists, Marshall and Story carved out a role for the Court that emphasized protecting the structure of government (e.g., federalism and the separation of powers) that the Framers and Ratifiers had endorsed. Under Marshall, the Supreme Court assumed a responsibility for policing the boundaries of constitutional authority between the nation and the states and among the branches of the national government.

Within this broad framework of government, Marshall argued, the Constitution vests judicial power and appellate jurisdiction directly in the Supreme Court. If Congress had not acted to regulate the Court's appellate jurisdiction, the Supreme Court would be free to exercise the entire jurisdiction that Article III confers. Once Congress has acted, however, the Court exercises its jurisdiction according to statutory regulations. In contrast to Marshall's view, Story argued that the Constitution vests the appellate jurisdiction directly in the Court, and that Congress has an affirmative duty to confer the entire appellate jurisdiction. Indeed, Story argued that Congress has a duty to vest the entire federal jurisdiction in some national judicial forum. The only legitimate exception that Congress could enact is a restriction that would protect the sovereignty and authority of the national government.

Despite the Court's various pronouncements on congressional authority to regulate and limit the Supreme Court's appellate jurisdiction, the pre-Marshall and Marshall courts' decisions do not sustain the argument that congressional power is plenary. In some cases, comments on congressional power are dicta since the decision turns on a question of statutory interpretation of the judiciary acts. Other cases involve questions of statutory rather than constitutional rights or claims. Some cases deal with regulating the mode of appeal rather than exceptions to the Court's appellate jurisdiction. Several cases rest on the Eleventh Amendment's limitation on the federal judiciary's jurisdiction rather than a statutory restriction. There is not one decision between 1789 and 1835 that supports the view that Congress has plenary power to prevent the Supreme Court from entertaining and deciding federal constitutional claims. Other than Story's opinion in *Martin*

v. *Hunter's Lessee*, there is also no judicial support for the mandatory view of the Court's appellate jurisdiction. Prior to the Taney Court, there are no binding opinions that define the scope of congressional authority to limit the Supreme Court's appellate jurisdiction to decide constitutional questions.

5

Congressional Power Over the Supreme Court's Appellate Jurisdiction: From Roger Taney to Earl Warren

....

During the pre-Marshall and the Marshall eras (1789–1835), the Supreme Court laid the foundation for its role as a coequal partner in the American constitutional system. Although Marshall's theory of judicial review (in *Marbury*) focused on the Court's authority to enforce constitutional limitations on Congress, Marshall and Story stressed the Supreme Court's role as an arbiter of federalism. In a series of decisions between 1816 and 1824, Story and Marshall enforced the constitutional authority of the national government over the states. Beginning with the congressional elections of 1826, Andrew Jackson's election to the presidency in 1828, and the appointment of new justices who did not share Marshall's nationalist convictions or his views of judicial power, the Court's influence waned.[1]

Despite internal dissension and external political opposition to the Court's decisions concerning the states' powers, Marshall continued to uphold the Supreme Court's authority to enforce constitutional supremacy, national authority, and a uniform interpretation of national law. While maintaining that Article III vests judicial power and appellate jurisdiction directly in the Supreme Court, Marshall acknowledged congressional power to regulate the appellate jurisdiction. However, he did not concede legislative authority to prevent the Court from deciding constitutional claims. Although Marshall's successor, Roger B. Taney, differed with the former chief on questions of judicial power, legislative authority, and the states' competence, both the Taney and subsequent courts have adhered to Marshall's views of the Supreme Court's appellate jurisdiction.

The Taney Era

Speaking for a unanimous Court, Taney adhered to the argument in *Barry* v. *Mercein* (1847) that the Supreme Court exercises its appellate jurisdiction only according to statutory regulation.[2] Barry had filed a petition for a writ of habeas corpus in the Circuit Court for the District of New York, to secure the release of his daughter from his estranged wife's custody. Judge Samuel Betts denied the petition, ruling that under the Judiciary Act of 1789, the circuit courts could issue writs of habeas corpus only in cases within their jurisdiction.[3] Indeed, Judge Betts denied that the case raised any questions that were within the competence of the federal courts. The original case, *In re Barry*, was a domestic relations dispute, entirely within the jurisdiction of New York's courts.[4]

On appeal, Taney refused to reexamine the habeas corpus issue, claiming that the Supreme Court lacked jurisdiction to review the circuit court's decision under section 22 of the Judiciary Act of 1789.[5] Although *Barry* v. *Mercein* rests on a statutory construction of the Judiciary Act of 1789, Taney explored the scope of congressional power over the Court's appellate jurisdiction. Unlike Marshall, Taney denied that the Constitution vested any appellate jurisdiction directly in the Supreme Court. "By the constitution of the United States," he noted, "the Supreme Court possesses no appellate power in any case, unless conferred upon it by act of Congress; nor can it, when conferred be exercised in any other form, or by any other mode of proceeding than that which the law prescribes."[6] Taney's statement concedes plenary power to Congress to regulate the mode of appeal as well as to make exceptions to the Court's appellate jurisdiction. Despite Taney's excessive deference to congressional authority over the Court, *Barry* v. *Mercein* remains an exercise in statutory interpretation. While *Barry* reveals a shift in the Court's attitude toward legislative authority, the narrow ruling does not alter earlier judicial precedent. Taney's remarks on congressional power under Article III may be interesting and informative, but they are dicta not binding on future courts.

During the January 1848 term of the Supreme Court, Taney wrote the majority's opinion in *United States* v. *Curry*,[7] an appeal from the District Court for the District of Louisiana involving title to a large tract of land. Not unlike *Barry*, *Curry* presented a question of statutory construction, namely, whether the Supreme Court had jurisdiction to hear the appeal under the act of May 26, 1824, as revived by the act of June 17, 1844, which placed a one-year time limit on Louisiana land claims cases.[8] Upon determining that the one-year time limit had elapsed, Taney dismissed the appeal for want of jurisdiction. Denying that the time limit was a mere technicality, Taney again deferred to congressional power to regulate the Court's jurisdiction.[9] Aside from demonstrating Taney's deference to Congress, *Curry* did not involve a question of the jurisdictional statute's constitutionality. Therefore, Taney's observations on congressional power to regulate appeals or to correct injustice are nonbinding dicta.

During 1850 the Supreme Court decided three cases that involved congressional power to regulate the federal courts' jurisdiction: *United States* v. *Boisdoire's Heirs, Sheldon* v. *Sill,* and *McNulty* v. *Batty.* The issue in the first case, *Boisdoire's Heirs,* was whether the Supreme Court had appellate jurisdiction in a Mississippi land claims case under the acts of 1824 and 1844. The precise statutory question was whether the act of 1844, extending the act of 1824 for five years, had expired with respect to appeals from the district court to the Supreme Court.[10] Although the language of the 1844 act seemingly placed a five-year limit on the life of the original act, Taney concluded that Congress had not intended this limitation to apply to the Court's appellate jurisdiction.[11] Pointing to an "obvious" inaccuracy in the language of the act, Taney remarked, "[t]his evident inaccuracy ought not, however, to embarrass the court in expounding the act, which, taken altogether, is sufficiently plain in its objects and intentions, as well as in its language."[12] By construing the entire act, rather than relying exclusively on the one inaccurate provision, Taney preserved the Court's appellate jurisdiction while claiming to uphold the basic congressional policy or purpose that lay behind the measure.[13]

At the same time, the chief justice acknowledged congressional power to control the Court's appellate jurisdiction.[14] Since the Supreme Court's jurisdiction had not expired, Taney's analysis of the effect of a jurisdictional statute's expiration on a pending case is dictum. In *Mc-Nulty* v. *Batty* (1850),[15] Justice Nelson followed Taney's dictum in *Boisdoire's Heirs* that if a statute conferring jurisdiction expires, the Supreme Court lacks appellate jurisdiction to review the lower court's decision, although the appeal or writ of error was pending at the time the act expired. With the admission of Wisconsin to the Union, on May 29, 1848, Congress provided that cases involving federal questions would be transferred to the new District Court for Wisconsin. Congress did not make any provision for the transfer of cases involving state questions. As Justice Nelson inferred from the relevant statutes, Congress intended to leave the regulation of such questions to the new state's government. Inasmuch as *McNulty* involved a debt action, normally within a state's competence, Justice Nelson reasoned that federal jurisdiction over the case had expired when Wisconsin became a state.[16]

Although Nelson subscribed to Taney's view that the Supreme Court can exercise only the appellate jurisdiction that Congress confers, as in *Boisdoire's Heirs*, *McNulty* rests entirely on a construction of the relevant statutes. Unlike *Boisdoire's Heirs*, there is no substantive federal claim or question in *McNulty*. Once Wisconsin became a state, congressional competence over all such matters ceased and devolved upon the state government. Therefore, *McNulty* is of doubtful precedential value since Congress could not conceivably confer federal jurisdiction over questions within a state's legislative and judicial competence.[17]

The third case that the Court decided during its 1850 term, *Sheldon v. Sill*,[18] involved the scope of congressional power to limit the lower federal courts' jurisdiction rather than the Supreme Court's appellate jurisdiction. Nevertheless, Justice Grier's opinion for a unanimous court includes several interesting observations on the exceptions and regulations clause. Adhering to well-established precedent, Grier maintained that Congress has plenary power to limit the lower federal courts' jurisdiction.[19] Since the Constitution does not mandate the existence of inferior courts, Grier observed, Congress has a right to prescribe as well as:

> [W]ithhold from any court of its creation jurisdiction of any of the enumerated controversies. Courts created by statute can have no jurisdiction but such as the statute confers. No one of them can assert a just claim to jurisdiction exclusively conferred on another, or withheld from all.[20]

Grier concluded that section 11 of the Judiciary Act of 1789 was constitutional and had not conferred jurisdiction on the circuit courts in the present case.[21]

Grier also dismissed the concept that Congress must confer "all the judicial powers not given to the Supreme Court" on some inferior court.[22] Implicitly, Grier dismissed Story's mandatory theory of federal jurisdiction. However, Grier left one interesting question unanswered. If, as he claimed, Congress has plenary power to regulate and limit the jurisdiction of any court that it creates statutorily, does it have an affirmative duty to assign the entire appellate jurisdiction to the Supreme Court, whose existence the Constitution prescribes and whose power and jurisdiction the organic law mandates? Grier's answer to this hypothetical question would be interesting but beyond the point, since *Sheldon* v. *Sill* rests on a statutory construction of the circuit court's jurisdiction rather than on a constitutional interpretation of the Supreme Court's appellate jurisdiction.

Although Roger B. Taney died on October 12, 1864, one of his most interesting opinions on judicial power, the judicial function, and congressional authority over the Supreme Court's appellate jurisdiction first appeared in 1885. Published posthumously, Taney's draft memorandum in *Gordon* v. *United States* (1864)[23] is less deferential toward congressional authority than his earlier opinions, *Barry* v. *Mercein*, *United States* v. *Curry*, and *United States* v. *Boisdoire's Heirs*. Sometime during the Supreme Court's recess, Taney prepared a draft of his views, which his brethren apparently considered in dismissing *Gordon* for lack of jurisdiction. As the Court's clerk remarked of the draft in 1885, "Irrespective of its intrinsic value, it has an interest for the court and the bar, as being the last judicial paper from the pen of Mr. Chief Justice Taney."[24]

An act of March 3, 1863, amending the act that established the Court of Claims, permitted either party to appeal the court's decision in any case exceeding $3,000. In effect, section 14 of the act provided that neither the Court of Claims nor the Supreme Court could enforce its judgment without executive and legislative approval. Taney acknowledged that the act posed no problems for the Court of Claims, which was an Article I court that Congress had created to facilitate legislative policy. However, section 14 of the act posed serious problems for the Supreme Court's judicial independence. If the Supreme Court granted jurisdiction, the terms of the act would render the Court subordinate to Congress and the secretary of the Treasury. By rendering a nonbinding, advisory opinion, the Court would be performing a nonjudicial function, a function beyond its judicial competence. In Taney's opinion, the act undermined the finality of the Supreme Court's judgment, from which there is no constitutional appeal, as well as its independence, coequal status, and the separation of powers.[25]

After establishing that Congress cannot confer power and jurisdiction that go beyond the limits of Article III, Taney asserted the Supreme Court's function as a final constitutional arbiter and its coequal status in the national government.[26] Casting deference to Congress and the states aside, Taney then asserted the Supreme Court's essential function as an arbiter between the national government and the states.[27] Despite his assertion of judicial power, Taney acknowledged that the Court's appellate jurisdiction was subject to congressional exceptions and regulations. However, he did not define either the scope of or limits on congressional power. If congressional power were plenary, Taney's view would collide with his analysis of the Court's status and essential functions, since Congress could employ the exceptions and regulations clause to impair the Supreme Court's power, status, and functions. In any event, *Gordon* v. *United States* involved legislative authority to expand the Court's jurisdiction beyond the limits of the Judiciary Article rather than restrict the exercise of the appellate jurisdiction within the confines of Article III. Even though Taney conceded congressional power over the Court's appellate jurisdiction, he concluded that any legislation that Congress might enact would be subject to judicial review under the supremacy clause,[28] a statement of judicial power equal to that of Marshall and Story.

During Roger B. Taney's tenure as chief justice, the Supreme Court decided at least seven cases touching on congressional power to limit its appellate jurisdiction. While Taney, Nelson, Grier, and Catron acknowledged broad, perhaps even plenary, power to limit the Court's appellate jurisdiction, the ratio decidendi in these cases did not rest on the constitutionality of congressional legislation. Several cases raised questions of statutory construction of jurisdictional statutes. In one case, Taney construed the act broadly, preserving the Court's appellate jurisdiction and avoiding any constitutional questions. In another case, Justice Grier's remarks on congressional power were dicta, since the decision involved a statutory construction of the lower court's jurisdiction rather than constitutional authority to limit the Supreme Court's appellate jurisdiction. In *Gordon* v. *United States*, the issue was congressional authority to expand rather than contract the appellate jurisdiction. Taney may have been more deferential to Congress in theory than in practice, but his opinion in *Gordon* represented a claim of judicial supremacy. As long as the Civil War raged and the Radical Republicans in Congress could remember Taney's opinion in *Dred Scott* v. *Sanford*,[29] it was best that his memorandum remained unpublished.

The Post–Civil War Era: The Chase Court

Immediately after the Civil War the Chase Court, laboring under the odium of the *Dred Scott* decision, faced a series of challenges to the congressional reconstruction program. Following the Supreme Court's decisions in *Ex parte Milligan* (1866), *Cummings* v. *Missouri* (1867), *Ex parte Garland* (1867), *Mississippi* v. *Johnson* (1867), *Ex parte Yerger*

(1868), and *United States* v. *Klein* (1872),[30] members of Congress introduced legislation to curb the Court's appellate jurisdiction. However, Chase's management of President Andrew Johnson's impeachment trial in the Senate (between March and May 1868) probably improved his personal prestige and, ultimately, helped restore congressional confidence in the Supreme Court.[31] His stewardship of the Court and a complete turnover of personnel between 1862 and 1874 also assuaged fears that the justices would pose a serious challenge to congressional policy and dominance of national politics.

Although the Radical Republicans feared that the Supreme Court would interfere with military reconstruction in the South, between 1866 and 1875 Congress expanded the federal courts' jurisdiction. Under the Civil Rights Act of 1866, Congress expanded the lower courts' jurisdiction and the Supreme Court's appellate jurisdiction to hear offenses against the statute. The act also provided for the removal of cases to federal courts in the event that individuals could not vindicate their rights in state courts.[32] Employing its authority under the Thirteenth, Fourteenth, or Fifteenth amendments, Congress continued to expand federal jurisdiction in a series of measures that included the Habeas Corpus Act of 1867, the Enforcement Act of 1870, and the Civil Rights Act of 1875.[33] In one sweep, Congress expanded the federal courts' jurisdiction to encompass virtually all federal questions in the Jurisdiction and Removal Act of 1875.[34] If Congress harbored doubts about the fidelity of the Supreme Court and the lower federal courts, the language and legislative history of these laws indicate that the nation's lawmakers distrusted the state courts to enforce constitutional supremacy, national authority, and the citizens' civil rights.

During the turbulent post–Civil War era, the Chase Court decided a series of cases touching on congressional power over the Supreme Court's appellate jurisdiction. Several cases, involving questions of statutory interpretation, were unrelated to the post–Civil War struggles between Congress and the Supreme Court. *Daniels* v. *Chicago and Rock Island Railroad Co.* (1865), for example, turned on whether Congress intended the jurisdictional statute to cover the present case. In *The Merchants Insurance Co.* v. *Ritchie* (1866), *The Assessors* v. *Osbornes* (1870), and *United States* v. *Tynen* (1871), the issue was whether repeal of the relevant statute terminated the Supreme Court's appellate jurisdiction. By contrast, *Ex parte McCardle* (1868), *Ex parte Yerger* (1869), *United States* v. *Padelford* (1870), and *United States* v. *Klein* (1872) arose out of the Civil War or postwar military reconstruction and raised fundamental questions regarding congressional power over the Supreme Court and the presidency.

The first group of cases did not pose constitutional questions for the Court. In *Daniels*, as Justice Swayne noted, the question was whether the Supreme Court had appellate jurisdiction under section 6 of the Judiciary Act of April 29, 1802. Under the act, the Supreme Court could issue a certificate of division to a circuit court in order to review "a question of law, and not of fact," in cases in which there was a division of opinion among the lower court's judges.[35] According to Swayne, *Daniels* involved both questions of law and fact. Inasmuch as these questions were inseparable, Swayne concluded, the Supreme Court lacked appellate jurisdiction.[36] Although *Daniels* rested on statutory interpretation of a jurisdictional act, Swayne commented on the scope of congressional power over the Court's appellate jurisdiction:

> To come properly before us, the case must be within the appellate jurisdiction of this court. . . . But it is for Congress to determine how far, within the limits of the capacity of this court to take, appellate jurisdiction shall be given, and when conferred, it can be exercised only to the extent and in the manner prescribed by law. In these respects it is wholly the creature of legislation.[37]

Swayne's views obviously parallel John Marshall's opinions in *Marbury* v. *Madison* and *Durousseau* v. *United States*, to which he referred. However, his views are dicta since the constitutionality of the act of 1802 was not before the Court.

In *The Merchants Insurance Co.* v. *Ritchie* (1867), *The Assessors* v. *Osbornes* (1870), and *United States* v. *Tynen* (1871),[38] the issue was whether the repeal of a statute conferring jurisdiction on the lower court also terminated the Supreme Court's appellate jurisdiction in a pending case. Speaking for a unanimous Court, in *Merchants Insurance Co.* Chief Justice Chase concluded that the Internal Revenue Act of 1866 had terminated the circuit courts' original jurisdiction in revenue cases between citizens of the same state.[39] Since the act of 1866 did not include a saving clause, jurisdiction over cases pending at the time of repeal ceased.[40] Therefore, the Court dismissed the appeal for want of jurisdiction. Chase's opinion affirms the principle established in *Norris* v. *Crocker* (1851), that repeal of a statute terminates a lower court's jurisdiction, in the absence of an explicit saving clause. *Merchants Insurance Co.* also implicitly supports the argument that congressional power over the lower federal courts' jurisdiction is plenary. In a second revenue case arising under the act of 1866, *The Assessors* v. *Osbornes*

(1870), Justice Clifford reaffirmed the principle of *Merchants Insurance Co.* that repeal of the jurisdictional statute terminates the federal courts' jurisdiction in a pending case.[41] He also reaffirmed the long-standing rule that congressional power over the lower courts' jurisdiction is plenary.[42]

In a third case, *United States* v. *Tynen* (1871), Justice Field dismissed a criminal indictment under an 1813 act defining offenses against the naturalization laws because Congress subsequently (1870) repealed the earlier act without preserving its criminal penalties.[43] Even though the repealer was implicit rather than explicit, Field affirmed the well-established principle that when two statutes conflict, the latter must prevail as the most recent expression of the legislative will.[44] Like *Daniels, Merchants Insurance Co.,* and *The Assessors, Tynen* rested on a statutory interpretation of the lower courts' jurisdiction. These cases did not present a question of congressional power to limit the Supreme Court's appellate jurisdiction. In the last three cases, the Court lacked appellate jurisdiction because Congress had repealed the lower courts' jurisdiction in a pending case. By contrast, in *Ex parte McCardle,* Congress repealed the Supreme Court's appellate jurisdiction in a case that was already before the Court.

Following the Supreme Court's decision in *Ex parte Milligan,* which denied the president's power to suspend the writ of habeas corpus and congressional power to establish martial law and try civilians by military commission outside the actual theatre of war, where civilian courts were open and functioning,[45] the Radical Republicans in Congress introduced legislation to curb the Court. During December 1866 and January 1867, as Charles Warren notes, Congress debated various measures designed to curb the federal judiciary. Representative John Bingham (R.-Ohio), for example, introduced a bill to completely abolish the Supreme Court's appellate jurisdiction.[46] The Supreme Court further enraged the Radicals on January 14, 1867, with two decisions, *Cummings* v. *Missouri* and *Ex parte Garland,* both test-oath cases arising out of the Civil War.[47] In both cases, the Court found that a legislative act denying Cummings and Garland the right to practice their professions constituted a bill of attainder, since the measure "declared the guilt of these persons and adjudged their punishment."[48] On April 5, 1867, pleadings began in *Mississippi* v. *Johnson,* in which Mississippi sought to enjoin the president from carrying out the reconstruction acts.[49]

Against this background of intense controversy between Congress and the Court, in February 1868 the justices heard oral argument in *Ex parte McCardle.*[50] The case was brought by a southern newspaper editor who had been tried for seditious libel by a military commission. After a circuit court had denied McCardle's petition for a writ of habeas corpus under the Habeas Corpus Act of 1867, on March 27, 1868, Congress repealed the previous measure (over the president's veto), which had been enacted to protect the Freedmen from their former masters. In fact, the Supreme Court had already agreed to review *McCardle*, but waited until the new act went into effect on March 27 before hearing oral argument "on the effect of the Repealer Act on the Court's jurisdiction to decide McCardle's appeal on the merits."[51] Since counsel were not available for oral argument, the Court postponed argument and did not announce its final decision until April 21, 1869.

The conventional interpretation of *McCardle* is that the Supreme Court recognized the plenary power of Congress to withdraw jurisdiction, even in a case pending before the High Court. Chief Justice Chase's opinion for the Court certainly provides evidence for the plenary view:

> We are not at liberty to inquire into the motives of the Legislature. We can only examine into its power under the Constitution; and the power to make exceptions to the appellate jurisdiction of this court is given by express words.[52]

Nevertheless, the repeal of the Habeas Corpus Act of 1867, which applied to persons in a state's custody, did not repeal the habeas corpus provision, section 14, of the Judiciary Act of 1789, which applies to persons in federal custody.[53]

Although Chase acknowledged congressional authority to regulate and make exceptions to the Supreme Court's appellate jurisdiction, the last paragraph of his opinion casts doubt on the conventional interpretation of *Ex parte McCardle*:

> Counsel seem to have supposed, if effect be given to the repealing act in question, that the whole appellate power of the court, in cases of *habeas corpus*, is denied. But this is an error. The act of 1868 does not except from that jurisdiction any cases but appeals from Circuit Courts under the act of 1867. It does not affect the jurisdiction which was previously exercised.[54]

Was Chase merely reminding counsel that an alternative avenue of appeal existed under section 14 of the Judiciary Act of 1789? Or was the chief justice implying that, if Congress had repealed the entire appellate jurisdiction over writs of habeas corpus, a serious constitutional question would exist? Namely, could Congress limit access to the writ of habeas corpus except in the manner that the Constitution prescribes? The language of Chase's opinion also implies that *McCardle* turns on a statutory construction rather than on a question of constitutional power to limit the Court's appellate jurisdiction. These ambiguities cast doubt on the precedential value of *McCardle*, since Chase did not determine whether the Court's appellate jurisdiction in habeas corpus cases is inherent.

In the face of congressional hostility, the Supreme Court retreated tactically from the field of battle. However, during the same term, the Supreme Court returned to the scope of congressional power to limit the appellate jurisdiction in habeas corpus cases. Speaking for the Court in *Ex parte Yerger*, on October 25, 1869, Chief Justice Chase acknowledged that the act of 1868 had not repealed the habeas corpus provision of the Judiciary Act of 1789.[55] In a clear reference to *McCardle*,[56] Chase implied but did not state unequivocally that, since the habeas corpus jurisdiction is derived directly from the Constitution, Congress cannot limit access to the Great Writ, except in conformity with Article I, section 9.[57] By the time the Court had decided *McCardle* and *Yerger*, the rebellion had ended. In any event, the act of 1867 merely changed the mode of appeal in habeas corpus cases from the lower courts, which implies that Congress may regulate, but not eliminate, access to the federal judiciary on a question of fundamental constitutional right. The Great Writ is so fundamental to human liberty,[58] as Chase emphasized, that attempts to limit access to the writ of habeas corpus require careful judicial scrutiny.

While Chase commented on congressional power to limit the Supreme Court's appellate jurisdiction, in both *Ex parte McCardle* and *Ex parte Yerger* he also suggested that Article I, section 9, imposes limitations on the scope of legislative authority. Some recent commentators have concluded that Chase acknowledged external constitutional restraints on congressional authority under the exceptions and regulations clause.[59] It is tempting to seize upon Chase's remarks as support for the external-restraint argument, but his comments are ambiguous. Conversely, his observations on the inherent nature of the habeas corpus jurisdiction suggest that the Court's deference to Congress was a tactical retreat rather than a concession of plenary power.[60] However jurists and scholars interpret Chase's opinions in the two cases, both *McCardle* and *Yerger* rest on statutory constructions of the Repealer Act of 1868. Therefore, his comments about congressional authority, the judicial function, and the inherent nature of the Supreme Court's habeas corpus jurisdiction are dicta. Neither case provides clear, unambiguous support for the argument that congressional power is plenary or that the Constitution imposes external restraints on the exercise of legislative authority under Article III, section 2.

If *McCardle* and *Yerger* cast doubt on legislative power to close the Supreme Court's door to petitioners seeking to vindicate fundamental constitutional rights, *United States* v. *Klein* (1872) raises serious questions about congressional authority to employ the exceptions and regulations clause as a means to promote an allegedly unconstitutional objective.[61] In July 1862, Congress authorized the president to pardon any persons who had participated in the rebellion, "with such exceptions and at such time and on such conditions as he may deem expedient for the public welfare."[62] In December 1863, President Lincoln issued a proclamation offering a full pardon to all persons (with some exceptions) who would take an oath swearing to support the Constitution and who would abide by congressional acts and presidential proclamations regarding slaves. Under the terms of the president's proclamation, the government promised to restore the individual's property rights, with the exception of slaves.[63]

Following the proclamation, on February 15, 1864, V. F. Wilson, who during the rebellion had voluntarily guaranteed the bonds of Confederate officials, took the oath of allegiance. Subsequent to Wilson's death, his administrator, Klein, petitioned the Court of Claims to recover $125,300 from the Treasury. On May 20, 1869, the Court of Claims issued a judgment for Klein, which the government appealed to the Supreme Court on December 11, 1869.[64] While the appeal was pending, on July 12, 1870, Congress passed an appropriations act, which provided that presidential pardons were inadmissable in the Court of Claims.[65] To sustain a claim, the Appropriations Act required independent proof of loyalty, irrespective of the pardon. If the Court of Claims had entered judgments on the basis of any other proof of loyalty, namely, a presidential pardon, the act required the Supreme Court to dismiss the appeal for want of jurisdiction. Finally, the Appropriations Act directed the Court to accept the presidential pardon as conclusive proof of the individual's disloyalty, in the absence of any independent proof of loyalty.[66] Under these circumstances, "the jurisdiction of the court [of claims] in the case shall cease, and the court shall forthwith dismiss the suit of such claimant."[67]

As Chief Justice Chase summarized the Appropriations Act, "[t]he substance of this enactment is that an acceptance of a pardon, without disclaimer, shall be conclusive evidence of the acts pardoned, but shall be null and void as evidence of the rights conferred by it, both in the

Court of Claims and in this court on appeal."[68] In other words, the act directed the Supreme Court and the Court of Claims to give a diametrically opposite effect to the pardon from the effect that the president had intended. According to Chase, the Court confronted two fundamental constitutional questions. First, could Congress infringe on the president's constitutional power to grant pardons by impairing the effect of a presidential pardon?[69] Second, could Congress employ its authority over the Court's appellate jurisdiction to "prescribe a rule in conformity with which the court must deny to itself the jurisdiction thus conferred, because and only because its decision, in accordance with settled law, must be adverse to the government and favorable to the suitor?"[70] If the Supreme Court had jurisdiction in this case, could Congress prescribe a rule for decision without interfering with the judicial power of the United States that Article III confers directly on the Court?

After determining that the Appropriations Act interfered with the president's pardon power (under Article II, section 1), Chase turned to the central questions of jurisdiction and judicial power.[71] First, he established that the Court of Claims was an Article III court, that it exercised the judicial power of the United States, and that the Supreme Court could exercise appellate jurisdiction over its decisions.[72] Although Chase clearly acknowledged that Congress had power to limit the Supreme Court's appellate jurisdiction in a particular class of cases, he denied that the legislature had merely enacted a jurisdictional statute:

> [T]he language of the proviso shows plainly that it does not intend to withold appellate jurisdiction except as a means to an end. Its great and controlling purpose is to deny to pardons granted by the President the effect which this court had adjudged them to have.
>
> * * * * *
>
> It is evident from this statement that the denial of jurisdiction to this court, as well as the Court of Claims, is founded solely on the application of a rule of decision, in causes pending, prescribed by Congress. The court has jurisdiction of the cause to a given point; but when it ascertains that a certain state of things exists, its jurisdiction is to cease and it is required to dismiss the cause for want of jurisdiction.
>
> It seems to us that this is not an exercise of the acknowledged power of Congress to make exceptions and prescribe regulations to the appellate power.[73]

By prescribing a rule for decision and requiring that the Court give a contrary effect to the evidence that the law required, Chase concluded that Congress had "inadvertently passed the limit which separates the legislative from the judicial power."[74] After reminding Congress that it could not use the exceptions and regulations clause to interfere with the president's pardon power and the Supreme Court's judicial power, Chase refused to deliver the coup de grace. The Supreme Court stopped short of declaring the provision of the Appropriations Act of 1870 unconstitutional. Concluding that the legislature had inadvertently inserted the provision in the Appropriations Act, the Court avoided a direct confrontation with Congress. The majority affirmed the Court of Claims' judgment, despite Justice Miller's dissent, claiming that the act was an unconstitutional interference with the president's pardon power in a "judicial proceeding in a constitutional court."[75]

While some authorities argue that *Klein* sustains the president's unconditional power to pardon crimes against the United States, other commentators argue that the decision implies that Congress cannot employ the exceptions and regulations clause for purposes that the Constitution otherwise prohibits. If Congress cannot use its authority (under Article III, section 2) to interfere with judicial and executive power, it cannot employ the provision to deny fundamental constitutional rights under the First, Fifth, and Fourteenth amendments. Still other authorities infer that Congress cannot use the exceptions and regulations clause to interfere with the Supreme Court's performance of its essential functions.[76] If *Klein* merely sustains the president's unconditional exercise of the pardon power, the decision is irrelevant in determining the scope of congressional authority over the Supreme Court's appellate jurisdiction. Even if *Klein* questions congressional authority to use Article III, section 2, for an unconstitutional purpose, the opinion is not binding, since the Court declined to declare the act unconstitutional. Although it is enticing to infer limitations on congressional authority from *United States* v. *Klein*, the opinion remains an interesting and informative period piece, another example of Chief Justice Chase's restoration of the Supreme Court's prestige and authority as a national political institution.[77]

Under Chief Justice Chase's stewardship, the Court avoided a direct confrontation with Congress over legislative control of national policy as well as the Supreme Court's appellate jurisdiction. In a series of decisions unrelated to the Civil War and Reconstruction, the Chase Court acknowledged congressional authority over its jurisdiction, but these decisions rested on statutory interpretations of the relevant jurisdictional acts. In dicta, the justices restated earlier opinions declaring that Article III enables the Supreme Court to receive jurisdiction over the persons and subject matter enumerated in section 2, but that Congress must act before the Court can exercise its jurisdiction. None of these decisions suggest that Congress can selectively withdraw subject matter from the Supreme Court's appellate jurisdiction in cases involving questions of constitutional right.

In a second series of cases arising out of the Civil War and Reconstruction, the Supreme Court acknowledged congressional power to withdraw jurisdiction over pending cases. However, neither *McCardle* nor *Yerger* involved a complete repeal of the Supreme Court's appellate jurisdiction over habeas corpus cases. Furthermore, the Court decided *McCardle* and *Yerger* on statutory rather than constitutional grounds. Thus conventional interpretations concede too much regarding congressional power to limit the Supreme Court's appellate jurisdiction. More recent interpretations claim too much regarding constitutional limitations on legislative power over the Court. In *Klein*, Chase implied that Congress cannot employ its authority for purposes that breach constitutional limitations, but the Court stopped short of declaring the Appropriations Act of 1870 unconstitutional. By stepping away from a direct confrontation with Congress, the justices restored the Court's influence, but left their successors without a binding precedent regarding the scope of congressional authority to limit the Supreme Court's appellate jurisdiction.

The Era of Industrialization and Transcontinental Expansion: The Waite and Fuller Courts

In the thirty-three years following the end of Reconstruction (1877), the Waite and Fuller courts turned to the problems of industrialization and transcontinental expansion. While the Waite and Fuller courts legitimized laissez-faire capitalism, overturning state legislation regulating business and industry, in the 1880s the Supreme Court generally sustained the congressional exercise of the commerce power vis-à-vis the states.[78] Despite criticisms of the Supreme Court's decisions overturning state legislation, congressional attacks on the Court's jurisdiction were unsuccessful. Even when the Court overturned congressional legislation, as it did in *United States* v. *E.C. Knight Co.* (1895) and *Pollock* v. *Farmers' Loan & Trust Co.* (1895),[79] Congress failed to curb judicial power. In fact, Congress continued to expand the federal courts' jurisdiction, enacting various removal statutes that allowed individuals and corporations to remove cases from state to federal courts. In March 1885, Congress reenacted the provisions of the Habeas Corpus Act of 1867.[80] By legitimizing laissez-faire capitalism and sustaining national power, the Court expanded its influence during the Waite and Fuller eras.

Under Waite and Fuller, the Court decided four cases involving questions of congressional power to limit its appellate jurisdiction: *Baltimore & Potomac Railroad Co. v. Grant* (1879), *The Francis Wright* (1882), *United States v. Bitty* (1908), and *St. Louis, Iron Mountain, & Southern Railway Co. v. Taylor* (1908).[81] Not one of these opinions suggests that Congress has unlimited power over the Supreme Court's appellate jurisdiction.[82] Although the Court acknowledged congressional authority to regulate and make exceptions to its appellate jurisdiction, in three cases these acknowledgements are dicta, since the decisions rested on questions of statutory construction. In the fourth case, *The Francis Wright*, the justices upheld the constitutionality of an act restricting appeals in admiralty to questions of law, but implied that other constitutional provisions limit the exercise of congressional authority under the exceptions and regulations clause.[83] As in earlier decisions, the Supreme Court was deferential to Congress, without conceding legislative power to bolt the Marble Palace shut to litigants presenting constitutional claims.

Citing *Durousseau v. United States* (1810), in *Railroad Co. v. Grant* Chief Justice Waite merely reaffirmed the maxim that the Court can exercise its appellate jurisdiction only when Congress affirmatively grants jurisdiction.[84] Three years after *Railroad Co.*, Waite delivered the Court's opinion in *The Francis Wright* (1882), a case that raised the issue of Congress's constitutional power to limit the appellate jurisdiction in admiralty to questions of law.[85] Relying on Ellsworth's majority opinion in *Wiscart v. D'Auchy* (1796), Chase conceded "that while the appellate power of this court under the Constitution extends to all cases within the judicial power of the United States, actual jurisdiction under the power is confined within such limits as Congress sees fit to prescribe."[86] Waite concluded:

> Undoubtedly, if Congress should give an appeal in admiralty causes, and say no more, the facts, as well as the law, would be subjected to review and retrial; but the power to except from—take out of—the jurisdiction, both as to law and fact, clearly implies a power to limit the effect of an appeal to a review of the law as

applicable to facts finally determined below. . . . The constitutional requirements are all satisfied if one opportunity is had for the trial of all parts of a case. Everything beyond that is matter of legislative discretion, not of constitutional right. The Constitution prohibits a retrial of the facts in suits at common law where one trial has been had by a jury (Amendment, art. 7); but in suits in equity or in admiralty Congress is left free to make such exceptions and regulations in respect to retrials as on the whole may seem best.[87]

Therefore, the Court found the act of February 16, 1875, confining appeals in admiralty to questions of law, constitutional.[88]

Although the Court sustained the constitutionality of the act, there was no denial of constitutional right since the parties had had an opportunity to try the facts before a jury, which satisfied the requirements of the due process clause of the Fifth Amendment. Under the Constitution and civil law, Waite argued, there is no right to retry the entire case. Indeed, Waite's remark concerning the right to trial by jury in common-law cases implies external constitutional restraints on congressional power to limit the Supreme Court's appellate jurisdiction. The chief justice's assurance that "constitutional requirements are all satisfied" underscores the limitation that the due process clause of the Fifth Amendment places on congressional authority under the exceptions and regulations clause. *The Francis Wright* sustains congressional power to limit the Supreme Court's appellate jurisdiction, but Waite's opinion does not support the argument that Congress can employ its authority to vitiate constitutional rights or prevent the Supreme Court from adjudicating constitutional claims.

If Waite intimated that other constitutional provisions limit the exercise of congressional power under the exceptions and regulations clause, John Marshall Harlan explicitly stated the principle. Acknowledging congressional discretion (under Article III, section 2) in *United States* v. *Bitty*, Harlan noted, "What such exceptions and regulations should be it is for Congress, in its wisdom, to establish, having of course due regard to all the provisions of the Constitution."[89] Although Harlan suggested that other constitutional provisions may limit congressional discretion, his suggestion remains dictum, since the Court failed to find any constitutional deprivation in *Bitty*. Harlan's suggestion is intriguing, but it is not binding on the Court.

During the same term, the Court decided *St. Louis, Iron Mountain, & Southern Railway Co.* v. *Taylor* (1908), an appeal from the Supreme Court of Arkansas.[90] In this case, the Supreme Court faced the threshold issue of whether there was a cognizable federal question under the jurisdictional statute. Does section 709 of the Revised Statutes authorize an appeal from a state court when that court construes a federal statute in a way that denies the appellant's right or immunity under federal law?[91] Speaking for the Supreme Court, Justice Moody concluded that the state court's decision presented a federal question reviewable under section 709.[92] In construing section 709, Moody reiterated the often-stated argument that, while the judicial power of the United States extends to all cases arising under the Constitution, laws, and treaties, the Court exercises its appellate jurisdiction according to the statutes. "Congress," Moody observed, "has regulated and limited the appellate jurisdiction of this court over the state courts by § 709 of the Revised Statutes, and our jurisdiction in this respect extends only to the cases there enumerated, even though a wider jurisdiction might be permitted by the constitutional grant of power."[93] According to Moody, there was no doubt that Congress intended the Court to exercise appellate jurisdiction in this case. Indeed, Moody observed that the exercise of appellate jurisdiction in such cases was indispensable in maintaining a uniform construction of national law throughout all the states.[94]

Not unlike *Grant* and *Bitty*, *St. Louis, Iron Mountain, & Southern Railway Co.* involved a question of statutory construction. Namely, did the jurisdictional statutes authorize review of the lower federal or state court's decision? These cases did not challenge the constitutionality of the jurisdictional statute. In *The Francis Wright*, the Supreme Court sustained the constitutionality of the act limiting appeals in admiralty to questions of law. However, Chief Justice Waite's opinion implies that constitutional limitations, external to Article III, may restrict the congressional exercise of power under the exceptions and regulations clause. The opinions of neither the Waite nor the Fuller court support the argument that Congress has plenary power over the Supreme Court's appellate jurisdiction.

The Era of Mature Capitalism, the Administrative State, and World Power: From Taft to Warren

While the Waite and Fuller courts confronted cases arising from the nation's emergence as an industrial and transcontinental power, following the First World War the Supreme Court faced problems posed by America's rapid industrialization and development as a world power.

Between William Howard Taft and Earl Warren, the Supreme Court faced an increasing volume of complex cases posed by the growth of public corporations, the concentration of economic power, the Great Depression, governmental regulation of business and industry, the proliferation of administrative and independent agencies, the development of administrative law, declared and undeclared wars, a prolonged period of cold war, and a myriad of seemingly intractable racial and social problems.

Responding to these problems, Congress continued to expand the jurisdiction of the Supreme Court and the lower federal courts. Despite periodic conflicts with the Court, Congress has not enacted legislation limiting the Supreme Court's authority to review lower court decisions presenting constitutional claims. Although the justices have continued to acknowledge broad congressional power over the Supreme Court's appellate jurisdiction, they have not conceded legislative authority to prevent litigants from presenting constitutional claims to the Court. With few exceptions, Congress and the Supreme Court have shown deference toward one another.

The Taft and Hughes Courts

During the interwar period (1918–1941) the Taft and Hughes courts decided only a few cases touching on congressional power over appellate jurisdiction. These were *Luckenbach S.S. Co. v. United States* (1926), *Federal Radio Commission v. General Electric Co.* (1930), and *Crowell v. Benson* (1932).[95] In *Luckenbach*, the Court sustained congressional legislation limiting review of Court of Claims decisions to questions of law. Speaking for the Court, Justice Van Devanter denied that the limitation on the Supreme Court's jurisdiction contravened the Fifth Amendment's due process clause.[96]

Inasmuch as there was no right to sue the United States and the Court of Claims had considered and weighed the evidence according to law, Van Devanter concluded, there was no basis for the Supreme Court to review the lower court's finding.[97] If there had been a right to sue for additional compensation or if the Court of Claims had failed to consider and evaluate the evidence, according to Van Devanter's view, there would have been a right to appeal the lower court's decision. On a more speculative note, if Congress had foreclosed any review of Court of Claims' decisions involving due process claims as an exercise of legislative power to limit the Supreme Court's appellate jurisdiction, would such a limitation pass constitutional muster? Given Justice Van Devanter's view that no constitutional deprivation had occurred, *Lucken-bach* remains an exercise in statutory interpretation rather than a test of congressional power to prevent the Court from deciding constitutional claims.

Speaking for the Court in a second case, *Federal Radio Commission* v. *General Electric Co.* (1930), Justice Van Devanter denied that the Supreme Court had appellate jurisdiction to review a decision of the Court of Appeals for the District of Columbia, on appeal from the Federal Radio Commission.[98] In denying jurisdiction, Van Devanter noted that the Court of Appeals for the District of Columbia is an Article I court that performs nonjudicial functions. In this case, the lower court acted as a "superior and revising agency."[99] Its proceedings were legislative and advisory, "because it was . . . instructing and aiding the commission in the exertion of power which was essentially legislative."[100] Although Congress can invest legislative courts with nonjudicial functions,

> this Court cannot be invested with jurisdiction of that character, whether for purposes of review or otherwise. It was brought into being by the judiciary article of the Constitution, is invested with judicial power only and can have no jurisdiction other than of cases and controversies falling within the classes enumerated in that article. It cannot give decisions which are merely advisory; nor can it exercise or participate in the exercise of functions which are essentially legislative or administrative.[101]

Federal Radio Commission simply did not present a case or controversy within the meaning of Article III. Therefore, the Court could not render a binding judgment. Furthermore, Congress could not invest appellate jurisdiction in the Supreme Court because the Court's exercise of such jurisdiction would breach the limits of judicial power. In reality, *Federal Radio Commission* addressed the problem of expanding the Court's appellate jurisdiction beyond the Judiciary Article's limits rather than restricting its jurisdiction under the exceptions and regulations clause.

Although *Crowell* v. *Benson* (1932) does not concern congressional power to withdraw whole classes of cases from the Supreme Court's appellate jurisdiction, Chief Justice Hughes's majority opinion raises several important questions concerning constitutional limitations on the scope of legislative power to delegate determinations of fact and law to administrative agencies.[102] Do Article III and the Fifth Amendment's due process clause require judicial determination of questions of law and of fact? The Longshoremen's and Harbor Workers' Compensation Act of 1927 provided for compensation to employees who had been injured or killed while performing work on the navigable waters of the United States. The suit was brought in the district court to enjoin the enforcement of an award in favor of Knudsen and against Benson, who claimed that Knudsen was not an employee at the time he was injured and was not, therefore, within the jurisdiction of the United States Employees' Compensation Commission.[103] While the deputy commissioner had authority to determine questions of fact and law, the act provided that "[r]ulings of the deputy commissioner upon questions of law are without finality. So far as the latter are concerned, full opportunity is afforded for their determination by the Federal courts through proceedings to suspend or to set aside a compensation order."[104]

Before determining the substantive merits of Knudsen's claim, Hughes examined a series of procedural and constitutional objections to the act. First, he denied that Benson was entitled to a jury trial simply because the claim arose under the admiralty and maritime jurisdiction of the federal courts.[105] Second, Hughes examined a series of due process claims. The chief emphasized that the statute permitted the federal courts to examine questions of law. He also noted that the act contained adequate procedural safeguards, including notice and a hearing on the facts, which preserved procedural due process. Furthermore, in exercising their admiralty and maritime jurisdiction, the federal courts had ample opportunity to determine the "fairness" of any administrative hearing. For example, was the administrator's finding without evidence, or contrary to the evidence, or was the hearing inadequate, unfair, or arbitrary in any way?[106]

Unlike common-law cases, in admiralty, Hughes continued, there is no right to a judicial determination of all the issues in a claim. Under Article I, Congress can assign the determination of private claims in admiralty to administrative agencies as long as the federal courts have an opportunity to review the agency's determination of questions of law and the jurisdictional facts upon which the claimant's constitutional rights depend.[107] Did Knudsen come within the deputy commissioner's jurisdiction? Was he an employee at the time he sustained the injury? Was he injured or killed while working on the navigable waters of the United States?[108] If any of these conditions had not been met, the case would not have come within the admiralty and maritime jurisdiction, which implies that congressional power to substitute administrative proceedings for an Article III court and, perhaps, a jury trial would be questionable.

Inasmuch as Congress had not explicitly provided that the deputy commissioner's determination of "fundamental or jurisdictional facts" should be final,[109] the majority concluded that the statute neither violated Benson's constitutional rights nor undermined the independence of the federal judiciary.[110] Nevertheless, the majority emphasized, "the essential independence of the exercise of the judicial power of the United States in the enforcement of constitutional rights requires that the Federal court should determine such an issue upon its own record and the facts elicited before it."[111] In sustaining judicial power, the majority argued that the due process clause imposes limits on congressional power to withdraw subject matter from the federal courts' jurisdiction. *Crowell* v. *Benson* is of limited value in determining the scope of congressional authority since the majority sustained the constitutionality of the act.[112] Nevertheless, *Crowell* raises the question of whether there is a right to the determination of constitutional claims in Article III courts rather than administrative agencies or state courts. If such a right exists, could Congress enact legislation limiting the Supreme Court's appellate jurisdiction to hear constitutional claims on appeal from state courts?

The Vinson and Warren Courts

During the post–World War Two period, the Supreme Court and the lower federal courts decided several disparate cases raising questions of congressional authority over the federal courts' jurisdiction. In *National Mutual Insurance Co.* v. *Tidewater Transfer Co.* (1949), the Court examined the scope of congressional power to extend the diversity jurisdiction to citizens of the District of Columbia.[113] Although Article III, section 2, extends the judicial power to controversies "between citizens of different States," on April 20, 1940, Congress conferred the diversity jurisdiction on the federal district courts in civil actions, involving no federal question, between citizens of the District of Columbia and citizens of the states and U.S. territories.[114] Since the Supreme Court's decision in *Hepburn & Dundas* v. *Ellzey* (1805), the diversity jurisdiction had been closed to citizens of the District of Columbia.[115]

Although Congress intended to create equal access to a federal forum in diversity cases, could it extend the diversity jurisdiction beyond the limits of Article III, or exercise its power under Article I (section 8, cl. 17) to govern the District of Columbia, for the same purpose without breaching the Judiciary Article's limits? The Court sustained the constitutionality of the act, but the majority was divided regarding the basis of congressional power. Justices Black and Burton joined Justice Jackson in announcing the Supreme Court's decision, but Justice Rutledge wrote a concurring opinion, in which Justice Murphy concurred. While the Jackson Three sustained the act as an exercise of Congress's Article I powers,[116] Rutledge and Murphy argued that Congress has authority to place citizens in the District of Columbia on an equal basis with citizens of the states by extending the diversity jurisdiction.[117] Upon examination of the Framers' intent, Rutledge "discovered" that the Constitution's authors did not preclude a broad construction of citizenship.[118] Apparently, Rutledge and Murphy preferred broadening the meaning of "citizen" to breaching the limits of judicial power and jurisdiction under Article III.

Vinson, Douglas, Frankfurter, and Reed dissented from the majority's opinions. Vinson, with Douglas concurring, argued that Congress lacked the power to extend federal jurisdiction beyond the Judiciary Article's limits. The records of the Federal Convention and the state ratifying conventions, as well as judicial precedent, Vinson wrote, clearly confirm that Article III states the maximum jurisdiction that Congress can confer on the federal judiciary.[119] Frankfurter, with Reed concurring, was equally certain that the Judiciary Article clearly delimits the federal courts' judicial power and jurisdiction.[120] The Framers imposed these restrictions, Frankfurter noted, to guard "against the self-will of the courts as well as against the will of Congress by marking with exactitude the outer limits of federal judicial power."[121]

Citing *Ex parte McCardle* as authority, Frankfurter asserted that congressional power over the federal courts' jurisdiction is plenary:

> Congress need not establish inferior courts; Congress need not grant the full scope of jurisdiction which it is empowered to vest in them; Congress need not give this Court any appellate power; it may withdraw appellate jurisdiction once conferred and it may do so even while a case is *sub judice.*[122]

In the same paragraph, however, Frankfurter asserted judicial power to determine the validity of congressional legislation affecting the federal courts' jurisdiction:

> If there is one subject as to which this Court ought not to feel inhibited in passing on the validity of legislation by doubts of its own competence to judge what Congress has done, it is legislation affecting the jurisdiction of the federal courts. When Congress on a rare occasion through inadvertence or generosity exceeds those

limitations, this Court should not good-naturedly ignore such a transgression of congressional powers.[123]

As in *Federal Radio Commission* v. *General Electric Co., National Mutual Insurance Co.* addresses the power of Congress to expand federal jurisdiction beyond the Judiciary Article's limits. In sustaining the act, three members of the majority rested their decision on Congress's Article I powers, while the other two justices redefined the meaning of citizenship with regard to diversity jurisdiction. Felix Frankfurter's comments on congressional power to limit federal jurisdiction appear in a dissenting opinion and are not germane to the decision. Frankfurter's remarks concerning the plenary power of Congress are gratuitous since he reserved the right to determine the constitutionality of any legislation affecting the federal courts' jurisdiction.

During Vinson's tenure as chief, the Court decided two other cases, *Bruner* v. *United States* (1952) and *De La Rama S.S. Co.* v. *United States* (1953), that dealt with congressional power to withdraw the federal courts' jurisdiction in a pending case.[124] Speaking for the majority in *Bruner*, Chief Justice Vinson noted that, absent a reserve or saving clause, jurisdiction over a pending case would cease, even after the Supreme Court had granted a writ of certiorari.[125] Vinson merely adhered to the well-established principle that "when a law conferring jurisdiction is repealed without any reservation as to pending cases, all cases fall with the law."[126] Vinson's opinion implies that, if the repealer had altered the appellant's property rights, a constitutional issue would exist.

In *De La Rama S.S. Co.* v. *United States*, the Supreme Court held that Congress had not deprived the district court of jurisdiction over a suit in admiralty to recover for the wartime loss of the M.V. Dona Aurora by repealing the War Risk Insurance Act of 1940.[127] Despite the repealer of July 25, 1947, the General Saving Statute preserved the ship owners' rights. Even without the General Saving Statute, Frankfurter wrote for the Court, the government's liability as an insurer would have survived the repealer.[128] If the repealer had merely altered the mode of proceeding by transferring such cases from the admiralty jurisdiction of the district court to the jurisdiction of the Court of Claims, there would be no question about congressional power to terminate the district court's jurisdiction. However, as the government admitted:

[T]o deny petitioner the opportunity to enforce its right in admiralty and to send it to the Court of Claims instead is to diminish substantially the recoverable amount, since in a district court sitting in admiralty interest accrues from the time of filing suit . . . while in the Court of Claims interest does not begin to run until the entry of judgment.[129]

Congress can change the forum as long as it does not alter or extinguish substantive property rights. Frankfurter's opinion implies that the Fifth Amendment imposes a limitation on congressional power to regulate the federal courts' jurisdiction. Frankfurter's opinion in *De La Rama* seemingly conflicts with his dissenting view in *National Mutual Insurance Co.*, that legislative power to limit the federal court's jurisdiction is plenary. Since Congress had enacted a general saving statute, however, Frankfurter's remarks regarding constitutional rights, absent congressional legislation, are dictum.

In the Vinson Court era, the courts of appeals for the Second Circuit and the District of Columbia Circuit decided two cases that questioned congressional authority to deny access to a federal forum, *Battaglia* v. *General Motors Corp.* (1948) and *Eisentrager* v. *Forrestal* (1949).[130] *Battaglia* was one of more than a hundred cases in which various litigants challenged the constitutionality of the Portal-to-Portal Pay Act of 1947. In 1938, Congress had enacted the Fair Labor Standards Act (FLSA), which established a minimum wage for workers and set a maximum work week of forty hours. The act provided that workers should be paid one and one-half times their ordinary hourly wage for more than forty hours of work in any work week.[131]

Disputes soon arose about the meaning of the "work week." Did it include time spent traveling to and getting ready for work? After the administrator of the Labor Department's Wages and Hours Division ruled that coal and iron-ore miners were entitled to compensation for time spent traveling from the mine surface to the work face, workers in other industries sued in the district courts, demanding that their pay be figured from "portal to portal," from the time they arrived until they left the company's premises. In a six-to-two decision, the Supreme Court ruled in *Anderson* v. *Mt. Clemens Pottery Co.* (1945) that the workers were entitled to portal-to-portal pay as well as penalties, interest, and retroactive compensation under the Fair Labor Standards Act.[132]

Following the 1946 election, a Republican-controlled Congress enacted the Portal-to-Portal Pay Act of 1947, which President Truman reluctantly signed. The 1947 act provided that the time spent traveling to and from the job and getting ready to work was not and had never been part of the statutory work week under the FLSA. Congress reversed the Supreme Court's decision by giving a precise and different meaning to the act. Moreover, Congress exercised its authority to limit the jurisdiction of the courts by providing that no state or federal court could hear future cases involving portal-to-portal pay under the FLSA.[133]

In *Battaglia*, the Court of Appeals for the Second Circuit sustained the constitutionality of the Portal-to-Portal Pay Act's termination of state and federal court jurisdiction in all pending and future cases arising under the FLSA. The circuit court found the 1947 act a reasonable exercise of the commerce power.[134] Since the right to portal-to-portal pay in this case arose from the Supreme Court's interpretation of the FLSA, Congress could exercise the commerce power to correct the Court's mistaken statutory interpretation. Furthermore, the right to portal-to-portal pay was a statutory rather than a constitutional right. Therefore, Congress could abolish state and federal court jurisdiction without breaching the Fifth Amendment's due process clause. The circuit court found no violation of the due process clause, but Judge Chase cautioned:

> We think, however, that the exercise by Congress of its control over jurisdiction is subject to compliance with at least the requirements of the Fifth Amendment. That is to say, while Congress has the undoubted power to give, withhold, and restrict the jurisdiction of courts other than the Supreme Court, it must not so exercise that power as to deprive any person of life, liberty, or property without due process of law or to take private property without just compensation. . . . Thus, regardless of whether subdivision (d) of section 2 [of the Portal-to-Portal Act] had an independent end in itself, if one of its effects would be to deprive the appellants of property without due process or just compensation, it would be invalid.[135]

Although the circuit court sustained the act's constitutionality, Judge Chase stated explicitly that the due process clause of the Fifth Amendment imposes limitations on congressional authority to restrict the federal courts' jurisdiction. Since the Portal-to-Portal Act merely left the courts without jurisdiction in future cases, without depriving any Fifth Amendment rights or encroaching on judicial power, Judge Chase's opinion regarding external constitutional limitations on congressional power, under the exceptions and regulations clause, remains an interesting but nonbinding invitation to the federal judiciary.

If Judge Chase issued an invitation in *Battaglia*, Judge Prettyman stated explicitly in *Eisentrager* v. *Forrestal* (1949) that the habeas corpus provision of Article I, section 9, imposes limits on congressional power over the federal courts' jurisdiction.[136] The writ of habeas corpus, Judge Prettyman argued, is an inherent common-law right, which Congress cannot suspend "except when, in cases of rebellion or invasion, the public safety may so require."[137] Even where the jurisdictional statutes fail to provide for a judicial forum, all persons, including enemy aliens in U.S. custody, have a right to the writ. The writ is an indispensable means to test the government's authority to deprive a person of life and liberty in any case arising under the Constitution, laws, and treaties of the United States.[138]

In reversing the district court's decision, the court of appeals held that any person in the custody of the United States government can seek a writ of habeas corpus to determine the validity of such confinement. Simply because Eisentrager was not confined within U.S. territory or because the jurisdictional statute failed to provide a judicial forum, Congress cannot suspend the privilege to the writ either by omission or affirmative action, except according to Article I, section 9.[139] Although there are no federal courts in Germany, Judge Prettyman observed, the District Court for the District of Columbia has jurisdiction over Eisentrager's immediate jailer and his commanding officers, including the secretary of defense.[140]

Quoting from *Johnson* v. *Zerbst*,[141] Judge Prettyman emphasized the indispensability of the Great Writ as the only means to enforce the Constitution's prohibitions on the exercise of governmental power:

> Of the contention that the law provides no effective remedy for such a deprivation of rights affecting life and liberty it may well be said—as in *Mooney* v. *Holohan* . . . that it "falls with the premise." To deprive a citizen of his only effective remedy would not only be contrary to the "rudimentary demands of justice" but destructive of a constitutional guaranty specifically designed to prevent injustice.[142]

In reference to the Great Writ, Judge Prettyman resurrected Justice Story's argument that Congress has an affirmative duty to vest the entire judicial power of the United States in some federal forum. "Upon the precise problem before us," Prettyman wrote, "we conclude that whatever may be the lack of forum in other cases, the Constitution specifically prohibits that result in respect to habeas corpus. Congress cannot suspend that privilege, unless there be invasion or rebellion."[143] Although the Supreme Court reversed *Eisentrager* v. *Forrestal* on other grounds,[144] Judge Prettyman's opinion remains a powerful statement of the right of access to a federal forum in habeas corpus cases.

In 1962, the Warren Court decided the last major case relating to questions of congressional power over the federal courts' jurisdiction, *Glidden Company* v. *Zdanok*.[145] In *Glidden*, the company's employees sued in a New York court to recover damages for breach of a collective bargaining agreement. Subsequently, the case was removed to the District Court for the Southern District of New York, on the basis of diversity of citizenship. On appeal, a divided panel of the court of appeals, including Judge J. Warren Madden, an active judge of the Court of Claims sitting by designation of the chief justice, sustained the employees' right to recover damages. In a second companion case, on appeal from the District Court for the District of Columbia, Judge Joseph R. Jackson, a retired judge of the Court of Customs and Patent Appeals, had presided over a criminal trial, also by designation.[146] In both cases, the petitioners alleged that they had been "denied the protection of judges with tenure and compensation guaranteed by Article III."[147] In other words, both petitioners claimed that they had been denied a hearing in an Article III court.

Speaking for the majority, Justice John Marshall Harlan rejected the claim, noting that on August 25, 1958, Congress had enacted legislation conferring Article III status on the Court of Claims and the Court of Customs and Patent Appeals. These courts are now constitutional courts. They exercise the judicial power of the United States, they no longer perform nonjudicial functions, and Article III guarantees their judges' salaries and tenure.[148] In rejecting the claim that Congress could not create specialized courts with limited jurisdiction, under Article III, Harlan affirmed congressional authority to restrict the lower federal courts' jurisdiction:

> The great constitutional compromise that resulted in agreement upon Art. III, § 1, authorized but did not obligate Congress to create inferior federal courts. . . . Once created, they passed almost a century without exercising any very significant jurisdiction. . . . Throughout this period and beyond it up to today, they remained constantly subject to jurisdictional curtailment.[149]

Furthermore, Harlan emphasized, "[n]o question can be raised of Congress' freedom, consistently with Article III, to impose such a limitation [i.e., the power to award damages, but not specific relief] upon the remedial powers of a federal court."[150] While Harlan acknowledged broad legislative authority over the federal courts, he remarked, "[t]he authority is not, of course, unlimited."[151] Distinguishing *Ex parte McCardle* from *United States* v. *Klein*, Harlan admitted that Congress could not employ its authority to regulate jurisdiction "to invade the judicial province by prescribing a rule of decision in a pending case."[152]

In a dissenting opinion, Justice Douglas, with Justice Black concurring, rejected the majority's view that the two courts were, in fact, Article III courts. Douglas argued that it would take a constitutional amendment to confer Article III powers and status on these courts and their judges, that is, to guarantee their judicial independence.[153] Douglas also implied a right to vindicate federally protected rights before an Article III court.[154] Finally, in a footnote, Douglas cast doubt on whether the Supreme Court's decision in *Ex parte McCardle* would pass constitutional muster today:

> The Court does great mischief in today's opinions. The opinion of my Brother Harlan stirs a host of problems that need not be opened. What is done will, I fear, plague us for years.
>
> First, that opinion cites with approval *Ex parte McCardle* . . . in which Congress withdrew jurisdiction of this Court to review a *habeas corpus* case that was *sub judice*, and then apparently draws a distinction between that case and *United States* v. *Klein*. . . . There is a serious question whether the *McCardle* case could command a majority view today.[155]

While Justice Harlan examined congressional power to restrict the lower federal courts' jurisdiction, the *Glidden* decision rests on other grounds, namely, legislative authority to confer Article III powers and status on federal tribunals of limited jurisdiction. *Glidden* does not raise questions of congressional authority to limit the Supreme Court's appellate jurisdiction under the exceptions and regulations clause. Harlan acknowledged broad legislative authority to regulate and restrict the lower courts' jurisdiction, but he also recognized both internal and external limits on the exercise of congressional power, as his reference to *United States* v. *Klein* explicitly indicates. Finally, Douglas's dissenting opinion casts doubt on the contemporary precedential value of *Ex parte McCardle* and suggests that there is a right to present constitutional claims in some federal forum.

In the era from William Howard Taft to Earl Warren, the Supreme Court remained deferential toward the congressional exercise of power over the federal courts' jurisdiction. The justices acknowledged broad congressional power over the Court's appellate jurisdiction, but never conceded plenary power to prevent litigants from vindicating their constitutional rights. In some cases, the Court's decisions involved statutory rather than constitutional rights (e.g., see *Lucken-*

bach S.S. Co. v. *United States*). Other decisions (e.g., *Bruner* v. *United States*) were exercises in statutory construction of jurisdictional acts that did not raise questions of constitutional authority to limit the Supreme Court's appellate jurisdiction or the jurisdiction of the lower federal courts. Several decisions concerned congressional regulation of the mode of proceeding (*Bruner* v. *United States*) rather than legislative power to restrict the federal courts' jurisdiction. A few decisions (*Federal Radio Commission* v. *General Electric Co.* and *National Mutual Insurance Co.* v. *Tidewater Transfer Co.*) turned on other constitutional issues. *Federal Radio Commission* rested on a construction of the case-and-controversy requirement of Article III. *National Mutual Insurance Co.* raised the question of congressional authority to expand federal jurisdiction beyond the Judiciary Article's boundaries.

Mostly in dicta and sometimes in dissenting opinions, various justices have acknowledged the existence of external limits on the exercise of congressional power under Article III, sections 1 and 2. Several opinions suggest that the Fifth Amendment's due process clause, the habeas corpus provision of Article I, section 9, and the prohibition on bills of attainder (Article I, section 9, cl. 3) impose external constitutional limits on Congress's exercise of its Article III powers to regulate and restrict federal jurisdiction. The Supreme Court's decision in *De La Rama S.S. Co.* v. *United States* and the courts of appeals' decisions in *Battaglia* v. *General Motors Corp.* and *Eisentrager* v. *Forrestal* imply a right to a remedy in a federal forum in cases involving substantive constitutional rights. Far from suggesting that Congress has plenary authority, recent cases imply important constitutional limitations on Congress's exercise of power to restrict the Supreme Court's appellate jurisdiction and the jurisdiction of the lower federal courts.

Conclusion

Throughout its history, the Supreme Court has acknowledged broad congressional power to regulate and limit its appellate jurisdiction and virtual plenary power to regulate the lower federal courts' jurisdiction. With the exception of Roger B. Taney, the justices have argued that the Constitution vests judicial power and jurisdiction directly in the Court, but the Court requires enabling legislation to exercise its appellate jurisdiction. The Supreme Court has adhered to John Marshall's "negative-pregnant" doctrine by refusing to infer jurisdiction that the statutes neither explicitly confer nor clearly imply. As a corollary, the Court has taken the position that statutes terminating jurisdiction apply to pending as well as future cases.

With the exception of Morrison Waite's opinion in *The Francis Wright*, the Court has not rendered a binding judgment on the scope of congressional power to limit its appellate jurisdiction in cases raising constitutional claims. Many of the Supreme Court's decisions involve questions of statutory construction of jurisdictional acts, while other decisions do not involve substantive constitutional claims. Some cases actually concern legislative power to expand the Court's appellate jurisdiction beyond the Judiciary Article's boundaries rather than congressional power to restrict such jurisdiction under the exceptions and regulations clause. Even though Waite acknowledged legislative authority to restrict the Court's appellate jurisdiction in admiralty to questions of law, he implied that the Fifth Amendment's due process clause imposes limits on congressional power under the exceptions and regulations clause.

Since *The Francis Wright*, various Supreme Court and lower federal court decisions have suggested that the Fifth Amendment, the habeas corpus provision, and the constitutional prohibition on bills of attainder impose external constitutional restraints on congressional power to regulate and make exceptions to the Supreme Court's appellate jurisdiction. A few recent opinions also imply that litigants presenting a constitutional issue have a right of access to a federal judicial forum to adjudicate their constitutional claim. From the perspective of the Marble Palace, there is no binding decision that sustains the plenary theory of congressional power over the Court's appellate jurisdiction.

From the Capitol, the view is equally unclear. Although Congress has restricted the lower courts' jurisdiction, it has not barred access to the Supreme Court to petitioners who seek to appeal the adverse decisions of state courts in cases raising federal constitutional claims. Even the habeas corpus repealer of 1868 left McCardle another avenue of appeal to the Supreme Court. Despite occasional congressional pique with the Court's decisions, generally Congress has expanded the jurisdiction of the Supreme Court and the lower federal courts. Although Congress has enacted some limits on the Supreme Court's appellate jurisdiction, until the 1950s these jurisdictional restrictions involved substantive questions of statutory rather than constitutional rights. Unlike earlier statutes that Congress has enacted, current proposals designed to prevent the federal courts from hearing and deciding school prayer, school busing, and state antiabortion cases involve claims of constitutional right. Do these proposals present a categorically unique challenge to the Supreme Court's power and function in the constitutional system?

6

Congressional Power Over the Court:
A View from the Capitol

....

The Supreme Court at the Storm Center

Since 1800 Congress, presidents, and state politicians have periodically assailed the U.S. Supreme Court's decisions. As Charles Warren has observed, the Jeffersonian Republicans criticized the Court for failing to declare the Sedition Law and the Charter of the Bank of the United States unconstitutional, while the Federalists attacked the Supreme Court's failure to declare Jefferson's Embargo Act unconstitutional. Between 1819 and 1831 the Court's congressional critics attacked its decisions sustaining the national government's power and limiting the states' exercise of their police powers to promote the public health, safety, and welfare. Before the Civil War Republican politicians attacked the Court for sustaining the Fugitive Slave Act, while after the war the Radical Republicans assaulted the justices for jeopardizing the congressional program of military reconstruction.[1] During the 1880s the Court's critics expressed anger over its decisions in *The Legal Tender Cases* and *The Civil Rights Cases*.[2]

In the period of industrial growth from 1890 to 1937, Populists, Progressives, New Deal Democrats, and other critics accused the Court of reaching for judicial supremacy and thwarting representative government and popular sovereignty by nullifying the mature policy judgments of Congress and the president.[3] Between 1953 and 1961 the Supreme Court's critics attacked its decisions in such diverse areas as public school desegregation, federal and state loyalty-security programs, congressional and state legislative investigatory powers, the states' powers to regulate professional employment, and the criminal defendant's rights.[4] Since 1962 congressional critics have expressed outrage over the Court's decisions on public school prayer, congressional districting and state legislative apportionment, mandatory school busing to achieve racial desegregation, the rights of conscientious objectors, and state antiabortion laws.

Although Congress has usually exercised restraint toward the Court, satisfying itself with rhetorical threats warning the justices to exercise self-restraint and show greater deference to congressional policy judgments, there have been successful efforts to restrain the Court. Congress has enacted legislation overturning the Supreme Court's "mistaken" statutory constructions, as in the portal-to-portal pay case.[5] Congress and the states have amended the Constitution, setting aside the Court's constitutional judgments in *Chisholm* v. *Georgia* (1793), *Dred Scott* v. *Sanford* (1857), *Pollock* v. *Farmers' Loan and Trust Co.* (1895), and *Oregon* v. *Mitchell* (1970).[6] Congress has considered and, occasionally, enacted legislation altering the structure of the federal judiciary. On seven occasions, Congress has altered the Supreme Court's size (1801, 1802, 1807, 1837, 1863, 1866, and 1869).[7] In 1802 Congress repealed the Judiciary Act of 1801, abolishing the new circuit courts, and enacted a second law postponing the Supreme Court's term until February 1803.[8] In addition to altering the Supreme Court's size and the structure of the lower courts, Congress has considered legislation that would require extraordinary majorities to declare acts of Congress and the state legislatures unconstitutional.[9]

Congress has considered and, in some cases, enacted legislation limiting the federal judiciary's jurisdiction and remedial powers. The Norris-La Guardia Act severely restricted the use of injunctions in labor-management relations disputes.[10] In the Portal-to-Portal Pay Act Congress foreclosed access to all state and federal courts in cases involving statutory rights to portal-to-portal pay under the Fair Labor Standards Act (FLSA) of 1938.[11] Although Congress has considered numerous proposals that would deny access to the Supreme Court or any other federal forum in cases involving constitutional claims, thus far it has not enacted such Draconian measures. Despite attempts to curb the Supreme Court's appellate jurisdiction over school prayer, school busing, and state antiabortion laws, Congress has exercised restraint regarding the Supreme Court's appellate jurisdiction.

These proposals are not unique, but since 1954 members of Congress have introduced hundreds of bills to limit or overturn the Court's decisions protecting the individual's right to be free from state sponsored, authorized, or endorsed prayer in public schools; de jure segregation of public school facilities; and state interference with a woman's decision to terminate a pregnancy. In addition to limiting the effect of the Supreme Court's decisions and, conceivably, making it more difficult for individuals to secure their constitutional rights, many of these proposals would alter the institutional relationship between Congress and the Court as well as the delicate balance of power between the national government and the states.

Inasmuch as Congress has a responsibility to consider the constitutional as well as the policy implications of proposals to curb the Supreme Court's appellate jurisdiction and remedial powers and the lower federal courts' jurisdiction, an inquiry into congressional perceptions of legislative authority, under Article III, sections 1 and 2, is germane to the continuing controversy over the scope of congressional power. In the absence of an authoritative judicial decision on the scope of congressional power, jurists and scholars should analyze congressional perceptions of legislative authority, the legislative history of attempts to limit the exercise of judicial power, and the constitutional-institutional effects of earlier proposals in evaluating the legitimacy of contemporary proposals to limit the Court's appellate jurisdiction in cases raising constitutional claims. While Congress may not have final authority to construe the scope of its own power over the Supreme Court, the justices would be foolhardy to ignore congressional perceptions of legislative power under the exceptions and regulations and ordain and establish clauses.

Aside from venting congressional and public hostility toward the Supreme Court, there are important rationales for legislative responses to the Court's decisions. First, members of Congress may be legitimately dissatisfied with the Court's policy judgments. They may perceive that the justices have misunderstood the legislative intent or policy judgment in a particular act. Congress's reversal of the Supreme Court's portal-to-portal pay decision, *Anderson* v. *Mt. Clemens Pottery Co.*,[12] represents an extreme but legitimate response to the justices' interpretation of congressional intent. In addition to reversing the Court's "mistaken" statutory construction, Congress rebuked the high court and removed all federal and state jurisdiction over portal-to-portal pay cases.[13]

Of course, an equally plausible interpretation is that Congress failed to define its intent precisely in the Fair Labor Standards Act, giving the administrator and the judiciary ample opportunity to fill in the interstices by defining the meaning of such vague terms as the "work week." At times, the justices guess incorrectly or, as in the portal-to-portal case, congressional majorities change. Following the 1946 elections, a Republican majority replaced the earlier Democratic majority that had enacted the FLSA, the last major social and economic legislation of the New Deal. Whether the Court erred or Congress was vague, a new legislative majority had ample opportunity to change national policy. The Supreme Court did not long frustrate either a legislative or a popular majority.

Second, the Court's congressional critics may perceive that the justices have either failed to consider fully the legislative intent or have focused on a statute's dominant purpose, ignoring the other purposes that Congress considered or stated explicitly. Evidently, in *Anderson v. Mt. Clemens Pottery Co.*, the Court ignored the established customs, practices, and contracts that Congress had considered in drafting the FLSA's broad provisions defining regular compensation for a normal forty-hour "work week." The Supreme Court's statutory constructions of the Social Security Act, the National Labor Relations Act, and the Nationality Act of 1940 also emphasized each measure's dominant purpose.[14] In each case, Congress soon reversed the Court's interpretation.[15] When the Court ignores the legislative purpose or fails to examine the various objectives and complex facts that Congress considered, the legislature has an opportunity to override the justices' policy judgments. Congressional legislation correcting judicial error in statutory construction is essential to a healthy dialogue between Congress and the Court. If the Supreme Court strays too far from congressional policy or the policy consensus changes following realignments in the American electorate and party system, Congress can, and sometimes does, inform the Court by reversing its statutory interpretations.

Third, in some cases the Court has defied Congress's manifest intent by simply ignoring the explicit provisions of congressional acts. Beginning with *Swann v. Charlotte-Mecklenburg* (1971),[16] the Supreme Court has ignored Congress's intent in the Civil Rights Act of 1964.[17] The act provided specifically that:

> [N]othing herein shall empower any official or court of the United States to issue any order seeking to achieve a racial balance in any school by requiring the transportation of pupils or students from one school to another or one school district to another in order to achieve such racial balance, or otherwise enlarge the existing power of the court to insure compliance with constitutional standards.[18]

Although the language of the Civil Rights Act clearly prohibits school busing and other remedial measures to change the racial balance of public schools, the Court has never declared section 2003 unconstitutional. It has, in fact, ignored the manifest intent of Congress by permitting and sometimes requiring mandatory busing to alter the existing racial balance of public schools. Inasmuch as the Supreme Court has defied the manifest intent of Congress repeatedly, there is little point in Congress's enacting additional legislation to correct the Court's judgment. Increasingly frustrated with the Court, members of Congress have introduced numerous constitutional amendments that would prohibit the use of race as a factor in assigning students to public schools.[19] Independent of legislative or judicial motivations, the introduction and enactment of constitutional amendments is another legitimate means of communication between Congress and the Supreme Court.

When the Supreme Court ignores the statutory policy judgments of Congress and the states' legislatures or declares an act unconstitutional, Congress and the states can propose and ratify constitutional amendments overturning the Court's judgments. Although constitutional amendments require extraordinary majorities that are difficult to mobilize, they are an accepted, legitimate means of reversing the Supreme Court's statutory and constitutional judgments. In response to the Court's decisions in the reapportionment case, *Reynolds* v. *Sims* (1964),[20] in July 1964 Senator Everett M. Dirksen (R.-Ill.) introduced a constitutional amendment designed to remove all federal court jurisdiction over state legislative districting and apportionment.[21] As Senator Dirksen recognized, the amendment process is the people's ultimate weapon in holding the judiciary accountable, however irrational, impassioned, or mistaken some scholars believe popular majorities can be. In a constitutional democracy that explicitly provides for change in the organic law through constitutional amendment, the people have an uncontestable right to alter the Court's substantive judgments as well as the structure of government through the amendment process.

However, when members of Congress perceive that the Supreme Court has overstepped its constitutionally prescribed role or functions, is there an equally persuasive rationale for ordinary jurisdictional legislation that would alter the Court's functions, its relationship to Congress and the president, the structure of the federal system, or judicially recognized constitutional rights? Do the members of Congress perceive judicial gerrymandering as an appropriate, legitimate response to a Supreme Court that has run riot? Since 1954 congressional proponents of jurisdictional gerrymandering have offered several rationales for their proposals.

First, the Supreme Court and the lower federal courts have overstepped their judicial function vis-à-vis Congress and the states. In response to *Roe* v. *Wade*,[22] for example, congressional critics have argued that the decision is an exercise in judicial policy making, wholly unwarranted by the language and history of the Fourteenth Amendment. Inasmuch as the due process clause does not explicitly or implicitly create a zone of privacy that includes a woman's right to obtain an abortion, the Supreme Court has invaded the states' authority, under the Tenth Amendment, to protect public health, safety, welfare, and morals.[23] Responding to *Roe*, Senator Orrin G. Hatch (R.-Utah) observed in 1981:

> The federal judiciary has been courting constitutional disaster by reading its own predilections into the nation's foundational document. The Supreme Court is the body charged with policing the bounds drawn by the Constitution. When the policeman violates the law, a higher authority must undertake to protect freedoms. The Constitution is that higher authority and has outlined the means to prevent overreaching [Article III, sections 1 and 2].[24]

As a response to decisions such as *Wesberry* v. *Sanders* (1963) and *Reynolds* v. *Sims* (1964), which involve congressional districting and state legislative reapportionment, and *Powell* v. *McCormack* (1969), which challenges the plenary power of the House of Representatives to exclude a congressman,[25] members of Congress argued that the Court had invaded areas that are textually committed to the exclusive judgment of Congress or the states. From the congressional perspective, the Supreme Court had interfered with the performance of core functions that the Constitution explicitly or implicitly assigns to representative political institutions. As a result, the Court had upset the Framers' plan of government, unilaterally altered federal-state relationships and the separation of powers, and disturbed the constitutional equilibrium of the American political system.

In breaching the separation of powers, the Court has made legislative rather than judicial determinations. Proponents of legislation curbing the federal courts' jurisdiction over busing, prayer, and abortion claim that since the Fourteenth Amendment does not authorize federal courts to order busing, prohibit prayer, or create abortion rights, the judiciary is inquiring into the motive, wisdom, and expediency of policy judgments that belong exclusively to representative political institutions accountable (i.e., responsive and responsible) to a broad electorate.[26] By substituting its judgment for the policy determinations of the people's representatives, the judiciary has frustrated the policy preferences of popular, electoral majorities, as expressed in periodic state, congressional, and presidential elections. Whether Congress and the state legislatures are "representative" and accountable or state and national elections are referenda on public policies, theoretically, legislatures are more directly accountable than an appointed federal judiciary that has life tenure. In theory, the federal judiciary is a nondemocratic, irresponsible institution, which should refrain from interfering in the democratic process unless Congress and the state legislatures have clearly exceeded their constitutional authority.[27]

Given the difficulties of constructing legislative coalitions, the federal courts should refrain from overturning legislative policies. Under the existing congressional rules and organization (for example, the committee system, the seniority system, the dilatory rules of procedure, and the bicameral structure of Congress), when the Court sets aside legislative policies, it may take Congress years to reconstruct the coalitions and negotiate the compromises necessary to crystalize a policy consensus. In the interim, the federal courts may frustrate the policy preferences of both legislative and popular majorities. Although there is considerable merit to the argument, as the child labor case *Hammer v. Dagenhart* (1918)[28] demonstrates, the existence of antimajoritarian congressional rules and organization belies the reasoning that the federal judiciary, alone, frustrates the operation of democratic processes and institutions.[29] Indeed, the Supreme Court's intervention in congressional districting and state legislative apportionment has probably made the House of Representatives and many state legislatures more responsive and responsible to popular majorities since 1964.

In addition to democratic theory and constitutional limitations, congressional critics of judicial adventurism argue that Congress and the state legislatures are superior fact finders to judges and juries.[30] Theoretically, the rules of evidence do not permit the judiciary to consider the broad range of economic, sociological, psychological, and other social-science evidence that legislatures can entertain. Even if judges could consider such evidence, they are not trained to evaluate extrajudicial facts. Frequently, judges do not have access to either the data or the expert staffs necessary to evaluate complex social, political, economic, technical, and other societal problems.[31] However theoretically convincing these arguments appear, advocates of the superiority of legislative fact finding necessarily assume that legislators decide on the basis of "the evidence" rather than on their political instincts (that is, their personal preferences and judgments about constituents', party leaders', or interest groups' political preferences). Unlike courts, legislatures need not make decisions on the basis of any evidence. They are called upon to make policy choices within the areas that the U.S. and state constitutions commit to their judgment.

As long as the federal courts perform their judicial function, congressional critics admit, Congress should defer to the judiciary's constitutional and statutory constructions. However, when judges substitute their values for the Framers' or the legislature's intent, Congress has ample authority under Article III, sections 1 and 2, and Article V (providing for constitutional amendments) to correct the judiciary's mistaken policy judgments and restore the balance of power between the nation and the states or among the branches of the national government that the courts have disturbed. The Framers and Ratifiers intended both Article V and the ordain and establish and exceptions and regulations clauses as democratic checks on an errant judiciary that has abandoned its function, interfered in the democratic process, and unilaterally altered the Framers' plan of government. Since 1962, the Court's opponents conclude, the federal judiciary rather than Congress has provoked a constitutional crisis threatening the political system's stability and legitimacy.

Congressional Responses to the Supreme Court

Judging from the frequency and volume of congressional criticism and proposals to curb the Supreme Court's powers since 1954, members of Congress regard rhetorical threats, statutory revision, constitutional amendments, and jurisdictional legislation as appropriate and legitimate means to modify, reverse, or prevent the implementation of particular, "objectionable" judicial decisions. Is the contemporary conflict between Congress and the Court categorically different from earlier clashes between the two institutions? Are current attempts to reverse the Supreme Court's prayer, busing, and abortion decisions within the range of methods that Congress has employed previously to alter the Court's policy judgments? Are contemporary proposals constitutionally different from earlier attempts to reverse judicial decisions? The answer to these questions depends, partially, on an assessment of legislative intent. What are the authors', sponsors', and supporters' remedial purposes? What are the constitutional consequences or effects of earlier and contemporary proposals regarding the Court's decisions, jurisdiction, powers, and functions?

The Pre-Marshall and Marshall Eras

Angered by the Supreme Court's decision in *Chisholm* v. *Georgia* (1793) that the federal courts had judicial power to decide controversies between a state and citizens of another state,[32] in 1798 the states ratified the Eleventh Amendment reversing the Court's decision. The Eleventh Amendment removed federal judicial power over "any suit in law or equity, commenced or prosecuted against one of the United States by citizens of another State, or by citizens or subjects of any foreign State."[33] While the amendment restricted national judicial power by restoring the states' sovereign immunity against such suits, both Congress and the states employed the constitutionally prescribed method (Article V) to reverse the Supreme Court's decision. In addition to reversing the Court's judgment, the Eleventh Amendment also had important structural-functional consequences for the federal judiciary. The amendment circumscribed the federal courts' power to protect citizens' and foreign nationals' rights against state infringements, but "Congress, in proposing the Eleventh Amendment, and the states, in ratifying it, had within a markedly short time equated the Court's interpretation of the Constitution with the document itself."[34] Congress and the states tacitly recognized that the only legitimate means to reverse the Supreme Court's constitutional interpretation is through the amendment process.

Despite swift congressional and state response to *Chisholm* v. *Georgia*, the 1790s were a decade of relative calm between Congress and the Supreme Court. However, with the Supreme Court's failure to declare the Sedition Law unconstitutional, the passage of the Judiciary Act of 1801, the Repealer Act of 1802, and *Marbury* v. *Madison* (1803), the Court returned to the center of the storm. In addition to establishing new circuit courts and reorganizing the district courts, the Judiciary Act of 1801 expanded the federal courts' jurisdiction. Congress granted the new circuit courts jurisdiction over U.S. criminal cases; cases arising under the U.S. Constitution, laws, and treaties; civil suits brought by the government; and prize cases. The act also granted the circuit courts bankruptcy jurisdiction, concurrently with the district courts, and provided for the removal of specified cases from the states' courts.[35] The "ill-fated" Judiciary Act of 1801, as William Crosskey noted, was designed to expand the national courts' jurisdiction and provide for the Supreme Court's supervision of the national judicial establishment.[36]

As indicated by Alexander Hamilton's response to Jefferson's message of December 8, 1801,[37] and the congressional debates on the Repealer Act of 1802,[38] the central question was the power and function of the federal judiciary in a representative democracy. The Federalists argued that an independent judiciary is essential to preserving individual liberty, restraining the arbitrary exercise of governmental power, maintaining national supremacy, and resolving disputes among the states. The Jeffersonian Republicans accused the federal courts of reaching for judicial supremacy and threatening individual liberty and representative government. The Jeffersonians also claimed that each branch of the national government has authority to interpret the Constitution in performing its functions. Moreover, under Article III, section 1, the Jeffersonians argued, Congress has plenary power to abolish as well as create lower federal courts.[39] Hamilton rejected the Jeffersonian's departmental theory of judicial review and their conception of legislative power over the judiciary, arguing that if Article III does confer plenary power over the lower courts, it is implicit rather than explicit.[40]

Congress passed the Repealer Act of March 8, 1802, by a strict party-line vote in both houses.[41] The act abolished the recently created circuit courts, terminating their jurisdiction. The repealer restored the jurisdiction of the old district and circuit courts under the Judiciary Act of 1789.[42] In a second act, of April 29, 1802, Congress delayed the next term of the Supreme Court until February 1803.[43] A week after the Supreme Court decided *Marbury* v. *Madison* (1803),[44] declaring section 13 of the Judiciary Act of 1789 unconstitutional, the Court declined in *Stuart* v. *Laird* (1803) to hold the Repealer Act of 1802 unconstitutional.[45] The Supreme Court retreated from a direct confrontation with Congress and the president.[46]

The act of 1802 was designed to curb the exercise of federal judicial power vis-à-vis Congress and the states. By abolishing the new circuit courts, terminating their jurisdiction, and restoring the old district- and circuit-court structure, Congress restricted the scope of federal judicial power to the limited jurisdiction of sections 9 and 11 of the Judiciary Act of 1789 (see chapter 4). The intensely partisan nature of the debate anathematized congressional efforts to rationalize the federal judicial structure until 1891. In abolishing the new circuit courts, Congress tied the size and function of the Supreme Court to the number of judicial circuits. Requiring the justices to ride circuit imposed an onerous duty on the Court and undermined its effective supervision of the federal judiciary. Although the Repealer Act of 1802 was a partisan measure that had serious consequences for federal judicial power, function, and structure, Congress was exercising its constitutional authority, under Article III, section 1, to organize the federal judiciary, which comprehends the power to establish and abolish the lower courts as well as terminate their jurisdiction.

In the ten years between *Marbury* v. *Madison* (1803) and *Fairfax* v. *Hunter* (1813),[47] there was relative quiescence between Congress and the Supreme Court. John Marshall's ruling (sitting as a circuit justice) in *United States* v. *Burr* (1807)[48] that the president is subject to judicial process provoked a congressional response. The Jeffersonians attempted to withdraw the Supreme Court's appellate jurisdiction in criminal cases and remove its habeas corpus jurisdiction, but these measures were unsuccessful.[49] The Court's decisions in *Fletcher* v. *Peck* (1810),[50] holding that the contracts clause of the Constitution prohibited the state of Georgia from rescinding a legislative land grant, and *Fairfax* v. *Hunter* (1813),[51] holding that the treaty of 1794 with England prohibited the state of Virginia from confiscating Lord Fairfax's property,[52] provoked considerable ire in Congress and the states. However, during this period Congress vented its frustration with the Court largely through rhetorical threats.

Beginning with *Martin* v. *Hunter's Lessee* (1816),[53] the sequel to the *Fairfax* decision, conflict between Congress and the Supreme Court intensified. *Martin* was followed by a series of decisions involving delicate economic and political issues as well as the Court's enforcement of national supremacy over the states. The Supreme Court's decisions in *McCulloch* v. *Maryland* (1819), *Dartmouth College* v. *Woodward* (1819), *Sturges* v. *Crowninshield* (1819), *Cohens* v. *Virginia* (1821), *Green* v. *Biddle* (1823), and *Osborn* v. *Bank of the United States* (1824)[54] exacerbated congressional irritation with the justices, but there was little serious support for attempts to curb the federal judiciary's powers.[55] Nevertheless, the Jeffersonians and, later, the Jacksonian Democrats made several attempts to alter the Supreme Court's internal decision-making process, its appellate jurisdiction, and its power vis-à-vis Congress and the states.

The Supreme Court's congressional critics attempted repeatedly but failed to repeal section 25 of the Judiciary Act of 1789, which had conferred appellate jurisdiction on the Supreme Court to review state court decisions that question the validity of congressional acts and international treaties, that question the validity of state acts, or that deny a litigant's claim to protection under the U.S. Constitution. In April 1822 Representative Stevenson of Virginia introduced a bill to repeal section 25. On January 2, 1824, Representative Wickliffe of Kentucky proposed that the House Judiciary Committee "inquire into the expediency of either repealing entirely the obnoxious Twenty-Five [*sic*] Section or modifying it."[56] Following the Supreme Court's decision in *Craig* v. *Missouri* (1830), in 1831 the House Judiciary Committee reported a similar proposal, which the House defeated by a vote of 138/51.[57]

In addition to repeated attempts to repeal section 25, there were several other proposals to curb the Supreme Court. On December 12, 1821, Senator Johnson of Kentucky introduced a constitutional amendment authorizing the U.S. Senate to review decisions of the Supreme Court involving questions of states' rights.[58] On December 10, 1823, Senator Johnson also introduced legislation requiring the concurrence of seven justices in any case challenging the validity of state or congressional acts.[59] In 1822 and 1823 Congress considered but did not enact legislation to confine the admiralty jurisdiction to the ebb and flow of the tides.[60] In 1826, as Charles Haines has observed, Congress again debated, but did not pass, legislation restricting the Court's powers.[61]

During the 1820s Congress considered proposals to alter the Supreme Court's internal decision-making process, its appellate jurisdiction over state court decisions, its power vis-à-vis Congress and the states, and specific decisions. Clearly, Senator Johnson's constitutional amendment would have altered the Court's relationship to Congress and would have impaired its function as an arbiter of federalism. Similarly, attempts to repeal section 25 of the Judiciary Act of 1789 were intended to undermine the Supreme Court's role as an umpire of the federal system. While Article V of the Constitution contemplates constitutional amendments, repeal of section 25 would have impaired the Court's authority to enforce the supremacy clause of Article VI. Many Jeffersonians viewed section 25 as an instrument of centralized power, but James Madison, who opposed Marshall's decisions, also opposed efforts to repeal this vital section of the Judiciary Act:

> A paramount or even a definitive authority in the individual States, would soon make the Constitution and laws different in different States, and thus destroy that equality and uniformity of rights and duties which form the essence of the compact; to say nothing of the opportunity given to the States individually of involving by their decisions the whole Union in foreign contests.[62]

Although Congress considered both simple legislation and constitutional amendments to curb the Supreme Court, it did not enact a single proposal changing the Court's function as an arbiter of federalism or its relationship to Congress. The Court retained its appellate jurisdiction to enforce national supremacy, provide a uniform construction of national law, and protect the individual's constitutional rights. The

Supreme Court's adversaries may have failed to curb its power, but after 1825 the justices retreated from a direct confrontation with Congress. John Marshall's Court had been battered by a series of confrontations with Congress, the president, and the states. During Marshall's last five years, the Court was also internally divided; this undermined its credibility. The evidence also suggests "that the Court was giving some consideration to what Mr. Dooley called 'election returns'."[63] In any event, the Supreme Court escaped relatively unscathed from its second major confrontation with Congress.

The Taney Court

Following congressional reaction to *Craig* v. *Missouri* (1830)[64] and Andrew Jackson's response to *Worcester* v. *Georgia* (1832),[65] criticism of the Court abated. Even before Roger Taney's tenure as chief justice, according to Haines, John Marshall and his colleagues "began to temper their decisions to accord more nearly to the prevailing public sentiment of the country."[66] Under Taney the Court generally conceded authority to Congress and the states. Aside from episodic rhetorical threats, there were virtually no serious efforts to curb the Supreme Court's jurisdiction or judicial power. After the Court's decision in *Kendall* v. *United States ex rel Stokes* (1838),[67] President Van Buren requested that Congress divest the federal courts of their jurisdiction to issue writs of mandamus.[68] With Taney dissenting in *Kendall*, the Supreme Court sustained the circuit court's authority to issue a writ of mandamus to the postmaster general. However, both the majority and dissenting opinions conceded Congress's plenary authority to regulate the circuit courts' jurisdiction.[69] Congress did not enact Van Buren's proposal, but it was clearly within the scope of legislative authority that the Court conceded to Congress.

Although Congress did not enact legislation limiting the federal courts' jurisdiction between 1838 and 1859, "the threats and the danger of sectional strife" were on the horizon.[70] Taney's opinions in *Dred Scott* v. *Sanford* (1857) and *Ableman* v. *Booth* (1859) provoked intense criticism.[71] Taney denied congressional power to prohibit slavery in the territories, under the Missouri Compromise of 1820, and in *Ableman* v. *Booth* he rejected the state of Wisconsin's authority to issue a writ of habeas corpus for the release of a prisoner in federal custody.[72] In enforcing the Fugitive Slave Law of 1850, Taney sustained the Supreme Court's authority to enforce national supremacy and a uniform interpretation of national law as well as the lower federal courts' exclusive jurisdiction.[73] Although Taney's opinions provoked a political storm, criticism was directed against the decisions rather than the Court's jurisdiction and judicial power.[74] With the destruction of Taney's reputation as a jurist and the Court's influence as a national political institution, it was unnecessary for Congress to enact legislation altering the Supreme Court's function.

The Civil War and Post–Civil War Era

With the exception of Chief Justice Taney's opinion in *Ex parte Merryman* (1861),[75] which President Lincoln ignored, during the Civil War the federal courts supported the president's exercise of extraconstitutional power.[76] Indeed, in *Ex parte Vallandigham* (1864), the Court avoided a direct confrontation with the president by denying its jurisdiction to review or revise the findings of a military commission.[77] Only after the Civil War ended did the Supreme Court in *Ex parte Milligan* (1866) challenge the president's authority to suspend the privilege to the writ of habeas corpus and substitute a military commission for a civilian court outside the actual theatre of military operations.[78] During its next term, in *Mississippi* v. *Johnson* (1867) and the *Test Oath Cases, Ex parte Garland* (1867) and *Cummings* v. *Missouri* (1867), the Court marched further into the political thicket, threatening to overturn the entire congressional program of military reconstruction. However, following congressional repeal (1868) of the Habeas Corpus Act of 1867, the justices backed away from a collision in the long awaited and much anticipated decision, *Ex parte McCardle* (1869). Although Chief Justice Chase asserted the Court's jurisdiction under the Judiciary Act of 1789, in *Ex parte Yerger* (1869) the justices retreated further. After Yerger's counsel and the attorney general entered into an agreement "by which Yerger was to be protected from the military," the case became moot.[79] *Yerger* was the Supreme Court's last challenge to Reconstruction.

The Radical Republicans in Congress reacted to the *Milligan* decision by introducing legislation to curb the Court's appellate jurisdiction and prevent further judicial interference with military government in the South. In the House, Representative John Bingham (R.-Ohio) proposed legislation to abolish the Supreme Court's appellate jurisdiction entirely and a constitutional amendment to abolish the Court.[80] The Supreme Court's decision in *Cummings* resulted in both rhetorical threats and various court-curbing proposals. In 1868 the House Judiciary Committee "reported a bill to provide that, in any case involving the validity of a law of Congress, two thirds of the Judges must concur in an opinion adverse to the law."[81] In the Senate, the Radicals introduced a bill to prohibit the Supreme Court from deciding any "political question." On March 26, 1868, Representative Thaddeus Stevens (R.-Pa.) sponsored a bill removing the Supreme Court's appellate jurisdiction over any case arising under the Reconstruction Acts.[82] Then, on March 27, 1868, Congress repealed the Habeas Corpus Act of 1867.

Although the Repealer Act marked the high point of Radical power, attacks on the federal judiciary continued through 1869. On December 9, 1869, Senator Lyman Trumbull (R.-Ill.) proposed legislation that would have abolished the Supreme Court's appellate jurisdiction over any case arising under the Reconstruction Acts.[83] According to Charles Warren, Trumbull's proposal "was in reality a bill to destroy the constitutional function of the Court."[84] In a vicious attack on the Court, Senator Charles Drake (R.-Mo.) proposed "a bill to provide that no Court created by Congress should have any power to adjudge invalid any Act of Congress, and to prohibit the Supreme Court in its appellate jurisdiction from affirming any such judgment of invalidity by an inferior Court."[85] The Supreme Court's decision in *Ex parte Yerger*, on October 25, 1869, defused the Radicals' campaign. Apart from the repealer act, other, more Draconian measures died with the Forty-first Congress.

The Fortieth and Forty-first congresses responded to the Supreme Court's post–Civil War decisions by considering legislation intended to alter the Court's jurisdiction, judicial power, constitutional function, and internal decision-making process. Both Bingham's and Drake's proposals would have destroyed the Court's constitutional function by insulating congressional legislation from judicial review. In addition to undermining the Framers' careful balance of power among the coequal branches of the national government, both proposals would have impaired the Supreme Court's authority to supervise the federal judiciary, promote a uniform construction of national law, and enforce constitutional supremacy under Article VI.

As the post–Civil War response to the Supreme Court's decisions indicates, Congress has considered serious limitations on the Court's appellate jurisdiction as a means of curbing judicial power and reversing specific decisions. The justices took the cue by retreating from the battlefield in *Ex parte Yerger*. Despite contemporary arguments over the meaning of the Repealer Act and *Ex parte McCardle*, in the post–Civil War era Congress did not enact legislation preventing the Supreme Court from deciding constitutional claims or impairing its function vis-à-vis Congress and the states. In fact, between 1866 and 1875 Congress expanded the federal courts' jurisdiction and role as an umpire of the federal system.

The Era of Judicial Nationalism

Even during the era of judicial nationalism and congressional expansion of federal jurisdiction (1875–1891), there were several attempts to curb the federal courts' powers. While the Senate Republicans favored expansion of federal judicial power to protect corporations against state regulation, the House Democrats began "a continuous effort to pull in the reins on federal judicial power" to prevent the federal judiciary from enforcing various civil rights laws.[86] In response to the Supreme Court's expanding exercise of judicial review of state and congressional acts, as Felix Frankfurter and James Landis wrote, "[i]n the Forty-fourth Congress (following the passage of the Act of March 3, 1875) bills were introduced in the House of Representatives to cut down jurisdiction on removal [of cases from state to federal courts]. Half a dozen bills with a like object appeared at the next Congress."[87]

Shortly after the Supreme Court's decision in *Ex parte Schollenberger* (1877)[88] extending the removal jurisdiction of the circuit courts, the House passed legislation restricting the removal of cases from state courts "in three successive Congresses, in 1880, 1883, and 1884; three successive Senates buried it."[89] Between 1884 and 1886 the Senate rejected proposals to curb the federal courts' jurisdiction, while the House of Representatives killed legislation to relieve the Supreme Court's crowded docket, reorganize the circuit courts, and improve the federal judiciary's efficiency.[90] In a series of compromises, between 1887 and 1891 Congress enacted minor restrictions on the Court's appellate jurisdiction[91] and reorganized the federal courts, establishing nine courts of appeals and shutting off a "flood of litigation" in the Supreme Court.[92] Despite occasional partisan attacks and rhetorical threats, congressional expansion of federal jurisdiction supported the Supreme Court's extension of national power over the states and protection of laissez-faire capitalism.

The Quest for Judicial Supremacy

"During [the] thirty years from 1888 to 1918," notes Charles Warren, "there were two radical extensions and two restrictions of the Court's jurisdiction through Congressional action."[93] Despite congressional pique with the Supreme Court's decisions restricting the use of the commerce power as a national police power and limiting the states' police power to regulate wages, hours, and working conditions in mining and manufacturing, there was general support for the Court's legitimation of laissez-faire capitalism.[94] *Pollock* v. *Farmers' Loan & Trust Co.* (1895), the income-tax case; *United States* v. *E.C. Knight Co.* (1895), the sugar-trust case; and *In re Debs* (1895), affirming Eugene Debs' conviction for his leadership of the Pullman strike,[95] were among the occasional cases that produced outbursts of criticism and calls for congressional restraint of the judiciary. Aside from the Sixteenth Amendment reversing the Court's income-tax decision, the Supreme Court's critics were unsuccessful in curbing its power and jurisdiction.

Once again, following the Court's decisions in *Lochner* v. *New York* (1905), to overturn New York's maximum-hour law for the bakery industry; *Hammer* v. *Dagenhart* (1918), to invalidate the congressional child-labor law; and *Adkins* v. *Children's Hospital* (1923), to void the congressional minimum-wage law for the District of Columbia,[96] there was renewed public criticism of judicial usurpation of legislative power. The lower federal courts' continuing use of their equity powers to enjoin strikes in labor-management-relations disputes also stimulated calls for limitations on the federal judiciary's power and jurisdiction. However, the Progressives and other critics were unable to crystalize public dissatisfaction into legislation. In Congress, as Walter Murphy argues, the critics engaged largely in verbal pyrotechnics, but their legislative proposals died in committee. The Supreme Court's congressional critics were so fragmented that they could not pose a serious challenge to the Court's power or jurisdiction.[97]

In the period between 1891 and 1932, congressional regulation, that is, expansion and contraction of the Supreme Court's appellate jurisdiction, was unrelated to dissatisfaction with particular decisions. Congressional legislation was motivated largely by concern for the effective operation of the federal judiciary. Beginning with the Judiciary Act of 1891, Congress attempted to rationalize the federal courts' organization, relieve the Supreme Court's overcrowded docket, and codify the various statutes regulating federal jurisdiction. The Judiciary Act of 1891, establishing the courts of appeals, restricted the Court's appellate jurisdiction,[98] but did not significantly relieve overcrowding of its docket. The Court of Customs Appeals Act of 1909 established a new Court of Customs Appeals and relieved the Supreme Court of appeals in customs cases.[99] However, an act of March 2, 1907, expanded the Court's appellate jurisdiction in criminal cases by permitting the government to appeal decisions in cases involving demurrers and other motions to quash indictments.[100] An act of December 23, 1914, expanded the Supreme Court's certiorari jurisdiction.[101] In the first major revision of section 25 of the Judiciary Act of 1789, Congress authorized appeals from the decisions of state courts invalidating the constitutionality of state laws.[102] Previously, section 25 had restricted review to state court decisions sustaining the constitutionality of such statutes. The act of 1914 represented an important addition to the Supreme Court's appellate jurisdiction and its function as an umpire of the federal system.

Before World War One it had become apparent that the Supreme Court could not keep abreast of its docket. "The aim of the Act of September 6, 1916," wrote Frankfurter and Landis, "was to enable the Court to keep more nearly abreast of its docket by shutting off cases of minor importance."[103] The act provided that the courts of appeals' decisions would be final in all cases arising under the Bankruptcy Act of July 1, 1898; the act of April 22, 1908, relating to injuries of railroad employees; the Railroad Eighteen Hour Act of March 1, 1907, governing the safety of employees and passengers; and the Railway Safety Appliance Act of March 2, 1893, regulating railway safety appliances.[104] Although Congress restricted appeals of statutory questions in these cases, the act of 1916 permitted the Supreme Court to issue writs of certiorari on questions of law.[105] In the act of 1916, Congress did not foreclose access to the Supreme Court in cases raising constitutional claims.

Despite congressional efforts to promote the Supreme Court's efficiency, the act of 1916 failed to stem the tide of judicial business coming to the Supreme Court.[106] The act also failed to restrict the Supreme Court's appellate jurisdiction and provide flexibility so that the Court could perform its essential functions of resolving conflicts among appellate courts and deciding "matters of national concern."[107] After William Howard Taft became chief justice he assumed the leadership in promoting judicial reform. Under his initiative, a committee of justices drafted the Judges Bill, which Congress enacted in 1925.[108] The act restricted appeals by right and granted the Supreme Court discretion in issuing writs of certiorari to the state and lower federal courts. As Frankfurter and Landis note, the Judges Act of 1925 reduced the Court's role as a court of last resort and stressed its "dominant function as adjudicator of vital constitutional issues."[109] While restricting the Supreme Court's appellate jurisdiction, the act gave the Court broad discretion over its case load. With relatively few exceptions, the act permitted the justices to determine which cases raise significant federal questions worthy of the Court's attention and resources. The act was designed to enhance rather than interfere with the Supreme Court's performance of its constitutional functions.

Between 1891 and 1932 the Supreme Court enjoyed broad public and professional support. Despite occasional attacks on its decisions regarding the national government's use of the commerce clause to regulate business and industry, the states' employment of their police powers for similar purposes,[110] and the lower federal courts' use of their equity powers to enjoin strikes, the Supreme Court's critics were singularly unsuccessful in curbing its power, jurisdiction, and function. During this period the Supreme Court was an integral member of the dominant political coalition that governed the United States. While the Court sometimes sustained congressional legislation regulating the new corporations' blatant abuses of economic power,[111] it continued to legitimate laissez-faire capitalism. As long as the Supreme Court's decisions supported the dominant political coalition's values, Congress, the president, and interest groups such as the American Bar Association insulated the justices from occasional attacks on their decisions and the Court's power, jurisdiction, and function.

The Decline of Judicial Supremacy

Between 1928 and 1936 a major realignment of the American party system fundamentally altered the prevailing policy consensus on government's power to regulate the economy, the appropriate relationship between the national government and the states, and the national government's responsibility to promote the individual's social and economic welfare. Against the background of the Great Depression, the national government assumed power and responsibility in many areas that, traditionally, the states and the private sector had controlled. Congress enacted legislation designed to promote employment security, income security, and restoration of the market place. To accomplish these objectives, Congress created an array of executive and independent agencies that mushroomed into an administrative state. The New Deal transformed the national government from a passive arbiter among competing interests into a positive force that reached into virtually every American home, farm, factory, business, village, town, and city to promote a vastly expanded concept of the national welfare. Although cash grants-in-aid had existed since the late nineteenth century, for the first time the national government awarded a grant directly to a municipality, the city of Chicago, bypassing the state government in Springfield. Employing the power to regulate interstate commerce and the taxing and spending power, Congress and the Roosevelt administration radically changed the role of government and the relationship between the nation and the states.

If Franklin Roosevelt and the Seventy-third Congress represented a new majority, the Hughes Court remained relatively oblivious to the fundamental transformation of American society and the national economic catastrophe. Between 1933 and 1937 the Supreme Court invalidated a series of national and state laws aimed at promoting economic recovery.[112] The constitutional crisis between the Court and the Roosevelt administration came to a head on May 27, 1935, Black Monday, when the Supreme Court declared two laws and a presidential order unconstitutional. In *Humphrey's Executor* v. *United States*,[113] the Court held that the president lacked authority under the Federal Trade Commission Act to remove a commissioner because he disagreed with the commissioner's policies. On the same day, the justices announced in *Schechter Poultry Corp.* v. *United States* (1935)[114] that the National Industrial Recovery Act was an unconstitutional delegation of power to the executive and a violation of the commerce clause, as applied to intrastate commerce. For good measure, the Court also voided the Frazier-Lemke Act, declaring its provisions for relief of distressed farmers, under the bankruptcy laws, a violation of the Fifth Amendment's due process clause.[115] During its 1935 term, the Supreme Court declared war against the New Deal, against the centralization of power and governmental control of the economy.

Although conflict between the administration and the Supreme Court reached another climax on February 5, 1937, when President Roosevelt sent his judicial reorganization plan to Congress,[116] between 1932 and 1937 Congress considered numerous proposals and enacted five major laws curbing the federal judiciary's jurisdiction and remedial powers. On March 23, 1932, Congress enacted the Norris–La Guardia Act, restricting the federal courts' jurisdiction to enjoin strikes in labor disputes.[117] In May 1934 Congress passed the Johnson Act, which restricted the federal courts' diversity jurisdiction in suits to enjoin the orders of state public utility commissions.[118] Three years later, on August 31, 1937, Congress enacted the Tax Injunction Act, limiting the district courts' jurisdiction to enjoin the assessment and collection of state taxes.[119] At the beginning of World War Two, Congress passed the Emergency Price Control Act of 1942, which established an Office of Price Administration (OPA) to regulate rents and the prices for services and commodities; created an Emergency Court of Appeals with exclusive jurisdiction over suits to enjoin the administrator's orders and regulations; and denied all other courts original jurisdiction over such suits.[120] Following the war, on May 14, 1947, Congress enacted the Portal-to-Portal Pay Act, abolishing the jurisdiction of state and federal courts to entertain any case involving portal-to-portal pay under the Fair Labor Standards Act.[121] In addition to the laws that Congress enacted, representatives and senators introduced both statutes and constitutional amendments to prohibit the federal courts from passing on the constitutionality of specific statutes. With the exception of the Emergency Price Control Act, a wartime measure designed to promote the national defense and security, the other measures reflected congressional and, perhaps, popular discontent with the decisions of the Supreme Court and the lower federal courts.

The Norris–La Guardia Act was designed to remove the federal courts from most labor disputes.[122] Under the act, Congress restricted the federal courts' jurisdiction to issue injunctions in "lawful" labor disputes, which the act defined,[123] but Congress did not insulate the act from judicial review. The Norris–La Guardia Act permitted federal courts to enjoin illegal disputes and prevent threats to private property. In such disputes, the act authorized federal courts to issue injunctions where no other legal remedy was available. The act preserved the complainant's right to procedural due process by requiring notice and guaranteeing a judicial hearing.[124] Section 10 of the act provided for review of a district court's decision, granting or denying an injunction or restraining order, in a court of appeals.[125] In the event that any person was charged with contempt of court for violating judicial orders in labor disputes, section 11 guaranteed the accused the right to a jury trial.[126]

Critics of the Norris–La Guardia Act argued that it limited the federal courts' jurisdiction and judicial power in cases involving constitutional claims. However, the withdrawal of the federal courts' injunctive powers did not deny any due-process rights since other remedies were available in illegal labor disputes, including suits for civil damages and criminal prosecution.[127] In *Lauf* v. *Shinner* (1938), the Supreme Court sustained the constitutionality of the act's limitation on the lower federal courts' jurisdiction.[128] With justices Butler and McReynolds dissenting, Justice Roberts, speaking for the majority, conceded congressional power to regulate the jurisdiction of the lower federal courts. "There can be no question," Roberts wrote, "of the power of Congress thus to define and limit the jurisdiction of the inferior courts of the United States."[129] Both the Norris–La Guardia Act and the Court's decision in *Lauf* v. *Shinner* are consistent with the Supreme Court's long-standing position that congressional authority to regulate the lower federal courts' jurisdiction is plenary.

Not unlike the Norris–La Guardia Act, the Johnson Act of 1934 limited the equity jurisdiction of the district courts in suits "to enjoin, suspend, or restrain the enforcement, operation, or execution of any order" of state public utility commissions in cases based on diversity of citizenship or raising constitutional claims.[130] Speaking for the majority, in *Yakus* v. *United States* (1944), Chief Justice Stone noted that the Johnson Act and other similar laws limiting the federal courts' power to grant injunctions were "not a denial of due process or a usurpation of judicial functions."[131] The Johnson Act preserved the complainant's right to procedural due process by requiring reasonable notice and a hearing. The act also required the availability of a "plain, speedy, and efficient remedy," either in law or equity, in the state courts.[132] Under the Johnson Act, Congress did not foreclose appeals to the Supreme Court in cases raising constitutional claims. Therefore, advocates of jurisdictional gerrymandering cannot claim the Johnson Act as legislative precedent for denying litigants access to a federal forum in which to vindicate constitutional rights.

Similarly, the Tax Injunction Act of 1937 does not offer legislative precedent for plenary power to limit the federal courts' jurisdiction. Under the act, Congress withdrew the district courts' jurisdiction over "any suit to enjoin, suspend, or restrain the assessment, levy, or collection of any tax imposed by or pursuant to the laws of any State where a plain, speedy, and efficient remedy may be had at law or in equity in the courts of such State."[133] Although the act limited the district courts' equity jurisdiction, Congress required the availability of an adequate state remedy and left the Supreme Court's door open to hear cases involving constitutional claims. In *Great Lakes Co.* v. *Huffman* (1943), Chief Justice Stone, speaking for the Court, observed that the Tax Injunction Act merely sanctioned the federal equity courts' practice of abstaining from such suits unless the state courts afford the taxpayer no adequate remedy.[134]

Although the Emergency Price Control Act of 1942 denied all other federal courts jurisdiction to enjoin the OPA's orders and regulations, Congress created an Emergency Court of Appeals with "exclusive jurisdiction to set aside such regulation, order, or price schedule, in whole or in part, to dismiss the complaint, or to remand the proceeding."[135] Congress restricted tests of the OPA's orders and regulations to the Emergency Court, with an appeal, on a writ of certiorari, to the Supreme Court.[136] Furthermore, Congress staffed the Emergency Court with Article III judges, preserving the complainant's right to challenge the legality of the administrator's orders in an Article III forum.[137] While Congress prevented private parties from seeking injunctions in the district courts, the act authorized the administrator to obtain injunctions in any district court against persons violating the OPA's orders and regulations.[138]

In *Lockerty* v. *Phillips* (1943), the Supreme Court sustained the provisions of the Emergency Price Control Act withdrawing the equity jurisdiction of the federal courts and conferring exclusive jurisdiction on the Emergency Court to enjoin the OPA's orders.[139] Chief Justice Stone noted:

> There is nothing in the Constitution which requires Congress to confer equity jurisdiction on any particular inferior federal court. All federal courts, other than the Supreme Court, derive their jurisdiction wholly from the exercise of the authority to "ordain and establish" inferior courts, conferred on Congress by Article III, § 1, of the Constitution. Article III left Congress free to establish inferior federal courts or not as it thought appropriate. It could have declined to create any such courts, leaving suitors to the remedies afforded by state courts, with such appellate review by this Court as Congress might prescribe.[140]

Stone also construed the statute as providing adequate opportunity to challenge the constitutionality of the administrator's orders and regulations. "We think it plain," he wrote, "that orders and regulations involving an unconstitutional application of the statute are 'not in accordance with law' within the meaning of this clause, and that the constitutional validity of the Act, and of orders and regulations under it, may be determined upon the prescribed review in the Emergency Court."[141] As the Court interpreted the act, complainants had sufficient opportunity to raise constitutional claims in an Article III forum, with an appeal from the Emergency Court to the Supreme Court.

During the next term, in *Yakus* v. *United States* (1944), the Court sustained the act's criminal provisions, regulating criminal prosecutions for violation of the administrator's orders and regulations. Noting that the act gave complainants adequate opportunity to challenge the legality of orders and regulations as well as the statute's constitutionality in administrative proceedings and in the Emergency Court, the Supreme Court found that the act's criminal procedures satisfied the Fifth Amendment's due process clause.[142] Specifically, the Court sustained sections of the act precluding defendants charged with violating administrative orders from raising the legality of such orders as a defense in a criminal proceeding. Since there was adequate opportunity to raise legal and constitutional claims before the OPA and in the Emergency Court, with an appeal to the Supreme Court, Chief Justice Stone reasoned that the act satisfied the requirements of due process.[143] In *Lockerty* and *Yakus*, Stone concluded that the Emergency Price Control Act provided a suitable Article III forum to determine constitutional claims and was within the scope of congressional power to regulate the lower federal courts' jurisdiction.

In contrast to the Emergency Price Control Act, in the Portal-to-Portal Pay Act the Eightieth Congress foreclosed access to state and federal courts in any statutory portal-to-portal pay case arising under the Fair Labor Standards Act of 1938. Since these suits involved statutory rather than constitutional claims, neither the Portal-to-Portal Pay Act nor the circuit court's decision in *Battaglia* v. *General Motors Corp.*[144] provide legislative or judicial precedent for the plenary view of congressional power over federal jurisdiction. Indeed, as construed by the federal courts, none of the five acts that Congress passed during the New Deal–Fair Deal eras supports the argument that Congress has plenary power to deny a federal forum to litigants seeking to vindicate their constitutional rights. These statutes involved questions of statutory rights or provided some federal forum in which litigants could present their constitutional claims. During the 1930s Congress employed its Article III powers to limit the federal courts' jurisdiction and remedial powers, but did not alter the Supreme Court's constitutional functions in the American federal system.

The Warren Court Era (1953–1969)

Following the Supreme Court's confrontation with the Roosevelt administration, the death or resignation of justices Sutherland, Butler, Hughes, Van Devanter, and McReynolds gave the president an opportunity to reshape the Court and its policies. With the appointments of justices Black, Reed, Frankfurter, Douglas, and Murphy, and the elevation of Stone to chief, the Court retreated from its collision course with Congress and the president. Roosevelt lost the battle to enlarge the Court, but, with the Grim Reaper's aid, the president won the war against the Four Horsemen (Butler, McReynolds, Sutherland, and Van Devanter). Between 1937 and 1941 the Supreme Court sustained the national government's broad use of the commerce and tax powers to promote economic recovery and the general welfare.

During World War Two the Court began to shift its focus from the protection of property rights to the vindication of other personal liberties. As Justice Stone urged in his famous footnote in *United States v. Carolene Products Co.* (1938),[145] the Court presumed the validity of social and economic legislation, deferring to legislative policy judgments unless Congress had made a clear mistake regarding its power. With regard to such personal rights as speech, religion, and the equal protection of racial and ethnic minorities, the Supreme Court moved almost imperceptibly toward a "more searching judicial inquiry" into legislation that infringed fundamental rights or impaired a minority's access to the political process.[146] Toward the end of World War Two, for example, the Court curtailed the government's power to detain and conditionally release innocent Japanese Americans from "detention" camps.[147] In 1944 the Court also overturned a Democratic white primary in Texas as abridging the right to vote on the basis of race.[148] In *Shelley* v. *Kraemer* (1948),[149] the justices found that state judicial enforcement of a discriminatory housing deed or covenant violated the Fourteenth Amendment's equal protection clause.

However, the Court did not precipitate another major confrontation with Congress until 1954, when it held in *Brown* v. *Board of Education of Topeka* that de jure racial segregation of public schools violated the Fourteenth Amendment.[150] *Brown* marked the beginning of a prolonged struggle between Congress and the Supreme Court over the Court's decisions on racial desegregation of schools and other public facilities,[151] state and federal loyalty-security programs,[152] the investigatory powers of Congress and the states,[153] the criminal defendant's rights,[154] the states' authority to regulate admission and practice of the licensed professions of law and teaching,[155] prayer in the public schools and the establishment of religion,[156] and congressional districting and state legislative apportionment.[157]

The congressional response focused on civil rights, civil liberties, the states' autonomy, and congressional power. Between 1953 and 1968 members of Congress introduced legislation to reverse the Court's statutory interpretations and alter its function and structure. During this period, according to John Schmidhauser and Larry Berg, there were seventeen bills to reverse specific decisions and nine direct attacks on the structure or function of the Supreme Court.[158] In both houses, members introduced constitutional amendments to curb the Supreme Court's power over school desegregation, loyalty-security, the defendant's rights, school prayer, and redistricting and reapportionment. During the same period, approximately sixty bills were introduced to curb the Court's appellate jurisdiction in these areas.[159] The objective was clear: namely, to reverse the justices' decisions, correct their extraconstitutional policy making, and prevent further judicial invasion of state and congressional authority. Despite the sound and fury, the Supreme Court's critics failed to enact a single bill curbing its appellate jurisdiction.[160]

The Rivers bill (1955), the Jenner-Butler bill (1957–1958), and the Tuck bill (1966) were characteristic of legislation to curb the federal courts' jurisdiction. Introduced in the Eighty-fourth Congress by Representative Mendel Rivers (D.-S.C.), H.R. 3701 employed congressional authority, under the exceptions and regulations clause, to deny the Supreme Court appellate jurisdiction over public-school desegregation suits. The chairman of the House Judiciary Committee, Emanuel Celler, who supported *Brown* v. *Board of Eduction*, pigeonholed Rivers's bill and all other measures to limit the federal courts' jurisdiction over school desegregation. Although Senator Herman Talmadge (D.-Ga.) urged the passage of a similar measure, in 1955 the Senate did not act on jurisdictional curbs.[161]

Responding to the Supreme Court's decisions in loyalty and security cases during 1957, Senator William Jenner (R.-Ind.) introduced S. 2646, which sought to restrict the Court's jurisdiction over "five types of cases: (1) contempt of Congress; (2) the Federal Loyalty-Security Program; (3) state antisubversive statutes; (4) regulations of employment and subversive activities in schools; (5) admission to the practice of law in any state."[162] While Jenner was irritated with specific decisions, the consequences of his proposal were structural and functional. Appearing before the Senate Internal Security Subcommittee, on August 7, 1957, Jenner testified that the Supreme Court had created extraconstitutional rights, that the justices had amended the Constitution, and that Congress had the authority, under Article III, section 2, to curb the justices' violation of their judicial oath. Jenner received some support for his proposal, but the Senate carried S. 2646 over to the second session. In 1958, Senator Butler (R.-Md.) amended Jenner's bill, deleting all but the jurisdictional limit on state bar cases. Even in this modified form the proposal was defeated. Seeking to avoid a serious breach within the Democratic Party during the 1958 congressional campaign, Lyndon Johnson quickly tabled the modified Jenner-Butler bill.[163]

Similar in approach to the Rivers and Jenner-Butler bills, Representative Tuck's proposal to curb the federal courts' jurisdiction over state legislative apportionment and districting had more far-reaching consequences. While the Rivers and Jenner-Butler bills insulated state and federal acts from the Supreme Court's constitutional review, the Tuck bill removed the appellate jurisdiction of the Supreme Court and the jurisdiction of the lower federal courts over all state legislative apportionment and districting cases and prevented federal court orders and implementation decrees from taking effect.[164] The Rivers and Jenner-Butler proposals would have altered the Court's relationship to Congress and undermined its authority to promote federal supremacy and a uniform interpretation of national law. However, the bills would have left some federal forum available to persons seeking to vindicate their constitutional rights. The Tuck bill would have denied any federal forum to litigants raising constitutional claims. Although Congress defeated all three measures, they have become a harbinger of recent attacks on the Supreme Court. The Rivers, Jenner-Butler, and Tuck bills have become models for the hundreds of proposals that senators and representatives have introduced to curb the federal courts' jurisdiction over school prayer, school busing, and state antiabortion cases.

Congress and the Court: The Legislative Record

Contemporary proposals to curb the Supreme Court's appellate jurisdiction and remedial powers over school prayer, school busing, and state antiabortion cases are not unique, but they are extraordinary, constitutionally questionable methods of reversing or limiting the effect of judicial decisions. Since 1954 the Court's congressional critics have focused on judicial decisions protecting personal rights against abridgement by the states and the national government. With increasing frequency, members of Congress have introduced limitations on the federal courts' jurisdiction and remedial powers that would place the primary burden of vindicating constitutional rights on the states. Inasmuch as many recent judicial decisions involve the exercise of the states' power vis-à-vis the individual, do proposals denying access to a federal forum or preventing a federal court from employing indispensable remedies burden those individuals seeking to protect their constitutional rights?

Prior to 1954 Congress sometimes reacted strongly to particular decisions, but it did not enact legislation curbing the Supreme Court's jurisdiction or remedial powers that would prevent the justices from deciding constitutional claims, shield state or congressional legislation from constitutional review, prevent the Court from enforcing national supremacy, or prevent it from promoting a uniform interpretation of national law. In many instances, members of Congress engaged in rhetorical threats, warning the justices not to march further into the political thicket. Frequently, Congress enacted legislation reversing the Court's statutory interpretations of various laws, occasionally delivering a stern warning and rejecting the justices' mistaken views. In four instances, Congress and the states adopted constitutional amendments reversing the Supreme Court's constitutional interpretation. None but the Eleventh Amendment altered the Court's function as a constitutional umpire. Nevertheless, the people's representatives have authority, under Article V, to reverse the justices' decisions through the constitutional-amendment process.

Congress also has reacted to the Supreme Court's decisions by making structural changes in the federal judiciary, altering the size of the Court and the structure of the lower courts. While some scholars and jurists may criticize congressional tampering with the federal judiciary's structure, there is little question about legislative authority to organize the Supreme Court and the lower federal courts. With the possible exception of the Judiciary (Repealer) Act of 1802, Congress has not interfered with the Supreme Court's performance of its constitutional functions.

Although Congress has considered numerous proposals to restrict the Court's appellate jurisdiction in cases presenting constitutional claims, thus far it has not enacted legislation that would prevent litigants from raising such claims either in the Supreme Court or in some other Article III forum. Except for the Habeas Corpus Repealer of 1868, legislative restrictions on the Supreme Court's appellate jurisdiction have involved questions of statutory rather than constitutional right and interpretation. Since the Judiciary Act of 1789 Congress has adhered to the principle that the Supreme Court's portal should remain open to litigants seeking to vindicate constitutionally protected rights.

As for the Court's remedial powers, Congress undoubtedly has the authority under Article III to choose among various remedies. However, if a federally protected right exists, some adequate remedy must be available. As long as other adequate remedies exist, Congress has the power to preclude the use of a specific remedy. However, does Congress have authority to deny the use of a particular remedy, if that remedy is demonstrably indispensable to the protection of a specific right? Does Congress, for example, have power to preclude the federal courts from using their equity powers to order school busing to achieve racial desegregation when and where all other remedies have failed to safeguard a constitutionally protected right? Finally, does Congress have authority to prevent the federal courts from employing a remedy that is more effective in protecting constitutional rights than other remedies available to the courts?

If Congress employs its authority over the federal courts' jurisdiction and remedial powers to vitiate constitutionally protected rights, such legislation would not be constitutionally palatable. Congress cannot do indirectly what the Constitution prohibits it from doing directly. Any other argument would reduce constitutional limitations on governmental power to a hollow promise. Moreover, simple legislation that alters the structure of government, the Court's coequal status, and its authority to enforce the supremacy clause vis-à-vis the states would also jeopardize the Framers' and Ratifiers' basic plan of government.

If various proposals to limit the Supreme Court's jurisdiction and remedial powers over school prayer, school busing, and state antiabortion laws employ legislative authority, under Article III, section 2, for the purpose of vitiating constitutionally protected rights, they would be suspect. It may be difficult to determine the collective intent of Congress, but a careful examination of the language, content, and legislative history of such proposals should cast light on the constitutional effects of proposed legislation curbing the Court's appellate jurisdiction and remedial powers. The timing and juxtaposition of jurisdiction-stripping bills, constitutional amendments, and other legislation also should illuminate the intent of their sponsors and supporters. Only careful case studies of the legislative struggles over school prayer, school busing, and state antiabortion cases can address the constitutionality of proposed limits on the Court's jurisdiction and remedial powers.

7

Congress, the Court, and School Prayer

....

In the twenty-five years since the Supreme Court decided that the New York State Regents' prayer constituted a religious establishment prohibited by the First and Fourteenth amendments, members of Congress have introduced hundreds of measures designed to restore prayer in the nation's public schools. Among these proposals are constitutional amendments, jurisdictional limitations, substantive legislation, and sense-of-congress resolutions. Ostensibly motivated by the belief that public schools have a responsibility to inculcate America's religious values and heritage, senators and representatives proposed more than 600 constitutional amendments and forty-five jurisdictional statutes to reverse the Supreme Court's decisions in *Engel* v. *Vitale* (1962) and *Abington* v. *Schempp* (1963) between 1962 and 1987.[1] In these two landmark opinions, the Court declared that the states can neither compose a prayer nor require school children to recite passages from the Bible or the Lord's Prayer during the regular school day.

A decade after *Abington*, however, the proponents of school prayer had not secured the congressional support necessary to propose a constitutional amendment to the states. Increasingly frustrated by their failure to pass an amendment, the opponents of *Engel* and *Abington* introduced legislation in 1974 to limit the federal courts' jurisdiction over school prayer cases. Despite their concerted effort, Congress has not passed a single bill restricting the federal courts' jurisdiction over school prayer cases. Defeated, but undaunted, proponents of public school prayer have focused their efforts on several substantive proposals to achieve their objective. For example, they have proposed restrictions on federal funding of schools that prohibit students from engaging in voluntary prayer. On August 11, 1984, Congress enacted the Equal Access Act, which protects the rights of secondary school students to exercise their religious beliefs.[2] However, the act does not achieve the objective of restoring prayer to the classroom as an integral part of the public schools' educational program.

To determine whether congressional attempts to limit the Supreme Court's appellate jurisdiction and the jurisdiction of the lower federal courts over school prayer cases breach the First Amendment's establishment clause, it is important to examine: (1) the Court's interpretation of the establishment clause regarding religious or devotional exercises in public schools; (2) the language and content of various proposed jurisdictional limitations; (3) the legislative history of these bills, including their sponsors' manifest objectives; (4) the juxtaposition of jurisdictional bills to constitutional amendments, substantive proposals, and sense-of-congress resolutions, which illuminate the remedial intent of jurisdictional limitations; (5) the similarities and differences among these methodologies; (6) the fungibility of methodologies; and (7) the constitutional implications of the methodologies that have been proposed to reverse the effects of *Engel, Abington*, and their progeny.[3]

As the Supreme Court has construed the applicability of the establishment clause to the states since *Everson* v. *Board of Education* (1947),[4] do various jurisdictional proposals vitiate the constitutional right to be free from an establishment of religion? By leaving the final determination of school prayer cases to the states' judiciaries, do jurisdictional limitations make it more difficult for individuals to vindicate this right than persons attempting to vindicate other "fundamental rights?" Do any of the proposed jurisdictional proposals alter the structure of government, that is, the constitutional relationship between Congress and the Supreme Court or between the states and the national government? Do any proposals limiting federal jurisdiction undermine the Supreme Court's authority to enforce the supremacy clause and promote a uniform construction of national law? Although these fundamental questions have been explored from the perspectives of the Framers, Ratifiers, Congress, and the Supreme Court, this and the next two chapters address recent legislative efforts to curb the federal courts' jurisdiction over school prayer, school busing, and state antiabortion cases.

The Scope of the First and Fourteenth Amendments: School Prayer and the Establishment Clause

Since the 1940s the Supreme Court has applied the First Amendment's guarantees that "Congress shall make no law respecting an establishment of religion or prohibiting the free exercise thereof" to the states. In *Cantwell* v. *Connecticut* (1940) the Court held that the state of Connecticut could not burden the exercise of religious liberty that the First and Fourteenth amendments protect.[5] Seven years later, in *Everson* v. *Board of Education*, the Supreme Court ruled that a New Jersey statute providing for the transportation of children to private schools, including sectarian or church-related schools, did not violate the establishment clause, as applied to the state through the Fourteenth Amendment's due process clause.[6] Finding that the statute had a public purpose, the justices ruled that the law did not constitute an establishment of religion. For the first time, the Court applied the establishment clause to the states.[7]

Congressional critics of subsequent establishment clause decisions criticize the Supreme Court's opinions from two perspectives. First, they argue that the Court has adopted a definition of religious establishment that is broader than the authors of the First Amendment intended. Second, they claim that the Fourteenth Amendment's Framers did not intend to incorporate the First Amendment's prohibition against religious establishment, however broadly or narrowly defined, into the concept of liberty that the Fourteenth Amendment embodies. The First Amendment, the argument continues, prohibits Congress from establishing a national church or state religion, but does not prevent the national government from permitting, encouraging, and supporting other religious activities. Thus Congress opens its sessions with prayer, pays military chaplains, and provides chaplains for federal prisoners without offending the establishment clause.[8]

Regarding the Fourteenth Amendment, the critics continue, neither its Framers nor its Ratifiers intended to apply the prohibition of a religious establishment to the states. The Fourteenth Amendment did not incorporate the First Amendment and other provisions of the Bill of Rights into the concept of liberty. Therefore, the states have authority, under the Tenth Amendment, to assist sectarian schools and require or encourage religious activities, including prayer, in public schools. The Court's critics point to the states' long-standing practice of granting tax exemptions to churches and other eleemosynary institutions that promote the public welfare. Given these long-standing practices, the states would not have ratified the Fourteenth Amendment had they realized that it might interfere with their promotion of religious values and institutions.[9]

Inasmuch as universal, compulsory education did not exist in 1791, it is difficult if not impossible to determine whether the Framers and Ratifiers of the First Amendment would have considered public school prayer an establishment of religion.[10] In the absence of either an explicit or implicit reference to public education, it is necessary to examine the values and broad purposes underlying the First Amendment to understand its Framers' intent. As the Supreme Court has construed the establishment and free exercise clauses, the Framers had several broad purposes in mind. First, they sought to avoid the sectarian strife that had riven England and Europe during the seventeenth century.[11] Second, they recognized the religious diversity that existed in the states.[12] Although nine of the colonies had established churches by 1770, religious diversity existed in all of the colonies. In Maryland, Pennsylvania, and Rhode Island, where there was complete religious freedom, Quakers, Baptists, Lutherans, Presbyterians, Congregationalists, and Roman Catholics lived in peace as neighbors. In the face of religious diversity, religious toleration was the only way to promote civil peace.[13] Recognizing the importance of religious toleration and diversity, the authors of the First Amendment prohibited the establishment of an official religion and guaranteed religious freedom.

To promote civil peace in a heterogeneous society, the authors of the First Amendment agreed that government should adopt a neutral stance toward religion. Neutrality, as Black argued in *Everson*, requires impartiality among religious sects as well as between the religious and the irreligious:

> The "establishment of religion" clause of the First Amendment means at least this: Neither a state nor the Federal Government can set up a church. Neither can pass laws which aid one religion, aid all religions, or prefer one religion over another.[14]

Social peace also requires a separation of the public and private sphere in religious affairs, a separation of church and state, as Black quoted Jefferson.[15] The First Amendment removes government from the realm of religious belief and practice so that the state can neither subvert nor manipulate religion to serve secular, public ends. A third requisite for social peace is that religion remain aloof from politics. By maintaining a neutral stance toward religion and avoiding close relationships or excessive entanglements with religious institutions, the state denies sectarian institutions the incentive to intervene in public controversies, which would rent the community.

As the Court has interpreted the free exercise clause, the Framers' essential purpose was to prohibit the state from interfering with the individual's freedom of belief and conscience. Neither the federal government nor the states, Black concluded:

> [C]an force nor influence a person to go to or remain away from church against his will or force him to profess a belief or disbelief in any religion. No person can be punished for entertaining or professing religious beliefs or disbeliefs, for church attendance or non-attendance.[16]

By restricting governmental power to interfere in matters of personal belief and conscience, the Framers sought to protect the individual's autonomy and integrity, promote religious toleration, and avoid the sectarian warfare that arises from public imposition of religious orthodoxy, especially in a pluralistic society.

From the Supreme Court's perspective, the First Amendment's free exercise and establishment clauses serve three basic, interrelated purposes in a society that has become heterodox. First, the religion clauses promote political and social stability by removing religion from the public sector. Second, they promote social pluralism, which some of the Constitution's Framers and Ratifiers believed essential to maintaining the political equilibrium on which the nation's fundamental charter rests.[17] Third, the religion clauses inhibit government from interfering with the individual's autonomy, which some Framers believed indispensable to maintaining limited, constitutional government.

As the continuing controversy over public school prayer demonstrates, there is considerable potential for conflict between the establishment and free exercise clauses. Since *Engel* and *Abington*, the Supreme Court and the lower federal courts have construed the establishment clause in a manner that virtually excludes any form of prayer or silent meditation from the public primary and secondary school curriculum. Regardless of the wisdom or historical accuracy of the Court's interpretation of the establishment clause, this does pose a barrier for some students who wish to engage in certain forms of prayer during the regular school day. Therefore, critics of the Supreme Court's "rigid" interpretation of the establishment clause claim that the justices have disregarded its Framers' intent and have infringed on the individual's religious liberty.[18]

While many legislative proposals (including constitutional amendments, jurisdictional limitations, substantive measures, and sense-of-congress resolutions) attempt to accommodate the free exercise and establishment clauses, the Court has adhered to a constitutional construction that virtually prohibits any religious or devotional exercise during the regular school curriculum. The Court's decisions rest on the tacit, if not explicit, assumption that the primary and secondary school environment is categorically different from that of other public institutions. Since all states have enacted compulsory attendance laws, children are required to attend either public or private schools, including church-related schools, that meet the states' educational standards. In the compulsory public school environment, school children are subject to the state's authority, as exercised by school boards, administrators, and teachers.[19] Under these circumstances, the state cannot compel, require, sanction, approve, sponsor, or encourage devotional activity during the school day. State laws and school board regulations that excuse students from devotional exercises or permit students to leave the classroom during periods of prayer or meditation are not a saving grace, since they single out, set apart, and stigmatize irreligious children or children who belong to nonconventional denominations. As a result, irreligious children, children who profess nonconventional beliefs, and the parents of such children face peer and community pressure, behind which looms the authority of the state. Therefore, in the compulsory environment of the public school, virtually all forms of prayer breach the Court's standards and the essential purposes of the establishment clause.

Although many of the Supreme Court's criteria for determining impermissible breaches of the establishment clause involve public assistance to sectarian schools and institutions, some are applicable to cases concerning prayer in public schools.[20] Since *Everson*, the Court has taken the position that state governments must maintain neutrality toward religion. State and local authorities may not authorize activities in public schools that either favor one religious denomination over another or promote religion over nonreligion (or vice versa). The neutrality standard, which the Court has employed, requires indifference rather than hostility toward religion.[21]

A second standard enjoins government from becoming excessively entangled in religion.[22] Similarly, the standard proscribes religious institutions from entangling themselves in government. Although the "excessive entanglement" standard is derived from cases concerning state assistance to church-related schools and institutions, at least one element is applicable to school prayer cases. That is whether the existence of religious activity in the public school classroom creates or exacerbates the sectarian strife that the Framers of the First Amendment sought to avoid.[23] Aside from chilling the legitimate political activities of religious organizations, in the public school setting the "excessive entanglement" standard requires a careful analysis of various devotional practices to determine whether a particular practice breaches the establishment clause.

The Court's third standard, the "secular-purpose" standard, is directly applicable to school prayer cases. The secular-purpose standard means that a statute, regulation or administrative practice must serve primarily secular ends that fall within the government's authority. If there is any benefit to religion, that benefit must be incidental rather than primary.[24] This standard also implies that the state should avoid employing religious means to achieve an otherwise permissible secular purpose, especially when secular alternatives are available. As the Court has applied the standard to school prayer, if the ostensible, secular purpose of a statute is to promote respect for the nation, state, community, parents, and teachers, the state may not use devotional prayer, since other means are available to inculcate these values and promote discipline in the classroom.[25] Thus far the Court's application of these standards to various forms of prayer and meditation has resulted in a constitutional prohibition of all prayer in public schools.

While the Court has developed many of these standards in relation to expenditure programs, they have also been applied to regulatory and other programs where public expenditures are often trivial and incidental. "No tax in any amount, large or small," wrote Justice Black, "can be levied to support any religious activities or institutions, whatever they may be called, or whatever form they may adopt to teach or practice religion."[26] Even though school prayer programs and other religious activities do not involve significant expenditures, they employ public facilities and personnel that are publicly funded. No matter how trivial the public expenditure, any program that violates any part of the Court's three-prong test would constitute an impermissible breach of the establishment clause. In employing these judicially established criteria, are there any devotional practices that Congress could sanction either directly or indirectly, without amending the Constitution?

Since *Everson*, the Supreme Court has found that a wide range of devotional activities in public schools offend the establishment clause. These activities include reading the Bible,[27] reciting prayers,[28] distributing Bibles,[29] religious instruction, requiring the teaching of creationism and forbidding the teaching of evolutionary theory,[30] the posting of wall plaques bearing the Ten Commandments,[31] and moments of silence and meditation.[32] At the same time, the Court has sustained some devotional practices, for example, prayers at commencement exercises, and the singing of the national anthem and recitation of the pledge of allegiance, both of which include references to God. In the forty years since *McCollum* v. *Board of Education* (1948),[33] however, the Supreme Court has broadened its definition of religious activities in public schools that offend the establishment clause.

School Prayer and Bible Reading

In 1962 and 1963 the Supreme Court extended the list of proscribed religious activities to include reciting prayers and reading the Bible during the school day. Concluding that the New York Regents' prayer breached the First and Fourteenth amendments, Justice Black, speaking for the majority, found "no doubt that New York's program of daily classroom invocation of God's blessings as prescribed in the Regents' prayer is a religious activity. It is a solemn avowal of divine faith and supplication for the blessings of the Almighty."[34] Neither the prayer's nondenominational character nor the fact that students were not required to recite the prayer and could leave the classroom during its recitation saved the program from the judicial ax. Although there was no "direct governmental compulsion,"[35] the New York law established an official religion. As Black commented, "When the power, prestige and financial support of government is placed behind a particular religious belief, the indirect coercive pressure upon religious minorities to conform to the prevailing officially approved religion is plain."[36]

Black also emphasized that the Framers of the First Amendment believed "that a union of government and religion tends to destroy government and to degrade religion."[37] As Black construed the establishment clause, the Regents' prayer violated the Framers' broad purposes by contributing to sectarian strife, creating an excessive entanglement of government and religion, and interfering with the individual's personal belief and conscience. Furthermore, the Regents' prayer endangered political and social stability and vitiated religious pluralism. By homogenizing prayer, Black claimed, the Regents' prayer debased religion, reducing sectarian liturgy to a bland petition "to whom it may concern." Or, as Yale Kamisar once recounted, the child of a suburban New York commuter recited daily, "Lead us not into Penn Station."[38]

Dissenting from the majority's opinion, Justice Potter Stewart denied

that the Regents' prayer constituted a religious establishment or interfered with anyone's free exercise of religion. He concluded that the
decision was at odds with many supplications to the deity in American
public life: prayers in Congress, the Supreme Court crier's petition
"God save the United States and this Honorable Court," various presidents' invocation of divine blessing, the national anthem, the pledge of
allegiance, and the words imprinted on every coin since 1865, "In
God We Trust."[39] Nevertheless, the majority concluded that, in the
compulsory public school setting, recitation of the Regents' prayer was
categorically different from these other practices.

Almost a year later, on June 17, 1963, the Court voided a Pennsylvania
statute requiring that "[a]t least ten verses from the Holy Bible shall be
read, without comment, at the opening of each public school on each
school day."[40] The law provided that any child could be excused from
reading or attending Bible reading at the written request of the parent
or guardian.[41] In *Murray* v. *Curlett* (decided together with *Abington*)
the Court found the Baltimore School Commissioners' rule providing
for "reading, without comment, of a chapter in the Holy Bible and/or
the use of the Lord's Prayer" offensive to the First and Fourteenth
amendments.[42] Although the school board had amended the rule to
provide for excused absence from daily exercises, the majority found
that these practices were religious and devotional, conducted by school
authorities and mandated by the state.

Arguing that the First Amendment prevents a fusion of church and
state, Justice Clark claimed that its prohibition encompasses any establishment of religion, not merely an established church.[43] Then Clark
introduced the "purpose and the primary effect" test, by asking:

> [W]hat are the purpose and the primary effect of the enactment?
> If either is the advancement or inhibition of religion then the
> enactment exceeds the scope of legislative power as circumscribed
> by the Constitution. That is to say that to withstand the strictures
> of the Establishment Clause there must be a secular legislative
> purpose and a primary effect that neither advances nor inhibits
> religion.[44]

Employing this standard, Justice Clark concluded that the Pennsylvania
practice clearly had the purpose and primary effect of advancing religion
in derogation of the First Amendment.[45] Despite the ostensible purpose
of promoting moral values, Clark also concluded that Baltimore's Bible-
reading program was a religious practice that did not serve secular
ends. While adhering to the neutrality standard, Clark denied that the

majority's opinion precluded the study of the Bible "as part of a secular program of education."[46] Studying the Bible for its literary and historic value, according to Clark, does not violate the First Amendment's mandate that "the Government maintain strict neutrality, neither aiding nor opposing religion."[47]

In concurring opinions, both justices Douglas and Brennan agreed that the First Amendment prohibits more than an established church. Although Douglas noted that the expenditure of public funds was negligible, he concluded that the First Amendment absolutely bars the use of tax dollars for religious purposes. Brennan recognized that Americans are a religious people,[48] but he noted that the severest test should be applied to the First Amendment in school prayer cases. Considering the unique environment of public schools, Brennan concluded, the establishment clause forbids religious exercises because they: "(a) serve the essentially religious activities of religious institutions; (b) employ the organs of government for essentially religious purposes; or (c) use essentially religious means to serve governmental ends, where secular means would suffice."[49]

Although the Supreme Court did not preclude all cooperation or accommodation between religion and government, in *Abington* and *Murray* the majority moved several steps toward prohibiting all religious activity in the classroom. In a dissenting opinion, Potter Stewart accepted the applicability of the establishment clause to the states, through the Fourteenth Amendment's due process clause,[50] but objected to the majority's "insensitive" and "mechanistic" definition of a religious establishment. He was particularly critical of the majority's failure to accommodate the right of children and their parents to freely exercise their religious beliefs.[51] The central value of the First Amendment and the Fourteenth Amendment's due process clause, Stewart concluded, "is the safeguarding of an individual's right to free exercise of his religion."[52] Justice Stewart conceded that school boards might eventually find it difficult to administer religious exercises in a constitutionally acceptable manner, but he remained optimistic that, through good will and inventiveness, some accommodation could be found.[53] Justice Stewart's optimism to the contrary, *Engel* and *Abington* still bar Bible reading and reciting prayers in the classroom, even when such devotional exercises are nonsectarian and school authorities excuse children from participation.

Following *Abington*, the Supreme Court and the lower federal courts faced numerous school prayer cases. In 1964, the U.S. Supreme Court unanimously reversed a Florida Supreme Court decision upholding a statute that authorized teachers to read from the Bible, without comment, during the school day.[54] Despite the state court's contention that the "statute was founded upon secular rather than sectarian considerations,"[55] the Court found the Florida practice an establishment of religion. Four years later, in *DeSpain* v. *DeKalb County Community School District* (1968), the Seventh Circuit Court of Appeals ruled that the compulsory recitation of a completely innocuous prayer constitutes an establishment of religion, according to the Supreme Court's standards.[56] A teacher in the DeKalb public schools had required kindergarten children to recite the following prayer, with their hands folded and eyes closed:

> We thank you for the flowers so sweet;
> We thank you for the flowers so sweet;
> We thank you for the food we eat;
> We thank you for the birds that sing;
> We thank you for everything.[57]

Although the teacher, Mrs. Watne, testified that she used the verse in her good citizenship and "thankfulness" program, the circuit court concluded that "the so-called 'secular purposes' of the verse were merely adjunctive and supplemental to its basic and primary purpose, which was the religious act of praising and thanking the Deity."[58] Speaking for himself and Circuit Judge Fairchild, Judge Swygert noted that, although the encroachment was minor, the First Amendment requires a high and impregnable wall between church and state.[59]

Similarly, in *Commissioner of Education* v. *School Committee of Leyden* (1971), the Supreme Judicial Court of Massachusetts held that voluntary religious exercises conducted on school property at the beginning of the school day, with the local school board's permission and in which teachers participated voluntarily, breached the establishment clause.[60] Citing *Abington*, Justice Cutter observed, "[t]he Supreme Court [of the U.S.] thus far has not limited the broad language with which (as in the *Schempp* case) it has held invalid substantially nondenominational and neutral religious observances on public school property."[61] As in *DeSpain*, the U.S. Supreme Court refused to review the lower court's decision.[62] As many critics of *Engel* and *Abington* correctly observe, most state and lower federal courts have applied the Court's decisions so broadly that even the most innocuous prayer recited on school property cannot survive the justices' First Amendment standards. As long as such prayers occur on school property, use school facilities, occur under a teacher's supervision, or in any way are authorized, sanctioned, and encouraged by state and local school authorities, they breach the Supreme Court's view of the establishment clause.

Moment-of-Silence Laws

In 1985 the Supreme Court extended its prohibition on prayer to an Alabama statute authorizing a period of silence for "meditation or voluntary prayer."[63] Delivering the Court's opinion, Justice Stevens observed that the First Amendment requires that a statute must have a clear secular purpose. "In applying the purpose test," he continued, "it is appropriate to ask 'whether government's actual purpose is to endorse or disapprove of religion.' "[64] As the evidence indicated, the statute's primary purpose was to promote religion. Indeed, according to Stewart, the statute had no secular purpose. Its sponsor, State Senator Donald Holmes, had stated that his legislative purpose was to "return voluntary prayer" to the classroom. In his testimony to the district court, Senator Holmes indicated that he had "no other purpose in mind" than returning voluntary prayer to Alabama's schools.[65] There was also a close relationship among the 1981 silent-meditation and voluntary-prayer statute, a 1978 law that authorized a one-minute period for meditation, and a 1982 act that "authorized teachers to lead 'willing students' in a prescribed prayer to 'Almighty God . . . the Creator and Supreme Judge of the world.'"[66] By juxtaposing the language of the predecessor and successor statutes, Justice Stevens concluded that "the State intended to characterize prayer as a favored practice. Such an endorsement is not consistent with the established principle that the government must pursue a course of complete neutrality toward religion."[67]

Although justices O'Connor and Powell concurred in the majority's decision, they agreed with one another that some moment-of-silence statutes might be constitutional. Powell questioned the adequacy of a single legislator's statements in determining the legislature's intent, but he could not find a clear secular purpose in the statute. Justice O'Connor agreed that "the text of the statute in light of its official legislative history leaves little doubt that the purpose of this statute corresponds to the purpose expressed by Senator Holmes at the preliminary injunction hearing."[68] However, she also took the position that some state statutes permitting a moment of silence without endorsing religion or favoring the "child who chooses to pray during a moment of silence over the child who chooses to meditate or reflect," might be constitutional.[69] Moreover, O'Connor recommended that her brethren refine their three-prong test, in *Lemon* v. *Kurtzman*, to find a different accommodation between the free exercise and establishment clauses.[70]

While Chief Justice Burger and Justice White denied that Alabama's moment-of-silence statute constituted an establishment of religion, Justice Rehnquist took the opportunity to challenge the Court's premises with regard to the establishment clause going back to *Everson*. Rehnquist challenged the Court's mistaken understanding of constitutional history, arguing that the Framers' essential purpose was to "prohibit the establishment of a national religion, and perhaps to prevent discrimination among sects."[71] He denied that the Framers intended "that the Government be absolutely neutral as between religion and irreligion."[72] Finally, Rehnquist denied that the *Lemon* tests had any basis in constitutional history or could be applied to yield principled results. Rehnquist concluded that "[n]othing in the Establishment Clause of the First Amendment, properly understood, prohibits any such generalized 'endorsement' of prayer."[73]

Creation Science

Although the teaching of creationism is not a devotional exercise equivalent to Bible reading, the recitation of prayers, or moments of silence, the Supreme Court's decision in *Edwards* v. *Aguillard* (1987)[74] indicates that justices Brennan, Marshall, Blackmun, Powell, and Stevens still adhere to the view that the state cannot use the public school curriculum to advance a particular religious doctrine. Louisiana's Balanced Treatment (Creationism) Act forbade "the teaching of the theory of evolution in public schools unless accompanied by instruction in 'creation science'."[75] Upholding the court of appeals' decision, the majority concluded that the legislature's "actual intent" was "to discredit evolution by counterbalancing its teaching at every turn with the teaching of creationism, a religious belief."[76] Justice Powell agreed with the majority's conclusion but filed a separate opinion, in which Justice O'Connor concurred. Powell argued that the act's legislative history revealed that the Louisiana legislature's primary purpose was to promote a religious belief.[77] However, he conceded that the Court's establishment-clause decisions do not prevent schools from teaching children about the nation's religious history and tradition.[78]

In contrast to the majority and concurring opinions, Justice Antonin Scalia (with whom Chief Justice Rehnquist concurred) denied that the legislature's primary "motivation" was to advance a religious belief. Indeed, Scalia argued that the majority's opinion ignored the statute's meaning and effect. By focusing exclusively on "motivation," the majority had ignored the statute's language, legislative history, and social and historical context. Simply because a statute coincides with, harmonizes the "tenets of some or all religions," or "benefits religion, even substantially," does not mean that its primary purpose and effect is to advance a religious belief. Referring to the Court's establishment-clause jurisprudence as "embarrassing," Scalia called upon his colleagues to introduce clarity, predictability, and some "principled rationale" into their decisions.[79]

As Rehnquist's and White's dissent in *Wallace*, O'Connor's concurring opinion in that case, and Scalia's dissent in *Edwards* indicate, there is growing dissatisfaction among the Court's members with the application of the neutrality principle to establishment-clause cases. Whether Rehnquist, White, O'Connor, and Scalia can persuade Justice Kennedy to join their ranks remains to be seen. If Kennedy should join his four colleagues, this will lead to a substantially different accommodation of the free exercise and establishment clauses. As the evidence suggests, a "new majority" may very well sustain moment-of-silence laws that do not favor a particular religious belief. Barring such a development, the establishment clause, as interpreted by the Supreme Court, many lower federal courts, and some states' appellate courts, prohibits school authorities from introducing virtually any form of prayer or devotional exercise into the classroom as part of the curriculum.

Congressional Response to the Court's School Prayer Decisions

In the twenty-five years since *Engel* and *Abington*, the Supreme Court's critics have employed four methodologies in their attempt to reverse the constitutional effects of the school prayer decisions: constitutional amendments, jurisdictional limitations, substantive legislation, and sense-of-congress resolutions. Although these methodologies differ with regard to constitutional requirements, legislative rules and procedure, policy implications, and constitutional effects, the ultimate objective remains fixed. Changes in congressional membership, the presidency, and the Supreme Court have not altered the primary objective of school prayer advocates, namely, to reverse the constitutional effects of *Engel*, *Abington*, and subsequent federal-court decisions banning prayer in the classroom. A secondary objective is to limit the federal courts' authority and restore the states' power to determine the religious content of educational programs.

The language and content of constitutional amendments and jurisdictional statutes, their legislative histories, and their authors' explicit statements leave little doubt about the remedial intent of most proposals. Since 1962, proponents of school prayer have regarded jurisdictional limitations, under Article III, sections 1 and 2, and constitutional amendments as alternative, interchangeable methods of achieving their strategic goal. On June 26, 1962, Representative Mendel Rivers (D.-S.C.) suggested a constitutional amendment requiring that Supreme Court justices stand for reelection every ten years. "Failing this," Rivers argued, "Mr. Chairman, it is time for the Congress to at least exercise its constitutional right under article III to drastically restrict and limit the appellate jurisdiction of this court which flaunts its authority in our very faces and it flaunts its authority because we have permitted them to run rampant over us."[80]

Concurring with Rivers's approach, Representative Howard Smith (D.-Va.), chairman of the House Rules Committee, remarked in July, "So far as the Supreme Court is concerned, the simplest and most practical remedy [to the school prayer decision] is that provision in the Constitution which authorizes the Congress to curtail the appellate powers of the Supreme Court and limit the Court's jurisdiction to those fundamental areas of review originally envisaged by the framers of the Constitution."[81] Specifically referring to *Engel*, "Judge" Smith argued that the Supreme Court had ignored the Framers' intent and usurped legislative power.[82] In addition to overturning *Engel*, Smith concluded, Congress should restore the separation of powers and the states' sovereignty.

On July 24, 1963, Senator Strom Thurmond (D.-S.C.) endorsed Dean Clarence E. Manion's national radio broadcast, entitled "Congress Should Strip the Supreme Court of its Appellate Jurisdiction." Manion, the former dean of the Notre Dame Law School and chairman of President Eisenhower's Commission on Intergovernmental Relations, remarked:

> These unfortunate Court ventures into policymaking and legislation in disregard for what the State justices called proper judicial restraint cannot be corrected by the slow process of constitutional amendment. . . . In the national interest, therefore, Congress should now exercise the authority given to it under article 3 of the Constitution and strip the Supreme Court of its appellate jurisdiction which it now exercises so prodigally to reverse the sound

judgments of all of the inferior courts in the country—State and Federal.[83]

While Manion suggested stripping the Supreme Court of its appellate jurisdiction, he proposed leaving "judicial review of due process of law" to the federal courts of appeals and the states' supreme courts. Nevertheless, Manion clearly regarded the constitutional-amendment process and jurisdictional legislation as fungible means of reversing the Court's constitutional interpretation.

Referring to *Abington*, on March 26, 1964, Representative August E. Johansen (R.-Mich.) argued that Congress should correct the Supreme Court's mistaken decision. Representative Johanson proposed a constitutional amendment, but he also suggested that Congress consider an alternative method: "In considering needed corrective action, attention should be given not only to possible amendment of the Constitution but also to possible exercise by the Congress of its constitutional authority to limit and regulate the appellate jurisdiction of the Supreme Court."[84] Johansen proposed both methods because he believed that the Supreme Court had distorted the meaning of the free exercise and establishment clauses and had ignored the nation's religious heritage. "I believe these decisions," he said, "if permitted to stand uncorrected, make inevitable far more radical, revolutionary, and disastrous violation of our religious heritage and reversal of our religious traditions."[85]

Ten years later, immediately following the defeat of Senator Thurmond's voluntary-prayer amendment, Senator Helms announced his intention of pursuing S. 784, a bill to limit and regulate the Supreme Court's appellate jurisdiction and the lower courts' jurisdiction. Admitting defeat in "Round 1," Helms announced, "there is more than one way to skin a cat, and there is more than one way for Congress to provide a check on arrogant Supreme Court Justices who routinely distort the Constitution to suit their own motions [sic] of public policy."[86] Senator Helms undoubtedly perceived jurisdictional legislation as a legitimate alternative to a constitutional amendment, for he remarked:

> It is this very difficulty of the amendment process which makes it a blunt instrument as a congressional check on a wayward judiciary. The framers never envisioned that the main congressional remedy for judicial abuse of power would be a constitutional amendment.
>
> If that were the case and Congress were relegated merely to proposing constitutional amendments whenever the Supreme Court dis-

torted the Constitution, then the amendment process would serve not to safeguard the text of the Constitution but to protect the Court's corruptions of it.

* * * * *

For these reasons I have advocated and will continue to advocate legislation to withdraw jurisdiction from the Supreme Court in those areas where it has clearly distorted the meaning of the Constitution. Although such legislation has yet to be enacted, it has met with some success.[87]

The sponsors' explicit statements as well as the language and legislative histories of jurisdictional proposals indicate that the justification for employing the jurisdictional methodology rests on constitutional as well as pragmatic rationales. The constitutional rationale for enacting jurisdictional limitations assumes that the Court has misconstrued the intentions of the First Amendment's Framers and Ratifiers. Simply stated, the justices have ignored the Framers' remedial intent and the nation's religious history and values. The Court has substituted its own values for the Framers' and Ratifiers' purposes. According to the Supreme Court's critics, the Framers had the limited objective of prohibiting a national church rather than proscribing all governmental support for religion. The Court's obsessive preoccupation with the establishment clause denigrates the free exercise clause and trenches on the people's religious liberty, which is a core value of the First Amendment. Neither the language and logic nor the framing and ratification of the First Amendment supports the justices' position.

Nor does the intent of the Fourteenth Amendment's Framers support the Court's incorporation of the establishment clause into the concept of liberty that the due process clause protects. Curiously, some proponents of jurisdictional limitations assume that the Fourteenth Amendment's due process clause does incorporate the free exercise clause. This inconsistency aside, the Fourteenth Amendment does not authorize the Court to give the due process clause a new, substantive meaning or create new rights that its Framers and Ratifiers never intended. Furthermore, the Fourteenth Amendment's enforcement provision, section 5, authorizes Congress rather than the Court to enforce whatever rights section 1—the privileges and immunities, due process, and equal protection clauses—creates.

If the Court has grossly misconstrued both the First and Fourteenth amendments, the Framers of the original Constitution have provided a legitimate alternative to the constitutional-amendment process to correct the Supreme Court's mistaken constitutional judgment. The exceptions and regulations and ordain and establish clauses of the Judiciary Article are a legitimate check on the Supreme Court's usurpation of congressional and state authority. Under Article III, sections 1 and 2, Congress has ample authority to reverse the Supreme Court's constitutional judgments, restore the Framers' and Ratifiers' intent, and redress the balance of power among the branches of the national government as well as between the states and the federal government.

Beyond these constitutional considerations, there are sound pragmatic arguments for advocating jurisdictional limitations. Despite determined and long-standing efforts to secure a constitutional amendment, the Court's critics admit that their endeavors have been fruitless. Although they have not achieved the two-thirds majority that is necessary to propose an amendment, on several occasions they have obtained the simple majority required to enact limitations on the federal courts' jurisdiction. In the interim, the Court's critics contend, the Court has eroded the nation's religious values and tradition. Unless Congress acts soon, the federal courts will destroy the people's religious liberty. Given the difficulties and time-consuming nature of the amendment process, it is imperative that Congress enact limitations on the federal courts' jurisdiction. If Congress does not employ its authority under Article III, the Court will continue to reduce the states "to a position of servitude at the Federal bar," in Jesse Helms's words, and deny the people's right to self-government.[88]

School Prayer Amendments

Although members of Congress have introduced more than 600 constitutional amendments on school prayer since 1962, many of these joint resolutions are identical or similar in language and content. They can be described according to (1) the locus of decision, (2) the form and content of devotional activity, and (3) the forum for prayer. Some joint resolutions leave the decision to participate in prayer with the individual, while other proposals return the locus of decision making to the states. Many voluntary prayer amendments prohibit the states from interfering with the individual's right to exercise his or her religious belief. Others authorize the states to permit voluntary prayer and emphasize that school authorities cannot compel participation in or presence during religious exercises. Still other resolutions require religious or devotional exercises but provide for excused absence from such activities.

A majority of proposed constitutional amendments address the form and content of devotional prayer. Some resolutions prescribe a particular prayer that the states may permit and/or require public school students to recite. In fact, some proposals include a "nonsectarian" or "nondenominational" prayer that schools may employ. While most prescribed prayers are "nondenominational," many joint resolutions prescribe the Lord's prayer or some "nonsectarian" verse. Another type of resolution prescribes Bible reading, but does not specify a particular version or edition of the Bible. In addition to resolutions prescribing form and content, there are other proposed amendments that describe neither. A few resolutions specifically prohibit the states and school authorities from prescribing or even encouraging a particular form or the content of school prayers. A number of joint resolutions permit a moment of silence, meditation, or prayer. Some moment-of-silence resolutions simply authorize a period for reflection without specifying a religious purpose.

Virtually all joint resolutions define the appropriate forum for public prayer. Most proposed amendments limit their reach to public or government-supported schools. Some include schools and other public buildings. Other resolutions merely provide for the right to pray in public buildings. A few proposals authorize government officials to set aside a place in schools and public buildings for prayer and meditation. In addition to describing the locus, form, and forum, some proposed amendments explicitly address the issue of group and individual prayer. Finally, a number of joint resolutions reach beyond the issue of prayer to authorize or permit the use of religious symbols on public buildings and public documents. Despite these differences, the overwhelming majority of proposed constitutional amendments introduced since 1962 seek to return some form of prayer to the public school classroom as an integral part of the educational program.

On June 27, 1962, two days after the Supreme Court's decision in *Engel* v. *Vitale*, Senator J. Glenn Beall (R.-Md.) introduced a constitutional amendment providing that "[n]othing contained in this Constitution shall be construed to prohibit the authority administering any school, school system, or educational institution supported in whole or in part from any public funds from providing for the voluntary participation by the students thereof in regularly scheduled periods of nonsectarian prayer."[89] Senator Beall's joint resolution was among the first of fifty-six amendments that members of Congress introduced in

1962. As the language of S.J. Res. 205 clearly indicates, its intent was to permit voluntary participation in nonsectarian prayer during the regular school day. The resolution granted state and local school officials discretionary authority to introduce devotional prayer into the schools' educational program.[90] Although Beall's proposed amendment differed somewhat in language and content from other joint resolutions, it typified the constitutional amendments that members introduced in the Eighty-seventh Congress. His measure had the effect of reversing *Engel*. Basically, the proposed amendment exempted several forms of school prayer from the Court's interpretation of the establishment clause and restored the states' authority to determine the religious content of the school curriculum. Without commenting on the wisdom, policy, or substantive merits of reintroducing school prayer, Senator Beall employed a legitimate constitutional methodology, under Article V, to reverse the Supreme Court's interpretation of the establishment clause.

This effort to amend the Constitution continued, uninterrupted, between 1962 and 1974. In the Eighty-eighth Congress, following *Abington*, members of both houses filed approximately 265 joint resolutions. Many were similar to earlier proposals, but several prescribed a particular prayer.[91] In contrast to these resolutions, other proposals emphasized the individual's right to freely exercise her or his religious beliefs. H.J. Res. 488, for example, simply permitted the states to set aside time for students to engage in religious worship.[92] Although the House and Senate judiciary committees held hearings on proposed constitutional amendments in 1962 and 1964, neither house adopted a school prayer amendment.

In 1966, the Senate Judiciary Committee conducted hearings on Senator Everett Dirksen's proposed amendment, S.J. Res. 148, which had forty-eight cosponsors. S.J. Res. 148 exempted voluntary prayers in public schools from the establishment clause, but prohibited school authorities from prescribing the form or content of any prayer.[93] However, Senator Dirksen's resolution would not have reversed either *Engel* or *Abington* since these decisions involved prescribed prayers that advanced a particular religious belief.[94] Indeed, the Dirksen amendment would have legitimated the Court's decisions in both cases. His amendment would have spawned endless litigation to determine the voluntary character of prayers that school authorities authorized or permitted. On September 21, 1966, the Senate defeated the resolution by a vote of 49/37.[95] While a majority of the senators voting supported the measure, Dirksen did not have the requisite two-thirds necessary to propose a constitutional amendment.

During the Ninetieth Congress (1967–1968) neither the Senate nor the House of Representatives held hearings on the fifty-three prayer resolutions that members put in the hopper. When Congress convened, on January 11, 1967, Senator Dirksen reintroduced his proposal.[96] Despite continuing conflict over the federal courts' application of *Engel* and *Abington*, Congress did not act on the proposed constitutional amendments. Dissatisfaction with the federal courts peaked again in the Ninety-first Congress, following the presidential election of 1968. Members of both houses introduced ninety-four constitutional amendments, most of which were identical to earlier proposals. Twice bloodied, but unbowed, Senator Dirksen reintroduced his voluntary prayer amendment.[97] As the tenor of the Senate's debate indicates, the prayer issue was alive and well among constituents.[98] However, the judiciary committees took no further action in 1969.

Frustrated by the Senate Judiciary Committee's inaction, in 1970 Senator Howard Baker (R.-Tenn.) took up the cudgel for Everett Dirksen. Circumventing the Judiciary Committee, Baker moved to amend S.J. Res. 264 (on equal rights), substituting a constitutional amendment on school prayer.[99] Baker's substitute amendment emphasized the individual's right "to participate in nondenominational prayer" in public buildings.[100] On October 13 the Senate accepted Baker's substitute (50/20).[101] As the vote indicated, the proponents of a prayer amendment had a majority but, once again, lacked the two-thirds necessary to amend the Constitution.

The proponents of school prayer failed to achieve their objective in the Ninety-first Congress, but they continued their drive in the Ninety-second, submitting another eighty amendments. In the Ninety-second Congress the campaign shifted to the House, where Charles Wylie (R.-Ohio) moved to discharge H.J. Res. 191 from the Judiciary Committee.[102] Almost identical to Senator Baker's resolution, H.J. Res. 191 emphasized the individual's right to exercise his religious beliefs in public buildings.[103] By September 21 Representative Wylie had secured the 218 signatures necessary to discharge his constitutional amendment from the Judiciary Committee. On November 8 the House voted to discharge by a vote of 242/157.[104] Both the vote and the number of signatures on the discharge petition revealed that a sizeable majority favored the joint resolution. However, on the final vote (240/163),[105] the advocates of voluntary prayer could not muster the support of two-thirds of their colleagues.

Following their unsuccessful campaign in 1971, advocates of school prayer apparently lost hope of securing a constitutional amendment.

During the next two sessions of Congress, the Supreme Court's critics celebrated the tenth anniversaries of *Engel* and *Abington* by submitting approximately eleven constitutional amendments. Toward the end of the Ninety-first and in the Ninety-second Congress several representatives introduced amendments providing for voluntary as well as silent prayer, meditation, and reflection.[106] Following the 1972 presidential election, for example, senators Schweiker and Scott proposed an amendment permitting voluntary, nondenominational prayer, similar to the Republican national platform.[107] In the House, Wylie reintroduced his voluntary prayer amendment, but by 1973 Watergate and Vietnam were preoccupying Congress and the nation.

After more than a decade of attempting to secure a constitutional amendment, advocates of school prayer changed their tactics in 1974. For the first time, senators Helms, Eastland, Thurmond, Curtis, and Bennett introduced a bill, S. 3981, to terminate the Supreme Court's appellate jurisdiction and the lower federal courts' jurisdiction over cases involving voluntary school prayer. Proponents of school prayer continued to introduce constitutional amendments, but they sponsored relatively few amendments between 1974 and 1985. During this period the proponents introduced approximately sixty-five constitutional amendments and at least forty-five bills limiting the federal courts' jurisdiction. They refined their tactics, focusing on fewer measures while simultaneously employing several methodologies to obtain their goal.

Jurisdiction-Stripping Bills and Related Legislation

Among the approximately forty-five bills that senators and representatives have introduced to restrict the federal courts' jurisdiction over school prayer cases, there are several important differences regarding scope and subject matter. Relying on congressional authority under Article III, sections 1 and 2, some bills would terminate the Supreme Court's appellate jurisdiction as well as the lower federal courts' jurisdiction over school prayer. Referring to legislative authority under the Judiciary Article's ordain and establish clause and, occasionally, Article I, section 8, other bills would terminate the lower courts' jurisdiction, but would permit appeals from state courts to the Supreme Court. A third group of proposed statutes would abolish the Supreme Court's appellate jurisdiction, leaving the final determination of school prayer cases with the states' appellate courts and the U.S. courts of appeals.

None of these jurisdictional proposals would deny access to all judicial forums, state and federal. Denial of access to any judicial forum would pose a serious due process question. Obviously, each type of legislation has different consequences for the functions of the Supreme Court, the lower federal courts, and the states' judiciaries. Various proposals also have consequences for the separation of powers, federal-state relationships, and the definition of constitutionally protected rights.

Beyond these differences in access to a judicial forum, various amendments to Title 28 of the U.S. Code differ regarding subject matter. One type of proposed legislation covers all forms of school prayer. A second type restricts the federal courts' jurisdiction over "voluntary" prayer cases. Presumably, the Supreme Court and the lower federal courts would retain jurisdiction over cases involving compulsory prayers. Similarly, the federal courts would have jurisdiction to determine whether various devotional exercises were, in fact, voluntary. If, for example, school authorities require children to recite prayers at the beginning of the school day, but excuse children from participating with their parents' or guardians' consent, would this practice constitute "voluntary" prayer within the meaning of the proposed jurisdictional statutes? Undoubtedly, statutes that restrict federal jurisdiction over "voluntary" prayer would spawn endless litigation and would require extensive judicial construction. Such proposals would involve the federal courts as deeply in school prayer cases as they have been since *Engel* and *Abington*. These measures are counterproductive from their sponsors' perspective, since they are likely to exacerbate the continuing controversy over school prayer.

With President Ronald Reagan's support, between 1981 and 1985 advocates of school prayer introduced jurisdictional measures, funding limitations, and equal-access bills as well as constitutional amendments to restore prayer in the nation's public schools. They realized, however, that they did not have the votes to adopt a constitutional amendment. Nevertheless, the continuing introduction of joint resolutions served several tactical and strategic objectives. First, the proponents could argue that they were making a good-faith effort to employ a constitutionally legitimate methodology. Second, they could demonstrate that a congressional majority supported their objective. Third, they could employ this double-barrel tactic to keep the issue alive, increasing pressure on the membership to support jurisdictional and substantive bills, which require only a simple majority for passage. If the gambit worked, the proponents anticipated that President Reagan would sign legislation restricting the federal courts' jurisdiction over school prayer cases.

If there was any doubt about the intent of the members who sponsored legislation to restrict the federal courts' jurisdiction, Senator Helms stated their position candidly in 1974 when he introduced S. 3981. In the ten years since *Engel* and *Abington*, he observed:

> [M]any of us have sought to reverse the Court's decision through the adoption of a constitutional amendment. But our efforts have not been successful. At this very moment, Senate Joint Resolution 84 is before the Senate Judiciary Committee . . . but I am also aware of the fact that this proposal has been before the committee for more than a year. The amendment process is time consuming and exceedingly difficult. The time has come to consider an alternative means of dealing with this problem.
>
> Fortunately, the Constitution provides this alternative under the system of checks and balances. In anticipation of judicial usurpations of power, the framers of our Constitution wisely gave Congress the authority, by a simple majority of both Houses, to check the Supreme Court through regulation of its appellate jurisdiction.[108]

As Helms's statement reveals, he regarded the goals of a constitutional amendment and his jurisdictional proposal as identical. Namely, he and his fellow cosponsors sought to reverse the constitutional effects of the federal courts' school prayer decisions.

Senator Helms's jurisdictional bill (S. 3981) provided that:

> [T]he Supreme Court shall not have jurisdiction to review, by appeal, writ of certiorari, or otherwise, any case arising out of any State statute, ordinance, rule, regulation, or any part thereof, or arising out of any Act interpreting, applying, or enforcing a State statute, ordinance, rule, or regulation, which relates to voluntary prayers in public schools and public buildings.[109]

Another section of the proposed bill abolished the jurisdiction of the U.S. district courts in voluntary prayer cases. Neither section applied to cases then pending in the federal courts.[110] If Senator Helms's introductory remarks or the language of the bill were ambiguous about the legislative intent, Senator Thurmond, a cosponsor, erased any doubt. "In my judgment," Thurmond observed, "this would restore the right of public school children to engage in voluntary prayers in public school buildings, without forced participation."[111] If both Helms and Thurmond assumed that federal-court decisions had proscribed voluntary prayer as an establishment of religion, their proposal and statements invited the states and their judiciaries to ignore the applicable federal judicial precedents and abdicate their responsibility under the supremacy clause.

Although Congress took no further action on Helms's proposal, the senator reintroduced his jurisdictional bill in 1975.[112] In a candid statement, similar to both earlier and later remarks, Senator Helms argued that the constitutional-amendment process was too cumbersome and time consuming, that Article III offered an alternative method to achieve his goal, and that the remedial intent of the statute was to "permit the recitation of voluntary, nondenominational prayers in the public schools. This bill has been made necessary by the judicial prohibition announced by the Supreme Court more than a decade ago in *Engel* v. *Vitale*."[113] In concluding his remarks, Helms again confirmed his specific, primary purpose: "The limited and specific objective of this bill, then, is to restore to the American people the fundamental right of voluntary prayer in the public schools."[114] Despite Senator Helms's determined efforts, neither house adopted jurisdictional legislation during the Ninety-fourth Congress (1975–1976).

During the Ninety-fifth Congress (1977–1978), members of Congress continued to introduce legislation limiting the federal courts' jurisdiction over voluntary school prayer.[115] In 1977 Senator William V. Roth, Jr., (R.-Del.) introduced, simultaneously, a bill to restrict federal jurisdiction (S. 1467) and a constitutional amendment (S.J. Res. 49) to permit voluntary school prayer.[116] Although he denied that his jurisdictional bill would overturn *Engel* and *Abington*, Senator Roth concluded his introduction of S. 1467 by saying:

> Mr. President, it is time that we quit denying our children the right to reaffirm their faith and dependence on God. It is time for the Congress to give effect to the public outcry for action.
>
> Mr. President, I now send to the desk my legislative package [S. 1467 and S.J. 49], in support of prayer in public schools.[117]

In 1978 Senator Helms reintroduced an identical version of his earlier jurisdictional proposal. Reiterating his argument, Helms stated:

> In my view, Mr. President, the American Government has a solemn duty to encourage religion among the people. With this in mind, I send to the desk a bill which will permit the recitation of voluntary,

nondenominational prayers in the public schools. This bill has been made necessary by the judicial prohibition announced by the Supreme Court in *Engel* v. *Vitale*.[118]

Helms emphasized that individuals would still have access to state courts to protect their religious freedom, but he immediately reasserted his original argument that the limited and specific intent of his bill was to restore voluntary prayer in the public schools. Apparently, Helms assumed that state judges would be more hospitable to school prayer than their brethren on the federal bench.[119]

At the beginning of the Ninety-sixth Congress (1979) Helms reintroduced his jurisdictional bill, offering the same rationale for its adoption.[120] Reminding his colleagues that litigants would still have access to state courts to protect their First Amendment rights, Helms restated his intent of restoring voluntary prayer in the classroom. Adding a new line to the well-known refrain, he concluded that public school children should have the right to pray because they "are a captive audience. They are compelled to attend school. Their right to the free exercise of religion should not be suspended while they are in attendance."[121]

Frustrated by the Judiciary Committee's inaction, on April 9 Helms offered his proposal as an amendment to the Supreme Court Jurisdiction Act of 1979. Reciting the familiar litany, Helms argued that Congress has constitutional authority to limit the federal courts' jurisdiction and that the state courts would retain jurisdiction to protect First Amendment rights.[122] In response to criticism, Helms again revealed his primary intent: "The purpose of this amendment is to restore to the American people the fundamental right of voluntary prayer in the public schools."[123] At the conclusion of the debate, the Senate accepted Helms's amendment by a vote of 51/40 and adopted the act by a vote of 61/30.[124] Although Jesse Helms had been successful for the first time, the House failed to enact his proposal. Toward the end of the session, on November 30, Senator Roth reintroduced his jurisdictional proposal and a constitutional amendment, but both measures died in the Ninety-sixth Congress.[125] Once again disclaiming that his jurisdictional bill would overrule *Engel* or *Abington*, Roth called on his colleagues to stop denying children the right to "reaffirm their faith and dependence on God. I now send to the desk my legislative package," Roth concluded, "in support of prayer in public schools."[126]

In 1980 the Republican Party and its presidential candidate, Ronald Reagan, endorsed voluntary school prayer, but the Senate did not act on Senator Helms's amendment to the Supreme Court Jurisdiction Act or any other bill limiting the federal courts' jurisdiction. In the House of Representatives, Philip Crane (R.-Ill.) filed a discharge petition, claiming that S. 450 had been languishing in the Judiciary Committee for more than nine months.[127] In a prepared statement, Crane asserted that his purpose in moving the discharge petition was to restore voluntary prayer. As in the past, during the Ninety-sixth Congress jurisdictional legislation died in the House of Representatives.

With Ronald Reagan's election in 1980, proponents of school prayer stepped up their efforts to limit the federal courts' jurisdiction. In 1981 various members of Congress introduced approximately eleven bills proposing limitations on federal jurisdiction in school prayer cases. Buoyed by Republican control of the Senate for the first time since 1955, on February 16, 1981, Helms introduced S. 481, "The Voluntary Prayer Act of 1981," which abolished the Supreme Court's appellate jurisdiction and the lower courts' jurisdiction over voluntary prayer cases.[128] Representative Ashbrook introduced a similar measure in the House, along with a second bill restricting only the district courts' jurisdiction.[129]

As the title of Helms's bill and the tenor of the debate reveal, nineteen years after *Engel*, advocates of school prayer had not abandoned their primary objective of assuring school children the right to pray "at all times and in all places."[130] In a related move, Senator Roger Jepsen (R.-Iowa) offered a "Voluntary Prayer and Religious Meditation Act," guaranteeing the individual's free exercise of religion, preventing the states and the national government from interfering with voluntary prayer and devotional reading in any federally supported school, and authorizing the U.S. district and state courts to hear cases involving attempts to interfere with these statutory rights.[131] Introducing his measure, Jepsen stated explicitly that it was "designed to reverse the last 19 years of Supreme Court decisions and subsequent case law regarding the constitutionality of State-sponsored religious exercises in the public schools."[132]

Having failed to enact any of the proposed jurisdictional measures, advocates of school prayer succeeded later in 1981 in amending the Commerce, Justice, State Appropriations Bill for Fiscal 1982 (H.R. 4169), prohibiting the use of federal funds "to prevent the implementation of programs of voluntary prayer and meditation in the public schools."[133] While the House agreed to the amendment (333/54), the Senate adopted a different amendment (93/0), providing that "nothing in this act shall be interpreted as the establishment of religion, or prohibiting the free exercise thereof."[134] The Senate's compromise amendment represented a partial victory for both sides, but did not accomplish the objective of restoring voluntary prayer in the classroom.

In 1981 the advocates of school prayer shifted their emphasis from a constitutional amendment to jurisdictional and substantive legislation. The language, legislative history, and debate on constitutional amendments, Senator Helms's jurisdictional proposal, Senator Jepsen's Voluntary Prayer Act, and Representative Walker's amendment to the Commerce, Justice, State Appropriations Bill underscore the common purpose and close relationship among these various legislative proposals. Proponents of school prayer still had their eyes fixed on the Polar Star: reversing the Supreme Court's decisions in *Engel, Abington,* and subsequent school prayer cases.

Feeling success within his grasp, Jesse Helms continued the struggle to curb the federal courts' jurisdiction during 1982.[135] Searching for a winning strategy, Helms offered his bill as an amendment to a temporary increase in the debt ceiling, which he knew was indispensable to continuing government operations. The Senate debated Helms's amendment extensively between September 19 and October 1. Unable to enact a cloture motion ending debate on his amendment (which was defeated 53/45),[136] Helms could nevertheless demonstrate that a majority now supported his position. Although he came closer to achieving his objective in 1982 than he had on any other occasion, Congress adjourned without enacting a bill limiting the federal courts' jurisdiction.

While summing up his agreement with Helms's objective of restoring school prayer, Senator David Durenberger (R.-Minn.) indicated that he could not support the methodology. Durenberger endorsed a constitutional amendment, but regarded court-stripping legislation as "a Pandora's box that can threaten all of our rights once it is opened up."[137] Like many colleagues, Durenberger questioned the constitutional legitimacy of legislation depriving the Supreme Court of jurisdiction to review laws affecting fundamental rights.[138]

Senator Helms introduced his Voluntary Prayer Act again in 1985.[139] In his opening remarks, he argued that his primary purpose was "to restore freedom to the States to allow voluntary prayer, Bible reading, and religious meetings in the public schools."[140] Since the Supreme Court had misconstrued the intent of the First Amendment, he continued, it was necessary to correct the justices' mistaken constitutional interpretation. Although a constitutional amendment is one way to correct judicial error, Helms concluded, Article III "provides several other more direct ways for Congress to check abuses of the judicial branch, including control of jurisdiction."[141] On a more pragmatic note, Senator Helms confessed that the constitutional-amendment process imposed "an extremely heavy burden" that he had been unable to meet.[142] After a lengthy debate in which Helms's opponents questioned the constitutional legitimacy of employing the ordain and establish and exceptions and regulations clauses, on September 10 the Senate voted to table Helms's proposal (62/36).[143]

Jesse Helms, Orrin Hatch, and other senators who advocate school prayer thus far have been unable either to secure a constitutional amendment or to limit the federal courts' jurisdiction. However, they have kept the issue alive, obviously striking a responsive chord in the American electorate. The Senate Judiciary Committee, under the chairmanship of Strom Thurmond, and its Subcommittee on Constitutional Amendments, chaired by Orrin Hatch, held hearings on school prayer amendments and legislation in every session of Congress between 1982 and 1985.

On February 3, 1983, Senator Denton introduced the Equal Access Act. As originally proposed, the act would have prevented the expenditure of federal funds to assist any public school that does not permit:

> [S]tudents, faculty, or groups of students and faculty, to engage in voluntary extracurricular activities on school premises of a public elementary or secondary school during noninstructional periods [or that denies] . . . equal access and opportunity to, or discriminates against, students or faculty or both, or groups of students, groups of faculty members, or both, that seek to engage in voluntary prayer, religious discussion or silent meditation on school premises during noninstructional periods.[144]

Although Congress took no further action on equal-access legislation in 1983, on August 11, 1984, it enacted the Equal Access Act.[145] The act prohibits secondary schools that receive federal funds from closing their facilities selectively to student religious groups, but the law does not authorize federal agencies to withhold financial assistance to any school. Thus far the Supreme Court has not determined the constitutionality of the Equal Access Act. However, in *Bender* v. *Williamsport Area School District* (1986),[146] the Court vacated a decision of the Third Circuit Court of Appeals holding that the Williamsport Area High School was not required to permit a religious club, Petros, to conduct meetings in the school.

Finding that the petitioner did not have standing to sue, the Supreme Court ruled that the court of appeals lacked jurisdiction. The Court's order, remanding the case to the court of appeals with instructions to dismiss, let the district court's decision stand.[147] The district court had decided that the First Amendment's establishment clause does not require the school district to deny Petros the opportunity to meet.[148] By denying Petros equal access to school facilities along with all other student organizations, school authorities had burdened these students' free-speech rights. Chief Justice Burger and justices White, Rehnquist, and Powell dissented, arguing that the majority should have decided *Bender* on the merits. While Burger would have decided the establishment-clause issue, Powell would have determined the students' free-speech claim.[149] In either event, with the appointment of justices Scalia and Kennedy, a new majority probably would sustain the equal-access methodology that Congress has employed.

Conclusion: Congressional Intent and the Constitutional Legitimacy of Jurisdiction Stripping

After twenty-five years of struggle, proponents of school prayer have secured only one measure, the Equal Access Act of 1984, which allows students to conduct religious activities during club or activity periods, set apart from the regular educational program, without a teacher's supervision, and in no way encouraged or sponsored by school authorities. Senator Helms and his allies have not succeeded in restoring prayer in the classroom. Having failed to secure a constitutional amendment, proponents of school prayer turned to jurisdictional and substantive bills to obtain their objective. Occasionally, some members also introduced sense-of-congress resolutions, which express congressional sentiment regarding the value of school prayer, but do not have any binding, legal effect on the federal and state courts.

When proposed limitations on the federal courts' jurisdiction are considered in relation to constitutional amendments and substantive measures, jurisdiction-stripping bills are clearly a subterfuge for reintroducing prayer in the nation's public school classrooms. The sponsors' statements, within the context of the legislative histories of jurisdictional proposals, leave little doubt that the primary purpose and effect of these bills is to reverse the Supreme Court's decisions in the school prayer cases. A secondary, related effect is to leave the final determination of school prayer cases and First Amendment rights to state courts, which the sponsors of jurisdictional limitations apparently believe will be less hospitable to *Engel, Abington,* and subsequent decisions than the federal courts. As such, proposed limitations on the federal courts' jurisdiction in school prayer cases attempt to accomplish indirectly what Congress cannot accomplish directly. These proposals burden a judicially defined constitutional right to be free from an establishment of religion.[150] If the Supreme Court has misconstrued the intent of the First and Fourteenth amendments, the Constitution provides a legitimate methodology, in Article V, to reverse the justices' mistaken constitutional interpretation. However, the methodologies that articles III (sections 1 and 2) and V describe are not fungible or interchangeable means to accomplish the primary objective of reinstating school prayer.

Most jurisdictional proposals have other constitutionally questionable effects. Although the Supreme Court would still retain jurisdiction to determine the constitutionality of jurisdiction-stripping proposals, such proposals alter the balance of power between Congress and the Court and the relationship between the states and the national government. If Congress enacts a series of such measures on prayer, busing, abortion, and other judicially defined constitutional rights, it will impair the Supreme Court's authority to enforce the supremacy clause, provide a uniform construction of national law, and protect fundamental rights against state infringement. Moreover, Congress could employ the same methodology to shield national legislation against judicial review. While some advocates of jurisdictional gerrymandering argue that the exceptions and regulations and ordain and establish clauses are a democratic check on judicial usurpation of state and congressional power, the Framers did not intend to arm Congress with authority to alter the structure of government by a simple majority.

Beyond these constitutional effects, proposals restricting the federal courts' jurisdiction in school prayer cases would not reverse the Supreme Court's decisions unless these measures are an open invitation to the states' judiciaries to ignore the standing precedents. Otherwise, under the supremacy clause, the state courts have a responsibility to enforce the Supreme Court's decisions on school prayer. Those proposals limiting the Supreme Court's appellate jurisdiction, but retaining the district courts' jurisdiction in school prayer cases, would have a curious legal effect. In any state, the U.S. district courts and the state courts could, conceivably, come to diametrically opposite conclusions regarding the constitutionality of school prayer. Without access to the Supreme Court, there would be no means to resolve conflict between state and federal courts. By removing the Supreme Court as an arbiter, proposals that retain the district courts' jurisdiction would sow controversy, undermine comity between the state and federal courts, and create confusion regarding the status of constitutionally protected rights.

Although jurisdictional gerrymandering is an attractive alternative to opponents of the Supreme Court's school prayer decisions, it is a constitutionally questionable methodology. By changing the level of decision making from the federal to the state courts, advocates of this methodology single out and burden the vindication of a judicially defined constitutional right to be free from an establishment of religion.[151] If the purpose and primary effect of jurisdictional gerrymandering is to burden a particular right, in addition to all other constitutional infirmities, such jurisdictional legislation poses serious equal-protection issues under the Fifth Amendment's due process clause.[152] While congressional authority to regulate the federal courts' jurisdiction under the Judiciary Article is broad, nevertheless, the First, Fifth, and Fourteenth amendments impose external, constitutional limitations on the exercise of legislative power.

8

School Desegregation and Court-Ordered Busing: Where There Is a Right, Is There a Remedy?

....

Since the Supreme Court's decision in *Swann* v. *Charlotte-Mecklen-burg Board of Education* (1971),[1] members of Congress have introduced numerous proposals to restrict the federal courts' authority in school desegregation cases. Many of these proposals would remove the lower federal courts' jurisdiction and the Supreme Court's appellate jurisdiction to make any decision requiring that public school students be assigned to schools on the basis of their race. Other proposals would restrict the federal judiciary's authority to employ busing as a remedial tool in school desegregation cases. These proposals rest on congressional authority to regulate the federal courts' jurisdiction and remedial powers under Article III and the enforcement clause (section 5) of the Fourteenth Amendment.

Although these proposals differ regarding the degree of congressional intrusion on federal judicial power, their common objective is to end court-ordered busing to achieve racial desegregation of the nation's public schools. Congressional opponents of the Supreme Court's desegregation decisions argue that the federal judiciary lacks both the authority and competence to impose massive busing on school districts in which de jure segregation exists. "Antibusing proponents" also allege that busing is destructive and counterproductive in achieving the goal of desegregation and improving educational quality.

Before assessing the constitutional implications of various "antibusing proposals," it is first necessary to examine the Court's perception of busing as a remedial tool in desegregation cases. Under what circumstances has the Supreme Court imposed busing plans on local school districts? To what extent has the Court found busing to be an indispens-able remedy in vindicating the Fourteenth Amendment right to be free from racial segregation in public education? Second, an examination of congressional opposition to desegregative busing will illuminate the remedial intent of proposals that senators and representatives have introduced to limit the federal courts' powers and jurisdiction in school desegregation cases. What are the bases of congressional dissatisfaction with court-ordered busing to end racial segregation in education? What is the range and scope of legal methodologies that senators and represen-tatives have proposed to prohibit the federal courts from interfering with the putative right of public school students to attend a neighbor-hood school?

Third, what is the scope of congressional power under section 5 of the Fourteenth Amendment to enact antibusing legislation? Does section 5 empower Congress to limit the federal courts' remedial pow-ers to vindicate Fourteenth Amendment rights? If there is a constitu-tional right to be free from public school segregation, can Congress prohibit the federal courts from employing either an indispensable or the most effective remedy necessary to vindicate that right? Although Congress has authority, under Article III and section 5 of the Fourteenth Amendment, to regulate the federal courts' jurisdiction and remedial powers, can Congress employ its authority to vitiate equal-protection rights, undermine the separation of powers, and circumvent the consti-tutional-amendment process (in Article V)?

A Constitutional Right—An
Indispensable Remedy

Supporters of antibusing legislation contend that since busing is a rem-edy rather than a constitutional right, congressional authority to limit or forbid its use is plenary. Furthermore, antibusing proponents claim, other effective desegregation remedies exist, for example, freedom-of-choice plans, which would not require the imposition of additional school busing.[2] Do these proposals merely attempt to remove one of several effective remedies or do they deny the federal courts the only constitutionally adequate remedy? To answer this question, one must examine the Supreme Court's decisions relating to the Fourteenth Amendment's equal protection clause and desegregation of the public schools.

Beginning in 1896 the Supreme Court read the "separate, but equal" doctrine into the Fourteenth Amendment when it validated a Louisiana statute requiring "equal, but separate, accommodations" for black and white railway passengers.[3] Speaking for the majority in *Plessy* v. *Furgusen*, Justice Henry Brown argued that legislation cannot overcome social prejudice. Separate-but-equal facilities, Brown continued, relate only to social equality rather than political or civil equality, which the Fourteenth Amendment's Framers intended to protect. "If one race be inferior to the other socially," Brown concluded, "the Constitution of the United States cannot put them upon the same plane."[4]

Not until 1954 did the Supreme Court explicitly reject the "separate-but-equal" doctrine in its landmark decision, *Brown* v. *Board of Education*.[5] In a unanimous decision, the Court held that de jure racial segregation in public schools is unconstitutional. Speaking for the Court, Chief Justice Earl Warren argued that it was impossible to determine whether the Fourteenth Amendment's Framers intended to prohibit segregated public school facilities. Despite the Framers' intent and the Court's decision in *Plessy* v. *Furgusen*, Warren contended that the Supreme Court "must consider public education in the light of its full development and its present place in American life."[6] Relying on the empirical evidence of educators and psychologists,[7] Warren concluded that "separate educational facilities are inherently unequal" and deny black children "the equal protection of the laws."[8] In articulating the doctrine that de jure[9] segregation in public education is repugnant to the Constitution, the Court applied the concept of equal protection to both the states and federal government.[10]

In *Brown II* (1955), the Court announced that school officials have the "primary responsibility" to "make a prompt and reasonable start" toward "a racially nondiscriminatory school system."[11] Speaking for the Court, Warren instructed that federal district courts supervise the implementation of schoolboard desegregation plans because of their "proximity to local conditions and the possible need for further hearings."[12] Warren stated that the district courts should formulate "equitable"[13] desegregation remedies to assure that dual school systems would be abolished "with all deliberate speed."[14]

Between 1955 and 1968, however, *Brown I* had little practical effect in desegregating many public schools. During this period, the Supreme Court decided only a few cases regarding the implementation of *Brown I*. In *Cooper* v. *Aaron* (1958),[15] for example, the Supreme Court reinstated a district court's desegregation order in Little Rock, Arkansas, despite resistance from the governor and other state officials, who argued that they were not bound by *Brown I*. In a forceful opinion for a unanimous Court, Chief Justice Warren declared that state authorities cannot disobey the Supreme Court's constitutional interpretations and deprive children of their right to equal protection of the laws "through evasive schemes for segregation whether attempted 'ingeniously or ingenuously'."[16]

In *Goss* v. *Board of Education* (1963),[17] the Court found that a minority-to-majority transfer plan was not a constitutionally adequate desegregation remedy. Writing for a unanimous Court, Justice Clark argued that since the transfer plan would perpetuate segregation[18] it could not satisfy the requirements of the equal protection clause. Also, in *Griffen* v. *Prince Edward County School Board* (1964),[19] the Court rejected the county's attempt to close public schools and subsequently fund white-only private schools. Writing for the majority in *Griffen*, Justice Black exemplified the Court's frustration with delays in public school desegregation: "There has been entirely too much deliberation and not enough speed in enforcing the constitutional rights" identified in *Brown I*.[20] The Court's decisions in *Cooper*, *Goss*, and *Griffen* notwithstanding, the pace of public school desegregation remained slow until the late 1960s.[21]

Thirteen years after *Brown I*, in *Green* v. *New Kent County School Board* (1968),[22] the Court expressly held that remedies in school desegregation cases are not limited to racially neutral measures. The Fourteenth Amendment, Justice Brennen wrote, imposes an "affirmative duty to take whatever steps might be necessary to convert to a unitary system in which racial discrimination would be eliminated root and branch."[23] Rejecting as inadequate a freedom-of-choice plan,[24] Brennen noted that "delays" in correcting Fourteenth Amendment violations and desegregation plans that fail to "provide meaningful assurance of prompt and effective disestablishment" are constitutionally deficient.[25] *Green* marked a major turning point in implementing *Brown I*. For the first time, the Supreme Court explicitly required *effective* desegregation measures.[26] Furthermore, the Court's decision in *Green* clarified that the Fourteenth Amendment does not simply require school boards to cease discriminatory actions. School boards have an "affirmative duty" to *integrate* their educational facilities and create a unitary system effectively and immediately.[27]

Three years later, in *Swann* v. *Charlotte-Mecklenburg Board of Education*,[28] the Supreme Court further delineated the scope of judicial authority to assure that school districts comply with equal-protection requirements. Speaking for a unanimous Court, Chief Justice Warren Burger identified several limitations on the use of the federal courts' equity powers in desegregation cases. First, Burger recognized that school boards have the primary responsibility for abolishing dual schools. Only when school boards fail to meet this constitutional obligation is judicial intervention justified.[29] He acknowledged that a federal-court desegregation decree is only justified "on the basis of a constitutional violation."[30] Burger concluded that "[t]he task is to correct . . . the condition that offends the Constitution. . . . As with any equity case, the nature of the violation determines the scope of the remedy."[31]

In identifying acceptable remedial tools in desegregation cases, Burger argued that an assignment plan "is not acceptable simply because it appears to be neutral."[32] Moreover, he stressed that judicial authority to dismantle dual schools includes racially conscious remedies, for example, "gerrymandering of school districts and attendance zones . . . pairing, 'clustering,' or 'grouping' of schools,"[33] that may be inconvenient, but constitutionally required:

> Absent a constitutional violation there would be no basis for judicially ordering assignment of students on a racial basis. All things being equal, with no history of discrimination, it might well be desirable to assign pupils to schools nearest their homes. But all things are not equal in a system that has been deliberately constructed and maintained to enforce racial segregation. The remedy for such segregation may be administratively awkward, inconvenient, and even bizarre in some situations and may impose burdens on some; but all awkwardness and inconvenience cannot be avoided in the interim period when remedial adjustments are being made to eliminate the dual school systems.[34]

Burger recognized busing as a remedial tool that may be indispensable in constructing a constitutionally adequate desegregation plan.[35] The chief justice concluded that the district court's record in *Swann* justified implementing a desegregation plan that included busing as essential to fulfill the promise of *Brown* and the Fourteenth Amendment. Acknowledging that "[d]esegregation plans cannot be limited to the walk-in school,"[36] Burger suggested that in some situations busing is a constitutionally indispensable remedy.

However, Burger cautioned, if the district courts employ busing, they must demonstrate that it is "reasonable, feasible, and workable" in furthering the goal of desegregation.[37] He also noted that time and distance might limit the use of school busing to the extent that these factors risk the health of school children or "significantly impinge on the educational process."[38] Finally, Burger recognized that any desegre-

gation remedy is an "interim corrective measure"[39] that would terminate once the constitutional violation had been corrected:

> Neither school authorities nor district courts are constitutionally
> required to make year-by-year adjustments of the racial composi-
> tion of student bodies once the affirmative duty to desegregate
> has been accomplished and racial discrimination through official
> action is eliminated from the system. This does not mean that
> federal courts are without power to deal with future problems; but
> in the absence of a showing that either the school authorities or
> some other agency of the State has deliberately attempted to fix or
> alter demographic patterns to affect the racial composition of the
> schools, further intervention by a district court should not be nec-
> essary.[40]

In three other cases decided on April 20, 1971, the Court addressed
the legitimacy of remedial busing in school desegregation cases.[41] In
Davis v. *Board of Commissioners*, the Supreme Court rejected the Fifth
Circuit Court of Appeal's desegregation plan as failing to end a dual
system because "inadequate consideration was given to the possible
use of bus transportation and split zoning."[42] The Court reasoned that
by failing to consider busing, the court of appeals had not adhered to
Green's requirement that desegregation plans must be effective.[43] The
Supreme Court's reasoning in *Davis*, as in *Green*, is straightforward;
that is, a remedy that does not effectively correct a constitutional
violation is no remedy at all. Without the use of busing as a remedial
tool, the desegregation plan considered in *Davis* was ineffective and
therefore inadequate in vindicating the constitutional right to be free
from educational segregation.

Similarly, in *North Carolina Board of Education* v. *Swann*, Burger
buttressed the premise that if busing were not available in desegregation
cases, it would be difficult, if not impossible, to correct the constitutional violation.[44] At the time, North Carolina's "Anti-Busing Law"
prohibited public school assignments on the basis of race and the use
of desegregative busing.[45] Writing for a unanimous Court, Burger stated
that:

> [I]f a state-imposed limitation on a school authority's discretion
> operates to inhibit or obstruct the operation of a unitary school
> system or impede the disestablishing of a dual school system, it
> must fall; state policy must give way when it operates to hinder
> vindication of federal constitutional guarantees.[46]

The chief justice concluded that the prohibition on desegregative bus-ing would "hamper the ability of local authorities to effectively remedy constitutional violations."[47]

In *Swann* the Court emphasized that the district courts could only remedy de jure, not de facto, segregation.[48] Until 1973, the Court's de jure/de facto distinction meant that desegregation decisions were applicable only to school districts that had segregated their educational facilities by statute or constitutional provision. Hence, most of the federal courts' desegregation orders were confined to school districts in the South.[49] However, in *Keyes* v. *School District No. 1* (1973) the Court opened the door for the desegregation of public schools in northern cities. In *Keyes*, the Court found that, although the Denver, Colorado, school system had never required separate but equal schools by statute, local school officials had gerrymandered school districts and selected school construction sites in a conscious effort to maintain racial segre-gation.[50] Writing for the majority, Justice Brennan argued that de jure racial segregation existed whenever local or state officials took purpose-ful action to segregate the public schools. After acknowledging that the Court's past desegregation decisions involved cases where dual schools were "compelled or authorized by statute,"[51] Brennan made the quan-tum leap:

> This is not a case, however, where a statutory dual system has ever existed. Nevertheless, where plaintiffs prove that the school authorities have carried out a systematic program of segregation affecting a substantial portion of the students, schools, teachers, and facilities within the school system, it is only common sense to conclude that there exists a predicate for a finding of the exis-tence of a dual school system.[52]

The Court also found that if purposeful segregation existed in a signifi-cant portion of the school district, there was a presumption that official discrimination had caused racial segregation in other portions of the school district.[53] Unless a school board could rebut this presumption, a federal court had authority to order a district-wide remedy.[54]

However, in *Milliken* v. *Bradley* (1974)[55] the Court refused to uphold a district court's multidistrict busing decree for the Detroit school system, absent a showing of de jure segregation in all of the school districts affected. After finding intentional discrimination in Detroit's school district, the district court concluded that a remedy which was limited to the Detroit inner-city district would be ineffective in achiev-ing a unitary system because of that district's large minority population.

On the basis of its assessment, the district court ordered a desegregative busing plan that included fifty-three surrounding school districts.[56]

Writing for the Court, Chief Justice Burger argued that the district court's plan could be justified if (a) de jure segregation existed in all outlying districts or (b) a constitutional violation in one district had a "significant segregative effect" in the other districts.[57] Since the evidence indicated that de jure segregation existed only in the inner-city district, Burger contended that the district court's plan "would impose on the outlying districts, not shown to have committed any constitutional violation, a wholly impermissible remedy."[58] He stressed that the remedial goal is "to restore the victims of discriminatory conduct to the position they would have occupied in the absence of such conduct."[59] The chief concluded that since discriminatory conduct had only occurred in the Detroit inner-city school system, "the remedy must be limited to that system."[60]

Similarly, in *Austin Independent School District* v. *United States* (1976)[61] and *Dayton Board of Education* v. *Brinkman* (1977)[62] (*Dayton I*), the Court ordered the district courts to reexamine their desegregation plans because the scope of the remedies ordered was broader than and unsupported by the extent of the violation. In remanding the cases, the Court instructed the district courts to reassess their determination according to *Washington* v. *Davis*,[63] in which the Supreme Court held that plaintiffs seeking to prove equal-protection violations must demonstrate that government officials acted with discriminatory intent.[64] Writing for the majority in *Dayton I*, Justice William Rehnquist argued that, to find a constitutional violation in school desegregation cases, a district court must demonstrate that the school board "intended to, and did in fact, discriminate against minority pupils, teachers, or staff."[65]

In *Pasadena City Board of Education* v. *Spangler* (1976),[66] the Court imposed another limitation on the federal courts' exercise of their equity powers in school desegregation cases. In *Spangler*, the Court held that a school system under a court-ordered desegregation plan cannot be forced to adjust attendance zones annually in response to racial shifts in residential patterns. In *Spangler*, the district court had required the school board to adjust its assignment plan every year "so that there would not be a majority of any minority" in a public school.[67] Writing for the majority, Justice Rehnquist reasserted the holding in *Swann* that there is no constitutional right to a particular racial mix in the public schools, merely a right to a unitary public school system.[68]

Three years later, in *Dayton Board of Education* v. *Brinkman* (1979)[69] (*Dayton II*) and *Columbus Board of Education* v. *Penick* (1979),[70] the

Supreme Court apparently expanded the scope of the federal courts' authority to remedy de jure segregation in public schools. Speaking for the majority in *Dayton II* and *Columbus*, Justice White held that if a school board had intentionally segregated its facilities at the time the Court decided *Brown I* (1954), district courts could attribute current racial segregation, in part, to that past discrimination. The trial record indicated that the Dayton and Columbus school boards not only failed to discharge their constitutional obligation to establish a unitary system, but had effectively perpetuated past racial discrimination.[71] White concluded that the evidence was sufficient to demonstrate a constitutional violation.[72]

In *Dayton II* and *Columbus* the Court also ruled that district courts may rely on disproportionate impact to demonstrate a discriminatory purpose: "[A]ctions having foreseeable and anticipated disparate impact are relevant evidence to prove the ultimate fact, forbidden purpose."[73] While some commentators have criticized this ruling for reviving "uncertainty over the proof required to show discriminatory intent in school desegregation cases,"[74] White emphasized that the decisions were consistent with precedent. Quoting from the district court's opinion, Justice White concluded:

> Adherence to a particular policy or practice, "with full knowledge of the predictable effects of such adherence upon racial imbalance in a school system is one factor among many others which may be considered by a court in determining whether an inference of segregative intent should be drawn." . . . The District Court thus stayed well within the requirements of *Washington* v. *Davis* and *Arlington Heights*.[75]

While *Pasadena City Board of Education* v. *Spangler* addressed the scope of a district court's authority to supervise its desegregation decree, two court of appeals' decisions in 1986, *Riddick* v. *Norfolk School Board*[76] and *Dowell* v. *Board of Education*,[77] addressed the question of how long a school district can be subject to a court-ordered desegregation plan. Or, as the Fourth Circuit phrased the issue: "Does judicial involvement end when unitary status is achieved or does judicial involvement continue in perpetuity to prevent resegregation absent a showing of intent to discriminate?"[78] The two courts arrived at apparently conflicting conclusions regarding this question.

After identifying the existence of de jure segregation in Norfolk, Virginia, in 1971, the district court implemented a desegregation plan requiring massive crosstown busing. Four years later, the district court declared that Norfolk had achieved "unitary"[79] status and returned jurisdiction over school assignments to the Norfolk School Board. In 1983 the Norfolk School Board abolished the district court's 1971 busing plan and initiated a neighborhood school assignment plan. In a suit to enjoin the school board's plan, the district court ruled that the finding of "unitariness" in 1975 effectively shifted the burden to the *plaintiffs* to demonstrate that the school board acted with discriminatory intent.[80] Concurring with the district court's decision, the Fourth Circuit sustained the reallocation of the burden of proof to the plaintiffs. The court of appeals held that "the burden of proving discriminatory intent attaches to a plaintiff once a de jure segregated school system has been found to be unitary. . . . [A]ny further judicial action . . . would amount to the setting of racial quotas, which have been consistently condemned by the Court."[81]

The Tenth Circuit confronted parallel circumstances in *Dowell*. In 1972 the district court ordered desegregative busing for the Oklahoma City school district. In 1977 the district court found the Oklahoma City system to be "unitary" and relinquished jurisdiction over school assignments. In 1985 plaintiffs moved to reopen the case, challenging the school board's reassignment, which would have eliminated desegregative busing for grades 1–4. Based on the 1977 finding of "unitariness" and the reasoning in *Riddick*, the district court denied the motion to reopen the case because the plaintiffs could not demonstrate that the school board intended to discriminate.[82] In overturning the district court's ruling, the Tenth Circuit emphasized that the finding of unitariness does not automatically vacate the district court's mandatory desegregation injunction.[83]

The Supreme Court's refusal to review these cases has left the apparent conflict between the Fourth and Tenth circuits unresolved. However, the disagreement between the circuits is limited to a narrow procedural question.[84] The procedural disagreement aside, neither decision supports the contention that a district court's desegregation decree must continue in perpetuity. *Spangler*, *Riddick*, and *Dowell* all support the earlier pronouncements in *Green* and *Swann* that a desegregation decree should end when, in the district court's judgment, the last vestiges of dual schools have been terminated root and branch.[85]

In *Brown I* and *Green*, the Court recognized that officially mandated separate-but-equal schools deprive black children of equal protection and that the Fourteenth Amendment places an affirmative duty on local school officials to abolish dual schools immediately. Although the Court found busing to be an indispensable remedial tool in the

Charlotte-Mecklenburg cases, it has adhered to several limitations on the use of busing that are consistent with the federal courts' exercise of their equity powers. First, district courts may impose busing on local school districts only to remedy de jure segregation, that is, officially mandated racial segregation in the public schools. Federal courts have no authority to remedy racial segregation in the schools that results solely from residential patterns. Statutory or constitutional provisions providing for separate-but-equal educational facilities are sufficient to demonstrate de jure segregation. In school districts without a prior history of statutory dual schools, a court must predicate a finding of a constitutional violation upon evidence of intentional discrimination. Disproportionate impact alone will not support a finding of intentional segregation. Hence, plaintiffs in desegregation cases bear the initial burden of proving discriminatory intent in attempting to demonstrate a constitutional violation.[86]

In redressing a constitutional violation, a district court can employ desegregative busing only when it can demonstrate that busing is a feasible, reasonable, and workable remedy that will not impinge significantly on the educational process or endanger the health of school children. Even when a district court employs desegregative busing, the court's order may not exceed the scope of the violation and must be designed to return plaintiffs to the position they would have occupied absent official discrimination. Desegregative busing is "remedial rather than punitive" and "simply is not equitable if it is disproportionate to the wrong."[87] After implementing a desegregation decree calling for busing, a district court cannot obligate a school board to make periodic adjustments in the plan, since there is no constitutional right to a particular racial balance in the schools.[88] Finally, when the constitutional violation has been redressed and a school district is operating a unitary system, a district court may terminate its desegregation decree and return authority over pupil assignments to the school board. If the plaintiffs allege that the school board's subsequent actions have the purpose and primary effect of reestablishing dual schools, the plaintiffs once again bear the initial burden of demonstrating that school officials have acted with segregative intent.

A fair reading of these decisions involving public school segregation reveals that the district courts can order school busing as a necessary or indispensable remedy to dismantle dual school systems. If busing is the only constitutionally adequate remedy in certain cases, opponents of court-ordered busing cannot argue that it is merely one of several equally effective remedies. As in Charlotte-Mecklenburg, North Carolina, where there was no other adequate remedy to vindicate the Fourteenth Amendment right to be free from educational segregation, busing is tantamount to a constitutional requirement. Absent an effective busing plan, in many communities, the Court's decision in *Brown* may be little more than a hollow promise.

The Controversy: Congressional Dissatisfaction with Court-Ordered Busing

Since *Swann* (1971), congressional opposition to court-ordered busing has been strident, but not unreasonable. Opponents of court-ordered busing argue that the federal judiciary has exceeded its constitutional authority in school desegregation cases. By enmeshing themselves in the educational process, the federal courts have usurped legislative and executive policy-making functions in violation of the separation-of-powers doctrine. Furthermore, the judiciary's critics argue, the federal courts have usurped the states' authority to regulate education, in derogation of the Tenth Amendment. Proposing H.J. Res. 20,[89] a neighborhood school constitutional amendment, Representative Frank Annunzio (D.-Ill.) argued that fashioning desegregation remedies requires a policy judgment, which is a legislative rather than a judicial prerogative.[90]

Despite congressional enactment of legislation limiting the use of school busing to achieve a racial balance, the Burger Court ignored the intent of § 2003 of the Civil Rights Act of 1964, which provides that:

> Nothing herein shall empower any official or court of the United States to issue any order seeking to achieve a racial balance in any school by requiring the transportation of students or pupils from one school to another. . . .
>
> "Desegregation" means the assignment of students to public schools and within such schools without regard to their race, color, religion or national origin.[91]

The Civil Rights Act notwithstanding, the Burger Court held that the Constitution may require racially conscious remedies, including busing, in school desegregation cases.[92]

Referring to the Court's busing decisions as a usurpation of congressional authority to enforce the Fourteenth Amendment, opponents of court-ordered busing argue that neither the language and logic nor the history of the Fourteenth Amendment supports the federal courts' use of their equity powers to bus children across cities and counties to achieve an artificial racial balance in the public schools. Moreover, the Court's "misguided" decision in *Swann* contradicts its earlier rationale that school authorities should be "color-blind" in assigning pupils to public schools.[93] Just as it is constitutionally impermissible for the states to assign students on the basis of race to maintain segregation, *Swann*'s critics argue, it is equally impermissible for the Supreme Court to use racial criteria, however benignly, to promote racial integration of the schools.

Citing public opinion polls, *Swann*'s congressional opponents have argued that a majority of Americans oppose court-ordered busing.[94] They make a plausible argument that the mass transportation of school children has undermined the quality of primary and secondary education.[95] The Supreme Court's critics contend that forced busing is divisive, disrupts the educational process, aggravates racial tension, and undermines the stability that students require to learn effectively. In addition, long bus rides deprive children of time to study, enjoy family life, and develop enduring friendships with their peers. Students who suffer long hours on a school bus cannot participate in extracurricular programs, including sports, clubs, and social activities that are important to their educational development. Desegregative busing also denies parents an opportunity to participate in parent-teacher associations, confer with their childrens' teachers, and attend functions in schools that are often remote from their homes. Inasmuch as busing entails additional financial burdens, without substantially raising taxes, busing opponents contend, school districts do not have the resources necessary to enhance educational programs for both black and white children.

To end the refrain, opponents of court-ordered busing claim that it is counterproductive to the goal of public school desegregation. Busing, they argue, frequently leads to "white flight," the residential migration of the white population away from school districts under busing orders, sometimes to suburban or rural public schools, at other times to private schools. As a result, school districts under court orders have become less racially balanced than they were prior to judicial intervention, and support for public education has dwindled.[96] Finally, the opponents argue, federal judges lack the training, expertise, and authority to legitimate a social theory that is without any constitutional foundation. With its superior fact-finding capability and its constitutional authority under section 5 of the Fourteenth Amendment, only Congress can evaluate psychological, sociological, and other nonjudicially cognizable evidence and fashion remedies to desegregate the public schools. Therefore, busing opponents conclude, Congress should reassert its constitutional policy-making role and protect the states' educational systems from judicial tyranny.

Congressional Attempts To Limit Federal Power To Require Busing

Members of Congress have pursued four major avenues to prohibit desegregative busing. Congressional dissatisfaction with busing is manifest in (1) bills to prohibit the Department of Health, Education, and Welfare (HEW; later, the Department of Education) from using federal funds to require busing, (2) bills to prohibit the Justice Department from initiating or joining suits leading to busing, (3) bills to restrict the federal courts' authority to order busing, and (4) resolutions proposing antibusing constitutional amendments. A brief historical review of these proposals will illuminate their remedial intent and constitutional implications.

Funding Restrictions

A decade after *Brown*, Congress enacted the first law to encourage local school authorities to assign children to public schools without regard to their race. The Civil Rights Act of 1964 authorized the federal government to bring suits, provide technical assistance, and withhold funds to assure that state and local school officials dismantle dual school systems. Until the mid-1970s, federal authorities emphasized withholding funds rather than providing technical assistance and bringing suits to end de jure segregation of public schools. Prior to 1968, HEW merely required written assurance from school districts that they were making a good-faith effort to terminate dual systems. HEW suggested two methods to desegregate public schools: assignment of students to the school geographically closest to their residence and freedom-of-choice plans. By 1968, however, HEW no longer viewed freedom-of-choice plans as an effective method of promoting desegregation. Following the Court's decision in *Green*, HEW established new guidelines for desegregation that included racially conscious remedies.[97] That same year, Congress amended the HEW Appropriations Act of 1968 to prohibit the use of funds to bus students, force attendance at a particular school, or close schools in conflict with parental choice "in order to overcome racial imbalance."[98]

Congress added similar restrictions to the HEW Appropriations Acts over the next several years, seeking to insulate freedom-of-choice plans from HEW interference.[99] Beginning in 1976 Congress imposed more stringent restrictions on HEW's authority to require school busing. Enacted over President Ford's veto, the Labor-HEW Appropriations Act of 1976 included the "Byrd amendment," which prohibited the use of funds to require "directly or indirectly, the transportation of any student to a school other than the school which is nearest the student's home."[100] Despite these restrictions, HEW circumvented the Byrd amendment by requiring busing to implement other desegregation plans. Responding to HEW's policy, Congress added the "Eagleton-Biden amendment" to the Labor-HEW Appropriations Act of 1978. The Appropriations Act amendment prohibited the use of federal funds to require busing beyond the neighborhood school to implement pairing, clustering, or building new school facilities.[101] Since 1978, Congress has included similar funding restrictions in HEW and Department of Education appropriation acts.[102]

In 1978 congressional opponents of busing focused their attention on restricting the Justice Department's involvement in desegregation litigation.[103] Although the House adopted Representative James M. Collins's (R.-Tex.) amendments to the 1979 and 1980 appropriations bills for the Justice Department, which prohibited the department from initiating or joining school busing suits, the conference committees dropped Collins's amendments in the final versions of both bills.[104] In 1980 Congress passed the State, Justice, Commerce, and Judiciary Appropriations Act of 1981 (H.R. 7584), which included the "Helms-Collins" amendment prohibiting the Justice Department "from bringing any sort of action that would require, directly or indirectly," the busing of public school children beyond the neighborhood school. However, on December 13, 1980, President Carter vetoed the bill. According to Carter, the Helms-Collins provision "would effectively allow Congress to tell a President that there are certain constitutionally-mandated remedies for the invasion of constitutional rights that he could not ask the courts to apply."[105] Carter reasoned that by prohibiting the executive branch from enforcing constitutional rights, the restriction violated the separation-of-powers doctrine.[106] Following Ronald Reagan's election, both Houses included an identical provision in the Justice Department Authorization bill of 1982 (S. 951). The Senate passed the bill, but the House Judiciary Committee buried the bill because of a controversial amendment restricting the federal courts' authority to issue busing orders.[107]

Jurisdictional Bills

Congressional dissatisfaction with busing is also manifest in bills attempting to restrict the federal courts' authority in school desegregation cases. Since 1971 members of Congress have introduced separate bills as well as riders to appropriations, education, and energy bills. These proposals include both jurisdictional and remedial limitations on the federal courts' authority.

While several jurisdictional proposals would deny the lower federal courts authority to close schools, transfer teachers, or assign students on the basis of race,[108] other measures simply would extinguish the lower federal courts' jurisdiction in any case involving the public schools.[109] However, the overwhelming majority of jurisdictional proposals would remove all federal jurisdiction to render any decision requiring attendance at a public school on the basis of race. Although the language of these bills is remarkably similar, there are several interesting variations among the proposals. H.R. 1211 would remove federal jurisdiction to make school assignments on the basis of race, creed, or gender.[110] Another variation, exemplified by H.R. 556, would prohibit the federal courts from requiring attendance at a public school for *any* reason. As introduced by Representative Larry P. McDonald (D.-Ga.), the bill provides that: "no court of the United States shall have the jurisdiction to make any decision, or issue any order, which would have the effect of requiring any individual to attend any particular school."[111] A third variation prohibits federal judicial review of state action relating to public school assignments based on race.[112]

A fourth variation would prevent the federal courts from interfering with student assignments to schools offering freedom-of-choice plans. One such bill introduced by Senator Jesse Helms (R.-N.C.) provides that "[n]o court of the United States shall have jurisdiction to make any decision . . . requiring any school board to make any change in the racial composition of the student body at any public school . . . to which students are assigned in conformity with a freedom of choice system."[113] Helms's bill also would remove all federal jurisdiction to transport students, close schools, or transfer faculty to affect the racial composition of a school with a freedom-of-choice plan.[114] A final variation would remove federal jurisdiction to make any decision leading to the busing of school children on the basis of race. In the Ninety-third Congress (first session) Senator Robert P. Griffin (R.-Mich.) introduced S. 179, which provided that: "No court of the United States shall have jurisdiction to make any decision . . . the effect of which would be to require that pupils be transported to or from school on the basis of their race, color, religion, or national origin."[115]

Remedial Bills

Congressional opponents of court-ordered busing have also introduced legislation that would restrict the remedial powers of the federal courts in school desegregation cases. These bills often cite congressional power both to regulate federal jurisdiction and to enforce the Fourteenth Amendment (section 5) as the constitutional authority for such legislation. The three major variations of remedial proposals include bills that would: (1) absolutely prohibit the assignment of students to public schools on the basis of race, (2) prescribe procedural or evidentiary rules that delay and/or make it more difficult to employ busing as a remedial tool in desegregation cases, and (3) restrict the permissible scope of busing orders.

Most remedial proposals would prohibit any federal court from compelling the assignment or transportation of students to public schools on the basis of race. As a direct response to *Swann,* in 1971 Representative Richard H. Fulton (D.-Tenn.) proposed a bill (H.R. 11401) that would have prohibited any federal court from ordering busing to promote desegregation.[116] Other remedial proposals include procedural or evidentiary requirements that would delay or impede the use of busing in school desegregation cases. Some proposals would postpone the implementation of busing orders until the courts of appeals and/or the Supreme Court enter final judgments in school desegregation cases or until the time permitted for an appeal has elapsed.[117] In 1977 Representative John D. Dingell (D.-Mich.) proposed H.R. 13534, a bill providing that:

> No court of the United States shall issue an order requiring the transportation of students or the merger of school districts as a means of eliminating racial segregation in schools if . . . the local educational agency affected has adopted a plan for its schools approved by the Secretary of Health, Education, and Welfare under section 2.[118]

Section 2 of the bill instructed the secretary of HEW to approve a local agency's desegregation plan that promised to improve educational quality and provided:

[F]or assignments of students to schools on a racially nondiscriminatory basis and in a manner which will result in the elimination of segregation in such schools to the maximum extent feasible without requiring the transportation of students, or their attendance in the schools of another such agency.[119]

Finally, several remedial proposals would employ congressional power under Article III and section 5 of the Fourteenth Amendment to restrict the use of court-ordered busing as a remedy in desegregation cases. The proposed Neighborhood School Act of 1981, for example, prohibits federal courts from ordering the assignment or transportation of students if (1) the total daily travel time exceeds 30 minutes or (2) the total daily distance traveled exceeds ten miles. The proposal also prohibits a busing order that would require "a student to cross a school district having the same grade level as that of the student."[120]

Since 1971 members of Congress have introduced numerous and diverse proposals seeking to limit the federal courts' powers in school desegregation cases, but only two measures have been enacted. Although the Education Amendments of 1972[121] and the 1974 amendments to the Elementary and Secondary Education Act of 1965[122] survived the legislative gauntlet, their final language was so weak that these acts have had only a negligible effect on the federal courts' powers. The Education Amendments of 1972 succeeded only in postponing busing orders "for the purposes of achieving a balance among students with respect to race" until litigants had exhausted all appeals, or until the time for appeals had tolled.[123] However, in *Drummond* v. *Acree*,[124] Justice Powell (sitting as a circuit justice) held that this restriction did not apply to remedies in cases involving de jure segregation.[125] The Equal Educational Opportunities Act of 1974 established remedial priorities for desegregation cases, placing busing at the bottom of the list as the remedy of last resort. The act also declared that no student shall be bused beyond the school "closest or next-closest" to her or his residence.[126] However, section 203(b) granted discretionary authority to the federal courts by providing that: "[T]he provisions of this title are not intended to modify or diminish the authority of the courts of the United States to fully enforce the fifth and fourteenth amendments to the Constitution of the United States."[127] Subsequently, the federal courts interpreted these statutory restrictions as not limiting the judiciary's powers in cases involving constitutional violations.[128]

In the twelve years following *Swann*, Congress considered numerous proposals attempting to limit the federal courts' jurisdiction and remedial powers. However, only four measures received serious legislative attention: (1) two bills that the Nixon administration sponsored in 1972, (2) a bill that senators Roth and Biden proposed in 1977, and (3) Senator J. Bennett Johnston's (D.-La.) amendment to the Justice Department Authorization bill of 1982. In 1972 President Nixon sent two bills to Congress. The first measure, the Equal Educational Opportunities Act, would have prohibited desegregative busing for grades 1–6 and restricted the use of busing in grades 7–12 unless a court found "clear and convincing evidence" that no other remedy would effectively dismantle a dual system.[129] A second proposal, the Student Transportation Moratorium Act, would have barred the implementation of all new busing orders until June 1, 1973, or until Congress enacted substantive busing legislation.[130] The administration argued that Congress had constitutional authority to enact both proposals under the Judiciary Article and under the Fourteenth Amendment's enforcement clause.[131] The Equal Educational Opportunities Act emerged from the House with a comprehensive ban on desegregative busing, except to the school "closest" or "next-closest" to a pupil's home. The House version also provided for reopening previous desegregation orders so that federal courts could modify earlier decrees to comply with the act's provisions. Following an extended filibuster and three unsuccessful attempts to pass a cloture motion, the House amendment died in the Senate.[132]

In 1977 the Senate Judiciary Committee reported (11/6) S. 1651, a bill sponsored by senators William V. Roth, Jr., (R.-Del.) and Joseph R. Biden. The Roth-Biden proposal would have prevented any federal court from ordering desegregative busing unless the court found that a "discriminatory purpose in education was a principle motivating factor in the constitutional violation for which such transportation is proposed as a remedy."[133] The bill also provided for the stay of district-court decisions ordering interdistrict busing until litigants had exhausted all appeals. In 1977 a threatened filibuster prevented S. 1651 from coming to the floor. Following a similar threat in 1978, the Senate tabled an identical amendment to the Elementary and Secondary Education Act extension bill (S. 1753).[134]

On June 19, 1981, Senator J. Bennett Johnston (D.-La.) introduced the Neighborhood School Act as an amendment to the Justice Department Authorization bill of 1982 (S. 951). The amendment prohibited any federal court from ordering busing beyond the school nearest a student's home unless such busing was "reasonable", that is, if the total daily distance involved did not exceed ten miles and/or the total daily time traveled did not exceed thirty minutes. The amendment also prohibited cross-district desegregative busing and authorized the attorney general to bring suits on behalf of students who believed that they were being bused in violation of the proposal's standards. After a lengthy filibuster and five attempts to invoke cloture, on March 2, 1982, the Senate finally passed the measure, including the Johnston amendment (57/37).[135] The House referred the bill to its Judiciary Committee, which never reported the measure.[136]

Although Congress never enacted the Nixon proposals, the Roth-Biden bill, or the Johnston amendment, these measures intruded least on the powers, jurisdiction, and functions of the federal courts. The proposed statutes included subtle procedural requirements and remedial limitations that would have made it more difficult to obtain busing orders in desegregation cases. In contrast to these proposals, most other bills would terminate federal jurisdiction over school busing or completely deny the federal courts remedial powers to order transportation in public school desegregation cases. Virtually all of these measures incorporate two common elements: (1) both jurisdictional and remedial proposals base their authority on congressional power to regulate the federal courts' jurisdiction under Article III, sections 1 and 2, and/or section 5 of the Fourteenth Amendment, and (2) the intent and primary effect of these proposals is to end court-ordered busing to desegregate the nation's public schools.

Constitutional Amendments

In addition to proposed jurisdictional and remedial statutes, Congress has considered numerous joint resolutions proposing constitutional amendments to end court-ordered busing. Senators and representatives have introduced joint resolutions that would prohibit (1) the federal courts from assigning students to public schools on the basis of their race,[137] (2) *any* governmental authority from assigning students to public schools on the basis of their race,[138] (3) governmental authorities from assigning students on the basis of their race to any public school other than the one closest to their residence,[139] (4) governmental authorities from assigning students to schools other than the one closest to their residence, without exception,[140] and (5) governmental interference with parents' or guardians' rights to choose a public school for their children.[141]

During the Ninety-second Congress (second session) the House Judiciary Committee held hearings on more than fifty constitutional amendments. One of the most visible proposals, Representative Norman Lent's (R.-N.Y.) H.J. Res 620, provided that "[n]o public school student shall, because of his race, creed, or color, be assigned to or required to attend a particular school."[142] Although the Rules Committee sent Lent's resolution to the floor,[143] the House leadership never scheduled H.J. Res. 620 for a vote. During April 1973 and October 1975 the Senate Judiciary Committee also conducted hearings on antibusing amendments, but the committee never reported a proposal to the Senate.[144]

In 1979 Representative Ronald M. Mottl (D.-Ohio) secured the 218 signatures necessary to discharge H.J. Res. 74 from the Judiciary Committee's grip. However, the House defeated the amendment by a vote of 209/206.[145] Representative Mottl's amendment stated: "No student shall be compelled to attend a public school other than the public school nearest to the residence of such student which is located within the school district in which the student resides and which provides the course of study pursued by such student."[146] Two years later, in 1981, Mottl attempted to discharge another amendment from the Judiciary Committee. His second resolution, H.J. Res. 56, provided: "[n]o court of the United States shall require that any person be assigned to, or be excluded from any school on the basis of race, religion, or national origin."[147] Since Mottl obtained only 195 of the 218 signatures necessary to act on a discharge petition, his constitutional amendment faded into oblivion along with the Ninety-seventh Congress.[148]

As the legislative record indicates, both senators and representatives have pursued various means to affect the assignment of students to the nation's public schools. Most of these proposals have the primary purpose and effect of insulating the assignment of children to neighborhood schools from the federal judiciary's racially conscious efforts to desegregate the public schools. Nevertheless, in specific cases, the Supreme Court has decided that the constitutional right to be free from racial discrimination in public education and the employment of racially conscious remedies are coterminous. As the language of proposed amendments, restrictions on federal jurisdiction, and limitations on the judiciary's remedial powers indicates, many members of Congress perceive these measures as fungible or interchangeable methods of depriving the federal courts of effective or indispensable remedies necessary to vindicate the constitutional right to be free from public school segregation.

The preliminary evidence indicates that there is little difference between remedial and jurisdictional proposals. If a bill prohibits the federal courts from making assignments or ordering the transportation of public school pupils on the basis of race, whether phrased in jurisdictional or remedial terms, the primary effect is to deprive the federal courts of the authority necessary to remedy a constitutional violation.[149] Chapter VI demonstrated that congressional power to enact such legislation under Article III is questionable. However, it is also necessary to examine congressional authority under section 5 of the Fourteenth Amendment. Does this constitutional provision grant Congress plenary authority to deny the federal courts remedies that the Supreme Court has deemed indispensable in vindicating Fourteenth Amendment rights?

Congressional Authority to Curb the Courts
Under Section 5 of the Fourteenth Amendment

Antibusing proponents claim that congressional authority to restrict the federal courts' jurisdiction and remedial powers in school desegregation cases exists under section 5 of the Fourteenth Amendment, which grants Congress "power to enforce, by appropriate legislation, the provisions of this article."[150] In *Katzenbach* v. *Morgan*[151] the Supreme Court recognized congressional power, under section 5, to remedy state violations of Fourteenth Amendment rights. The Supreme Court sustained an amendment to the Voting Rights Act of 1965 providing that the states could not deny Puerto Ricans who had completed a sixth-grade education in an accredited Spanish-language school in Puerto Rico the right to vote because they could neither read nor write English. The Voting Rights amendment was in direct conflict with New York's statute requiring English literacy as a requirement for voter eligibility. Apparently, the voting rights provision also contradicted the Supreme Court's earlier refusal to void a similar literacy requirement as a violation of the equal protection clause.[152]

Interpreting section 5 as an affirmative grant of discretionary power to Congress to determine "whether and what legislation is needed to secure the guarantees of the Fourteenth Amendment,"[153] the Supreme Court sustained section 4(e) of the Voting Rights Act. Speaking for the majority, Justice Brennan argued that the Court should defer to congressional judgment as long as it could "perceive" some rational basis for the legislative policy.[154] In addition to recognizing Congress's "specially informed legislative competence"[155] and superior fact-finding capabilities, Brennan suggested that section 5 authorizes Congress to define the "substantive scope"[156] of equal-protection rights that section 1 of the Fourteenth Amendment guarantees against state infringement. As a result, some members of Congress have read Brennan's opinion in *Morgan* as conceding legislative authority to enact antibusing legislation, pursuant to section 5 of the Fourteenth Amendment. However, Brennan emphasized that Congress could employ its enforcement powers to expand but not contract judicially defined equal-protection rights. Responding to Justice Harlan's dissenting opinion, which suggested that if Congress could expand equal-protection rights it could also "dilute" these rights,[157] Brennan stated:

> § 5 does not grant Congress power to exercise discretion in the other direction and to enact "statutes so as in effect to dilute equal protection and due process decisions of this Court." We emphasize that Congress' power under § 5 is limited to adopting measures to enforce the guarantees of the Amendment; § 5 grants Congress no power to restrict, abrogate, or dilute these guarantees. Thus, for example, an enactment authorizing the States to establish racially segregated systems of education would not be—as required by § 5—a measure "to enforce" the Equal Protection Clause since that clause of its own force prohibits such state laws.[158]

Whether Congress or the Supreme Court has authority to expand on the core of rights that the equal protection clause protects, clearly neither the legislature nor the judiciary possesses constitutional power to diminish an individual's right to the equal protection of the law. Insofar as congressional antibusing proposals restrict, dilute, or abrogate equal-protection rights, they are constitutionally deficient.[159] Recently, several members of the Court have denied that *Morgan* legitimates congressional authority to define the substantive content of the equal protection clause. Dissenting in *EEOC* v. *Wyoming*,[160] Chief Justice Burger, joined by justices Powell, Rehnquist, and O'Connor, concluded that Congress may not "define rights wholly independently of our case law."[161] The dissenting justices denied that section 5 authorizes Congress to conclude that a state law mandating the retirement of game wardens at age 55 violates the equal protection clause. Burger stressed that "[a]llowing Congress to protect constitutional rights statutorily that it has independently defined fundamentally alters our scheme of government."[162]

Although there is considerable debate concerning congressional power to expand equal-protection rights statutorily, as recently as 1982 the Court reaffirmed the principle that Congress cannot employ section 5 to dilute these rights. In *Mississippi University for Women* v. *Hogan*,[163] the Court invalidated the university's policy of excluding males from its nursing program. The university asserted that Congress intended to exempt undergraduate schools that have traditionally had single-sex admissions policies from the requirements of Title IX of the Education Amendments of 1972, which forbade gender discrimination in higher education. Writing for the majority, Justice O'Connor doubted that Congress had intended to exempt the university from its obligation to enforce the Fourteenth Amendment. According to O'Connor, Congress lacks authority to grant states exemptions from their constitutional obligation to enforce the Fourteenth Amendment's guarantee of equal protection to all persons. Congress could not justify such a statute as a valid exercise of its power to enforce the Fourteenth Amendment, since section 5 grants the legislature affirmative power to "enforce the guarantees of the Amendment; § 5 grants Congress no power to restrict, abrogate or dilute these guarantees. . . . Although we give deference to congressional decisions and classifications, neither Congress nor a State can validate a law that denies the rights guaranteed by the Fourteenth Amendment."[164]

Morgan, EEOC v. *Wyoming*, and *Hogan* illuminate the Court's analysis of legislative authority vis-à-vis the states under section 5 and the equal protection clause. However, legislative proposals limiting the federal courts' jurisdiction and remedial powers involve different considerations of congressional authority over the federal judiciary. Ronald Rotunda argues that the Fourteenth Amendment gives Congress, rather than the federal courts, the power to limit the authority of the states. But Congress cannot employ section 5 to prevent the federal judiciary from enforcing the Fourteenth Amendment's guarantees:

> Whatever the reach of section 5 as a vehicle for augmenting the power of Congress to regulate matters otherwise left to the states, it provides no authority for Congress to interfere with the execution or enforcement of federal court judgments or to overturn federal judicial determinations of the requirements of the fourteenth amendment. The entire fourteenth amendment increased congressional power at the expense of the states, not of the federal courts.[165]

If the judiciary's province is "to say what the law is,"[166] then Congress's independent authority to define the substance of Fourteenth Amendment rights is doubtful. As a minimum, section 5 does not empower Congress to restrict, dilute, or abrogate judicial interpretations of the equal protection clause. Since most antibusing proposals interfere with the federal judiciary's authority to dismantle the nation's dual-school systems, such proposals vitiate rather than fulfill the promise of equal protection. As the evidence and analysis (here and in chapter 6) suggest, there are no judicial precedents that support congressional power to enact antibusing proposals that rely on Article III, sections 1 and 2, or section 5 of the Fourteenth Amendment. Indeed, the cases that proponents of antibusing legislation cite actually suggest that most antibusing proposals exceed congressional authority under the Fourteenth Amendment and the Judiciary Article. As a minimum, the Supreme Court's decisions indicate that Congress cannot employ its legislative authority under the Fourteenth Amendment and Article III to shield antibusing proposals from other constitutional requirements and limitations. Undoubtedly, antibusing proposals would be subject to the Supreme Court's constitutional scrutiny. Would most antibusing proposals survive the Supreme Court's equal-protection standards? Would they breach the Supreme Court's understanding of the constitutional separation of powers?

Equal Protection and the Antibusing Proposals

As with other congressional legislation, antibusing proposals are subject to the Supreme Court's scrutiny under the equal-protection doctrine. Although the language of the Fourteenth Amendment applies to state action denying equal protection, the Court has applied the equal-protection concept to the federal government through the Fifth Amendment's due process clause. Speaking for the majority in *Bolling* v. *Sharpe* (1954),[167] Chief Justice Warren denied that the concepts of equal protection and due process are interchangeable. However, he emphasized that "discrimination may be so unjustifiable as to be violative of due process."[168] While Warren conceded that the national government could restrict the citizen's liberty to accomplish "a proper governmental objective," he stated categorically that "[s]egregation in public education is not reasonably related to any proper governmental objective."[169] In concluding his opinion for a unanimous Court, Warren stressed that the Fifth and Fourteenth amendments impose an equal duty on the states and the national government to protect the individual's right to be free from segregation in the public schools.[170]

Both in *Shapiro* v. *Thompson* (1969)[171] and *Dunn* v. *Blumstein* (1972),[172] the Supreme Court decided that statutory classifications unduly burdening previously recognized constitutional rights are suspect under the equal-protection doctrine. In *Shapiro* the Court held that lengthy waiting periods that deny "welfare benefits to otherwise eligible applicants solely because they have recently moved into the jurisdiction"[173] burden the citizen's right to travel freely throughout the United States.[174] Similarly, in *Dunn* the Supreme Court ruled that lengthy residency requirements as prerequisites to register to vote unconstitutionally burden the citizen's right to travel. The Court concluded in both cases that "[a]bsent a compelling state interest, a State may not burden the right to travel in this way."[175] Although *Shapiro* and *Dunn* apply to state actions that burden equal-protection rights, a federal statute that denies the federal courts' authority to order desegregative busing is similarly suspect. By denying the federal courts' authority to employ either the only adequate or the most effective remedy in public school desegregation cases, Congress could burden the individual's right, albeit indirectly, to be free from racial segregation in public education.[176]

Proponents of antibusing proposals respond by arguing that as long as state courts are available to protect Fourteenth Amendment rights, restrictions on the federal courts' jurisdiction and remedial powers are constitutionally acceptable. In fact, antibusing proposals do not prohibit the state courts from employing busing to end public school segregation. Since state courts are required to enforce the Supreme Court's public school desegregation decisions, under the supremacy clause,[177] antibusing proponents conclude, litigants have an appropriate judicial forum in which to vindicate Fourteenth Amendment rights. However, unless antibusing proposals are an invitation to ignore *Brown*, *Swann*, and subsequent decisions, they would have the curious effect of sabotaging their sponsors' manifest objectives. Antibusing proposals that invite the states to ignore standing federal precedents or freeze the Supreme Court's constitutional construction of the equal protection clause are either constitutionally suspect or politically counterproductive from their sponsors' perspective.

Some antibusing proponents anticipate that state judges will be more reluctant to order massive busing to achieve racial desegregation of public schools than their brethren on the federal bench. As Senator William V. Roth (R.-Del.) intimated in introducing a bill (S. 2937) to deny the lower federal courts jurisdiction to order busing of students and teachers to carry out racial desegregation plans, "State courts, which are closer to the people and more cognizant of the local impact of court-ordered remedies, would retain jurisdiction. Hopefully, the judges in State courts would be more thoughtful in their deliberations before ordering sweeping social reforms for the State over which they preside."[178] Many state judges are subject to popular pressure through periodic elections. In deciding controversial school busing cases, state judges may have one eye on the election returns, to paraphrase Mr. Dooley. Unlike their federal brethren, state judges do not possess the protection of the life-tenure and judicial-compensation provisions that the Constitution guarantees to Article III judges.[179] In states and communities where desegregative busing is unpopular, aggrieved racial minorities may find it more difficult to vindicate their constitutional rights in state courts than federal courts.[180] Only by ignoring the realities of American political life can one argue that individuals who suffer racial discrimination have the same opportunity to vindicate their rights to equal protection in state as in federal courts.

In addition to jeopardizing a fundamental right, antibusing proposals discriminate against racial minorities. In assessing whether legislation impermissibly burdens racial minorities, the Supreme Court has examined legislators' motives as well as the language and legislative history of measures that are not facially discriminatory.[181] However, jurists or scholars need not engage in highly subjective motivational analyses to demonstrate that most antibusing proposals violate the equal-protection concept. Measures restricting the federal courts' remedial powers in school desegregation cases embody *explicit* racial classifications that imply discriminatory motives. Speaking for the majority in *Personnel Administrator of Massachusetts* v. *Feeny*,[182] Justice Stewart remarked: "Certain classifications . . . in themselves supply a reason to infer antipathy. Race is the paradigm. A racial classification, regardless of purported motivation, is presumptively invalid and can be upheld only upon an extraordinary justification."[183]

Proponents of antibusing legislation argue that their proposals (1) do not discriminate against racial minorities and (2) do not embody racial classifications. Antibusing proposals, they continue, would affect only litigants seeking busing decrees and would not necessarily burden racial minorities. Armed with numerous public opinion polls, school busing opponents argue that an overwhelming majority of both blacks and whites favor preserving the neighborhood school. Attitudes toward desegregative busing, they conclude, are racially neutral.[184] However, the Supreme Court rejected this proposition in *Washington* v. *Seattle School District No. 1*:[185] "[T]he United States . . . maintains that busing for integration . . . is not a peculiarly "racial" issue at all . . . we are not persuaded . . . desegregation of the public schools . . . at the bottom inures primarily to the benefit of the minority, and is designed for that purpose."[186]

In *Seattle*, the Court considered a state initiative that prohibited school boards from requiring a student to attend a school other than the one geographically closest to her or his residence. Writing for the majority, Justice Blackmun found that Initiative No. 350 violated the equal protection clause because the law made it more difficult for a racial minority to achieve its policy objectives than other groups. By reallocating governmental power on this one issue, the initiative used the racial nature of school busing "to define the governmental decision-making structure" and, therefore, imposed "substantial and unique burdens on racial minorities."[187] The Court penetrated the initiative's superficial neutrality, stating that:

> Noting that Initiative 350 nowhere mentions "race" or "integration," appellants suggest that the legislation has no racial overtones; they maintain that . . . the initiative simply permits busing for certain enumerated purposes while neutrally forbidding it for all other reasons. We find it difficult to believe that appellants' analysis is seriously advanced, however, for despite its facial neutrality there is little doubt that the initiative was effectively drawn for racial purposes.[188]

In *Seattle* the Supreme Court reaffirmed the principles established in *Hunter* v. *Erickson* (1969)[189] and *Lee* v. *Nyquist* (1970).[190] In *Hunter*, the Court invalidated a city-charter provision that subjected antidiscrimination housing ordinances to local referenda, a procedure that did not apply to other housing matters. The Court held that the provision violated the equal protection clause because, on its face, the charter discriminated against racial minorities by "treating racial housing matters differently from other racial and housing matters."[191] The fact that the charter did not mention race was irrelevant to the Court's finding. As Justice White noted in the majority's opinion: "[a]lthough the law on its face treats Negro and white, Jew and gentile in an identical manner, the reality is that the law's impact falls on the minority."[192]

One year later, a three-judge federal court applied *Hunter* to New York's antibusing law. In *Nyquist* the district court voided a New York statute that prohibited the state commissioner of education from implementing "plans designed to alleviate racial imbalance in the schools except with the approval of a local elected board or upon parental consent." By creating "a single exception to the broad supervisory powers the state Commissioner of Education exercises over local public education," the New York law established an explicit racial classification that constitutes "an invidious denial of equal protection."[193] As the district court concluded in *Nyquist*: "[T]he state creates an explicitly racial classification whenever it differentiates between the treatment of problems involving racial matters and that afforded other problems in the same area."[194]

A fair reading of *Seattle, Hunter,* and *Lee* suggests that the antibusing proposals embody impermissible racial classifications that are "inherently suspect"[195] under the equal-protection doctrine. Antibusing proposals draw an invidious distinction between racial minorities that seek to prevent racial discrimination in public education and other groups that seek judicial remedies to protect constitutional rights. Furthermore, antibusing proposals attempt to allocate judicial power according to the racial nature of an issue. If desegregative busing is indispensable to ensuring a minority's right to equal protection, by precluding the federal courts from employing this remedy in school desegregation cases most antibusing proposals place additional burdens on racial minorities that already suffer constitutional deprivations.[196]

A statute that requires black litigants to raise equal-protection claims in state courts, but permits white litigants to raise constitutional claims in state or federal courts, would constitute an impermissible racial classification. Similarly, a statute that differentiates among litigants indirectly according to their race suffers from the same constitutional infirmity. In effect, most antibusing proposals embody racial classifications that "discriminate against minorities, and constitute a real, substantial, and invidious denial of the equal protection of the laws."[197]

The Separation of Powers

Antibusing proposals that restrict the federal judiciary's remedial powers also raise serious separation-of-powers questions. In *United States v. Klein,*[198] the Supreme Court held that Congress cannot employ its legislative power, under Article III, to interfere with the judiciary's and executive's performance of their constitutional functions. In *Klein,* the Court concluded that the Appropriations Act of July 12, 1870, interfered with the federal judiciary's power because it prescribed a "rule of decision"[199] in a particular case. Although the Court's ruling in *Klein* concerned congressional interference with executive power, the decision is applicable to most antibusing proposals. The Appropriations Act of 1870 invalidated Supreme Court decisions sustaining the president's exercise of the pardon power. Similarly, antibusing proposals would effectively invalidate judicial orders implementing the Supreme Court's interpretation of the Fourteenth Amendment. If the "great and controlling purpose"[200] of antibusing legislation is to prevent the federal courts from enforcing the High Court's constitutional rulings, these proposals transgress the scope of legislative authority.

In 1972, for example, Representative John D. Dingell (D-Mich.) introduced H.R. 13534, which would prohibit any federal court from ordering desegregative busing if the local educational agency involved had adopted a desegregation plan approved by HEW. In testifying before the House Judiciary Committee, Dingell stated that his proposal was "an attempt to guide the hands and ways of the courts into perhaps the most expeditious and satisfactory conclusion to the cases before them."[201] As Representative Dingell's testimony on H.R. 13534 implied, the bill was designed to alter the federal courts' decisions in school desegregation cases. "This bill," Dingell candidly admitted, "represents a very carefully drafted piece of legislation whose purpose is to find us a way out of this thicket in which we seem to have wandered, of requiring court enforced busing or merger of school districts."[202] Similarly, in introducing S. 1147, a bill prohibiting the federal courts from ordering student assignments based on race, Senator Slade Gorton (R.-Wash.) testified to the Senate Judiciary Subcommittee on the Separation of Powers that "we are not attempting directly to reverse Supreme Court decisions but, to put it more delicately, simply to guide the Supreme Court into a slightly different channel."[203] Despite Senator Gorton's felicitous phraseology, S. 1147 would encroach on the judiciary's core functions.

Two other significant proposals, the Roth-Biden bill (S. 1651) and President Nixon's Equal Educational Opportunities Act of 1972, incorporate decision rules that defy *Klein*. S. 1651 mandates evidentiary rules and procedural requirements that make it more difficult to obtain busing orders. The Roth-Biden bill provides that:

> [N]o court of the United States shall order directly or indirectly the transportation of any student on the basis of race, color, or national origin unless the Court determines that a discriminatory purpose in education was a *principal* motivating factor in the constitutional violation for which such transportation is proposed as a remedy.[204]

If adopted, this provision would impose a higher standard of proof in school desegregation cases than in other equal-protection cases. As the Court stated in *Arlington Heights* v. *Metropolitan Housing Corporation*,[205] it is difficult, if not impossible, to demonstrate that racial discrimination is the sole or principal motivation in equal-protection cases. Speaking for the majority in *Arlington Heights*, Justice Powell stated:

[*Washington* v. *Davis*] does not require a plaintiff to prove that the challenged action rested solely on racially discriminatory purposes. Rarely can it be said that a legislature or administrative body operating under a broad mandate made a decision motivated solely by a single concern or even that a particular purpose was the "dominate" or "primary" one. In fact, it is because legislators and administrators are properly concerned with balancing numerous competing considerations that courts refrain from reviewing the merits of their decisions absent a showing of arbitrariness or irrationality. But racial discrimination is not just another competing consideration. When there is a proof that a discriminatory purpose has been a motivating factor in the decision, the judicial deference is no longer justified.[206]

Albeit subtly, the Roth-Biden bill elevates the standard of proof by requiring that racial discrimination must be a *principal* motivating factor in school desegregation cases before a court could grant equitable relief.

Similarly, President Nixon's Equal Educational Opportunities Act prescribed cumbersome decision rules designed to end court-ordered busing in desegregation cases. Testifying against the proposal, William Van Alstyne stated that the separation of powers "precludes Congress from directing an Article III Court to apply a different and more restrictive interpretation of the Constitution than that which the Supreme Court has already determined to be required."[207] Also testifying against the proposal, Senator William M. McCulloch (R.-Ohio) asserted that Congress "cannot prostitute the courts for an unconstitutional end."[208]

Defending congressional authority to regulate the federal courts' remedial powers, antibusing proponents claim that the federal courts rather than Congress have violated the separation-of-powers doctrine. Since the federal courts are not competent to evaluate the social science evidence offered in desegregation suits, they should defer to the superior fact-finding expertise of Congress. Testifying before the Senate Judiciary Committee's Subcommittee on Constitutional Rights, Senator Slade Gorton (R-Wash.) asserted, "I am convinced that much of the reason that the U.S. Supreme Court has gone in the way that it has, authorizing and sometimes even requiring mandatory busing, is that it has not had all of the facts . . . the Court is very likely to defer to us in this respect."[209] Testifying in favor of President Nixon's antibusing proposals, Acting Attorney General Richard G. Kleindienst urged Congress to exercise its "expertise" and "lay down a guideline that would be binding upon the 400 Federal district judges in this sensitive area."[210] However, if the Supreme Court has determined that "[n]o rigid guidelines as to student transportation can be given for application to the infinite variety of problems presented in thousands of situations,"[211] can Congress establish a uniform decision rule without impairing the judiciary's authority to fashion adequate remedies in cases that are within its jurisdiction?

Assuming that Congress has power under the Judiciary Article and the Fourteenth Amendment to prescribe decision rules that alter the federal courts' remedial powers to enforce equal-protection rights, can Congress expand as well as contract the judiciary's remedial powers? Although opponents of school busing argue that Congress can limit the federal judiciary's remedial powers, they deny that Congress has authority to expand these powers. A colloquy between Assistant Attorney General Theodore B. Olson and Representative Harold S. Sawyer (R-Mich.) on the proposed Neighborhood School Act of 1981 illustrates the constitutional dilemma that opponents of school busing confront. Noting the Supreme Court's refusal to extend judicial remedies beyond school districts that have engaged in de jure segregation,[212] Sawyer observed that the Court's failure to order metropolitan-wide busing in these cases had accelerated white flight to the suburbs. Under these circumstances, confining judicial busing orders to inner-city school districts promotes racial segregation rather than desegregation of public schools.

If the federal courts had authority to extend busing orders to suburban districts within the metropolitan commuting radius, there would be little incentive for whites to flee from their homes and jobs. When Sawyer queried Olson about the scope of congressional power to authorize the federal courts to issue metropolitan-wide busing orders whenever desegregative busing is employed, the assistant attorney general responded, ironically, that such a statute would be unconstitutional. Olson contended that Sawyer's suggestion was in conflict with the Supreme Court's decisions that prohibit metropolitan-wide busing absent a showing of de jure segregation in suburban school districts.[213] Testifying in favor of the Neighborhood School Act, Olson argued that section 5 of the Fourteenth Amendment empowers Congress to prescribe rules for a judicial proceeding, even though these statutory rules might deny remedies that the Supreme Court has deemed indispensable to enforcing constitutional rights.[214] However, Olson added hurriedly that section 5 does not grant Congress power to *expand* the federal court's authority to order desegregative busing, because such legislation would conflict with the constitutional holding in *Milliken* v. *Bradley*.

Olson's inconsistency to the contrary, the separation of powers prohibits Congress from extinguishing remedies that the Supreme Court recognizes as indispensable to enforcing equal-protection rights. Inasmuch as most antibusing proposals would impair the federal judiciary's authority to end de jure racial segregation in public education, such proposals interfere with the federal courts' performance of their constitutional functions. Antibusing proposals that prohibit the federal courts from employing remedies in public school desegregation cases that the Supreme Court deems indispensable are a subtle, indirect interference with the exercise of judicial power and undermine the Supreme Court's performance of its constitutional role as a coequal branch of government.

Circumventing the Constitutional Amendment Process

The language and legislative histories of antibusing proposals indicate a manifest intent to end court-ordered busing to achieve racial desegregation of the nation's public schools. Hence, these proposals seek to reverse the Supreme Court's decisions in *Swann* v. *Charlotte-Mecklenburg Board of Education* and subsequent decisions. While Congress can reverse the Court's decisions through a constitutional amendment, can it employ the Judiciary Article and the Fourteenth Amendment to accomplish the same objective? As their statements, the language of various proposals, and the close juxtaposition of constitutional amendments, jurisdiction-stripping bills, and remedial limitations indicate, opponents of desegregative busing regard these methodologies as fungible means to reverse "obnoxious" Supreme Court decisions. However, if these methodologies were genuinely fungible, why would the Court's critics even bother to introduce constitutional amendments, which require extraordinary majorities and involve cumbersome, time-consuming procedures to reverse the constitutional effects of the Supreme Court's decisions? In fact, the methodologies are not fungible since they are subject to different constitutional requirements and legislative rules.

Admitting that their idée fixe is to reverse the effects of *Swann*, the Court's critics concede that they are circumventing the cumbersome and time-consuming process that constitutional amendments require. Testifying before the Judiciary Committee's Subcommittee on Constitutional Rights on his proposal (S. 287) to remove the lower federal courts' jurisdiction to hear cases or controversies involving the public

schools, Senator William L. Scott (R-Va.) stated, "While I favor a constitutional amendment to prevent the busing of children to obtain a racial
balance, it may be difficult to obtain the necessary two-thirds vote in
each body of the Congress and I am glad the committee is considering
alternate proposals."[215] During the time needed to propose and ratify a
constitutional amendment, antibusing proponents argue, federal courts
will continue to inflict damage on the states' educational systems.
During the same hearings before the Subcommittee on Constitutional
Rights, Senator William Brock (R.-Tenn.) stated:

> As you know, I have introduced Senate Joint Resolution 14, a
> constitutional amendment to forbid the assignment of children to
> a particular school on the basis of race, color, or creed. However,
> it has become painfully obvious that my amendment faces serious
> obstacles. At best its passage will require a lengthy period of time,
> during which the abuse will continue should no other action be
> forthcoming.
>
> It is the need for more immediate redress of this grievance that
> causes my appearance before you today. This subcommittee has
> before it four proposals [jurisdiction statutes removing federal court
> authority to order busing], each of which attempts to deal with
> the complex problem of achieving equality of opportunity for all
> children without the imposition of court-ordered busing.[216]

Opponents of desegregative busing also view the constitutional-
amendment process as a "fall back" position. Testifying in support of
the Neighborhood School Act of 1981, Representative W. Henson
Moore (R.-La.), who attempted to secure an antibusing amendment in
1981, argued that the Neighborhood School Act is a quick and easy way
to accomplish the same end as passing a constitutional amendment. If
the federal courts declare the act unconstitutional, Moore observed,
Congress can always "fall back" to the amendment process:

> [I]f I had my druthers . . . I would rather have the constitutional
> amendment, which settles the issue completely once and for all.
> As a practical matter, I don't think that this is going to happen any
> time soon. . . . If we are going to bring about some kind of remedy
> to partially limit what I think is excessive use of busing, I think
> legislation like this is the quickest way. . . .
>
> Then, we would let it go through the courts. If they rule, no, we
> can't attack remedies, then we know that the only thing you can
> do is a busing amendment.[217]

The close juxtaposition between various constitutional amendments and statutory antibusing proposals indicates that their sponsors' remedial purposes are similar, if not identical. During testimony before the Judiciary Subcommittee on Constitutional Rights, Senator Roth indicated that Congress could enact either a constitutional amendment or statutory measures to end court-ordered busing:

> I have supported the neighborhood school concept ever since I have been in Congress and will continue to do so as long as I am here. I would prefer that this matter be handled by legislation, however. As this appears not to be possible, I believe we should move forward with a constitutional amendment because, after all, this is a long slow process. Should subsequent events prove such an amendment unnecessary, nothing will have been lost.[218]

Often, members who introduce constitutional amendments also offer jurisdictional and remedial legislation to end or impede court-ordered busing. During the Ninety-fourth Congress, first session (1975), Senator Roth introduced a constitutional amendment that provided: "No public school pupil shall be transported to a particular school because of his or her race, color, national origin, creed, or sex."[219] During the second session (1976) Roth offered a bill (S. 2937) to extinguish the lower federal courts' jurisdiction to order desegregative busing. Having failed to garner the votes necessary for a constitutional amendment, Roth turned to the statutory alternative of gerrymandering the federal courts' jurisdiction and remedial powers. Roth's opposition to court-ordered busing was manifest:

> Busing for desegregation has become the symbol of a massive reformist effort by the Federal courts . . . to integrate the schools by means of a socially disruptive, financially burdensome, and administratively unfeasible regime of race quotas. . . . Through the imposition of an ill-conceived theory of social justice, these judges . . . have distorted the spirit of democratic Government to achieve an end mandated neither by logic or constitutional guarantee. The result has been intrusive Federal intervention into local affairs and the watering down of educational standards.[220]

In 1977 the Senate Judiciary Committee reported the Roth-Biden bill (S. 1651), which prescribed procedural and evidentiary rules in desegregation cases. Commenting on S. 1651, Roth expressed the hope that his proposal would "negate the court decisions that have moved in the direction of purely racial balance."[221]

Another outspoken opponent of school busing, Senator Sam Ervin, Jr., (D.-N.C.), also advocated both legislation and constitutional amendments to reverse *Swann* and its progeny. Endorsing Senator Edward Gurney's (R.-Fl.) vow to "actively support any effort, statutory or constitutional"[222] prohibiting court-ordered busing, Ervin stated:

> I might add that I favor statutes to put an end to this tyranny immediately, and a constitutional amendment to put an end to it forever.
>
> I am reminded somewhat of a story about the man who was away from home and received a telegram from his undertaker saying, "Your mother-in-law died today, shall we cremate or bury?" He wired back and said, "Take no chances: Cremate and bury."
>
> I would cremate first by legislation and then bury by constitutional amendment.[223]

Representative Ronald M. Mottl (D.-Ohio), another sponsor of constitutional amendments prohibiting busing, supported the Neighborhood School Act of 1981, claiming that the act would achieve the same purpose as a constitutional amendment:

> Since coming to Congress in 1975, I have advocated a neighborhood school constitutional amendment, to insure once and for all that public education is colorblind. . . .
>
> Still, I wholeheartedly endorse the busing provisions of S.951. This legislation offers a creative approach toward getting the federal courts out of busing. . . . I would actually prefer the constitutional amendment. However, if we cannot get that through, I would be in complete accord and endorse this proposal as a sound means in which to severely hamper the remedy of court ordered busing.[224]

Evidently, many proponents of antibusing legislation view the amendment process (Article V) and congressional authority to regulate the federal courts' jurisdiction and remedial powers under Article III (sections 1 and 2) and section 5 of the Fourteenth Amendment as interchangeable methods to reverse the Supreme Court's school busing decisions. However, Article V requires that constitutional amendments run the gauntlet in Congress and the state legislatures. By attempting to reverse the Supreme Court's constitutional interpretation statutorily, antibusing proponents are circumventing the amendment process for reasons of political expediency, while denying the states their right to participate in amending the Constitution.

If antibusing proposals that limit the federal courts' jurisdiction and remedial powers in public school desegregation cases discourage state courts and school boards from employing effective remedies to end de jure segregation, is there a substantive distinction between statutory proposals and constitutional amendments that restrict or prohibit desegregative busing? As former United States Attorney General Benjamin Civiletti recognized, antibusing bills would prohibit the federal courts and, implicitly, discourage state courts and local school boards from busing children to end de jure segregation of public schools:

> The question that you would ask is why? Why would that legislation be passed if the State courts are going to be following the Supreme Court precedent, if the State courts are more subject to pressure, because they are not appointed for life and independent in their salaries perhaps. Why would the Congress determine to shift exclusively jurisdiction from the Federal lower court to the State court unless it was to send a message or signal that somehow the State courts were going to be deciding matters more in tune with what the Congress perceived to be the majority view and be more reluctant to order busing than what they perceive the Federal courts to be. And that is a troublesome proposition.[225]

Undoubtedly, many school boards and state courts would be reluctant to employ remedies that Congress disfavors and prohibits federal courts from employing.[226]

Some of *Swann*'s supporters argue that court-ordered busing is not an appropriate topic for a constitutional amendment. On the one hand, proponents of school busing claim that Congress lacks authority to restrict the federal courts' remedial powers since busing is indispensable to vindicating a constitutional right. Testifying against President Nixon's antibusing legislation, Alexander Bickel observed: "[If] the Court should accept the command of Congress that it may not administer what it regards as the essential remedy, the Court will have accepted a more far-reaching limitation on judicial power, a greater qualification of the power of judicial review established by *Marbury* v. *Madison* than ever before in its history."[227] On the other hand, Bickel also testified against H.J. Res. 620, a constitutional amendment to end busing, arguing that Congress should not clutter the Constitution with specific remedial provisions:

> [I]t trivializes the constitution to deal by constitutional amendment with a subject enmeshed in so many variables and so local in nature. A constitutional amendment dealing with busing would

be preposterously out of place in comparison with the momentous structural and substantive provisions with which the rest of our constitution, after a fashion proper to a constitution, was written to deal. Nor do any of the amendments so far made to the Constitution, saving only prohibition and its repeal, fail to deal with subjects of the proper magnitude. We must not set foot on the road to converting our Constitution into a code of detailed regulation, dealing with a myriad passing grievances, after the fashion of so many state constitutions, which are then every so often scrapped whenever it seems advisable to make a fresh start.[228]

If both of Bickel's arguments are correct, Congress is powerless to alter the Supreme Court's constitutional judgments. Bickel's position would promote judicial supremacy, a form of tyranny that the Framers of the original charter sought to prevent. Furthermore, a constitutional amendment prohibiting desegregative busing is no more or less specific than amendments conferring the right to vote at age eighteen, prohibiting the states from interfering with the voting rights of blacks and women, or granting the national government power to tax income without apportioning taxes among the states on the basis of population. Reasonable individuals may disagree about the wisdom of desegregative busing, but the people have an indisputable right, through the amendment process, to reverse the Supreme Court's constitutional judgments.

Conclusion: Desegregative Busing and Constitutional Legitimacy

Although Congress has broad authority to regulate the federal courts' jurisdiction and remedial powers, neither Article III nor the Fourteenth Amendment's enforcement provision grants Congress power to vitiate the individual's right to equal protection. Section 5 of the Fourteenth Amendment empowers Congress to prevent state interference with the individual's right to equal protection rather than to restrict the Supreme Court's interpretation of section 1 or the lower federal courts' powers to enforce the Court's constitutional construction. Furthermore, the Framers of the original charter did not grant Congress authority under the Judiciary Article to nullify the Supreme Court's constitutional interpretation. Neither the framing of Article III nor subsequent judicial precedents suggest that Congress can employ its authority to regulate the federal courts' jurisdiction and remedial powers as a subterfuge to nullify the Court's constitutional judgments.

Many antibusing proposals are suspect because they embody racial classifications. They attempt to reallocate governmental power, that is, change the decision-making arena in school busing cases in a manner that burdens a racial minority in violation of *Washington* v. *Seattle School District No 1*. Other antibusing proposals attempt to dictate or direct decisions in public school desegregation cases, in violation of the separation-of-powers doctrine. Most antibusing legislation interferes with judicial power and independence by nullifying the Supreme Court's constitutional constructions in derogation of the amendment process (in Article V).

Neither Article III nor section 5 of the Fourteenth Amendment grants Congress authority to amend the Constitution by simple majorities. Neither provision empowers Congress to insulate antibusing proposals from judicial scrutiny. Nor is a congressional preference for the neighborhood school a sufficiently compelling interest to justify the proscription of judicial remedies that are necessary to end de jure racial segregation of the nation's public schools. If Congress doubts the wisdom or constitutionality of the Supreme Court's decisions in *Brown* v. *Board of Education, Swann* v. *Charlotte-Mecklenburg,* and subsequent cases, it can propose a constitutional amendment to prohibit desegregative busing.

9

The Undying Issue: Congress, the Court, and Abortion Rights

....

Since the Supreme Court decided in *Roe* v. *Wade* (1973)[1] that the Fourteenth Amendment's due process clause encompasses a qualified right to privacy that includes a woman's decision to terminate her pregnancy,[2] the abortion issue has divided Congress, the Court, and the nation. Public opinion polls and continuing legislative efforts to circumscribe the Supreme Court's abortion decisions indicate a lack of consensus on the moral, social, ethical, religious, legal, and constitutional questions that these decisions have posed to the American people.[3] In response to *Roe* and subsequent decisions, members of Congress have introduced numerous constitutional amendments, funding restrictions in appropriations and authorization bills, limitations on the federal courts' jurisdiction and remedial powers, and various other statutory measures attempting to limit the effects of the Court's abortion decisions.

Following *Roe*, both Congress and the states have enacted legislation to circumscribe and circumvent the Supreme Court's decision. In a continuing dialogue with Congress and the states, the Court has sustained some measures as a legitimate expression of governmental interest in protecting maternal health and "potential life," while it has voided others as an illegitimate interference with the woman's constitutional right to privacy. As the current dockets of the Supreme Court and the lower federal courts indicate, the effort to find some accommodation between the woman's right and the government's compelling interest will continue in the foreseeable future.

As in the school prayer and school busing controversies, congres-

sional critics of *Roe* dispute the Supreme Court's constitutional interpretation, substantive policy judgments, and institutional authority to
decide abortion cases. According to *Roe*'s critics, neither the Fifth nor
the Fourteenth amendment encompasses a right to privacy that includes a woman's decision to end her pregnancy. The language and
framing of the Fifth and Fourteenth amendments provide neither explicit nor implicit support for the justices' policy judgments.[4] Indeed,
the due process clauses of the Fifth and Fourteenth amendments impose
an affirmative duty on government to protect human life throughout
every stage of biological development beginning with conception.

Lacking any constitutional basis for its decision in *Roe*, the Court
has conceived a new substantive right to an abortion that is no more
justifiable than earlier decisions that created economic rights. According to the critics, *Roe* v. *Wade* and *Lochner* v. *New York*[5] are equally
unwarranted judicial exercises that have transformed the due process
clauses into substantive guarantees that the Framers and Ratifiers of
the Fifth and Fourteenth amendments never contemplated. In creating
substantive due process rights, the Court has trammeled on congressional authority to promote the general welfare and regulate interstate
commerce and the states' authority to protect the public's health,
safety, welfare, and morals. The Supreme Court, its critics conclude,
has abandoned self-restraint, usurped the legislative powers of Congress
and the states, and exceeded the constitutional scope of judicial power.

Arguing that the Court has exceeded its judicial function under Article III and the Fourteenth Amendment, opponents of *Roe* and subsequent decisions claim that the exceptions and regulations and ordain
and establish clauses authorize Congress to limit the Supreme Court's
appellate jurisdiction and the federal district courts' jurisdiction and
remedial powers in abortion cases. In addition, section 5 of the Fourteenth Amendment empowers Congress rather than the federal judiciary to enforce the due process and equal protection clauses. Congress
can employ its powers under section 5 to define the fetus as a person
deserving due process and equal protection, prohibit the states from
denying these rights to the unborn, and limit the federal courts' authority to enjoin the states from prohibiting abortions and interfering with
fetal rights.

Unlike legislation limiting the federal courts' remedial powers in
busing cases, some of *Roe*'s critics observe, Congress could employ its
enforcement powers (in section 5) to define those persons entitled to
due process and equal protection. Since such legislation does not define
the substantive meaning of due process, it would not interfere with the

Supreme Court's authority to interpret the meaning of due process. Even if such legislation defines substantive due process rights, it expands rather than contracts Fourteenth Amendment guarantees. Therefore, legislation requiring the states to protect the fetus' due process rights would not conflict with Justice Brennan's suggestion in *Katzenbach* v. *Morgan*[6] that Congress has authority to expand, but not contract, Fourteenth Amendment rights.[7] However, these arguments ignore the effect of congressional legislation on a woman's judicially defined right to choose an abortion over giving birth. Finally, proponents of legislation resting on section 5 evade potential congressional interference with the district courts' judicial powers to enforce previously defined constitutional rights.

Although *Roe, Doe* v. *Bolton*,[8] and other federal-court decisions establish a zone of privacy that government can breach only when it demonstrates a compelling interest in maternal welfare and potential life, these decisions do not impose an affirmative duty on the states or the federal government to pay for abortions from the public purse. Even in cases of therapeutic or medically necessary abortions, neither the states nor the federal government has an obligation to pay for an indigent woman's abortion through Medicaid programs. Absent an affirmative duty to fund abortions, both the states and the federal government can adopt spending programs that favor childbearing over abortions.

Congress can also restrict the expenditure of federal funds through authorization and appropriation acts that prohibit federal agencies from funding abortions. As long as there is no constitutional duty to finance abortions, Congress and the states can exercise their respective legislative powers to circumscribe access to abortions. Because the Supreme Court does not recognize indigence as a suspect classification or the public funding of abortions as a fundamental right, funding restrictions do not violate the equal protection and due process clauses. Funding restrictions, the Court's critics conclude, are a constitutionally permissible, albeit indirect, means to limit the practical effect of *Roe* v. *Wade*.

Since 1973 congressional opponents of the Supreme Court's abortion decisions have employed four basic methodologies in their struggle to reverse, circumvent, or circumscribe *Roe* v. *Wade*. Citing congressional authority under Article V, they have introduced constitutional amendments that limit or define state and congressional power to restrict, regulate, or prohibit abortions. A second methodology employs legislative authority under the Judiciary Article to limit the Supreme Court's appellate jurisdiction and the jurisdiction of the lower federal courts in abortion cases. A third methodology employs the legislative powers of

Congress to restrict federal funding of abortions. Finally, there are various statutory proposals, including informed-consent bills, human life bills, and measures protecting the rights of medical personnel and facilities to refuse to perform abortions, that rest on congressional authority to enforce the Fourteenth Amendment.

Even a cursory examination of congressional reaction to the Supreme Court's abortion decisions reveals that the legislative response is more varied, differentiated, and complex than congressional attempts to reverse the Court's school prayer and school busing decisions. Nevertheless, each of the four methodologies that senators and representatives have employed poses several common questions. Do these methodologies impinge on rights that the Supreme Court has defined as fundamental under the Fifth and Fourteenth amendments? Alternatively, are these methodologies legitimate expressions of a compelling governmental interest in protecting maternal health and potential life that do not infringe on a woman's right to choose between an abortion and childbearing? Furthermore, what are the effects of various methodologies on the relationship between Congress and the Supreme Court? Do these methodologies undermine the Court's authority to enforce the supremacy clause? Do they alter the constitutional relationship between the states and the national government? Do these methodologies impair the Supreme Court's constitutional function of providing a uniform construction of national law? Are they constitutionally legitimate means to reverse the effects of *Roe* and subsequent decisions? Only a careful examination of the Supreme Court's decisions concerning the scope of a woman's right to end her pregnancy and congressional responses to *Roe* will illuminate the permissible range of legislative authority to circumscribe or reverse the federal courts' abortion decisions.

Privacy, Abortion, and the States' Authority: The Supreme Court Intervenes

As the Supreme Court acknowledged in *Roe* v. *Wade*, prior to its decision on January 22, 1973, laws regulating abortions varied considerably among the states. Despite these variations, until the late 1960s all but a few states and federal jurisdictions prohibited abortions except when necessary to save a mother's life. Alabama and the District of Columbia, Justice Blackmun noted, permitted abortions to protect a woman's health, while Massachusetts, Pennsylvania, and New York authorized their courts to determine whether an abortion was lawfully justified.[9]

Following the guidelines of the American Law Institute's Model Penal Code, between 1967 and 1972 nineteen states liberalized their abortion laws. The Model Penal Code permitted "justified" abortions, but recommended that abortions be performed in licensed hospitals, except in emergencies.[10] By 1972 nineteen states permitted therapeutic, but not elective, abortions.[11]

Abortion and the Right to Privacy

Despite the trend toward enactment of more permissive abortion laws, in 1973 approximately thirty states prohibited abortions unless necessary to save the mother's life.[12] The Texas Penal Code, for example, made it "a crime to 'procure an abortion . . .' or to attempt one, except with respect to 'an abortion procured or attempted by medical advice for the purpose of saving the life of the mother'."[13] Claiming that the Texas statute interfered with "her right of personal privacy, protected by the First, Fourth, Fifth, Ninth, and Fourteenth Amendments,"[14] in March 1970, Norma McCorvey, a single woman, sought an injunction to restrain the district attorney of Dallas County from enforcing the Texas law. Although the Constitution does not explicitly confer a personal right to privacy, McCorvey was relying on a series of decisions in which the Supreme Court had inferred zones of privacy from various constitutional amendments.

Since 1923 the Supreme Court has discovered zones of privacy in the Fourteenth Amendment's due process clause as well as other constitutional provisions.[15] According to the Court, the concept of liberty encompasses a zone of privacy that includes the right to marry and procreate, the right of married and unmarried persons to use contraceptives, and the right of parents to rear and educate their children. Although the Supreme Court has never declared these rights to be absolute, it has required the states to demonstrate at least a reasonable interest in enacting public policies that do not intrude on the individual's privacy.

Dissenting in *Olmstead* v. *United States* (1928),[16] a case involving Fourth and Fifth amendment privacy rights, Justice Brandeis expressed the philosophy inherent in the Court's decisions concerning marital, familial, and procreative privacy. The Framers of the Bill of Rights, Brandeis emphasized, "sought to protect Americans in their beliefs, their thoughts, their emotions and their sensations."[17] Attempting to secure conditions favorable to the individual's pursuit of happiness, the Framers "conferred, as against the Government, the right to be let alone—the most comprehensive of rights and the right most valued by civilized men. To protect that right, every unjustifiable intrusion by the Government upon the privacy of the individual, whatever the means employed, must be deemed a violation of the Fourth Amendment."[18]

Beginning with *Meyer* v. *Nebraska* (1923),[19] the Supreme Court has recognized that the concept of liberty embodied in the Fourteenth Amendment's due process clause:

> [D]enotes not merely freedom from bodily restraint but also the right of the individual to contract, to engage in any of the common occupations of life, to acquire useful knowledge, to marry, establish a home and bring up children, to worship God according to the dictates of his own conscience, and generally to enjoy those privileges long recognized at common law as essential to the orderly pursuit of happiness by free men.[20]

While the Supreme Court has acknowledged that the concept of liberty embraces an individual's right to marry,[21] a parent's right to rear and educate her or his children,[22] and a family's right to domestic privacy,[23] the Court has emphasized its obligation to balance these privacy rights against the state's legitimate interest in protecting the public's health, safety, welfare, and morals. In the sixty-five years since *Meyer*, however, the Court has subjected the state's interest to closer scrutiny. In cases involving fundamental rights or suspect classifications (e.g., race and national origin) the Supreme Court has required the states to show a compelling interest rather than merely a reasonable interest in enacting and administering a public policy.

In addition to acknowledging zones of marital, familial, and parental privacy, the Supreme Court has recognized a fundamental right to procreative privacy.[24] The Court's early decisions linked procreative privacy to marriage and family life,[25] but more recent decisions have extended the zone of procreative privacy beyond conventional marital relationships sanctioned by the state. In *Eisenstadt* v. *Baird* (1972),[26] the Supreme Court struck down a Massachusetts law that prohibited physicians and pharmacists from administering, prescribing, or furnishing contraceptives to anyone but a married person. Writing for the majority, Justice Brennan rejected the state's contention that the statute was a justifiable public health measure. Its purpose, Brennan noted, is to deter premarital sexual relations. If married persons have a right to procure contraceptives, then unmarried individuals must enjoy the same right. Going beyond the equal-protection argument, Brennan focused on the individual's right to procreative privacy:

It is true that in *Griswold* the right of privacy in question inhered in the marital relationship. Yet the marital couple is not an independent entity with a mind and heart of its own, but an association of two individuals each with a separate intellectual and emotional makeup. If the right of privacy means anything, it is the right of the *individual*, married or single, to be free from unwarranted governmental intrusion into matters so fundamentally affecting a person as the decision whether to bear or beget a child.[27]

Prior to *Roe* v. *Wade* the Supreme Court had disengaged the right of procreative privacy from marriage and the family relationship. The Court transformed this liberty into a fundamental, individual right to decide whether to bear children. In earlier decisions, such as *Meyer* and *Pierce* v. *Society of Sisters* (1925), the Supreme Court required the state to demonstrate a reasonable interest in the public's health, safety, welfare, and morals to justify intrusions on familial privacy. In recent decisions, such as *Loving* v. *Virginia* (1967), *Eisenstadt*, and *Roe*, the Court has required the states to demonstrate a significant or compelling interest to justify intrusions on the individual's right to privacy.

Although *Eisenstadt* focused on the woman's right to prevent conception, it foreshadowed the Supreme Court's decision in *Roe*, which protected the woman's right to decide whether to terminate an unwanted pregnancy by abortion. Just as *Skinner* v. *Oklahoma* (1942) and *Griswold* v. *Connecticut* (1965) emphasized earlier judicial values of familial privacy and autonomy, *Eisenstadt*, *Roe*, and subsequent decisions stress recent judicial values of individual privacy and autonomy.[28] These decisions also demonstrate that the Supreme Court has transformed the due process clause from a guarantee of procedural fairness in judicial proceedings into a substantive protection against "unwarranted" government interference with the individual's right to privacy. Moreover, the Court has transformed the due process clause into a new elastic clause, which the justices can expand or contract according to their views of fundamental rights and the legitimate scope of governmental authority.

The Right to an Abortion v. The State's
Compelling Interest: Roe and Its Offspring

As Justice Blackmun stated in *Roe* v. *Wade* (1973), a woman does not have an absolute right to an abortion.[29] Speaking for the majority, Blackmun acknowledged that the state may have "important interests in safeguarding health, in maintaining medical standards, and in protecting potential life."[30] As Blackmun summarized the majority's position: "We, therefore, conclude that the right of personal privacy includes the abortion decision, but that this right is not unqualified and must be considered against important state interests in regulation."[31] In delineating a woman's right to privacy and the state's interest, Blackmun conceded that at some point in a pregnancy the governmental interest becomes "sufficiently compelling to sustain regulation of the factors that govern the abortion decision."[32]

According to the majority's opinion, the state must demonstrate that its interest in protecting maternal welfare and potential life is compelling and that its legislative enactments are "narrowly drawn to express only the legitimate state interests at stake."[33] As in other due process cases involving "fundamental rights," the Supreme Court subjected the state's policy to the same searching standard that it applies to equal-protection cases involving suspect racial classifications. Or, as Justice Rehnquist argued in his dissenting opinion, the majority transposed the compelling-state-interest test "from the legal considerations associated with the Equal Protection Clause of the Fourteenth Amendment to this case arising under the Due Process Clause of the Fourteenth Amendment."[34]

Denying that the term "person" in the Fourteenth Amendment includes the unborn, the majority ignored the fetus's right to life, apart from the state's interest in protecting potential life at the point of viability.[35] Unable to resolve "the difficult question of when life begins,"[36] the Court merely recognized the existence of divergent religious and philosophical views, but disclaimed that the judiciary could answer the question.[37] Conceding that it lacked the competence to decide when life begins, the Court also denied that it need resolve this conundrum, since a fetus is not a person deserving the protection of the Fourteenth Amendment's due process clause. Therefore, in balancing the individual's right to due process and the state's compelling interest in protecting maternal health and potential life, the majority did not incorporate the fetus into its equation.

After recognizing the state's interest in protecting the pregnant woman's health and preserving potential human life, Blackmun noted, the state's interest grows substantially "as the woman approaches term"[38] and as the fetus approaches viability. At some point during pregnancy, the state's interest becomes compelling. In each stage of pregnancy the state has an obligation to define its interest narrowly to express "only the legitimate state interests at stake."[39] In a statement that reads more like a report of the American College of Obstetricians and Gynecologists than a judicial opinion, Blackmun attempted to define the state's legitimate interest during each stage of pregnancy.

During the first trimester, the Court concluded, the state has virtually no interest in interfering with a woman's decision, in consultation with her physician, to obtain an abortion. Since an abortion during the first trimester is safer than carrying to term, Blackmun observed, there is no compelling justification for the state to interfere with a woman's decision to terminate her pregnancy. According to current medical knowledge, Blackmun wrote:

> [F]or the period of pregnancy prior to this "compelling" point, the attending physician, in consultation with his patient, is free to determine, without regulation by the State, that, in his medical judgment, the patient's pregnancy should be terminated. If that decision is reached, the judgment may be effectuated by an abortion free of interference by the State.[40]

Other than assuring that licensed physicians perform abortions under medical conditions that meet the state's general standards for similar medical procedures, the majority's opinion leaves no discretion to the legislature.

Beginning in the second trimester, "a State may regulate the abortion procedure to the extent that the regulation reasonably relates to the preservation and protection of maternal health."[41] This means that the state may regulate (1) the qualifications of persons performing abortions, (2) the licensure of persons performing abortions, (3) the type of medical facility in which the procedure is performed, and (4) the licensure of such facilities as hospitals and clinics.[42] Since Blackmun merely provided a few examples rather than a comprehensive enumeration of acceptable regulations, the scope of legislative authority remained indeterminate. However, the state cannot exercise its legitimate authority as a subterfuge to deter women from obtaining an abortion or to invade a judicially protected right to privacy.

Turning to the "[s]tate's important and legitimate interest in potential life," Blackmun noted that "the 'compelling' point is at viability."[43] Since the fetus is capable of "meaningful life outside the mother's womb" at the point of viability, the state may regulate and even proscribe an abortion during the third trimester, except when necessary to preserve the mother's life and health.[44] In addition to conditioning the state's authority to proscribe abortions, Blackmun cautioned that only appropriate medical personnel could determine the risks to a woman's life and health in deciding to perform an abortion.[45] At no point did Blackmun define the meaning of the terms "potential life" and "health." Once again, the Court provided the states with little guidance regarding their authority to regulate third-trimester abortions.

Throughout his opinion, Blackmun attempted to balance the competing and seemingly irreconcilable interests of the woman's right to privacy and the state's authority to preserve maternal health and potential life. Searching for the middle ground, Blackmun fashioned a shifting standard that attempts to weigh these distinct and competing interests differently in each stage of pregnancy. "The decision," he concluded, "leaves the State free to place increasing restrictions on abortion as the period of pregnancy lengthens, so long as those restrictions are tailored to the recognized state interests."[46] However, Blackmun failed to define the permissible scope of state regulation following the first trimester. By simply declaring the Texas statute unconstitutional, the Court's opinion left the states with few guidelines in exercising their legitimate interests in preserving maternal health and potential life.[47]

In *Doe v. Bolton* (1973),[48] the companion case to *Roe*, the Supreme Court began the arduous and apparently endless task of defining the permissible range of state and congressional authority to enact regulations protecting maternal health and preserving potential life. Between 1973 and 1987 the Court would confront the complex task of distinguishing between permissible regulations and legislative attempts to chill or restrict the right to privacy that it articulated in *Roe*. Following *Roe*, the Supreme Court decided more than forty cases involving various aspects of the abortion controversy.

In many cases the Court faced challenges to state laws requiring physicians and medical facilities to obtain a patient's informed consent prior to performing an abortion. Some of these cases involved minor women who challenged the authority of parents and husbands to withhold their consent to an abortion. While some cases concerned minor women capable of making an informed judgment, others involved immature minors who, in the state's view, were unable to make a decision. Still other suits raised such issues as the physician's right to practice and to make professional judgments about a patient's health or the potential viability of the fetus. In another series of cases, the Supreme Court confronted challenges to state regulations of medical facilities that performed abortions. Several cases presented issues involving the right of medical personnel and facilities to refuse to perform abortions. One case challenged state restrictions on the right to advertise abortion services. *Roe* v. *Wade* and *Doe* v. *Bolton* marked the beginning of a flood of litigation that continues today, as the Supreme Court attempts to define the permissible scope of state authority to regulate abortions.

In *Doe* v. *Bolton*, a twenty-two-year-old married woman and her physician challenged Georgia's criminal abortion statute, which prohibited abortions unless a licensed physician determined that, in his best clinical judgment, the procedure was necessary because:

(1) A continuation of the pregnancy would endanger the life of the pregnant woman or would seriously and permanently injure her health; or

(2) The fetus would very likely be born with a grave, permanent, and irremediable mental or physical defect; or

(3) The pregnancy resulted from forcible or statutory rape.[49]

In addition to these conditions, the statute required that (1) any woman seeking an abortion be a legal resident of Georgia, (2) the physician performing the abortion obtain written certification from two other licensed physicians that the abortion is necessary, according to the statutory conditions, (3) the physician perform the procedure in a hospital accredited by the State Board of Health and the Joint Commission on Accreditation of Hospitals, and (4) a committee of the hospital's medical staff approve the procedure in advance. In cases of rape, the law required the woman to file a sworn, detailed report to the appropriate law enforcement agency.[50]

Speaking for the Court, Justice Blackmun sustained the statutory provision leaving the decision to perform an abortion to the attending physician's best clinical judgment. Denying that the provision was unconstitutionally vague, Blackmun argued that the law gives the physician adequate discretion to exercise his best medical judgment. As for the requirement that all abortions, including first-trimester abortions, must be performed in an accredited, licensed hospital rather than a licensed clinic, Blackmun noted that the state had failed to show that only the former could protect the patient's health. The state simply had not demonstrated any compelling interest in maternal health by applying this requirement to first-trimester abortions. However, the Court did not restrict the state's authority to require that second- and third-trimester abortions be performed in a fully licensed hospital.[51]

Second, Blackmun noted, the state failed to show any compelling interest in requiring a hospital committee to approve abortions. This requirement interfered with the woman's right to receive medical care "in accordance with her licensed physician's best judgment."[52] With regard to the state's interest in protecting potential life, Blackmun found the hospital committee's judgment redundant since the attending physician had already made a first-hand professional medical judgment. Furthermore, the state's criminal law did not subject any other surgical procedure to a hospital committee's prior approval.

Similarly, the Court struck a provision requiring the concurrence of two other physicians prior to performing an abortion. Blackmun argued that this third requirement unduly interfered with the attending physician's best clinical judgment that the abortion is necessary. Noting that Georgia's criminal code subjects no other voluntary medical or surgical procedure to a similar requirement, Blackmun concluded that the law infringes on the physician's right to practice.[53] Finally, the majority declared the Georgia residency requirement unconstitutional. Since the requirement applied to private facilities and physicians as well as state-supported hospitals, Georgia could not demonstrate any "policy of preserving state-supported facilities for Georgia residents."[54]

As applied to Mary Doe, who sought an abortion in the ninth week of her pregnancy, and her physician, the Court found the Georgia criminal abortion act an unconstitutional interference with Doe's right to privacy and her physician's right to practice his profession according to his best clinical judgment. According to *Doe*, the state cannot require the performance of a first-trimester abortion in an accredited full-service hospital rather than a licensed clinic or other medical facility. Nor can the state interpose the judgments of other physicians and hospital committees between the patient and her physician. The state cannot interfere with the citizen's right to travel to obtain medical services. Nevertheless, the Court's decision denies an absolute right to an abortion and permits the state to enact legislation to protect maternal welfare and preserve potential life in the later stages of pregnancy.

In *Roe* v. *Wade* the Court articulated several general principles regarding a woman's right to terminate her pregnancy and the state's interest in protecting maternal health and preserving potential life. However, the majority's opinion did not provide specific standards for weighing and balancing these distinct and competing interests. *Doe* v. *Bolton* suggested that the states could not interfere with the physician's medical judgment concerning his patient's health or regulate abortion procedures differently from other medical and surgical procedures. According to Justice Blackmun, the state could not demonstrate a compelling interest in maternal health that outweighed the woman's privacy interest during the first trimester of pregnancy. In subsequent decisions the Court attempted to delineate these distinct and competing interests.

These cases involve complex state regulations of abortions, reveal deep divisions among the justices regarding the legitimacy of various state regulations, and demonstrate the difficulties inherent in deciding intricate medical, scientific, and other public policy questions according to judicial standards. To delineate permissible state regulations from unacceptable intrusions on the judicially defined right to privacy, these cases are presented by the types of regulations that states have enacted rather than by chronology. The Court's decisions are categorized according to regulations that (1) impinge on the woman's right to decide to have an abortion, (2) restrict the physician's right to practice and make professional judgments about a patient's health and the viability of the fetus, (3) limit the hospital's authority to administer the performance of abortions, and (4) restrict the use of public funds to finance abortions. Although this analysis does not follow the evolution of judicial policy, it illuminates the permissible scope of congressional and state responses to the abortion decisions.

State Regulation of the Woman's Decision

On June 3, 1974, the Supreme Court confronted the first challenge to a spousal or parental consent statute.[55] A Florida law required physicians to obtain the consent of a woman's husband or the parent of a pregnant, unmarried minor prior to performing an abortion. In addition to making no distinction between first-trimester abortions and those performed later in pregnancy, the Florida law gave "husbands and parents the authority to withhold consent for abortions for any reason or no reason at all."[56] Although the district court recognized the husband's interest in protecting the embryonic life of his child, it denied the state's authority to interfere with the mother's decision prior to the point of viability. Similarly acknowledging the parents' interest in their daughter's health and the fetus's potential life, the district court held that the statute interfered with the woman's right to privacy during the first trimester. Citing *Roe* and *Doe* as precedents, the district court concluded that "the pregnant woman's right of privacy is 'sole' during the first trimester."[57]

After the Supreme Court dismissed Florida's appeal,[58] on August 18, 1975, the Fifth Circuit Court of Appeals sustained the district court's decision.[59] The court of appeals noted that the state had failed to demonstrate a sufficiently compelling interest to interfere with the woman's right to privacy during the first trimester. Although the court of appeals acknowledged the state's interest in prohibiting illicit teenage sex, preserving the marital relationship, protecting the husband's procreative rights, and promoting the family's privacy and integrity, it denied that these interests were either sufficiently compelling or clearly related to the governmental interest in preserving maternal welfare and the life of the fetus in the early stage of pregnancy. The circuit court concluded that the "right to abortion is a very personal right exercised by the woman as an individual,"[60] a right that neither the state, nor a husband, nor a minor woman's parents can limit during the first trimester by exercising a blanket veto over her decision to obtain an abortion.

On July 1, 1976, two years after the Supreme Court dismissed *Gerstein*, the Court decided *Planned Parenthood of Missouri* v. *Danforth*,[61] a case in which two physicians challenged the constitutionality of various provisions of Missouri's abortion act of 1974. The Court sustained the section requiring the woman's written consent prior to an abortion, but held the spousal and parental consent requirements unconstitutional. Speaking for the majority, Justice Blackmun argued that, although Missouri did not require a patient's prior consent for virtually any other surgical procedure, the written-consent requirement during the first twelve weeks of pregnancy "is not in itself an unconstitutional requirement."[62] Blackmun observed that "[t]he decision to abort, indeed, is an important, and often a stressful one," which should "be made with full knowledge of its nature and consequences."[63] The state, he concluded, has a legitimate interest in assuring that a woman make this important decision voluntarily and with a full awareness of its significance.[64] Although justices White, Rehnquist, and Stevens and Chief Justice Burger concurred and dissented in part, none of the dissenting statements took exception with Blackmun's conclusion sustaining the informed-consent provision.

Addressing the spousal-consent provision, Blackmun concluded that "the State cannot 'delegate to a spouse a veto power which the state itself is absolutely and totally prohibited from exercising during the first trimester of pregnancy'."[65] While Blackmun recognized the husband's interest and the importance of the marital relationship, he reiterated that during the first trimester a woman has the right to make this decision unilaterally.[66] White, Burger, and Rehnquist dissented, arguing that the state should have discretion in balancing the mother's interest in terminating her pregnancy and the father's interest in having a child.[67] Thus, six justices concluded that the state cannot delegate a veto power to the spouse, while three members of the Court rejected judicial interference with the legislature's policy judgment.

Turning to the parental-consent requirement, Blackmun denied that the state has a significant interest in conditioning a pregnant minor's decision to terminate her pregnancy during the first trimester. Although Blackmun acknowledged the state's authority to regulate a minor's activities, he denied that Missouri could grant parents absolute authority to veto the decision of a physician and his minor patient to terminate her pregnancy. "Any independent interest the parent may have," Blackmun noted, "in the termination of the minor daughter's pregnancy is no more weighty than the right of privacy of the competent minor mature enough to have become pregnant."[68] However, Blackmun did recognize the state's interest in assuring that the minor woman, in consultation with her physician, is mature enough to "give effective consent for termination of her pregnancy."[69] By failing to distinguish between the mature and the immature minor, the state had failed to justify the parental-consent requirement.[70] Although Stewart and Powell acknowledged the state's authority to provide for parental advice and consultation, they agreed that the statute was constitutionally deficient because it imposed "an absolute limitation on the minor's right to obtain an abortion."[71]

White, Burger, and Rehnquist dissented, arguing that the statute was a valid method to assure that an unmarried minor woman make an intelligent decision "by requiring parental consultation and consent."[72] Justice Stevens agreed with his dissenting brethren. He argued that the state has authority to protect "a young pregnant woman from the consequences of an incorrect decision" by providing for parental participation in the decision to secure an abortion.[73] While Blackmun, Brennan, and Marshall found the parental-consent requirement patently unconstitutional, Stewart and Powell questioned only the absolute nature of the parental veto. The difference between Blackmun's and Stewart's opinions suggests that less blanket parental-consent provisions might withstand the Court's compelling-interest standard, even during the early stages of pregnancy.

On the same day that the Supreme Court decided *Danforth*, it vacated a decision of the District Court for Massachusetts enjoining the operation of a 1974 statute that required parental consent prior to performing an abortion on an unmarried minor woman (under eighteen).[74] The Court remanded *Bellotti* v. *Baird* (*Bellotti I*, 1976) to the district court pending the statute's construction by the Supreme Judicial Court of Massachusetts.[75] Although the appellees contended that the statute provided for a parental veto,[76] the state's attorney general argued that the law allowed a minor to obtain a court order permitting an abortion without parental consultation and consent.[77] As the state argued, the law even permitted an immature, unmarried woman to obtain a court-ordered abortion without parental consultation and consent, "where there is a showing that the abortion would be in her best interests."[78] If the state's interpretation were correct, the statute would not constitute an impermissible parental veto. Since the Massachusetts law was susceptible to a constitutionally acceptable interpretation, the Supreme Court ordered the district court to abstain, pending a decision of the Supreme Judicial Court of Massachusetts.[79] Following the Supreme Judicial Court's decision in *Baird* v. *Attorney General* (1977),[80] the district court again found the Massachusetts statute unconstitutional.[81]

Speaking for the majority in *Bellotti II*, Justice Powell acknowledged that a state can adjust its legal system to deal differently with minors than adults, but emphasized that, with respect to many Fourteenth Amendment due process rights, "the child's right is virtually coextensive with that of an adult."[82] The Court had previously recognized that the state has authority to protect a minor's welfare and can limit a child's right to make "important, affirmative choices with potentially serious consequences."[83] In limiting a child's freedom of choice, government can defer to parental judgment and guidance in making important decisions.[84] However, the state cannot give parents an absolute veto over a minor woman's decision to terminate her pregnancy.[85] Although a state may involve parents in a minor woman's choice to obtain an abortion, it must provide an alternative procedure to demonstrate either (1) that she is capable of making a mature, informed choice in consultation with her physician or (2) that, even if she cannot make such a choice, an abortion is in her best interest.[86] "In sum," Powell stressed, "the procedure must ensure that the provision requiring parental consent does not in fact amount to the 'absolute, and possibly arbitrary, veto' that was found impermissible in *Danforth*."[87]

Justice Powell concluded that the Massachusetts statute as interpreted by the Supreme Judicial Court was constitutionally wanting. First, the statute failed to distinguish between mature and immature minors. Second, the state must provide access to a court to determine whether an abortion is in the minor's best interest. The state may not condition a minor's access to a court by requiring that she must first notify and consult her parents.[88] Third, the state cannot give its courts a judicial veto over a mature and competent minor's decision to seek an abortion.[89]

Almost two years after *Bellotti II*, the Court decided *H. L.* v. *Matheson* (1981),[90] a case involving a pregnant minor who lived with her parents. In a class-action suit, the young woman, H.L., challenged the constitutionality of a Utah law providing that prior to performing an abortion a physician " *'[n]otify, if possible, the parents or guardian of the woman upon whom the abortion is to be performed, if she is a minor* or the husband of the woman, if she is married.' "[91] Distinguishing the notification provision from the parental-consent requirements in *Danforth* and *Bellotti II*, Chief Justice Burger found the procedure constitutional as applied to an unmarried, dependent minor who had "made no claim or showing as to her maturity."[92] Denying that the Utah law imposed a blanket parental veto, Burger argued that a mere notification requirement "does not violate the constitutional rights of an immature, dependent minor."[93] Rather than granting the parents or a judge a veto, Utah merely attempted to assure the family's integrity, the parents' right to provide "essential medical and other information" to the young woman's physician, and the parents' authority to " 'direct the rearing of their children'."[94] As applied to an unemancipated minor, Burger concluded that the Utah statute was narrowly drawn to serve the state's legitimate interests in protecting the woman's health and preserving potential life.[95]

Marshall, joined by Brennan and Blackmun, dissented from the majority's view that the appellant lacked standing. He concluded that "the Utah notice requirement is not necessary to assure parents [the] traditional child-rearing role, and that it burdens the minor's fundamental right to choose with her physician whether to terminate her pregnancy."[96] Despite Marshall's objections, the majority and concurring opinions suggest that if a state draws a statute narrowly, it can justify a compelling interest in protecting an unemancipated minor's health. Although the state cannot grant parents or courts authority to veto a mature minor's decision to end her pregnancy, it can provide for parental notice in cases that involve immature, dependent minors. *Matheson* strengthens the states' authority as well as the parents' responsibility for promoting minor children's health and welfare.

A decade after *Roe* v. *Wade*, in *Akron* v. *Akron Center for Reproductive Health* (1983),[97] the Supreme Court invalidated sections of Akron's "Regulations of Abortions" ordinance regarding parental and informed consent. The Akron ordinance prohibited physicians from performing abortions on minors (under eighteen) without providing the young woman's parents or guardian at least twenty-four hours notice prior to performing such an abortion. In the event that the physician could not locate the parents or guardian, the ordinance required that he provide "constructive notice" by certified mail at least seventy-two hours before performing the procedure, unless a court having jurisdiction over the minor had ordered the abortion. The ordinance also prohibited physicians from performing an abortion on a woman under fifteen years of age without (1) her written consent, (2) the written consent of her parents or guardian, or (3) an order from the court having jurisdiction over the minor woman. The ordinance's consent procedures did not distinguish between mature and immature minor women.[98]

In obtaining a woman's written, voluntary, and informed consent, the ordinance required that the attending physician provide a detailed, prescribed statement to assure that her consent is truly informed. The prescribed statement required the attending physician to inform the pregnant woman, among other things: (1) that she is actually pregnant, (2) the time that had elapsed since conception, (3) that the unborn child is a human life from the moment of conception, (4) a detailed description of the child's anatomical and physical characteristics at the time of abortion, (5) that in the event that the child is viable the physician has a legal responsibility to preserve its life, (6) the serious complications that can result from abortion, including the psychological effects, (7) a list of agencies that provide birth-control information, and (8) a list of agencies that can assist her during pregnancy and after birth, including adoption agencies.[99] The ordinance left the attending physician no discretion in providing the prescribed information.

Speaking for the majority in *Akron*, Justice Powell found that both the parental and informed-consent provisions unconstitutionally burdened the woman's due process rights. First, the Akron ordinance made "a blanket determination that *all* minors under the age of 15 are too immature to make this decision or that an abortion never may be in the minor's best interests without parental approval."[100] Second, unlike *Bellotti II*, the Akron ordinance did not provide for an alternative judicial proceeding to determine the minor woman's maturity or whether an abortion is in her best interests. The ordinance failed to distinguish between the mature and immature minor pregnant woman.

Addressing the informed-consent section, Powell recognized the state's interest in protecting the pregnant woman's health, but concluded that the ordinance went "beyond permissible limits."[101] By prescribing a specific statement, the ordinance interfered with the physician's professional responsibility to "ensure that appropriate information is conveyed to his patient, depending on her particular circumstances."[102] Various consent procedures, Powell noted, interfered with the physician's responsibility to protect his patient's health. The ordinance attempted to influence the woman's decision "between abortion or childbirth" rather than protect her health.[103] Suggesting that abortion is a "particularly dangerous" procedure, the ordinance included a "parade of horribles" designed to dissuade women from choosing an abortion.[104] These provisions burdened the women's constitutionally protected right to obtain an abortion during the first trimester, which the state could not justify as a legitimate interest in protecting maternal health.

In a scathing dissenting opinion, Justice Sandra Day O'Connor, joined by justices White and Rehnquist, attacked the Court's approach in balancing the state's interest and the woman's right differently in each stage of pregnancy. O'Connor argued that throughout pregnancy the Court should apply the same judicial standard, namely, whether the regulation imposes an undue burden on the woman's right.[105] When a regulation does not burden a fundamental right or liberty, the state merely needs to demonstrate that there is some rational relationship between the law and a legitimate purpose within the state's competence.[106] In determining whether the state has unduly burdened a fundamental right or liberty, O'Connor emphasized the legislature's role in balancing competing interests. Legislatures, rather than courts, she commented, " 'are ultimate guardians of the liberties and welfare of the people'."[107] Employing these standards, the minority concluded that the Akron ordinance was a reasonable expression of the state's legitimate interest in protecting maternal welfare and potential life.[108]

On the same day, the Supreme Court sustained the parental-consent provision of a Missouri statute regulating abortions. Justice Powell, who delivered the Court's opinion in *Planned Parenthood Association* v. *Ashcroft* (1983),[109] noted that the "State's interest in protecting immature minors will sustain a requirement of a consent substitute, either parental or judicial."[110] Since the Missouri law provided an alternative judicial procedure to determine whether the minor woman "is sufficiently mature to make the abortion decision herself or that, despite her immaturity, an abortion would be in her best interests,"[111] the statute conformed to the Court's judgment in *Bellotti II*. As interpreted by the court of appeals, the Missouri law was constitutionally permissible. Dissenting in part from the majority's opinion, Justice Blackmun, joined by justices Brennan, Marshall, and Stevens, interpreted the Missouri statute as giving third parties—parents and courts—an absolute veto over an unemancipated minor's decision to obtain an abortion.[112]

Thus five members of the Court (Powell, Burger, O'Connor, White, and Rehnquist) sustained the Missouri law's parental-consent provision.

Three years after *Ashcroft*, the Court confronted a challenge to the Pennsylvania Abortion Control Act of 1982, which included an informed-consent provision similar to the Akron ordinance. Acknowledging the state's authority to ensure that a woman has given voluntary and informed consent to an abortion, Justice Blackmun, speaking for the majority in *Thornburgh* v. *American College of Obstetricians and Gynecologists* (1986),[113] found that the informed-consent procedures were "nothing less than an outright attempt to wedge the Commonwealth's message discouraging abortion into the privacy of the informed-consent dialogue between the woman and her physician."[114] Dissenting, Chief Justice Burger claimed that the informed-consent requirement was a legitimate measure to ensure that a woman make a knowledgeable judgment, aware of the risks and alternatives. Burger argued that the Court had legitimated abortion on demand,[115] a demand that "will not even have to be the result of an informed choice."[116] In a second dissenting opinion, White also argued that the informed-consent procedure did not "directly infringe the allegedly fundamental right at issue—the woman's right to choose an abortion."[117] Writing a third dissenting opinion, O'Connor argued that the procedure was "rationally related to the State's interests in ensuring informed consent and in protecting potential human life."[118]

White also denied that the Fourteenth Amendment either textually or implicitly encompasses a woman's right to end her pregnancy. He rejected the argument that the due process clause includes the liberty that the Court discovered in *Roe* v. *Wade*. Since the right to end a pregnancy is not a fundamental right, White noted, there is no need to subject state regulation of abortion to strict scrutiny and require that the state justify its legislation by demonstrating a compelling interest in protecting maternal health and preserving potential life.[119] If a woman's decision to end her pregnancy is not a fundamental right, he argued, "[s]tate action impinging on individual interests need only be rational to survive scrutiny under the Due Process Clause, and the determination of rationality is to be made with a heavy dose of deference to the policy choices of the legislature."[120] The time had come, White concluded, to overrule *Roe* v. *Wade*!

Indeed, the time to narrow or reverse *Roe* may have come. On January 9, 1989, the Supreme Court granted a writ of certiorari to the Eighth Circuit Court of Appeals in *Webster* v. *Reproductive Health Service*.[121] The appellees (pregnant women, health-care professionals, and abortion-counseling services) had challenged provisions of Missouri's Abortion Regulation Statute (1986), which declares that human life begins at conception and "that unborn children have protectable interests in life, health, and well-being."[122] Both the district court and the court of appeals found that the legislature had adopted a particular theory of life to justify the regulation of abortion in conflict with *Roe* and subsequent decisions.[123] If the Supreme Court reverses the lower courts' judgment, the states will be free to adopt laws regulating, restricting, or prohibiting the performance of abortions. By sustaining Missouri's statutory declaration that human life begins at conception, the Court would return the nation to the status quo ante *Roe*.

Alternatively, the Supreme Court could void the statutory declaration while sustaining other provisions that prohibit the use of public funds, personnel, or facilities to counsel, encourage, assist in, or perform abortions.[124] Since the Missouri law applies to women who compensate public facilities for abortion services,[125] *Webster* is distinguishable from *Harris* v. *McRae* (1980)[126] and *Maher* v. *Roe* (1977),[127] which involve public expenditures for abortions. Although the states are not required to spend public funds to favor abortion over childbearing, the Missouri regulation attempts to discourage women from seeking information and obtaining an abortion even when they can afford to pay for such services. Therefore, it would be difficult for the Court to sustain the statute as a legitimate expression of the state's interest in promoting childbearing.[128] Unless the Supreme Court overturns *Roe* directly, the Missouri statute represents an attempt to burden a woman's right to make a knowing and intelligent choice about abortion and childbearing.

Without sustaining the declaration of policy, it will also be difficult to uphold other statutory provisions that require doctors (1) to perform abortions after the sixteenth week of pregnancy in a hospital and (2) to perform tests to determine whether the fetus is viable before performing an abortion on any woman whom a doctor believes is in the twentieth week of pregnancy.[129] As the court of appeals noted, these provisions erect obstacles to the meaningful exercise of the woman's rights, prevent doctors from exercising their best medical judgment, and interfere in the dialogue between doctor and patient.[130] In sum, the court of appeals ruled that the Missouri statute discourages women from exercising their due-process rights as interpreted "in *Roe* and its progeny."[131] Inasmuch as the statutory regulations are contingent on and inseparable from the declaration, the only principled way to reverse *Roe* is to sustain the policy that human life begins at conception.

Until the Supreme Court reverses *Roe* v. *Wade*, it has acknowledged that the states have a compelling interest in protecting a pregnant woman's health, which may justify some informed-consent and parental-consent requirements. If a statute is narrowly drawn to assure that a pregnant woman's consent to an abortion is informed and voluntary, the Court will sustain the legislative policy as a legitimate expression of the state's interest. However, if the law is designed to dissuade a woman from seeking an abortion, it burdens the woman's fundamental liberty or right to privacy that the Court established in *Roe*.

The Court has also recognized the interests of states and parents in assuring that pregnant minor women make an informed judgment regarding the abortion decision. However, neither a parent, guardian, husband, nor a court can exercise an absolute or unqualified veto over the young woman's decisions. In the event that the state adopts a parental-consent requirement, it must provide for an alternative judicial proceeding to determine whether the minor woman is mature and capable of making the decision to end her pregnancy. Even a pregnant, dependent, immature minor has a right to seek a court order to end her pregnancy, without prior parental consultation and consent. The court has a responsibility to determine whether an abortion is in the immature minor's best interests. The Supreme Court's decisions suggest that protection of the young woman's health is the criterion it will employ in determining whether the state's regulation expresses a legitimate interest or burdens the fundamental Fourteenth Amendment right to privacy.

The Physician's Right to Practice and Exercise
Professional Medical Judgment

Although the Supreme Court's abortion decisions recognize the states' authority to regulate the practice of medicine, these decisions also acknowledge the physician's indispensability to a pregnant woman's decision to have an abortion. Without the physician's knowledge, advice, and liberty to exercise his best clinical judgment, the woman's fundamental right to decide and obtain an abortion would be a hollow promise. In counseling women and performing abortions, it is the licensed physician who actually strikes the balance between protecting his patient's health and preserving potential human life. How far can the state intrude on the physician's professional judgment and the patient-doctor relationship without infringing on the right to privacy that the Court established in *Roe*? The Court's decisions involving the physician's role in abortions raise issues such as the state's authority to (1) license medical personnel, (2) restrict the performance of abortions to physicians, (3) limit the attending physician's discretion in providing information, which, according to professional judgment, a pregnant woman requires to make an intelligent choice, (4) prevent a physician from using the safest method of inducing an abortion in each stage of pregnancy in order to preserve potential life, (5) restrict the physician's medical judgment in determining the actual or potential viability of the fetus, and (6) intrude on the physician's ultimate obligation to protect a patient's life and health. Just as the Court denies that a woman has an absolute right to obtain an abortion, it denies that a physician has an absolute obligation to perform an abortion against his best clinical judgment concerning a patient's health.

On January 13, 1975, the Supreme Court affirmed a decision of the District Court for the Eastern District of Louisiana[132] invalidating a provision of Louisiana's Medical Practice Act, which authorized the suspension or revocation of a doctor's license for "procuring, aiding or abetting an abortion," unless the procedure was necessary to save the pregnant woman's life. In *Rosen* v. *Louisiana State Board of Medical Examiners*,[133] the district court held that the statute violated the Fourteenth Amendment: "[I]n that it impermissibly regulates abortion without regard to pregnancy stage, limits abortion to a life-saving procedure without regard to other fundamental rights of the woman, and interferes with the physician's medical judgment respecting his patient."[134] However, the district court denied that the woman and her physician have "an unqualified right to perfect an abortion subsequent to the first trimester."[135] As the district court conceded, after the first trimester Louisiana has greater discretionary authority to restrict abortions as long as the state tailors its law to the legitimate interests of protecting maternal health and preserving potential life.[136]

"The Court has also recognized," Justice Powell remarked in *Akron*, "because abortion is a medical procedure, that the full vindication of the woman's fundamental right necessarily requires that her physician be given 'the room he needs to make his best medical judgment'."[137] As Powell observed, the physician requires discretion in "assisting the woman in the decisionmaking process and implementing her decision should she choose abortion."[138] However, the Court also acknowledged the state's power to enact regulations during the first trimester. Nevertheless, the state must demonstrate that its regulations (1) serve important health objectives and (2) do not interfere with "physician-patient consultation" or with "the woman's choice between abortion and child-birth."[139]

In *Akron*, the Court found that the informed-consent procedure intruded on the physician's discretion, interfered with the patient-doctor dialogue, and deprived the physician's right to exercise his best medical judgment in determining the precise information that each patient needs to make an intelligent decision.[140] By requiring the doctor to read a specific litany to each patient, the ordinance inhibited the pregnant woman from obtaining the advice and information she needs to decide between abortion and childbirth. Powell also denied that the state has authority to insist that a physician, rather than other competent, licensed personnel, provide counseling. The state can satisfy its legitimate interest by requiring the physician to certify that a woman has received the information necessary to make an informed decision rather than requiring the physician to personally counsel the woman.[141] The Akron ordinance, Powell concluded, interfered with the woman's right and did not serve any legitimate state interest.

In balancing the competing and distinct interests of protecting maternal health and preserving potential human life, some states have adopted laws that regulate the methods or techniques that physicians may use to induce an abortion. States have also adopted statutes mandating that physicians preserve the life of a viable or potentially viable fetus during the later stages of pregnancy. These laws require physicians to make difficult professional judgments concerning fetal viability and to take measures to preserve the unborn child's life. Some laws proscribe the use of particular abortifacients, while other regulations mandate the presence of a second physician to deliver and care for the newborn child. How far can the state interfere with the attending physician's professional judgment, in order to protect potential life, without compromising the primary responsibility to preserve a patient's life and health?

As Justice Blackmun stated in *Danforth*, the state cannot prohibit the physician from using a safe technique "on the ground that the technique 'is deleterious to maternal health.'"[142] Section 9 of the Missouri abortion statute prohibited the use of saline amniocentesis, a method used in approximately seventy percent of abortions performed after the first twelve weeks of pregnancy.[143] In effect, the statute required the physician to employ a technique that incurred greater risks than the technique of choice, saline amniocentesis, or giving birth.[144] Therefore, the Court concluded, section 9 was not "a reasonable regulation for the protection of maternal health."[145] In a dissenting opinion, Justice White, joined by Justice Rehnquist and Chief Justice Burger, disputed the majority's "factual" findings as well as its conclusion that the Missouri law inhibited women in later stages of pregnancy from deciding in favor of abortion. Concluding that the legislature has the primary responsibility to enact public health policy, White denied the Court's competence to make complex medical findings "unless we purport to be not only the country's continuous constitutional convention but also its *ex officio* medical board with powers to approve or disapprove medical and operative practices and standards throughout the United States."[146]

In *Colautti* v. *Franklin* (1979)[147] the Court invalidated sections of the Pennsylvania Abortion Control Act of 1974, which required a physician to determine whether the fetus is or may be viable.[148] If the physician failed to determine whether the fetus was viable and failed to exercise professional care in preserving the life of a potentially viable fetus, the act subjected him to serious civil and criminal penalties. Although the act permitted the physician to choose an abortifacient necessary to preserve his patient's life or health, it conceivably placed him in the position of making a "trade-off" between protecting the woman's health and increasing the fetus's chances of survival.[149]

The statute afforded little discretion to the physician's judgment, did not adequately define the term "potentially viable," and subjected the physician to charges of criminal homicide for " 'intentionally, knowingly, recklessly or negligently caus[ing] the death of another human being'."[150] In addition to violating the physician's right to due process, Blackmun remarked, the law "could have a profound chilling effect on the willingness of physicians to perform abortions near the point of viability in the manner indicated by their best medical judgment."[151] Blackmun concluded that, because the physician has no way of knowing whether his actions caused the death of a potentially viable fetus, "the statute is little more than 'a trap for those who act in good faith'."[152] The majority also concluded that "the standard-of-care provision" was impermissibly vague.[153] By requiring the physician to use abortive techniques likely to preserve the life of the fetus, the state conceivably interferes with the physician's medical judgment and primary responsibility to protect his patient's life and health. The statute failed to define the physician's primary duty with precision,[154] and, once again, subjected him to criminal penalties for failing to take appropriate care in preserving fetal life. By interfering with the physician's best professional judgment, the act infringed on the privacy right that the Court had established in *Roe*.

Four years later, in *Ashcroft*,[155] the Court sustained Missouri's "second-physician requirement." The Missouri statute required the attendance of a second physician to preserve the unborn child's life, providing that this requirement did not "pose an increased risk to the life or health of the woman."[156] Sustaining the Missouri statute, Justice Powell remarked:

> [G]iven the compelling interest that the State has in preserving life, we cannot say that the Missouri requirement of a second physician in those unusual circumstances where Missouri permits a third-trimester abortion is unconstitutional. Preserving the life of a viable fetus that is aborted may not often be possible, but the State legitimately may choose to provide safeguards for the comparatively few instances of live birth that occur. We believe that the second-physician requirement reasonably furthers the State's compelling interest in protecting the lives of viable fetuses.[157]

While O'Connor, White, Rehnquist, and Burger concurred with Powell regarding the second-physician requirement, Blackmun, Brennan, Marshall, and Stevens dissented. The dissenters claimed that most postviability abortions are emergency procedures that usually employ dilation and evacuation, in which case there is no chance for fetal survival. Therefore, the presence of a second physician is superfluous, adds cost to the procedure, and burdens the woman's rights without advancing an interest in preserving potential life.[158] As the majority, concurring, and dissenting opinions indicate, the Court has persisted in acting as a continuing College of Obstetricians and Gynecologists, second-guessing the legislature's policy judgments on abortion procedures.

In *Thornburgh*[159] the Supreme Court again faced the issue of postviability care due the unborn child. Section 3210(b) of the Pennsylvania Abortion Control Act of 1982 mandated that the physician exercise "that degree of care 'which such person would be required to exercise to preserve the life and health of any unborn child intended to be born and not aborted'."[160] Section 3210(b) required the physician to use an abortion technique that "'would provide the best opportunity for the unborn child to be aborted alive unless,' in the physician's good-faith judgment, that technique 'would present a significantly greater medical risk to the life or health of the pregnant woman'."[161]

As Justice Blackmun interpreted these provisions, the act required the mother to bear "an increased medical risk" to save her unborn child's life. "Like the Missouri statute," Blackmun concluded, "the Pennsylvania act contains no express exception for an emergency situation."[162] Unlike the Missouri law, the Pennsylvania act did not even imply an intent "to protect a woman whose life may be at risk."[163]

Therefore, the majority (Blackmun, Brennan, Marshall, Powell, and Stevens) concluded that "[a]ll the factors are here for chilling the performance of a late abortion, which, more than one performed at an earlier date, perhaps tends to be under emergency conditions."[164] Although the majority's opinion rested on a detailed analysis of medical and scientific information as well as the legislature's intent, Blackmun reasserted the basic premise of *Roe* v. *Wade*:

> [T]hat the Constitution embodies a promise that a certain private sphere of individual liberty will be kept largely beyond the reach of government. . . . That promise extends to women as well as to men. Few decisions are more personal and intimate, more properly private, or more basic to individual dignity and autonomy, than a woman's decision—with the guidance of her physician and within the limits specified in *Roe*—whether to end her pregnancy. A woman's right to make that choice freely is fundamental. Any other result, in our view, would protect inadequately a central part of the sphere of liberty that our law guarantees equally to all.[165]

In attempting to express its legitimate interests in protecting maternal health and preserving potential life, the states, according to the Supreme Court, cannot intrude on the patient-physician relationship and interfere with the licensed physician's professional judgment in providing pregnant women with the information necessary to choose between abortion and childbirth. State laws that prescribe in detail the information that a doctor must provide his patient interfere with the free dialogue necessary to a woman's decision. In some instances, the Court has found, informed-consent provisions are designed to dissuade a woman from choosing abortion, serve no state health interest, and vitiate the right to privacy established in *Roe* v. *Wade*.

Similarly, the states have a legitimate interest in preserving the life of a viable fetus, but they cannot employ their authority to discourage women from obtaining postviability abortions or require physicians to employ abortion techniques that increase risks to the mother's life and health, use techniques that are less safe than carrying to term, or employ methods that interfere with the physician's primary responsibility to protect his patient's life and health. In balancing the competing interests of the mother and the fetus, the Court maintains, the states have an obligation in all stages of pregnancy to preserve the woman's life and health. However, the Court has sustained some measures to preserve the unborn child's life insofar as these medical and surgical procedures do not interfere with the doctor's primary responsibility to his patient or burden the woman's fundamental right.

The State's Authority to Regulate Medical Facilities

Just as the states have authority to license and regulate the physician's practice of medicine, they have a legitimate public health interest in regulating the operation of hospitals, clinics, and other medical facilities that perform abortions. Granted the state's legitimate health interests, can it regulate abortions differently from other medical and surgical procedures that hospitals perform? Can the state mandate the type of facility that can perform abortions at every stage of pregnancy? Can it require hospitals to file pathology reports regarding the fetus at every stage of biological development? In various cases involving state regulation of hospitals, the Court has attempted to determine whether the statute expresses a compelling interest in maternal health and fetal viability. Alternatively, the Court has asked whether the statute unjustifiably burdens the woman's fundamental right as expressed in *Roe* v. *Wade*.

In *Sendak* v. *Arnold* (1976)[166] the Supreme Court affirmed, without comment, the decision of a three-judge district court voiding an Indiana statute requiring doctors to perform first-trimester abortions in a licensed hospital or other licensed medical facility. Both in *Akron* (1983) and *Ashcroft* (1983), the Supreme Court invalidated provisions of an Akron ordinance and a Missouri law requiring doctors to perform second-trimester abortions in a critical-care hospital. The Court acknowledged the state's authority to require that physicians perform abortions in licensed medical facilities, but denied that either Akron or Missouri had demonstrated a compelling state interest in mandating a full-service, acute-care hospital. Inasmuch as neither Akron nor Missouri had demonstrated even a rational relationship between its regulation and its interest in protecting maternal health, the Court found that both laws unconstitutionally burdened the woman's fundamental right.[167] However, on the same day, in *Simopoulos* v. *Virginia* (1983),[168] the Court held that Virginia's law requiring physicians to perform second-trimester abortions in licensed hospitals, including outpatient hospitals, was a reasonable health regulation.[169] Justice Powell argued that Virginia's law was not an unreasonable means of furthering its compelling interest in protecting maternal health.[170] After a careful evaluation of recognized medical practice, the nation's "*ex officio* medical board" determined that the Virginia statute had not burdened the woman's fundamental right!

Finally, in *Akron* and *Ashcroft*, the Court determined whether the states have an important health interest in requiring a fixed waiting period prior to an abortion and a pathology report following the procedure. In *Akron*, Justice Powell argued, the city had failed "to demonstrate that any legitimate state interest is furthered by an arbitrary and inflexible waiting period."[171] The city presented no evidence to demonstrate that the waiting period is beneficial to all women seeking an abortion. Again, Powell emphasized the importance of leaving these determinations to a physician in consultation with his patient.[172]

While the Supreme Court has rejected fixed waiting periods prior to an abortion, it has sustained regulations requiring pathology reports following an abortion. Speaking for the Court in *Ashcroft*, Justice Powell observed that such reports may be medically useful and necessary since they often indicate serious or fatal disorders.[173] Second, the Missouri statute applied to most surgical procedures, whether performed in a hospital or other medical facility.[174] Third, in weighing the balance between the additional cost and protecting the woman's health, the Court could not conclude "that the Constitution requires that a State subordinate its interest in health to minimize to this extent the cost of abortions."[175] In other words, the requirement furthered a legitimate state interest without significantly burdening the pregnant woman's decision to obtain an abortion.[176]

Does Government Have an Affirmative Duty to Fund Abortions?

If government cannot burden a woman's fundamental right to decide to have an abortion, without demonstrating a compelling state interest in maternal health or fetal viability, does government have an affirmative duty to fund abortions for indigent women? In *Singleton* v. *Wulff* (1976)[177] the Supreme Court granted standing to two physicians who sued the state of Missouri for compensation, under the state's Medicaid Program, for abortions they had performed for needy women. Under the Missouri statute, the state refused to reimburse physicians for abortions unless they were "medically indicated" rather than elective procedures.[178] Although the Court granted standing, it declined to decide the case on its merits since Missouri had not had an opportunity to defend the statute in the court of appeals. *Singleton* raised, but did not answer, the basic question of whether the state's refusal to fund abortions for indigent women burdens their fundamental right under *Roe* v. *Wade*.

A year later, in *Beal* v. *Doe* (1977),[179] the Court ruled that Title XIX of the Social Security Act, which established the Medicaid program, does not require the states to fund nontherapeutic abortions. Speaking for the Court, Justice Powell noted that "[a]lthough serious statutory questions might be presented if a state Medicaid plan excluded necessary medical treatment from its coverage, it is hardly inconsistent with the objectives of the Act for a State to refuse to fund *unnecessary*—though perhaps desirable—medical services."[180] Indeed, Powell argued that "the State has a valid and important interest in encouraging childbirth."[181] There is nothing in the act's language or legislative history that demonstrates a congressional intent to require that states fund nontherapeutic abortions as a condition of participation in the Medicaid program.[182] At the time that Congress passed Title XIX in 1965, most states prohibited nontherapeutic abortions. The Department of Health, Education, and Welfare subsequently stated that "Title XIX allows—but does not mandate—funding for such abortions."[183] Therefore, the majority ruled that Pennsylvania's refusal to cover nontherapeutic abortions was not inconsistent with Title XIX of the Social Security Act.[184]

On the same day, in *Poelker* v. *Doe* (1977),[185] the Supreme Court ruled that the Constitution did not prohibit the city of St. Louis, Missouri, from "providing publicly financed hospital services for childbirth," while refusing to provide similar services for nontherapeutic abortions.[186] The Court rejected the court of appeals' view that denial of such services burdened the rights of indigent pregnant women established in *Roe* v. *Wade* and *Doe* v. *Bolton*. In its *per curiam* opinion, the Court denied that the city's refusal to provide nontherapeutic abortions for indigent women constituted invidious discrimination prohibited by the Fourteenth Amendment.[187] Dissenting in *Poelker*, justices Brennan, Marshall, and Blackmun argued that the city's policy coerced poor women into childbirth in violation of *Roe* v. *Wade*.[188] Hinting at an equal-protection argument, the dissenters observed that the Court's decision would pose a serious inconvenience to poor women.

In a third decision announced on June 20, 1977, *Maher* v. *Roe*,[189] the Supreme Court ruled that Connecticut's refusal to fund nontherapeutic abortions for indigent women during the first trimester did not violate the Fourteenth Amendment's equal protection and due process clauses. Since the state's policy did not deny equal protection or burden a fundamental right, the Court ruled, Connecticut need only demonstrate that its welfare policy has a rational relation to the state's legitimate interest in promoting childbirth. Referring to *Beal*, Justice Powell observed that the Medicaid program did not require Connecticut to pay for nontherapeutic abortions.[190] Citing *San Antonio School District v. Rodriguez*,[191] Powell rejected the claim that "financial need alone identifies a suspect class for purposes of equal protection analysis."[192] Hence, he denied that Connecticut has an obligation to accord equal treatment to abortion and childbirth in providing medical assistance to poor women.[193]

Although *Roe* v. *Wade* prohibited the state from burdening a woman's right to privacy and recognized her right to make the abortion decision free from compulsion,[194] it did not imply a limitation:

> [O]n the authority of a State to make a value judgment favoring childbirth over abortion, and to implement that judgment by the allocation of public funds. . . .
>
> There is a basic difference between direct state interference with a protected activity and state encouragement of an alternative activity consonant with legislative policy.[195]

Absent a denial of equal protection or a fundamental right, the state can express its legitimate interest in promoting human life by denying medical assistance for nontherapeutic abortions while providing assistance for childbirth.[196] Finally, Powell acknowledged Congress's discretionary authority to "require provision of Medicaid benefits for [nontherapeutic] abortions as a condition of state participation in the Medicaid program."[197]

If, as Justice Powell acknowledged in *Maher*, Congress has authority to require the payment of Medicaid benefits for nontherapeutic abortions, can it refuse to reimburse the states for funding medically necessary abortions? In *Harris* v. *McRae* (1980),[198] the Court sustained the Hyde Amendment to Title XIX of the Social Security Act, which provided that:

> "[N]one of the funds provided by this joint resolution shall be used to perform abortions except where the life of the mother would be endangered if the fetus were carried to term; or except for such medical procedures necessary for the victims of rape or incest when such rape or incest has been reported promptly to a law enforcement agency or public health service."[199]

Does Title XIX require the states to provide assistance for medically necessary abortions, even though the Hyde Amendment denies them compensation for such abortions, except when the mother's life is endangered or in cases of rape or incest? In the event that the states are not obliged to provide assistance for most medically necessary abortions, does the Hyde Amendment impinge on various rights that the First Amendment's establishment clause and the Fifth Amendment's due process clause protect?

Speaking for the majority in *Harris*, Justice Stewart first disposed of the statutory questions concerning Title XIX and the state's obligation to finance Medicaid programs for which Congress withholds federal funding.[200] Examining the legislative history of Title XIX within the context of cooperative federalism, Stewart concluded that Congress did not intend to require a participating state to "assume the full costs of providing any health services in its Medicaid plan."[201] As Stewart construed Congress's intent:

> Title XIX was designed as a cooperative program of shared financial responsibility, not as a device for the Federal Government to compel a State to provide services that Congress itself is unwilling to fund. Thus, if Congress chooses to withdraw federal funding for a particular service, a State is not obliged to continue to pay for that service as a condition of continued financial support of other services.[202]

Having disposed of the statutory questions, Stewart focused on the constitutional questions that Cora McRae posed to the Court. McRae, a New York medicaid recipient who wished to end her pregnancy during the first trimester, declared that the Hyde Amendment violated her fundamental rights under the due process clause. After summarizing the privacy right established in *Roe* v. *Wade*, Stewart argued that the Hyde Amendment does not place a "governmental obstacle in the path of a woman who chooses to terminate her pregnancy" by abortion.[203] The fundamental right established in *Roe*, Stewart concluded, does not include a constitutional right to governmental compensation for an abortion. Since the government did not create Cora McRae's indigence, it is not responsible for eliminating the financial obstacles she faced in exercising the full range of choices that *Roe* created.[204] As long as the government does not interfere with Cora McRae's decision, it has no affirmative constitutional duty to subsidize her choice to have an abortion.[205]

The Court also rejected a claim that the Hyde Amendment violates the equal-protection concept implicit in the Fifth Amendment's due process clause. Inasmuch as the amendment did not impinge on any fundamental right, Congress need only show that the legislation has a rational relation to a legitimate governmental purpose, namely encouraging childbirth over abortion. However, did the amendment promote invidious discrimination? Did it incorporate a suspect classification that would require the Court to apply a compelling-interest standard?[206] Since the Court previously had determined that poverty is neither a suspect classification nor the result of governmental action, the majority denied the equal-protection claim. Stewart concluded that, absent a due process or equal-protection claim, the Court could sustain the Hyde Amendment as a rational expression of the government's legitimate interest in protecting the potential life of the fetus.[207] In *Harris* v. *McRae*, the Court applied its decisions in *Maher* v. *Roe* and *Beal* v. *Doe* to medically necessary abortions. In effect, the Court left the question of funding abortions for indigent woman to legislative discretion.

For the fourth time since 1977, justices Brennan, Marshall, and Blackmun took strong exception to the Court's decision. They argued that the decision vitiated the fundamental right to privacy established in *Roe* v. *Wade*. Criticizing the Court's decision, Brennan commented:

> The fundamental flaw in the Court's due process analysis, then, is its failure to acknowledge that the discriminatory distribution of the benefits of governmental largess can discourage the exercise of fundamental liberties just as effectively as can an outright denial of those rights through criminal and regulatory sanctions.[208]

In a separate dissenting opinion, Marshall criticized the majority for failing to recognize "the undeniable fact that for women eligible for Medicaid—poor women—denial of a Medicaid-funded abortion is equivalent to denial of legal abortion altogether."[209] Forced to turn to "back-alley butchers," Marshall argued, a significant number of poor women would die or suffer serious "health damage."[210] Finally, Marshall urged the Court to apply equal-protection standards to the poor, to the most powerless, defenseless class in America, with regard to the protection of fundamental rights.[211] As a class, Marshall observed, indigent poor women seeking abortions include a "substantial proportion [who] are members of minority races."[212]

In two additional dissenting opinions, Blackmun and Stevens were equally critical of the majority's failure to recognize the disproportionate effect of the Hyde Amendment on the poor. Albeit indirectly, the Hyde Amendment either deprives the poor woman of an effective choice between abortion and childbirth or forces her to obtain abortions that may impair her life and health.[213] In either event, the dissenters concluded that the Court's decision vitiated the right established in

Roe v. *Wade*. Indeed, the majority's opinion reads like Anatole France's comment on "the majestic equality of the laws, which forbid rich and poor alike to sleep under bridges, to beg in the streets, and to steal their bread."[214]

Abortion Rights and the Scope of Legislative Authority

Although the Supreme Court has declared that the Fourteenth Amendment's due process clause encompasses a zone of privacy that includes a woman's right to end a pregnancy rather than bear a child, the Court has never acknowledged that this fundamental liberty is absolute. It has recognized compelling state interests in promoting the woman's life and health and, at the point of viability, of preserving potential human life. As a pregnancy continues and approaches term, the Court has recognized greater scope for legislative regulation than during the early stages of pregnancy. During later stages of pregnancy, the states' interest in maternal welfare and potential life may justify more extensive regulation of medical practices concerning abortions. However, the state cannot express its legitimate interest in preserving potential life by enacting legislation that endangers the woman's life or health. In balancing these competing interests, the Supreme Court has weighted the scales in favor of the woman's health and fundamental right to privacy. Insofar as the states impinge on these fundamental rights, they must demonstrate a compelling interest that outweighs the right to privacy established in *Roe* v. *Wade*.

Nevertheless, both Congress and the states have considerable latitude in enacting policies to ensure that a woman's consent to an abortion is voluntary and informed. Congress and the states can regulate a physician's practice of medicine to assure that only licensed medical personnel perform procedures under safe conditions. However, neither Congress nor the states can adopt policies that interfere with a woman's right to decide freely or her physician's exercise of professional judgment in advising a patient or performing an abortion. Neither can prevent a physician from using safe methods and techniques, that is, abortion procedures that are safer than bearing a child or less safe than other procedures.

Finally, neither the Fifth and Fourteenth amendments nor the Court's decision in *Roe* v. *Wade* requires the states or the federal government to provide public assistance to indigent women seeking an abortion. Insofar as governmental regulations do not burden a woman's choice, the states and the national government must demonstrate only a reasonable relationship between their enactments and a legitimate governmental objective. Thus government can employ its taxing and spending powers to promote childbirth rather than abortion. While government cannot burden a fundamental right, protected by the due process clauses of the Fifth and Fourteenth amendments, it does not have an affirmative duty or obligation to favor abortion over childbirth, except, perhaps, in cases where the woman's life is in jeopardy or in cases of rape and incest. However, even these exceptions may lie within the discretionary authority of the state and national governments.

The Supreme Court's abortion decisions offer Congress amplitude in adopting substantive legislation concerning the practice of and access to abortions. Undoubtedly, Congress and the states have authority to adopt and ratify constitutional amendments reversing *Roe* and its progeny. However, does Congress have authority under Article III, the Fourteenth Amendment, or Article I to adopt jurisdictional and substantive legislation infringing on the fundamental right to procreative privacy that the Supreme Court has discovered in the due process clauses of the Fifth and Fourteenth amendments?

Congressional Responses to the Supreme Court's Abortion Decisions

Congressional critics have pursued four major methodologies in attempting to reverse, qualify, or circumscribe *Roe* v. *Wade*, *Doe* v. *Bolton*, and subsequent judicial decisions. While some senators and representatives have proposed constitutional amendments, others have introduced amendments to appropriations and authorization bills restricting the use of federal funds for abortions. In addition, some members of Congress have proposed various substantive measures to ensure that a woman's consent to an abortion is voluntary and informed, to protect the life and rights of the unborn, and to guarantee the rights of medical personnel who refuse to perform abortions for reasons of conscience and religious conviction. Finally, some members have introduced legislation restricting the Supreme Court's appellate jurisdiction and the lower federal courts' jurisdiction to decide abortion cases.

Although proposed constitutional amendments require little justification, they illuminate the remedial intent of related substantive and jurisdictional bills. However, some proposed constitutional amendments have serious consequences for federal-state relationships and require careful consideration. Similarly, according to the Court's decision in *Harris* v. *McRae* (1980),[215] federal funding restrictions do not pose serious due-process or equal-protection issues, despite dissenting judicial and congressional opinions to the contrary. Some substantive proposals attempt to reverse the effect of the Supreme Court's constitutional interpretation of the Fourteenth Amendment, while other measures apparently do not infringe on the privacy rights established in *Roe* v. *Wade*. Finally, bills limiting the federal courts' jurisdiction raise serious questions regarding the scope of congressional authority vis-à-vis the federal judiciary under Article III and section 5 of the Fourteenth Amendment. All four methodologies present serious questions about the appropriate institutional relationship between Congress and the Supreme Court, as well as the relationship of the states to the national government. Aside from proposed constitutional amendments, many substantive proposals present serious questions about the legitimacy of reversing the Supreme Court's constitutional interpretation by simple legislative majorities.

Reversing Roe v. Wade *by*
Constitutional Amendment

Since 1973 senators and representatives have introduced four basic types of constitutional amendments. These amendments would: (1) restore the states' authority to regulate abortions or give Congress and the states concurrent authority to restore the status quo ante, (2) authorize Congress and the states to protect human life at every stage of biological development, (3) prohibit Congress and the states from interfering with human life at every stage of development, or (4) define the fetus as a person within the meaning of the Fifth and Fourteenth amendment's due process clauses and extend due process rights to the unborn child.

During the Ninety-fourth Congress, first session (1975), the Senate Judiciary Subcommittee on Constitutional Amendments considered S.J. Res. 91, which simply reserved power to the states "to regulate the circumstances under which pregnancy may be terminated."[216] As the resolution's sponsor, Senator William L. Scott (R.-Va.), testified before the subcommittee, S.J. Res. 91 simply recognized the constitutional system's federal character. In a system of dual sovereignty, Scott argued, "the right to regulate the health and morals of the people, marriage and divorce, property rights, and other day-to-day matters affecting the lives of citizens is in the States."[217] Aside from reversing *Roe* and *Doe*, Scott's proposed amendment did not fundamentally alter the structure of government or the role of the Supreme Court. In this respect, Scott's resolution was similar to previous constitutional amendments that reversed specific judicial decisions.

Six years later, in 1981, Senator Orrin Hatch (R.-Utah) proposed S.J. Res. 110, a constitutional amendment that would have conferred concurrent authority on Congress and the states to restrict or prohibit abortions.[218] Senator Hatch's amendment differed from Scott's proposal in several important dimensions. First, S.J. Res. 110 went far beyond restoring the status quo ante *Roe*, since nineteen states had liberalized their abortion laws by 1973. Unlike Scott's permissive proposal, S.J. Res. 110 authorized Congress and the states to restrict or prohibit abortions. In the event that the states enacted more restrictive abortion laws than Congress, the resolution provided that the states' laws would prevail. S.J. Res. 110 reversed the logic of the supremacy clause, which provides that in the event of a conflict between a valid congressional act and an otherwise valid state act, the former must prevail. As Professor Donald Regan testified before the subcommittee, Hatch's proposed amendment would have created "an almost unprecedented . . . situation in which Congress has a power to legislate but not a supreme power."[219]

In effect, S.J. Res. 110 handed the states a one-way ratchet wrench that Congress could not have reversed without securing a constitutional amendment. On March 10, 1982, the Judiciary Committee consented to the resolution by a vote of 10/7.[220] Dissenting from the committee's report, senators Patrick J. Leahy (D.-Vt.) and Max S. Baucus (D.-Mont.) noted that the resolution's consequences were similar to jurisdiction-stripping bills pending in the Ninety-seventh Congress:

> While this proposal does not act directly to limit court jurisdiction in the manner of some school busing, school prayer, and abortion bills now pending in the Senate, the spirit and the effect of S.J. Res. 110 are identical.

* * * * *

> S.J. Res. 110 not only weakens the judicial branch of government as effectively as the court-stripping legislation now before the Senate, but it would enshrine the change in the Constitution, where it would not be easily altered when it became clear once more that the courts are best guardians of personal rights.[221]

During the Ninety-eighth Congress, first session, Senator Hatch once again introduced his "human life federalism amendment," S.J. Res. 3.[222] As originally referred to committee, S. J. Res. 3 was identical to S.J. Res.

110. Chairing the Senate Judiciary Subcommittee on the Constitution, Hatch conducted hearings on his resolution on February 28 and March 7. Hatch admitted that his objective was to:

> [R]everse *Roe* cleanly, completely, and in a manner that conforms with the basic constitutional tenets adopted by the Framers. By a "clean" reversal of *Roe,* I mean we are seeking to nullify the decision without disrupting unrelated legal doctrines. By a "complete" reversal, I mean we are seeking to nullify the decision to the full extent that it protects an abortion liberty. . . . Finally, by a "conforming" reversal, I mean we are seeking to nullify the decision in a manner that fully respects the basic principles of federalism, checks and balances, limits on government authority, and other fundamental tenets of the constitutional scheme of governance.[223]

Appearing before the subcommittee, Senator Thomas F. Eagleton (D.-Mo.) endorsed the principle of S.J. Res. 3, but recommended that the subcommittee delete all but the first ten words of the resolution. As modified, S.J. Res. 3 read: "A right to abortion is not secured by this Constitution."[224] Senator Eagleton's version of S.J. Res. 3 simply restored the status quo ante, leaving the states free to regulate, restrict, or prohibit abortions.[225] Eagleton's proposed revision would have reversed *Roe* v. *Wade* and all subsequent decisions regarding the fundamental right to privacy and abortion.[226]

Endorsing Eagleton's proposal during the floor debate, Senator Hatch explained the remedial intent of S.J. Res. 3:

> By deconstitutionalizing the issue of abortion, the proposed amendment would allow the States a wide variety of options with respect to this matter. In their best judgment, the States might choose to have no policy regarding abortion or might restrict and condition it in a variety of ways.[227]

Hatch then examined the constitutional consequences of S.J. Res. 3:

> First. It would nullify the special right to abortion created by the Supreme Court in 1973.
> Second. It would prevent the creation of any other right to abortion in the harbor of the Constitution.
> Third. It would avoid any unnecessary repudiation of the doctrine of privacy. The use of the careful phrase "right to abortion" clarifies that the amendment only repeals the abortion decisions.
> Fourth. It would mean that State statutes concerning abortion

would be subject to ordinary standards of judicial review, that is, the rational basis test instead of the compelling State interest test. Fifth. It would restore to the States their general police power to restrict and prohibit abortion, or—and I think this is important for those who are against my position—elect to refrain from doing so. The States would be restored to the legal status they enjoyed prior to Roe.

Sixth. It would reenfranchise the people, acting through their elected State representatives to participate in the formation of abortion policy.

Seventh. It would restore the constitutional balance of powers between the States and Federal Government and between the legislative and judicial branches. In sum, it would restore the status quo ante Roe insofar as the power and responsibility to resolve abortion issues is concerned.[228]

Following a limited debate on June 27 and 28, the Senate defeated S.J. Res. 3 by a vote of 49/50. The human life federalism amendment did not obtain a simple majority, let alone the two-thirds vote necessary to recommend a constitutional amendment.[229] Unable to support the measure, but unwilling to vote against the joint resolution, Senator Helms simply answered "present" as the clerk called the roll. As Helms's remarks indicate, the Hatch human life federalism amendment did not go far enough in protecting the right to life. The determined pro-life advocates wanted to ban abortions totally rather than divest the decision to the states.

While the proposed human life federalism amendments would authorize the states to regulate and prohibit abortions, a second type of joint resolution would empower Congress and the states to protect human life at every stage of biological development.[230] None of these resolutions defines whether, in the case of a conflict, state or congressional policy shall prevail. Undoubtedly, the supremacy clause would govern such conflicts. However, these amendments invite judicial construction, which would enmesh the Supreme Court in abortion controversies. None of the proposed amendments indicates the scope of congressional and state authority to preserve human life in relation to the states' obligation to protect the woman's life and health. Therefore, this second type of resolution encourages further litigation to balance the competing interests of the pregnant woman and the unborn child. To what extent could Congress and the states employ their new constitutional authority to burden a woman's right to choose an abortion?

A third type of resolution denies the power of the states and the national government to interfere with human life at all stages of biological development. Reflecting divergent religious and philosophical views, these amendments define the beginning of life in various terms, namely, with conception, fertilization, or the first heartbeat. Since the Ninety-third Congress Senator Helms and his allies in both houses have introduced approximately eighteen versions of human life amendments.[231] Leading the opposition to the Supreme Court's abortion decisions in 1975, Senator Helms introduced two amendments, S.J. Res. 6 and S.J. Res. 130. The first resolution guaranteed the right to life from the moment of fertilization and granted Congress and the states concurrent power to enforce the amendment.[232]

S.J. Res. 130 was identical, but also contained a section that prohibited the states and the national government from depriving "any human being of life on account of illness, age, or incapacity."[233] Presumably, Senator Helms's resolution sought to prohibit euthanasia as well as abortion. These human life amendments pose several constitutional and political questions. To what extent do they impinge on various rights protected by *Roe*? Do they invite federal judicial construction to reconcile human life amendments with Fourteenth Amendment privacy rights? If these amendments invite judicial construction, are they not counterproductive from their sponsors' perspective? If Senator Helms's objective is to get the federal courts out of this political thicket, are his various proposals self-defeating?

Between 1973 and 1986, senators and representatives opposed to the Court's abortion decisions offered approximately seventy-five joint resolutions defining the fetus as a "person" within the meaning of the Fifth and Fourteenth amendments.[234] These proposed amendments extend the right of due process of law to the fetus. Virtually all of these amendments permit abortions under several circumstances, such as when the mother's life or health is at risk or in cases of rape.[235] Unlike the Fourteenth Amendment's enforcement clause, this type of joint resolution authorizes both Congress and the states "to enforce this article by appropriate legislation within their respective jurisdictions."[236]

It requires no Cassandra to prophesy that the last type of amendment would raise myriad problems. Since the amendment provides for concurrent enforcement, it is not clear whether it exempts enforcement legislation from the supremacy clause. Like other types of joint resolutions providing for concurrent enforcement, this last type invites judicial intervention in abortion controversies. By authorizing Congress and the states to enforce its provisions, the proposed amendment creates the potential for conflict between state and congressional laws protecting human life. Unless the Court's critics deprive the federal judiciary of jurisdiction regarding these amendments, the federal courts will have an opportunity, under the supremacy clause, to determine (1) whether there is a conflict between state and national laws, and (2) which legislation will prevail.

As the number and variety of proposed constitutional amendments indicate, the congressional critics of *Roe* v. *Wade* and its progeny do not share a common legislative purpose. While some amendments prohibit abortions, with few exceptions, other resolutions devolve abortion decisions to the states. Many proposed amendments focus on protecting the life and rights of the unborn. Finally, some proposals authorize Congress and the state legislatures to regulate abortion issues concurrently.

Although the people have a fundamental right to change their Constitution, including the rights that it protects, some amendments have serious implications for the Framers' basic plan of government. Amendments that authorize concurrent regulation of abortion create judicially cognizable questions under the supremacy clause of Article VI. Other amendments, which authorize the states and Congress to protect human life, create opportunities for the judiciary to determine the scope of legislative authority to limit the privacy right established in *Roe* v. *Wade*. Contrary to their sponsors' manifest intent, many proposals further insinuate the federal judiciary into abortion decisions.

Statutory Responses to Roe v. Wade

In addition to offering constitutional amendments, critics of the Supreme Court's abortion decisions have proposed various statutory measures to limit or circumscribe the effects of *Roe* v. *Wade*. These statutory proposals include funding restrictions, informed-consent requirements, right-of-conscience guarantees to physicians and other medical personnel, restrictions on fetal experimentation, and straightforward statutory reversals of the Court's decisions. While funding restrictions apparently do not pose serious constitutional questions, statutory attempts to reverse the Court's mistaken constitutional judgments in *Roe* and subsequent abortion decisions circumvent the amendment process. Once again, the variety and volume of statutory proposals and public laws reflect the frustration, deep divisions, and divergent objectives that exist among *Roe*'s congressional critics.

Funding Restrictions Since 1973 Congress has enacted at least twenty-five public laws restricting the use of federal funds for abortions. Authorization and appropriation acts for the departments of Health, Education, and Welfare (later Health and Human Services), and Defense, the U.S. Civil Rights Commission, the government of the District of Columbia, and Medicaid grant-in-aid programs to the states include various restrictions (sometimes referred to as Hyde-type amendments) on public expenditures for abortions. In 1973 and 1978, Congress prohibited the expenditure of any public funds for abortions in the Foreign Assistance Act of 1973 and the International Development and Food Assistance Act of 1978.[237] While these funding restrictions imply no exceptions, neither act applied to domestic programs. The two Hyde-type amendments prohibited the Agency for International Development and other public agencies from funding any abortions for women in developing countries, even when necessary to save their lives and protect their health. Admittedly, Congress has plenary authority to adopt foreign aid programs that impose American values on other nations that accept U.S. assistance.

Following *Maher* v. *Roe* (1977),[238] but prior to *Harris* v. *McRae* (1980),[239] Congress enacted the first in a series of somewhat less restrictive laws that prohibited federal agencies from using public funds for abortions. The Appropriations Act of 1976 for the departments of Labor and Health, Education, and Welfare, provided that: "None of the funds contained in this Act shall be used to perform abortions except where the life of the mother would be endangered if the fetus were carried to term."[240] Between 1981 and 1983 Congress adopted five other appropriations acts that incorporated similar provisions.[241]

Supported by the Court's decision in *Harris*, Congress employed its taxing and spending powers to restrict the availability of abortions for poor women. According to *Harris*, Congress does not have an affirmative duty or responsibility to assist indigent women in choosing abortion over childbirth. Since the Court's decisions deny that poverty is a suspect classification and that restrictions on public funds for abortions do not burden a fundamental right,[242] Congress can favor childbirth over abortion by providing funds to assist the former while denying funds to promote the latter. Exercising its discretionary authority, Congress has adopted ten other public laws that restrict the expenditure of public funds for abortions. However, these appropriations acts contain several exceptions to the general prohibition.[243] According to the Court's decision in *Harris*, congressional expansion of exceptions to the general prohibition is a matter of legislative grace rather than a constitutional mandate.

During the late 1970s Congress adopted three public laws that incorporate somewhat broader exceptions to the general prohibition than other appropriations and authorization acts include. The Continuing Appropriations Act for fiscal year 1978, the Department of Defense Appropriations Act for fiscal 1979, and the Labor-HEW Appropriations Act for fiscal 1979[244] permit these agencies to use funds for abortions (1) in the event that the mother's life is endangered by carrying to term, (2) in reported incidents of rape and incest, or (3) if two physicians determine that carrying a pregnancy to term would result in "severe and long-lasting physical health damage to the mother."[245] As a matter of congressional policy, the last exception offers physicians some professional discretion in advising their patients and performing abortions.

These variations in congressional policy on funding abortions reflect the inherent difficulty of developing legislative policies that involve distinct and competing interests. Congress's seemingly mercurial policy also mirrors the divisions that exist among *Roe*'s critics, shifting majority coalitions in the Senate and House of Representatives, changes in presidential policy and partisan control of the White House, a lack of legislative and national consensus on funding abortions for the poor, and the continuing struggle between proabortion and antiabortion forces to find some legislative compromise in this intractable conflict. Nevertheless, the decision to provide public assistance to poor women seeking an abortion remains a policy decision committed to the people's elected representatives rather than a constitutional judgment reserved for black-robed federal judges and Supreme Court justices.

The "Informed Consent Act". On January 6, 1987, senators Gordon J. Humphrey (R.-N.H.) and Jesse Helms introduced two identical "informed-consent" bills, S. 272 and S. 273.[246] As introduced, the "Informed Consent Act" (S. 272) prohibited persons employed in medical facilities operated by the Department of Health and Human Services or employed in any facility supported by federal funds from performing an abortion without first obtaining the pregnant woman's consent.[247] The bill prohibits the facility from releasing the consent form to anyone but the woman, the person performing the abortion, or a third party whose consent may be required prior to performing the procedure. The act permits the woman to release the consent form, but also allows federal or state courts to release such information.[248] Finally, in emergency situations, the bill permits a physician to perform an abortion if in his "best medical judgment . . . a medical emergency exists that complicates the woman's pregnancy in a manner which requires an immediate abortion."[249]

Except for section 3(c)(3), the informed-consent provision seems facially valid. However, section 3(c)(3) presents two important constitutional questions. Can a state or federal court order the release of detailed information that would compromise the woman's right to privacy and confidentiality?[250] If this section also implies that third parties, for example, parents or husbands, can veto a woman's decision, it would conflict with *Roe* v. *Wade, Doe* v. *Bolton,* and subsequent decisions. If this section is a covert means to require all minor pregnant women, without regard to their maturity, to consult with and obtain their parents' consent prior to an abortion, the provision probably conflicts with the Court's decisions in *Danforth,*[251] *Bellotti II,*[252] and *Akron.*[253] The vague, imprecise language of section 3(c)(3) raises serious constitutional questions that its authors fail to address.

Section 7(a), which requires the secretary of HHS to provide a specific list of information that physicians must present to each woman seeking an abortion to ensure that her judgment is intelligent and that she has weighed the risks and benefits of having an abortion, is also constitutionally questionable. Section 7(a) requires the physician to present a specific litany[254] that is similar to the provisions of *Akron's* "Regulations of Abortion" ordinance and Pennsylvania's Abortion Control Act of 1982, which the Court found constitutionally unacceptable.[255] Several essential provisions of the proposed "Informed Consent Act" seem incompatible with the pregnant woman's freedom to decide, the inviolability of the physician-patient relationship, and the physician's exercise of his best medical judgment regarding his patient's health. Sections 3(a)(3) and 7 attempt to nullify the Court's constitutional interpretation through ordinary legislation, which circumvents the constitutional-amendment process of Article V.

Right-of-Conscience Laws. Since 1973 Congress has enacted four statutes that prohibit courts, public officials, and public agencies from compelling physicians, medical personnel, and medical facilities that receive federal funds to perform abortions. Although these laws may have the effect of restricting access to abortions, they guarantee the First and Fourteenth Amendment rights of medical personnel whose religious beliefs or moral convictions proscribe abortion. The Health Programs Extension Act of 1973, the Legal Services Corporation Act of

1974, the Public Health Service Amendments of 1977, and Senator Danforth's amendment (No. 1877) to the Civil Rights Restoration Act (which Congress passed over President Reagan's veto on March 22, 1988), contain "right-of-conscience" provisions.[256] Although Danforth's amendment to the Civil Rights Restoration Act does not contain explicit "right-of-conscience" language, the senator stated that his intent was to protect the individual's freedom of conscience rather than restrict access to abortions.[257]

Conceivably, in some communities with limited medical facilities, a hospital's refusal to perform abortions would effectively restrict a woman's freedom of choice and impinge on her constitutionally protected right to decide in favor of abortion rather than childbirth. Under these circumstances, the federal courts would face a conflict between the woman's right to privacy and the physician's freedom of religion and conscience. Thus far, the Supreme Court has not intruded on the balance that Congress struck between the competing First and Fourteenth Amendment rights of privacy and religious freedom.

The Protection of Unborn Children. Beginning in 1982 senators Hatfield, Helms, and Jepsen and representatives Robert K. Dornan (R.-Cal.), Charles F. Dougherty (R.-Pa.), Hyde, Romano L. Mazzoli (D.-Ky.), and Fernand J. St. Germain (D.-R.I.) offered legislation "[t]o affirm the intrinsic value of all human life, to recognize the humanity of unborn children, and to ensure that the Federal Government not participate in or support abortions."[258] Despite the Supreme Court's finding in *Roe* v. *Wade* that the states lack authority to override the pregnant woman's rights "by adopting one theory of life,"[259] legislative proposals protecting unborn children explicitly recognize that human life begins before birth. These bills include policy statements that are at war with the Court's opinion that government cannot adopt a particular religious theory infringing on a woman's liberty to decide in favor of abortion. Indeed, several "right-to-life" bills that Senator Helms has introduced specifically reject the Court's constitutional judgment in *Roe*. In 1982 Helms introduced S. 2148, which declared that "scientific evidence demonstrates that the life of each human being begins at conception."[260] On January 3, 1985, Senator Helms offered his "Unborn Children's Civil Rights Act," proclaiming that "a right to an abortion is not secured by this Constitution."[261] Helms's legislation also rebuked the Supreme Court's failure to recognize that life begins at conception.[262]

Despite Senator Helms's verbal pyrotechnics, bills protecting the unborn child may be compatible with the Supreme Court's decision in

Harris v. *McRae.* If Congress does not have an affirmative duty to finance abortions, it can, theoretically, withhold federal funds for abortions to protect the lives of unborn children. Congress has a legitimate interest in protecting human life. Senator Helms's "Unborn Children's Civil Rights Act of 1985," for example, would prohibit the federal government from using public funds to "take the life of an unborn child," encourage and counsel women to terminate pregnancy, or support research on procedures to take an unborn child's life. Both sections include exceptions that permit public assistance for medical procedures necessary to prevent "the death of either the pregnant woman or her unborn child so long as every reasonable effort is made to preserve the life of each."[263] Two earlier bills that senators Hatfield and Helms introduced, S. 2372 and S. 2148 (1982), would also prohibit all federal agencies from performing abortions or entering into insurance contracts that reimburse patients for abortions, except when the mother's life would be endangered by carrying a child to term.

The "Unborn Children's Civil Rights Act" contains a "right-of-conscience provision" that would prohibit federally supported institutions from discriminating against employees who refuse to take an unborn child's life or who refuse to participate in insurance programs that cover such procedures. Employing congressional authority under section 5 of the Fourteenth Amendment, Helms's earlier bill (S. 2148) would obligate the states to recognize that human life begins at conception and prohibit the states from depriving all persons, including the unborn, of life without due process of law. Not unlike Senator Hatfield's 1982 proposal, the "Unborn Children's Civil Rights Act" provides that, should a lower federal court enjoin the enforcement of a state law or local ordinance protecting an unborn child's life, "any party in such a case may appeal to the Supreme Court."[264]

Clearly, the "Unborn Children's Civil Rights Act of 1985" and several earlier bills would forbid the federal government from performing or funding abortions, except in cases where the woman's or the fetus's life is at risk. Helms's previous bill (S. 2148) would require the states to recognize the senator's theory that human life begins at conception and would prohibit the states from denying the fetus's right to life without due process. While the funding restrictions probably would pass constitutional muster, the provision prohibiting federally operated facilities from performing abortions might in some circumstances (e.g., in the District of Columbia, federal territories, and U.S. military hospitals abroad) effectively limit a woman's right to obtain an abortion. Provisions requiring the states to recognize Senator Helms's theory of human life and prohibiting them from interfering with the fetus's right to life without due process would also run afoul of *Roe*. To the extent that such provisions interfere with a woman's privacy, that is, her right to choose abortion over childbirth, the proposed legislation is a statutory reversal of *Roe* v. *Wade*, a reversal that circumvents the constitutional-amendment process. By extending the Supreme Court's appellate jurisdiction to cases involving state and local "right-to-life" laws, Senator Helms and his congressional cohorts are inviting the Court to reopen the basic issues adjudicated in *Roe*.

The Legitimacy of Statutory Reversals of the Supreme Court's Constitutional Judgments

Statutes that reverse the Supreme Court's constitutional judgments in *Roe* and other abortion cases violate the constitutional-amendment process. They also interfere with the Court's function of promoting constitutional supremacy and the woman's fundamental right to privacy. However, most funding laws and several other statutes that Congress has enacted since 1973 are consistent with the Supreme Court's decisions in *Maher* v. *Roe* and *Harris* v. *McRae*. Some provisions of "informed-consent" statutes interfere with a woman's right to choose abortion free from governmental coercion. Right-of-conscience laws demonstrate the difficulty of balancing distinct and competing interests that the First and Fourteenth amendments protect. Several bills seeking to protect the rights of unborn children are difficult, if not impossible, to reconcile with the fundamental rights that the Court articulated in *Roe* v. *Wade* and *Doe* v. *Bolton*. Senator Helms's "Unborn Children's Civil Rights Act" is an open invitation to a new Supreme Court majority to reopen and reverse *Roe*.

Between 1973 and 1988 *Roe*'s congressional opponents have employed virtually every legislative device to limit the effects of the Court's abortion decisions. However, it would be erroneous to view the Court's critics as a monolithic bloc possessing a common legislative objective. While some members of Congress believe that the Supreme Court's abortion decisions are morally indefensible, others argue that the justices have misinterpreted the meaning of the term "liberty" in the Fourteenth Amendment. Still other senators and representatives believe that the justices should have exercised judicial self-restraint by leaving these complex and divisive public policy decisions to the people's elected representatives. Inasmuch as the Court has exercised its constitutional judgment, however mistaken, can members of Congress achieve their diverse policy objectives by restricting the federal courts' jurisdiction to decide future cases involving abortion rights?

Restrictions on the Federal Courts' Jurisdiction

Since 1974 a small but active group of senators and representatives has proposed restrictions on the federal courts' jurisdiction to decide abortion cases. Claiming authority under the exceptions and regulations and ordain and establish clauses,[265] representatives Phillip M. Crane (R.-Ill.), William L. Dickinson (R.-Ala.), John D. Dingell (D.-Mich.), Keith G. Sebelius (R.-Kan.), and Joseph D. Waggoner (D.-La.) have offered approximately fourteen bills to restrict the Supreme Court's appellate jurisdiction and the lower federal courts' jurisdiction to entertain cases involving state antiabortion laws.[266] Senator Hatch and representatives Ashbrook and David C. Treen (R.-La.) have submitted legislation to restrict the district courts' jurisdiction to enjoin any state or federal law that regulates abortions or limits the public funding of abortions.[267] Senator Helms and representatives Harold V. Froelich (R.-Wisc.), Hyde, and Mazzoli have proposed "human life" bills incorporating limitations on the district courts' jurisdiction to issue injunctions in cases involving state laws that regulate abortions, protect life from conception to birth, or prohibit the public funding of abortions.[268] In addition to claiming authority under the Judiciary Article, Senator Helms has cited section 5 of the Fourteenth Amendment as authority for his "human life" bill.

The first group of proposals is similar to bills removing the federal courts' jurisdiction over cases involving school prayer and school busing. During the Ninety-sixth Congress (1979), Representative Crane introduced H.R. 993, which provided that:

> [T]he Supreme Court shall not have jurisdiction to review, by appeal, writ of certiorari, or otherwise, any case arising out of any State statute, ordinance, rule, regulation or any part thereof, or arising out of any Act interpreting, applying, or enforcing a State statute, ordinance, rule, or regulation, which relates to abortion. The district courts shall not have jurisdiction of any case or question which the Supreme Court does not have jurisdiction to review [regarding abortion].[269]

Crane's proposal would deny litigants access to any federal forum to vindicate constitutional claims relating to state antiabortion laws. H.R. 993 and similar bills would leave the final determination of abortion rights to the states' judiciaries. These bills would vitiate the Supreme Court's authority to enforce the supremacy clause and provide a uniform interpretation of national law.

Almost four years before Crane introduced H.R. 993, in 1975, he called for legislation to strip the federal courts of their jurisdiction over state antiabortion cases. In addition to claiming constitutional authority and judicial precedent, Crane argued that jurisdictional legislation is an acceptable alternative to the more demanding and time-consuming process of amending the Constitution: "[T]his approach has the advantage of being easier to pass and quicker to implement. Instead of requiring a two-thirds vote of Congress plus ratification by three-fourths of the States, as would be required by a constitutional amendment, only a majority vote by both Houses of Congress and signature by the President is necessary."[270] Crane also intimated that his remedial objective was to reverse *Roe* v. *Wade,* but he doubted that the members opposed to the Court's decision had the votes necessary to prohibit abortion directly:

> Finally, it must be said that, from a political standpoint, an abortion measure that permits diversity stands a much better chance of passage than one which enunciates a hard-and-fast rule. Given the past precedents, it would seem to me that there is no reason why we should not proceed with a bill limiting Federal and Supreme Court jurisdiction over abortion as soon as possible.[271]

As Crane's remarks indicate, jurisdictional limitations would, in his judgment, free state courts to ignore the Supreme Court's decision in *Roe.*

Commenting on various jurisdiction-stripping proposals, Peter Rodino, chairman of the House Judiciary Committee, noted in May 1981:

> I find this approach to admittedly difficult legal and social policy issues to be totally without merit. The supremacy of the U.S. Constitution and the Supreme Court which interprets it cannot be altered by Members of Congress who are bent on trying to "correct" Supreme Court decisions with which they may disagree. There is an established procedure for amending the Constitution. . . . The back-door approach to creating change in constitutional law can only wreak havoc on the rights of citizens, the role of the courts, and the balance of powers between the Congress and the other equal branches.[272]

Echoing Rodino's comments, in February 1982 Senator Levin noted the opposition of the Conference of Chief Justices (of the states) to jurisdiction-stripping proposals. At their Midyear Meeting in Williamsburg, Virginia, on January 30, the conference adopted a resolution stating the reasons for its opposition. Without commenting on the merits of the Supreme Court's decisions, the chief justices argued that such bills presume that state judges "will not honor their oath to obey the United States Constitution, nor their obligations to give full force to controlling Supreme Court precedents."[273] Nevertheless, the chief justices concluded, the supremacy clause requires state judges to "give full force" to the Supreme Court's decisions. Jurisdiction-stripping proposals, therefore, would freeze the Court's current precedents. Absent a constitutional amendment, *Roe* v. *Wade* would remain "beyond the reach of the United States Supreme Court or state supreme courts to alter or overrule."[274]

Even some of the Court's critics have expressed serious reservations about legislation restricting the federal courts' jurisdiction. Commenting on such proposals in February 1982, Senator Barry Goldwater (R.-Ariz.) voiced his criticism:

> Now, I happen to believe the Federal courts have wrongly decided these subjects. I am strongly opposed to the breakup of neighborhood schools. I think the unborn baby is entitled to some legal protection. And I believe schoolchildren should be allowed a few moments of voluntary prayer.
> In my view, the Supreme Court has erred. But we should not meet judicial excesses with legislative excesses.
> It is contrary to the will of the framers. It is destructive of the Federal system. And it will result in the reverse outcome of what the Court's critics wish.[275]

In addition to arguing that the Framers granted Congress only limited housekeeping authority over the federal courts (under Article III, sections 1 and 2), Goldwater claimed that the Bill of Rights and the Thirteenth, Fourteenth, and Fifteenth amendments impose external limitations on congressional power. These external limitations, he observed, "point to the Federal judiciary as the intended arbiter of the Constitution."[276] In his judgment, jurisdiction-stripping proposals would irreparably harm the federal system by undermining the Supreme Court's function as the final arbiter of state legislation under the supremacy clause.[277] Furthermore, jurisdiction-stripping proposals are attempts to accomplish indirectly what the Constitution forbids Congress to do directly, namely, reverse the Supreme Court's constitutional interpretation through ordinary legislation.[278] Predicting that the proponents of such bills would rue the day they introduced legislation to curb the federal courts' jurisdiction, Goldwater concluded, "As sure as the sun will rise over the Arizona desert, the precedent will return to oppress those who would weaken the courts. If there is no independent tribunal to check legislative or executive action, all the written guarantees of rights in the world will amount to nothing."[279] Proposals that extinguish all federal jurisdiction over state antiabortion cases are inherently flawed because they alter the Framers' basic plan of government, change the balance of power between Congress and the Supreme Court, impair the Court's authority to enforce the supremacy clause, vitiate the individual's judicially protected constitutional rights, and circumvent Article V, which mandates that the states as well as Congress participate in amending the Constitution.

In contrast to the first type of jurisdictional legislation, which extinguishes all federal jurisdiction over state antiabortion cases, a second type prohibits the lower federal courts from issuing:

[A]ny restraining order or temporary or permanent injunction in any case

(a) involving or arising out of any Federal or State law or municipal ordinance that prohibits, limits, or regulates abortion (including any such law or ordinance relating specifically to abortion clinics or persons that provide abortions); or

(b) involving or arising out of any Federal or State law or municipal ordinance that prohibits, limits, or regulates the provision at public expense of funds, facilities, personnel, or other assistance for the performance of abortions.[280]

Senator Hatch's anti-injunction bill (S. 2138), which is similar to other proposals, presents several constitutional questions. As the bill applies to federal laws relating to abortion, S. 2138 would require a pregnant woman to seek a remedy against federal officials in a state court. However, according to the Supreme Court's decisions in *Ableman* v. *Booth* (1859)[281] and *Tarble's Case* (1872),[282] state courts are powerless to enjoin federal officials or interfere with their exercise of authority under federal law. As applied to federal laws restricting abortions, Hatch's bill leaves the pregnant woman seeking an abortion two options: (1) carry the child to term and challenge the act's constitutionality after she has given birth, or (2) have an illegal abortion and subject herself to criminal charges in order to challenge the constitutionality of the act. Both options burden the woman's constitutionally protected right to decide in favor of abortion free from compulsion. In effect, Senator Hatch's proposal requires a pregnant woman desiring an abortion to employ remedies that defeat the vindication of her fundamental right.

As applied to state laws prohibiting or restricting abortions, the pregnant woman who seeks an abortion must rely on state remedies to vindicate her right. Without assuming that state judges will be less hospitable than their federal brethren to women seeking abortions, the federal anti-injunction bill invites state legislatures to limit the remedies available to vindicate federally protected rights. In states that restrict or prohibit abortions, the legislature could also insulate restrictive abortion laws from the state courts' judicial scrutiny. Thus Senator Hatch's proposal conceivably leaves many women without an effective remedy either in a state or a federal court. The Hatch anti-injunction bill is an indirect means of burdening the vindication of a constitutionally protected right.[283]

While proponents of restrictions on the lower federal court's jurisdiction cite the Norris–La Guardia Act as precedent for anti-injunction bills, the act did not deny any due process rights, since other remedies were available in illegal labor disputes, including suits for damages and criminal prosecution.[284] Similarly, the Johnson Act of 1934, the Tax Injunction Act of 1937, and the Emergency Price Control Act of 1942 protected the individual's due process rights by leaving other effective remedies available to vindicate these rights. The Hatch proposal encourages the states to insulate their own laws from state-court review and leaves women without an effective remedy to challenge federal laws restricting abortions. Senator Hatch's approach is diabolically clever, but constitutionally tainted.

During the decade following *Roe* v. *Wade*, Senator Helms and representatives Froelich, Hyde, and Mazzoli offered a series of "human-life" bills. Although Representative Froelich offered the first "human-life" bill in 1973, Congress did not take any action until 1981, when the Senate Judiciary Committee reported Senator Helms's proposal, S.158.[285] As reported by the Judiciary Committee, S. 158 defined human life as beginning with conception. The bill then declared that the Fourteenth Amendment protects "all human beings."[286] Citing section 5 of the Fourteenth Amendment as authority for the legislation, S. 158 enjoins the states from depriving "persons of life without due process of law," from the time of conception.[287] The bill further acknowledges the states' compelling interest in protecting all persons "whom the State rationally regards as human beings." Similar to other human life legislation, S. 158 makes a series of findings that conflict with the Supreme Court's decision in *Roe* v. *Wade*. Senator Helms's proposal requires the states to give legal cognizance to a particular theory of life.

Unlike other simple human life bills, S. 158 proceeds to remove the lower federal courts' jurisdiction:

> [T]o issue any restraining order, temporary or permanent injunc-
> tion, or declaratory judgment in any case involving or arising from
> any State law or municipal ordinance that (1) protects the rights of
> human persons between conception and birth, or (2) prohibits,
> limits, or regulates (a) the performance of abortions or (b) the provi-
> sion at public expense of funds, facilities, personnel, or other assis-
> tance for the performance of abortions[.][288]

However, Senator Helms's bill does not restrict the Supreme Court's jurisdiction to review abortion cases arising in the states' courts. Finally, S. 158 provides for accelerated review of any challenges to the enforcement or constitutionality of the proposed act.[289]

Aside from the apparent conflict between the bill's findings and the Court's constitutional findings in *Roe*, the measure suffers defects similar to Senator Hatch's "anti-injunction" proposal. Essentially, S. 158 would require a pregnant woman seeking an abortion to turn to the states' courts for a remedy. Once again, state legislatures that enact restrictive abortion laws would have an opportunity to shield these enactments from the state courts' judicial scrutiny. Under these circumstances, a pregnant woman would face the same option that Hatch's proposal offers, namely, carry the child to term or challenge the state's law in a criminal proceeding following an illegal abortion. In either event, S. 158 burdens the due process right the Supreme Court established in *Roe* v. *Wade*.

If Senator Helms's human life bill burdens the pregnant woman's constitutional right to privacy under the due process clause, does section 5 of the Fourteenth Amendment authorize Congress to enact S. 158 and similar proposals? In *Katzenbach* v. *Morgan*,[290] Justice Brennan stressed that Congress could employ its enforcement powers to expand but not contract judicially defined equal-protection rights.[291] Applying the same analysis to fundamental due process rights, Congress lacks authority to diminish the judicially defined rights that the due process clause confers.[292] Furthermore, as Ronald Rotunda has argued, section 5 authorizes Congress to limit the states' interference with Fourteenth Amendment rights rather than restrict the federal judiciary's authority to interpret the scope of the privileges and immunities, due process, and equal protection clauses.[293] Section 5 does not grant Congress power to define Fourteenth Amendment rights and insulate human life bills from judicial review.

Conclusion: Justice Blackmun's Invitation
to a National Debate

On January 22, 1973, the United States Supreme Court invited Congress, the states, and the nation to debate abortion rights. By interpreting the Fourteenth Amendment's due process clause to include a right to privacy that encompasses a woman's decision of whether to end her pregnancy or bear her child, the Supreme Court invited politicians, theologians, lawyers, academicians, and the American people to respond to *Roe* v. *Wade*. Often cited, infrequently read, and usually misunderstood, *Roe* elevated the question of abortion from a state and local political issue to a national controversy that will not die. Justice Blackmun's majority opinion pricked the moral consciousness of the American people in a way that few Supreme Court decisions have since *Dred Scott*.

In *Roe*, the Court expanded the concept of privacy, which has evolved since 1923 to include marital, familial, and procreative rights. While the Supreme Court has declared that the right to marry, to use contraceptives, and to rear and educate one's children are fundamental liberties, it has denied that these rights are absolute. However, the Court has required the states to demonstrate that they have a compelling interest in regulating marriage, contraception, and procreation that justifies burdening fundamental liberties. Furthermore, the Supreme Court has applied strict scrutiny in determining whether the state's interest is genuinely compelling and whether the state's regulations are narrowly drawn to achieve its legitimate objectives. Finally, shortly before *Roe*, the Court transformed the right to privacy into an individual rather than a marital or familial liberty. For the first time, in *Roe*, the Court included a woman's right to end her pregnancy in a general and continually evolving concept of privacy rooted in the Fourteenth Amendment. As in other privacy cases, the Court denied specifically that a woman's right to decide in favor of abortion over childbirth is absolute. By creating a conditional right, the Supreme Court invited Congress and the states to test the legitimate scope of legislative power to regulate abortions. As the cases following *Roe* demonstrate, both Congress and the states have accepted the invitation. The current dockets of state and federal courts indicate that there will be a continuing dialogue between the Court and the people's representatives.

Since 1973 the Supreme Court has sustained some state regulations of abortion as legitimate expressions of a compelling governmental interest in protecting maternal health and preserving potential life. The Court has recognized the states' authority to restrict the performance of abortions to licensed physicians, to assure that physicians perform abortions under safe conditions, and to impose on physicians a duty to preserve potential life without increasing risks to the mother's life and health. However, the justices have voided regulations that burden the woman's right and that are not specifically related to a state's legitimate health policies. Finally, the Court has also sustained state and congressional authority to prohibit the use of public funds for both elective and therapeutic abortions. Since there is no affirmative governmental duty to fund abortions, the states and the national government can employ their taxing and spending powers to favor childbirth over abortion. As long as the government's funding policies do not interfere with the fundamental right or deny equal protection, the states and the national government need only demonstrate a rational relation between their policies and a legitimate interest in promoting human life.

In evaluating the legitimacy of congressional responses to *Roe* v. *Wade*, there are constitutional and institutional considerations that extend far beyond the Supreme Court's decisions. Although Congress and the states have plenary authority to amend the Constitution within the framework of Article V, some proposed antiabortion amendments would alter the relationship between the national government and the states. Proposals that confer concurrent power would invite judicial intervention in this political thicket, which is counterproductive to their sponsors' intentions. Some joint resolutions that confer concurrent power to restrict abortions in effect grant the states sovereign power to adopt more restrictive abortion laws than Congress, which could undermine the constitutional supremacy of national law in this area.

Legislative proposals to curb the federal courts' jurisdiction raise serious constitutional questions about the scope of congressional authority under Article III (sections 1 and 2) and section 5 of the Fourteenth Amendment. To the extent that these proposals burden judicially defined fundamental rights by making it more difficult for a woman to decide in favor of abortion, they are constitutionally suspect. Proposals that potentially deprive women of effective remedies to vindicate their rights are equally suspect. If there is any doubt about the remedial objectives of jurisdictional limitations on the federal courts' powers over abortion cases, Senator Helms's human life bill, S. 158, should satisfy a doubting Thomas. The human life bill rejects the Court's findings, declares the unborn to be persons under the due process clause, and removes the lower courts' jurisdiction to enjoin restrictive abortion laws.

Proposed limitations on the federal courts' jurisdiction should be examined in relation to other substantive legislation designed to restrict the effect of *Roe* and subsequent abortion decisions. Although funding restrictions are constitutionally palatable under *Harris* v. *McRae*, they have the effect of restricting the poor woman's ability to obtain an abortion. Most informed-consent proposals are reasonable measures to ensure that a woman's decision is voluntary and intelligent, but Humphrey's and Helms's bill includes a provision requiring a physician to recite a parade of horribles, which is designed to dissuade a woman from seeking an abortion. Many bills designed to protect the lives and rights of unborn children reject the Court's findings in *Roe*, proclaim that human life begins at conception or some other point prior to birth, embody a particular religious belief concerning the beginning of life, and infringe on the woman's right to decide in favor of abortion. Finally, freedom-of-conscience proposals attempt to reconcile competing First and Fourteenth Amendment rights, but, under particular circumstances, may prevent women from exercising their right to decide in favor of abortion.

Congress lacks authority under the Judiciary Article and the Fourteenth Amendment to adopt jurisdictional bills that burden judicially protected constitutional rights. Nor does it have legislative power under Article I, section 8, to adopt substantive measures that reverse the Supreme Court's constitutional judgments. Nothing in Article I, Article III or the Fourteenth Amendment authorizes Congress to circumvent the constitutional-amendment process, vitiate judicially protected constitutional rights, undermine the Court's function of maintaining constitutional supremacy and a uniform construction of national law, or alter the basic relationship between Congress and the Supreme Court. By reversing the Supreme Court's constitutional judgments through simple legislative majorities, *Roe's* opponents would alter the Framer's plan of government, evade the legitimate process of amending the Constitution, and deprive the states of their constitutional right to participate in changing the nation's fundamental law.

Epilogue
Constitutional Democracy, Judicial
Review, and Congressional Power
Over the Federal Courts
....

"Reconciling judicial review with American representative democracy," wrote Jesse Choper, "has been the subject of powerful debate since the early days of the Republic."[1] While advocates of judicial review argue that the federal judiciary has a responsibility to protect individuals and minorities against repressive, intemperate, and often transitory majorities, opponents criticize this uniquely American institution as inherently undemocratic. Constitutional review of popular choices by an irresponsible (appointed) and unresponsive (independent) judiciary vitiates governmental accountability to the people and undermines popular sovereignty. Alexander Bickel, for example, has criticized judicial review as "a deviant institution in the American democracy."[2]

As Choper admits, the continuing controversy over the legitimacy of judicial review partially depends on the disputants' theories of democracy, which are frequently vague and abstract. At a minimum, representative democracy requires that government is accountable to a broadly based electorate through regular and periodic elections. Second, government should be responsive to popular opinion, which finds expression through the electoral process. Third, electoral choices and governmental decisions are made according to the principle of majority rule, which requires that citizens' and representatives' votes receive equal weight or value. Although the people delegate specific powers to government, they retain sovereignty, that is, the ultimate power of decision. Popular sovereignty also implies that government derives its legitimacy from the people.

As an instrument of popular sovereignty, the legislature is the corner-stone of a representative democracy. The legislature's core function is to translate popular preferences into public policy. Despite various antimajoritarian features of the legislative process, Congress derives its primacy from the fact that it is a representative governmental institu-tion, that it operates according to principles of majority rule, and that legislators are subject to periodic, popular elections. Indeed, majority-rule democrats argue that the Framers were so committed to popular sovereignty that they deliberately assigned most of the national govern-ment's policy-making powers to Congress.

Despite legislative primacy in policy making, the Framers did not vest sovereign power in Congress or any other governmental institu-tion. Unlike the British Parliament, Congress does not possess preroga-tive power to alter the Constitution unilaterally or suspend its provis-ions during periods of emergency. Both the original Constitution and subsequent amendments place limitations on the exercise of legislative power. Moreover, the amendment process restricts majority rule and popular sovereignty by requiring extraordinary majorities to change the nation's fundamental charter. For two centuries, Americans have accepted restrictions on popular sovereignty by constitutionalizing ba-sic values, that is, by placing basic values beyond the reach of ordinary majorities.

The American constitutional system is an amalgam of liberal and democratic values; it is a compromise between majority rule and indi-vidual liberty. Congress has primacy in policy making, but it does not possess unlimited legislative power. The U.S. Constitution restricts the scope of congressional policy-making authority. Article I, section 9, for example, explicitly prohibits Congress from issuing bills of attain-der, taxing exports, or creating titles of nobility. Similarly, section 10 explicitly limits the states' powers. As every school child knows, the Bill of Rights restricts the exercise of congressional power. Today the Fourteenth Amendment imposes similar restrictions on the states' ex-ercise of power vis-à-vis individuals and minorities.

Conceding legislative primacy in policy making and Congress's repre-sentative character, is it possible to reconcile judicial review with popu-lar sovereignty? If a constitutional democracy incorporates competing principles of popular sovereignty and limitations on the popular will and the exercise of legislative power, the answer is "yes." Within the context of a constitutional democracy, the federal judiciary's core func-tion is to enforce constitutional norms and values, which include polic-ing the boundaries among governmental institutions as well as limiting the exercise of governmental power vis-à-vis individuals and minorities.

The federal judiciary's authority to enforce constitutional norms flows from the Judiciary Article, the supremacy clause of Article VI, the debates of the Federal Convention and the state ratifying conventions, and the language and the framing of the Judiciary Act of 1789. Despite the absence of an explicit textual commitment to the federal judiciary of constitutional review of congressional and state acts, the concept of judicial review is fundamental to the political system and pervades the framing of the Constitution. The Framers' basic remedial objective was to provide for constitutional supremacy and national authority, which were lacking under the Articles of Confederation. Rejecting a Council of Revision and congressional review of state acts, the Framers opted for judicial review as a means of promoting both constitutional supremacy and national authority.

Although some purists reject judicial review as incompatible with representative democracy, other majority-rule democrats accept the need to reconcile judicial review with popular sovereignty. As long as the federal judiciary derives its constitutional interpretations from the Constitution's text, some argue, there is little risk that the courts will interfere with Congress's performance of its core functions. If the federal judiciary exercises self-restraint, it will also avoid conflict with Congress, which will promote the courts' legitimacy, sustain public confidence in their neutrality and fundamental fairness, and enhance their ability to enforce judicial decisions. Or, as Justice Frankfurter argued, dissenting in *Baker* v. *Carr* (1962):

> The Court's authority—possessed of neither the purse nor the sword—ultimately rests on sustained public confidence in its moral sanction. Such feeling must be nourished by the Court's complete detachment, in fact and in appearance, from political entanglements and by abstention from injecting itself into the clash of political forces in political settlements.[3]

Admitting that the Constitution is often ambiguous, some "interpretivist" jurists concede the legitimacy of judicial construction based on the Framers' and Ratifiers' intent as well as the Constitution's text. In their attempt to reconcile judicial review and representative democracy, interpretivist scholars have devoted considerable energy to divining both the Framers' and Ratifiers' intent. While it is possible to discern their broad, remedial purposes, the search for the Framers' and Ratifiers' specific intentions is, often, a fruitless enterprise. Their record is fragmentary; they recorded little, and much has disappeared in the last two centuries.

On many important issues, the Framers and Ratifiers disagreed intensely with one another. Unable to reconcile their differences, the Framers chose ambiguous language. As Gouverneur Morris later admitted, he drafted various provisions of the Judiciary Article with deliberate ambiguity to secure their adoption without further cavil. Under the circumstances, it is impossible to determine the Framers' and Ratifiers' collective intent regarding the great clauses distributing power among the national government's branches and between the nation and the states.

If neither the text of the Constitution nor the Framers' and Ratifiers' discernible intentions provides the federal judiciary with a yardstick for its constitutional interpretation, in a constitutional democracy should appointed judges embody either their own or contemporary societal values in their constitutional judgments? Most interpretivists reject noninterpretivist judicial review as an interference with popular sovereignty and representative government. Unless the Framers and Ratifiers constitutionalized certain values, interpretivists claim, the federal courts should not interfere with policy judgments that the Constitution leaves to the discretion of Congress, the president, or the states. In the absence of a constitutional mandate, the federal judiciary should exercise restraint vis-à-vis representative institutions. Or, as District Judge Arlin Adams observed in *Atlee* v. *Laird* (1972), "courts serve democracy best by leaving the principal issues confronting the citizenry for decision to the political branches of the government."[4]

"[E]ven where original intent is clearly known to us," David Fellman wrote, "it may be wise to look upon it as only an aid to construction, and not as supplying a binding rule of interpretation."[5] Referring to *Coyle* v. *Smith* (1911), a case involving the equal status of the states in the union, Fellman argues that the decision was politically wise, despite the Convention's rejection of a proposal requiring Congress "to admit new states into the union on a plane of equality with existing states."[6] Although the Supreme Court's decision in *Coyle* is incompatible with the Framers' manifest intent, Fellman argues, it is a politically and constitutionally wise decision because the Court recognized the desirability of promoting "harmony among the states." In this case, Fellman concludes, "original intent provided the wrong answer."[7] Unlike the interpretivists, Fellman regards original intent as a yardstick or guideline rather than a binding rule of decision.

Not unlike Fellman, John Hart Ely accepts the necessity and desirability of noninterpretivist judicial review in maintaining the democratic process and protecting the rights of insular minorities. There are rights that deserve protection, Ely notes, even though the Constitution does not mention them. These rights—freedom of political expression, the right to vote without interference, the right to equal treatment and participation in the political process—are indispensable to maintaining representative democracy. Thus Ely defends the Warren Court's intervention in First Amendment cases involving freedom of expression since popular sovereignty requires an informed electorate, capable of judging congressional performance and holding the membership accountable for its decisions.

Similarly, Ely justifies the Supreme Court's decisions in the reapportionment and voting rights cases as assuring "that our elected representatives will actually represent."[8] As long as the Court's decisions promote democratic values, institutions, and processes, Ely argues, noninterpretivist judicial review is compatible with representative democracy and popular sovereignty. Indeed, Ely concludes that appointed judges rather than elected legislators should determine whether the democratic process has malfunctioned since judges are "comparative outsiders," need not worry about reelection, and can make more objective judgments than the people's representatives.

If the Court engages in noninterpretivist judicial review, Ely might argue, the justices should confine their intervention in the political process to maintaining the rules of representative democracy. Should the Supreme Court or the lower federal courts stray from their functions, there are legitimate checks that Congress can impose on errant justices and judges. In a constitutional democracy, congressional checks on the federal judiciary are the price of noninterpretivist judicial review. Congress has authority to propose amendments that reverse the constitutional judgments of the Supreme Court and the lower federal courts. Congress can expand or contract the size of the Supreme Court and other federal tribunals. Over time, the president and the Senate can alter the federal judiciary's personnel through the process of nomination, confirmation, and appointment of judges. Congress possesses the ultimate power to impeach and remove federal judges. As Gerald Ford once observed, "[A]n impeachable offense is whatever a majority of the House of Representatives considers it to be at a given moment in history; conviction results from whatever offense or offenses two-thirds of the other body [the Senate] considers to be sufficiently serious to require removal of the accused from office."[9] Admittedly, some democratic checks on the judiciary require extraordinary majorities to curb abuses of judicial power, but there is little question about the constitutional legitimacy of these methodologies.

Impatient with the constitutional process, the Supreme Court's critics argue that there is another effective, legitimate check on a judiciary that abuses its authority. The Constitution's Framers and Ratifiers, the critics claim, granted Congress authority to curb the Supreme Court's appellate jurisdiction and the lower federal courts' jurisdiction in cases involving constitutional as well as statutory claims. The ordain and establish and exceptions and regulations clauses are legitimate, democratic checks on a judiciary that has run riot. Employing this rationale, members of Congress have introduced hundreds of jurisdiction-stripping proposals since 1954. Thus far, Congress has not enacted a single measure restricting the Supreme Court's authority to decide cases involving constitutional claims.

The critics' claims to the contrary, a careful examination of the Constitution's framing and ratification does not reveal a clear intent to arm Congress with the power to restrict the Supreme Court's appellate jurisdiction in cases involving constitutional issues. Although the Framers and Ratifiers granted Congress plenary power to regulate the lower federal courts' jurisdiction, attempts to abolish all federal jurisdiction over specific constitutional claims would undermine the Framers' basic objectives. By closing the federal courts to litigants seeking to vindicate their constitutional rights, jurisdiction-stripping proposals would undermine constitutional supremacy, a uniform interpretation of national law, and the federal judiciary's obligation to protect the individual's rights against the incursions of the states and the national government. Jurisdiction-stripping proposals would also alter the basic relationship between Congress and the federal judiciary. Congress could employ such measures to shield its acts from the federal courts' constitutional review. Of course, Congress could allow the states' judiciaries to serve as the final arbiter of national legislation, which would undermine the basic logic of American federalism.

In addition to undermining the separation of powers, Congress could alter the federal system by shielding state acts from the Supreme Court's constitutional review. By stripping the Court of its appellate jurisdiction to review state acts, Congress would make the states the final arbiters of their own acts, which would invert the logic of American federalism. Congress could avoid this absurd outcome by granting the U.S. district courts and courts of appeals authority to determine the constitutionality of state actions. While this solution would preserve national authority, it would not promote a uniform construction of fundamental, constitutional rights. In many areas of policy making, federalism appropriately permits and encourages diversity. However, can a federal system long endure disparate and sometimes conflicting interpretations of constitutional rights? Such a system would vitiate the legal and political equality upon which majority rule and representative government rest. Moreover, conflicting constitutional interpretations would promote disharmony among the states. By gerrymandering the Supreme Court's appellate jurisdiction, proponents of jurisdiction-stripping legislation would restore the governmental principles of the Article of Confederation, whose defects were patently clear to the Constitution's Framers.

Considering the Framers' basic objective of assuring constitutional supremacy and the national government's authority over national, international, and transstate problems, it is highly improbable that they would have granted Congress the power to undermine the basic plan or structure of government. However, neither the language nor the Judiciary Article's framing and ratification clarifies the precise scope of congressional power over the federal courts' jurisdiction. Despite the ostensible clarity of the language of the ordain and establish and exceptions and regulations clauses, both provisions should be read in relation to the broad purposes of Article III and the supremacy clause of Article VI. Article III defines the subject matter over which the judiciary has jurisdiction in enforcing the hierarchy of law that the supremacy clause establishes. The drafting of Article III and the supremacy clause also affirms the Framers' understanding that the national judiciary would employ its power of judicial review to maintain the federal structure of government, police the boundaries among governmental institutions, and restrain the arbitrary exercise of power. A critical reading of the Convention's debates, a comparison of successive drafts of the Judiciary Article and other relevant constitutional provisions, and an analysis of the Framers' remedial intent and constitutional objectives indicate that Congress has broad, but not unlimited, authority to control the Supreme Court's appellate jurisdiction and the jurisdiction of the lower federal courts.

Throughout its history the Supreme Court has acknowledged broad congressional authority to regulate its appellate jurisdiction and virtually plenary power to control the lower federal courts' jurisdiction. However, the justices have never recognized congressional power to prevent the Court from entertaining and deciding constitutional claims. Despite differences between John Marshall and Joseph Story concerning the inherent nature of the Supreme Court's appellate jurisdiction, both carved out a role for the Court in protecting the Framers' and Ratifiers' plan of government, that is, federalism, the separation of powers, and limitations on governmental power vis-à-vis the individual. Both Marshall and Story assumed that the Court has a constitutional duty to police the boundaries between the states and the national government and among the national government's branches.

During John Marshall's tenure as chief justice (1801–1835) the Supreme Court adopted a theory of judicial review that emphasizes judicial enforcement of constitutional supremacy over Congress and the states. As an ardent nationalist, Marshall employed judicial review to enforce national authority over the states and create a uniform construction of national law. In fact, there is no decision between 1789 and 1835 holding that Congress has plenary power over the Supreme Court's appellate jurisdiction, and there is no decision holding that Congress has an affirmative duty to vest the entire federal jurisdiction in some Article III court.

Despite the Court's pronouncements suggesting that Congress has plenary power, these comments are dicta, since the cases turn on questions of statutory rather than constitutional construction. Some cases involve regulation of the mode of appeal rather than congressional power to restrict the Supreme Court's appellate jurisdiction. Several cases rest on the Eleventh Amendment's limitation on the federal judiciary's jurisdiction rather than the constitutionality of statutory restrictions under the exceptions and regulations clause. None of these cases involves questions of constitutional right. During the pre-Marshall and Marshall eras there were no binding precedents on the scope of congressional power to limit the Supreme Court's authority to decide constitutional questions.

With the exception of Morrison Waite's opinion in *The Francis Wright* (1882), since Marshall's tenure the Court has not rendered a binding decision on the scope of congressional authority over its appellate jurisdiction. Although Waite acknowledged congressional power to restrict the Supreme Court's appellate jurisdiction in admiralty to questions of law, he implied that the Fifth Amendment's due process clause imposes limitations on the exercise of congressional power under the exceptions and regulations clause. Since *The Francis Wright*, various Supreme Court and lower federal-court opinions imply that the habeas corpus provision, the prohibition on bills of attainder, and the Fifth Amendment impose limitations on congressional power. However, no federal court has imposed binding restrictions on Congress's authority to make exceptions to the Supreme Court's appellate jurisdiction.

Beginning with the enactment of the Judiciary Act of 1789, Congress acknowledged the Supreme Court's authority to promote constitutional supremacy, national power, and the individual's liberty. Although the authors of the Judiciary Act of 1789 left the determination of most federal questions to the states' judiciaries, they provided for appeal to the Supreme Court in those cases in which state courts uphold the constitutionality of state acts in preference to the U.S. Constitution, laws, and treaties. Despite various attempts to curb the Supreme Court's appellate jurisdiction, prior to 1868 Congress did not deprive litigants of an opportunity to vindicate their constitutional rights in a federal forum. Many jurists and scholars interpret the repealer act of 1868 as a restriction on the Court's habeas corpus jurisdiction. However, Chief Justice Chase interpreted the act as a regulation of the mode of appeal rather than an exception to the High Court's appellate jurisdiction.

Following the Civil War some members of Congress expressed their dissatisfaction with the federal judiciary by introducing legislation to curb federal jurisdiction. However, Congress steadily expanded the federal courts' jurisdiction and remedial powers. In addition to the civil rights acts, Congress enacted the Judiciary Act of 1875, which greatly enlarged the federal judiciary's federal-question jurisdiction. Between 1891 and 1932 Congress enacted legislation both contracting and enlarging the Supreme Court's appellate jurisdiction, but these acts were unrelated to dissatisfaction with the Court's decisions and did not interfere with the performance of its constitutional functions. Indeed, the Judges Act of 1925 promoted the Supreme Court's efficiency and function as an arbiter of American federalism by expanding the justices' discretionary power over their docket. Since 1789 Congress has not denied litigants seeking to vindicate their constitutional rights access to some federal forum.

Although recent attempts to curb the Supreme Court's appellate jurisdiction and the lower federal courts' jurisdiction and remedial powers are not unique, they are extraordinary and constitutionally questionable methods of expressing congressional dissatisfaction with the Court's constitutional judgments. Most jurisdiction-stripping proposals would Balkanize the federal judiciary, deprive the political system of a single, final arbiter of constitutional rights and powers, profoundly disturb the federal system's equilibrium, and burden individuals seeking to vindicate their constitutional rights. Some proposals would not alter the federal courts' jurisdiction concerning particular constitutional rights, but would deny the federal judiciary effective and, in some cases, indispensable remedies, without which the U.S. district courts could not protect the individual's rights. Jurisdictional and remedial legislation that alters the constitutionally mandated governmental structure or burdens individuals' fundamental rights represents an attempt to accomplish indirectly what the Constitution prohibits Congress from doing directly. These proposals are a subterfuge that circumvents the constitutional-amendment process, which is the only legitimate methodology to reverse the Supreme Court's constitutional judgments.

Frustrated in their attempts to secure constitutional amendments reversing the Supreme Court's school prayer, school busing, and abortion-rights decisions, congressional critics of *Engel* v. *Vitale* (1962), *Swann* v. *Charlotte-Mecklenburg* (1971), *Roe* v. *Wade* (1973), and subsequent decisions have pursued various legislative "alternatives" to reverse the effects of the Court's decisions. They have introduced bills to limit the Supreme Court's appellate jurisdiction over prayer, busing, and abortion. The critics have also proposed and Congress has enacted restrictions on the use of federal funds to promote desegregative busing and support nontherapeutic as well as therapeutic abortions. To the extent that these funding restrictions do not burden the individual's exercise of judicially protected constitutional rights, they are legitimate expressions of congressional dissatisfaction with the Court's decisions.

In addition to proposing constitutional amendments, jurisdictional restrictions, and funding restrictions, the Court's critics have sponsored measures to prohibit the federal district courts from using their equity powers to enforce the Supreme Court's abortion and school busing decisions. While Congress has authority to regulate the federal courts' remedial powers, can it employ legislative authority to prevent the federal judiciary from enforcing previously established constitutional rights? To the extent that Congress precludes the federal courts from employing either the most effective or indispensable remedies, it is interfering with the judiciary's power and core function of protecting the individual's constitutional rights in cases over which the federal judiciary has jurisdiction. Such legislation would burden the individual's enjoyment of constitutional rights, violate the separation of powers, and compromise judicial independence.

Similarly, Congress lacks authority to enact substantive measures, either under Article I, section 8, or section 5 of the Fourteenth Amendment, that reverse the Supreme Court's constitutional judgments through ordinary legislation. Senator Jesse Helms's "Unborn Children's Civil Rights Act," for example, would reverse *Roe* v. *Wade* by embodying a particular religious theory of human life and prohibiting the states and the national government from interfering with the fetus's right to life without due process. Helms's proposal burdens the pregnant woman's right to privacy and circumvents the constitutional-amendment process. Congress cannot use its legislative powers under Article I or its enforcement powers under section 5 of the Fourteenth Amendment to undermine or reverse the Supreme Court's interpretation of the rights that section 1 of the amendment protects. As the framing and ratification of the Fourteenth Amendment indicate, it is a restriction on the states' power to interfere with the rights of individuals and citizens rather than a limitation on federal jurisdiction and judicial power. If Congress disagrees with the Supreme Court's constitutional interpretation of the due process, equal protection, or other clauses, it can propose a constitutional amendment to reverse the justices' judgments. Although the amendment process is vexatious, it has the advantage of involving the states, whose interests the Courts' critics claim to represent.

Despite the different substantive and constitutional issues present in the school prayer, school busing, and abortion rights controversies, proponents of jurisdictional gerrymandering share a common objective, namely, reversing the Supreme Court's decisions. The proponents' tactics may vary according to the issue, but their primary objective remains constant, like Polaris. The Court's critics are committed to restoring prayer in the nation's public schools, prohibiting the use of school busing to achieve racial desegregation of the public schools, and either prohibiting most abortions or allowing the states to determine the availability of abortions. A secondary, related purpose is to curb the Supreme Court's power, that is, to prevent the justices from deciding issues that either Congress or the states should determine. When the Court exceeds its constitutional function, the critics conclude, Congress has authority to curb judicial usurpation of power by limiting the Supreme Court's appellate jurisdiction.

If the Supreme Court's critics are correct that the justices have exceeded their constitutional authority, usurped congressional and state power, interfered with other governmental institutions' performance of their core functions, and created rights that the Constitution does not warrant, their methodology for restraining the Court is questionable. Assuming that the Framers of the First Amendment would not have considered public school prayer a religious establishment, that the Fourteenth Amendment's authors did not intend to apply the establishment clause to the states, that the amendment's equal protection clause does not prohibit public school segregation, and that its due process clause does not encompass a woman's right to choose abortion over childbirth, the framing and ratification of the Judiciary Article belie the claim that congressional power over the Supreme Court's appellate jurisdiction is plenary. As long as the Supreme Court's critics adhere to their self-professed belief in original intent, they cannot support jurisdictional gerrymandering as a constitutionally legitimate methodology that the Framers' and Ratifiers' intended.

Despite the impassioned debate over the Framers' and Ratifiers' intent, the continuing struggle between Congress and the Supreme Court is more than an abstract debate among jurists, politicians, and constitutional scholars concerning original intent. It is a struggle over the Court's authority to define and enforce constitutional norms, values, and limitations on the exercise of governmental power in a constitutional democracy. It is a struggle for judicial independence that will continue long after the conflicts over school prayer, school busing, and state antiabortion laws have passed into oblivion.

Notes

....

Introduction

1   370 U.S. 421 (1962).
2   374 U.S. 203 (1963).
3   402 U.S. 1 (1971).
4   410 U.S. 113 (1973).
5   410 U.S. 179 (1973).
6   347 U.S. 483 (1954).
7   Bolt, Robert, *A Man For All Seasons* (New York: Vintage Books, 1966), at 37–38.

1   Congress, the Courts, and Federal Jurisdiction: Theoretical Perspectives

1   For an analysis of the many bills introduced in the mid-to-late 1950s limiting federal jurisdiction on federal and state loyalty and security programs as well as the defendants' rights and the administration of criminal justice, see Murphy, Walter F., *Congress and the Court: A Case Study in the American Political Process* (Chicago, Ill.: Univ. of Chicago Press, 1962); hereinafter cited as Murphy, *Congress and the Court*; see also Bator, Paul M., Paul J. Mishkin, David L. Shapiro, and Herbert Wechsler, *Hart and Wechsler's The Federal Courts and the Federal System*, 2nd ed. (Mineola, N.Y.: Foundation Press, 1973), at 360-362; hereinafter cited as Bator, *The Federal Courts*. Bator et al. claim that between 1953 and 1968 approximately sixty bills were introduced limiting federal jurisdiction in various areas. See also Schmidhauser, John R., and Larry L. Berg, *The Supreme Court and Congress: Conflict and Interaction; 1945–1968* (New York: The Free Press, 1972); hereinafter cited as Schmidhauser, *The Supreme Court*; and Pritchett, C. Herman, *Congress versus the Supreme Court: 1957–1960* (Minneapolis, Minn.: Univ. of Minnesota Press, 1961); hereinafter cited as Pritchett, *Congress versus the Supreme Court*.

Having failed to enact a constitutional amendment permitting prayer in public schools between 1962 and 1978, in 1974 the Supreme Court's critics introduced legislation curbing federal-court jurisdiction over the subject. In virtually every session of Congress since 1981 numerous jurisdictional bills have been introduced, but defeated.

With regard to desegregative busing, since the 92nd Congress, 1st Session (1971), several approaches have been advanced, including: constitutional amendments, e.g., H.J. Res. 620, 92d Cong., 1st Sess. (1971); limitations on the use of busing as a remedial tool, e.g., S. 528, 97th Cong., 1st Sess. (1981); and limits on federal-court jurisdiction over school busing, e.g., H.R. 81, 99th Cong., 1st Sess. (1985). Despite numerous efforts, Congress has not succeeded in depriving the federal courts of authority to order busing as a remedy for de jure segregation.

Similarly, regarding state antiabortion statutes members of Congress have introduced constitutional amendments, e.g., S.J. Res. 119, 93d Cong., 1st Sess. (1973), legislation restricting federal-court jurisdiction over the subject, and other statutory methods intended to limit the Court's abortion decisions. As early as 1973, Representative Froehlich introduced legislation limiting federal-court jurisdiction [H.R. 8682, 93d Cong., 1st Sess. (1973)].

2 Donald Morgan, Herman Pritchett, and John Schmidhauser generally argue that these jurisdictional proposals were responses to particular Supreme Court decisions. See Morgan, Donald G., *Congress and the Constitution: A Study of Responsibility* (Cambridge, Mass.: Belknap Press, 1966), at 5; hereinafter cited as Morgan, *Congress and the Constitution*; Pritchett, *Congress v. the Supreme Court*, at vii, 3–4, and 33–34; and Schmidhauser, *The Supreme Court*, at 4, 31–32, 148, and 149.

3 Walter Murphy recognizes that court-curbing legislation strikes at particular decisions, but also stresses the institutional consequences of such proposals. The Jenner-Butler bill [S.2646, 85th Cong., 1st Sess. (1957)], for example, was a response to the Supreme Court's decisions in *Watkins* v. *United States*, 354 U.S. 178 (1957), and *Yates* v. *United States*, 355 U.S. 66 (1957), but also represented an attack on judicial independence. See Murphy, *Congress and the Court*, at 161.

4 370 U.S. 421 (1962).

5 374 U.S. 203 (1963).

6 402 U.S. 1 (1971).

7 410 U.S. 113 (1973).

8 Since Henry Hart's lead article on congressional power over federal jurisdiction in 1953, there have been no fewer than fifty major law journal articles on this issue. See Hart, Henry M., Jr., "The Power of Congress to Limit the Jurisdiction of Federal Courts: An Exercise in Dialectic," 66 *Harv. L. Rev.* 1362–1402 (1953). [After the first entry all law journal articles are subsequently cited in the following manner: Hart, 66 *Harv. L. Rev.*] For a comprehensive list of the scholars who have drawn swords on the subject see Clinton, Robert N., "A Mandatory View of Federal Court Jurisdiction: A Guided Quest for the Original Understanding of Article III," 132 *U. Pa. L. Rev.* 741–855 (1984), n. 3, at 742–44. Subsequent to Clinton's article others have entered the list, including Amar, Akhil R., "A Neo-Federalist View of Article III: Separating the Two Tiers of Federal Jurisdiction," 65 *B.U.L. Rev.* 205–72 (1985); Castro, William R., "The First Congress's Understanding of Its Authority Over the Federal Courts' Jurisdiction," 26 *B.C.L. Rev.* 1101–26 (1985); Gunther, Gerald, "Congressional Power to Curtail Federal Court Jurisdiction: An Opinionated Guide to the Ongoing Debate," 36 *Stan. L. Rev.* 895–922 (1984); McAffee, Thomas B., "Berger v. The Supreme Court—The Implications of His Exceptions-Clause Odyssey," 9 *Dayton L. Rev.* 219–73 (1984); Nathanson, J. Edmond, "Congressional Power to Contradict the Supreme Court's Constitutional Decisions: Accommodation of Rights in Conflict," 27 *Wm. & Mary L. Rev.* 331–70 (1986).

9   Beginning with Alexander Bickel's *The Least Dangerous Branch* there has been a running battle over the Supreme Court's power of judicial review in a democracy. See Bickel, Alexander M., *The Least Dangerous Branch: The Supreme Court at the Bar of Politics* (Indianapolis, Ind.: Bobbs-Merrill Co., 1962); hereinafter cited as Bickel, *The Least Dangerous Branch*. In 1980, two important works appeared on this topic: Choper, Jesse, *Judicial Review and the National Political Process: A Functional Reconsideration of the Role of the Supreme Court* (Chicago, Ill.: Univ. of Chicago Press, 1980); hereinafter cited as Choper, *Judicial Review*; and Ely, John Hart, *Democracy and Distrust: A Theory of Judicial Review* (Cambridge, Mass.: Harvard Univ. Press, 1980).

10 The plenary view is often traced to Chief Justice John Marshall's opinion in *Cohens v. Virginia*, 19 U.S. (6 Wheat.) 264 (1821).

11 The mandatory view finds its parentage in Justice Joseph Story's opinion in *Martin v. Hunter's Lessee*, 14 U.S. (1 Wheat.) 304 (1816).

12 For an analysis on the limits of congressional power to control the Supreme Court's appellate jurisdiction and the jurisdiction of the lower federal courts, see, e.g., Sedler, Robert A., "Limitations on the Appellate Jurisdiction of the Supreme Court," 20 *U. Pitt. L. Rev.* 99–115 (1958); Eisenberg, Theodore, "Congressional Authority to Restrict Lower Federal Court Jurisdiction," 83 *Yale L.J.* 498–533 (1974); Rotunda, Ronald D., "Congressional Power to Restrict the Jurisdiction of the Lower Federal Courts and the Problem of School Busing," 64 *Geo. L.J.* 839–67 (1976); and Sager, Lawrence G., "The Supreme Court 1980 Term; Forward: Constitutional Limitations on Congress' Authority to Regulate the Jurisdiction of the Federal Courts," 95 *Harv. L. Rev.* 17–89 (1981).

13 Berger, Raoul, "Insulation of Judicial Usurpation: A Comment on Lawrence Sager's 'Court-Stripping' Polemic," 44 *Ohio St. L.J.* 611–47 (1983), at 611, 612; Alexander, Larry A., "Modern Equal Protection Theories: A Metatheoretical Taxonomy and Critique," 42 *Ohio St. L.J.* 3–68 (1981), at 11, 12; Perry, Michael J., "Noninterpretive Review in Human Rights Cases: A Functional Justification," 56 *N.Y.U. L. Rev.* 278–352 (1981), at 331; Black, Charles L., *Decision According to Law* (New York: W.W. Norton, 1981), at 17–19; hereinafter cited as Black, *Decision According to Law*; Lockhart, William B., Yale Kamisar, and Jesse H. Choper, *The American Constitution: Cases and Materials*, 5th ed. (St. Paul, Minn.: West Publishing Co., 1981), at 16; hereinafter cited as Lockhart, *The American Constitution*.

14 The due process clause of the Fifth Amendment may guarantee judicial process, but the supremacy clause provides that "the judges in every state be bound [by the Constitution], . . . anything in the constitution or the laws of any State to the contrary notwithstanding." U.S. Const. art. VI, § 2.

15 See Justice Story's opinion in *Martin v. Hunter's Lessee*, 14 U.S. (1 Wheat.) 304 (1816), at 328, 329.

16 Stebbins, Albert K., "The 'Vested' Powers of the United States Supreme Court," 10 *Marq. L. Rev.* 204–11 (1926), at 209; Crosskey, William W., *Politics and the Constitution in the History of the United States* (Chicago, Ill.: Univ. of Chicago Press, 1953), at 811–14; hereinafter cited as Crosskey, *Politics and the Constitution*; Clinton, 132 *U. Pa. L. Rev.*, at 845; and Caron, Wilfred R., "Federal Judicial Power: The Constitutionality of Legislative Encroachment," 34 *De Paul L. Rev.* 663–87 (1985), at 665, 674–75; Beck, Leland E., "Constitution, Congress, and Court: On

the Theory, Law, and Politics of Appellate Jurisdiction of the United States Supreme Court," 9 *Hastings Const. L.Q.* 774–850 (1982), at 833.

17 See n. 12 *supra.* for references to leading articles on external constitutional restraints on congressional power to regulate federal-court jurisdiction under Article III, sections 1 and 2.

18 Braveman, Daan, "The Standing Doctrine: A Dialogue Between the Court and Congress," 2 *Cardozo L. Rev.* 31–69 (1980), at 31; Sedler, 20 *U. Pitt. L. Rev.* at 109, 111–12; and Fraenkel, Osmond K., "The Functioning of the Lower Federal Courts as Protectors of Civil Liberties," 13 *Law & Contemp. Probs.* 132–43 (1948), at 137.

19 U.S. Const. art. III, §§ 1 and 2.

20 *Ex parte McCardle*, 74 U.S. (7 Wall.) 506, at 514 (1869).

21 Wright, Charles A., *Law of the Federal Courts*, 3rd ed. (St. Paul, Minn.: West Publishing Co., 1976), at 26; hereinafter cited as Wright, *The Federal Courts*; Friendly, Henry J., *Federal Jurisdiction: A General View* (New York: Columbia Univ. Press, 1973), at 1–2; hereinafter cited as Friendly, *Federal Jurisdiction*; Kent, James, *Commentaries on American Law*, 4 vols., edited by William M. Lacy (Philadelphia, Pa.: Blackstone Publishing Co., 1889), vol. I, at 361; hereinafter cited as Kent, *Commentaries*; and Rawle, William, *A View of the Constitution of the United States of America* (Philadelphia, Pa.: H. C. Carey and I. Lea, 1825), at 220.

22 Under the Judiciary Act of 1789 the jurisdiction of the federal district courts and circuit courts was rather limited. Section 8 of the act conferred exclusive jurisdiction on the district courts in U.S. criminal cases, admiralty and maritime cases, and suits against consuls and vice consuls. The district courts had jurisdiction concurrently with the states' courts in all suits that the U.S. Government brought where the amount was in excess of $100. Under section 11, the circuit courts had jurisdiction concurrently with the state courts in all civil cases at common law in excess of $500, suits involving aliens, and admiralty and maritime cases. They were granted exclusive jurisdiction in some U.S. criminal cases and jurisdiction concurrently with the district courts in other criminal cases. Finally, the circuit courts had removal jurisdiction from the states' courts in suits against aliens and in diversity cases. The federal courts were not granted general federal-question jurisdiction until the Judiciary Act of 1875. The Judiciary Act of 1789, ch. 20, 1 Stat. 73, 76–79 (1789).

23 Rostow, Eugene V., *The Sovereign Prerogative: The Supreme Court and the Quest for Law* (New Haven, Conn.: Yale Univ. Press, 1962).

24 On the conflict between majoritarian democracy and judicial review, see Choper, *Judicial Review*, chap. one, 4–59, esp. at 5; and Bickel, *The Least Dangerous Branch*, at 16, 18, 19.

25 Thayer, James B., "The Origin and Scope of the American Doctrine of Constitutional Law," 7 *Harv. L. Rev.* 129–56 (1893), at 144.

26 See Keynes, Edward, *Undeclared War: Twilight Zone of Constitutional Power* (University Park, Pa.: Penn State University Press, 1982), at 60–83, for an analysis of the plan of government, the political-question doctrine, and judicial self-restraint; hereinafter cited as Keynes, *Undeclared War*.

27 *Id.*, at 83.

28 Michael Perry observes that the ordain and establish and exceptions and regulations clauses are, perhaps, the only means that Congress can employ to reject noninterpretive judicial review. Thus, Congress and the president can reject the Supreme

Court's extraconstitutional value judgments. See Perry, 56 *N.Y.U. L. Rev.*, at 331. See also Black, *Decision Making According to Law*, at 17–18.

29   Schmidhauser, *The Supreme Court*, at 7; Pritchett, *Congress Versus the Supreme Court*, at vii; and Nagel, Stuart S., *The Legal Process from a Behavioral Perspective* (Homewood, Ill.: The Dorsey Press, 1969), at 275–79. Nagel's work is a careful empirical analysis of the relationship between congressional attempts to curb federal jurisdiction and judicial retreat from the very decisions that provided the stimulus for congressional action.

30   Wright's statement from the *Cornell Law Review* (1968) is reprinted in Lockhart, *The American Constitution*, at 15.

31   For a comprehensive statement of the interpretivist position, see Berger, Raoul, *Government by Judiciary: The Transformation of the Fourteenth Amendment* (Cambridge, Mass.: Harvard Univ. Press, 1977); hereinafter cited as Berger, *Government by Judiciary*. But, see Brest, Paul, "The Misconceived Quest for the Original Understanding," 60 *B.U.L. Rev.* 204–38 (1980), for a critique of the interpretivist argument. Brest rejects "strict textualism" and "strict intentionalism" as unworkable. While he accepts "moderate originalism," he concludes that a nonoriginalist approach is more effective in resolving contemporary conflicts. See Brest, 60 *B.U.L. Rev.* at 205.

32   Perry, Michael J., *The Constitution, the Courts, and Human Rights* (New Haven, Conn.: Yale Univ. Press, 1982).

33   Berger, *Government by Judiciary*, at 169, 170–71, 176–77, 181, 191–92, and 212–14. Berger articulates a narrow view of equal protection and due process. He defines both terms exclusively according to the Civil Rights Act of 1866 and interprets due process as entirely procedural. By adopting a broader view of equal protection and due process, he concludes, the Supreme Court has given the Fourteenth Amendment a wholly unintended substantive meaning and has invaded the states' and congressional authority.

34   U.S. Const. art. XIV, § 5. See also Hurst, Willard, "The Role of History," in Cahn, Edmond, ed., *Supreme Court and Supreme Law* (Bloomington, Ind.: Indiana Univ. Press, 1954), at 60.

35   However broad congressional power may be under section 5, Congress could not employ its authority to limit or vitiate the rights covered by section 1 of the Fourteenth Amendment. On congressional versus judicial power to define and protect the rights covered by section 1, see the following decisions: *South Carolina v. Katzenbach*, 383 U.S. 301 (1966); *Katzenbach v. Morgan*, 384 U.S. 641 (1966); and *Oregon v. Mitchell*, 400 U.S. 112 (1970). See also Wechsler, Herbert, "The Courts and the Constitution," 65 *Colum. L. Rev.* 1001–14 (1965), at 1005–6.

36   Ratner, Leonard G., "Congressional Power Over the Appellate Jurisdiction of the Supreme Court," 109 *U. Pa. L. Rev.* 157–202 (1960), at 157–59, 171–72, 173; Hart, 66 *Harv. L. Rev.*, at 1365. Hart notes that "an exception" should not be interpreted to allow Congress to destroy "the essential role of the Supreme Court in the constitutional plan." See also Eisenberg, 83 *Yale L.J.*, at 504–5.

37   247 U.S. 251 (1918). The decision continued to frustrate legislative efforts to regulate labor conditions until 1941, when the Court reversed its position in *United States v. Darby*, 312 U.S. 100 (1941).

38   As Harrison Tweed wrote in 1951, "What is at stake is a highly prized possession— a written Constitution with a Congress working under it as conscientiously as it

will and a Court sitting alongside it to assure that it acts as conscientiously as it should." Tweed, Harrison, "Provisions of the Constitution Concerning the Supreme Court of the United States," 31 *B.U.L. Rev.* 1 (1951), at 46. See also Kaufman, Irving R., "Maintaining Judicial Independence: A Mandate to Judges," 66 *A.B.A. J.* 470–72 (1980), at 470.

39 See Crosskey, *Politics and the Constitution*, at 642, 644–45; Strong, Frank R., "Rx for a Nagging Constitutional Headache," 8 *San Diego L. Rev.* 246 (1971), at 277, 279–80; Sager, 95 *Harv. L. Rev.*, at 43, 45–49.

40 See Choper, *Judicial Review*, chap. 4, 171–259.

41 Holmes, Oliver Wendell, *Collected Legal Papers* (New York: Harcourt, Brace, and Howe, 1920), at 295–96.

42 In a speech to the Kentucky State Bar, Associate Justice Stanley Reed pointed to the Court's function as an arbiter of federalism and the separation of powers. Reed, Stanley F., "Our Constitutional Philosophy Concerning the Significance of Judicial Review In the Evolution of American Democracy," 21 *Ky. B.J.* 136–46 (1957). See also Ratner, 109 *U. Pa. L. Rev.*, at 166, 184, 201; and Clark, Tom C., "The Court and Its Functions," 34 *Alb. L. Rev.* 497–502 (1970). Justice Tom Clark and Professor Ratner also stress that both Congress and the Court have recognized their independence in policing the federal system by acting with mutual restraint.

43 *Martin* v. *Hunter's Lessee*, 14 U.S. (1 Wheat.) 304, at 329–30 (1816).

44 See Stebbins, 10 *Marq. L. Rev.*, at 205–7; Crosskey, *Politics and the Constitution*, at 811–12, 813, 814.

45 *Martin*, 14 U.S. (1 Wheat.) at 329–30; Kent, *Commentaries*, vol. 1, at 346–48; Crosskey, *Politics and the Constitution*, at 809–17; Beck, 9 *Hastings Const. L.Q.*, at 832–34; Clinton, 132 *U. Pa. L. Rev.*, at 749–50, 838–39, 840; and Caron, 34 *De Paul L. Rev.*, at 669–70.

46 Caron, 34 *De Paul L. Rev.*, at 671–73.

47 On the exceptions and regulations clause as a distributing clause, see *id.*, at 669–70; Crosskey, *Politics and the Constitution*, at 915; and Clinton, 132 *U. Pa. L. Rev.*, at 844–45.

48 On the right of access to a federal forum, see Sedler, 20 *U. Pitt. L. Rev.*, 109, 113–14; and Sager, 95 *Harv. L. Rev.*, at 74.

49 Prescott, Arthur T., *Drafting the Federal Constitution: A Rearrangement of Madison's Notes, etc.* (Baton Rouge, La.: Louisiana State Univ. Press, 1941). John Rutledge, Roger Sherman, Luther Martin, and Pierce Butler opposed the creation of lower federal courts. *Id.*, at 654–57.

50 *Id.* James Madison, James Wilson, John Dickinson, Nathanial Gorham, and Gouverneur Morris argued the necessity for creating lower federal courts. Gorham, in particular, cited the prize courts under the Articles of Confederation as precedent for a federal judiciary.

51 Farrand, Max, ed., *The Records of the Federal Convention of 1787*, rev. ed. (New Haven, Conn.: Yale Univ. Press, 1966), vol. 2, 431 (Madison, August 27), 433 (Mason, August 27); hereinafter cited as Farrand, *Records of the Federal Convention*. As the records indicate, there were differences of opinion regarding the scope of congressional power to limit jurisdiction over questions of law versus questions of fact. Paul Bator argues that the exceptions and regulations clause is probably best understood as giving Congress some control over the Supreme Court's power to reverse a jury's verdict in civil cases. Bator, *Federal Courts*, at 21. However, this

view is hotly disputed. See also Justice Story's opinion in *Martin* v. *Hunter's Lessee*, 14 U.S. (1 Wheat.) 304, at 330 (1816) for a succinct statement of the mandatory view.

52 See Hamilton, Alexander, James Madison, and John Jay, *The Federalist*, edited by Jacob E. Cooke (Middletown, Conn.: Wesleyan Univ. Press, 1961), at 521–30 (No. 78, Hamilton); hereinafter cited as Hamilton, *Federalist*. See also Kaufman, 66 *A.B.A. J.*, at 470, 472; Ratner, 109 *U. Pa. L. Rev.*, at 160–61.

53 Alexander, 42 *Ohio St. L.J.*, at 11, 12; Berger, 44 *Ohio St. L.J.*, at 612–13; Perry, 56 *N.Y.U. L. Rev.*, at 331–34; Black, *Decisions According to Law*, at 17–18, 37–38; and Perry, *The Constitution*, at 128–30.

54 410 U.S. 113 (1973).

55 *Id.* See Justice Rehnquist's dissenting opinion, at 171–77. Rehnquist criticizes the majority's opinion for creating rights that the Fourteenth Amendment's Framers and Ratifiers never contemplated, for reviving the discredited due-process analysis of *Lochner*, and for invading the states' power to enact public health regulations.

56 See Bickel, *Least Dangerous Branch*, at 16, 18, 19; and Choper, *Judicial Review*, at 4–6.

57 Bickel disputes this position, noting, "The anxiety [exists], not so much that the judicial judgment will be ignored, as that perhaps it should but will not be." *Least Dangerous Branch*, at 184.

58 See, for example, John Francis Mercer's "Essays By a Farmer," Essay No. 6 (April 1, 1788), in Storing, Herbert J., ed., *The Complete Anti-Federalist* (Chicago, Ill.: Univ. of Chicago Press, 1981), vol. 5, at 53–54; hereinafter cited as Storing, *The Complete Anti-Federalist*. See also Samuel Chase's "Notes of Speeches Delivered to the Maryland Ratifying Convention," April 1788, in Storing, vol. 5, at 84–85; "Letters of Agrippa," probably James Winthrop (Massachusetts Gazette, January 1, 1788), in Storing, vol. 5, at 88–89; Federal Farmer, "Letters to a Republican," (Letter No. 3, October 10, 1787), in Jensen, Merrill, ed., *The Documentary History of the Ratification of the Constitution* (Madison, Wisc.: State Historical Society of Wisconsin, vols. 1–2, 1976; vol. 3, 1978; vol. 13, 1981; vol. 14, 1983), vol. 14, at 41–42; hereinafter cited as Jensen, *Documentary History*; George Mason, in the Virginia Convention (June 11, 1788), in Elliot, Jonathan, *The Debates in the Several State Conventions on the Adoption of the Federal Constitution*, 5 vols. (Philadelphia, Pa.: J.B. Lippincott Co., 1836), book 1, vol. 3, at 266, 521–22; hereinafter cited as Elliot, *Debates in the State Conventions*; and Luther Martin, to the Maryland House of Representatives (November 29, 1787), in Farrand, *Records of the Federal Convention*, vol. 3, at 152, 156.

59 Hamilton, *Federalist*, 522–23 (No. 78, Hamilton); James Madison, in the Virginia Convention (June 20, 1788), emphasized the concurrent jurisdiction of state courts over federal questions, in Elliot, *Debates in the State Convention*, book 1, vol. 3, at 535–36; Roger Sherman, New Hampshire Gazette (December 4, 1788), underscored the limited jurisdiction of federal courts, in Ford, Paul L., *Essays on the Constitution of the United States* (Brooklyn, N.Y.: Historical Printing Club, 1892), at 240–41; and James Wilson, in the Pennsylvania Convention, focused on judicial power as a means of promoting popular sovereignty by checking congressional and presidential abuses of power, in Elliot, at 445–46. The federalist argument is somewhat disingenuous since elsewhere Hamilton, Madison, and Wilson describe the federal courts as instruments of national sovereignty, a protection against the

states' encroachment on national power, and a safeguard against local bias and interstate conflict.

60 See *McCulloch* v. *Maryland,* 17 U.S. (4 Wheat.) 316, at 407 (1819).

61 In a letter from Gouverneur Morris to Timothy Pickering (December 22, 1814), in Elliot, *Debates in the State Conventions,* vol. 1, 507.

62 Taylor, Telford, "Limiting Federal Court Jurisdiction: The Unconstitutionality of Current Legislative Proposals," 65 *Judicature* 199–207 (1981), at 200; Hart, 66 *Harv. L. Rev.,* at 1364–65.

63 See Ratner, 109 *U. Pa. L. Rev.,* at 941–42; and Eisenberg, 83 *Yale L.J.,* at 504–6.

64 Merry, Henry J., "Scope of the Supreme Court's Appellate Jurisdiction: Historical Basis," 47 *Minn. L. Rev.* 53–69 (1962), at 63. Merry states that the Judiciary Act of 1789 affirms the Supreme Court's broad jurisdiction to review questions of law.

65 Ch. 20, 1 Stat. 73, at 85–86 (1789).

66 Crosskey, *Politics and the Constitution,* at 818–20, 1029–33.

67 Braveman, 2 *Cardozo L. Rev.,* at 53; Sager, 95 *Harv. L. Rev.,* at 68–70, 78–80; Brilmayer, Lea, and Stefan Underhill, "Congressional Obligation to Provide a Forum for Constitutional Claims: Discriminatory Jurisdictional Rules and the Conflict of Laws," 69 *Va. L. Rev.* 819–49, at 820, 821. See also Gunther, 36 *Stan. L. Rev.* Gunther challenges the argument that the states' courts will defend individual rights less vigorously than the federal courts. Indeed, judges in California and New York have been more vigorous than their brethren on the federal bench.

68 Paul Bator reports that between 1953 and 1968 members of Congress introduced more than 60 bills to limit federal-court jurisdiction, but none were enacted. See Bator, *The Federal Courts,* at 360.

69 Norris-La Guardia Act, Ch. 90, 47 Stat. 70 (1932); Johnson Act, Ch. 283, 48 Stat. 775 (1934); Tax Injunction Act, Ch. 726, 50 Stat. 738 (1937); Emergency Price Control Act, Ch. 26, 56 Stat. 767 (1942); Portal-to-Portal Act, Ch. 52, 61 Stat. 84 (1947).

70 159 F. 2d 254 (2nd Cir. 1948).

71 80 U.S. (13 Wall.) 128, at 146–47 (1872).

72 Even Ralph Rossum, who supports the plenary view, admits that the Court has addressed this issue directly only once, in *Ex parte McCardle.* See Rossum, Ralph A., "Congress, the Constitution, and the Appellate Jurisdiction of the Supreme Court: The Letter and the Spirit of the Exceptions Clause," 24 *Wm. & Mary L. Rev.* 385–428 (1983), at 394.

73 73 U.S. (6 Wall.) 318 (1868), denial of motion to dismiss; 74 U.S. (7 Wall.) 506 (1869), decision reported.

74 *Id.,* at 514.

75 Judiciary Act of 1789, Ch. 20, 1 Stat. 73 (1789).

76 At the very end of his opinion, Chase implied that *McCardle* turns on a statutory construction rather than a question of congressional power to limit the Court's appellate jurisdiction. *McCardle,* 74 U.S., at 515.

77 75 U.S. (8 Wall.) 85 (1869).

78 *Id.,* at 102–3.

79 U.S. Const. art I, § 9. See, e.g., Ratner, 27 *Vill. L. Rev.;* Rotunda, 64 *Geo. L.J.*

80 See Black, Charles L., *Structure and Relationship in Constitutional Law* (Baton Rouge, La.: Louisiana State Univ. Press, 1969); hereinafter cited as Black, *Structure and Relationship;* Wisdom, John Minor, "The Frictionmaking, Exacerbating, Politi-

cal Role of the Federal Courts," 21 *Sw. L.J.* 411–28 (1967); Parker, John J., "Federal Jurisdiction and Recent Attacks Upon It," 18 *A.B.A. J.* 433–39, at 479 (1932); Ratner, 109 *U. Pa. L. Rev.*; Beck, 9 *Hasting Const. L.Q.*

81 See Ratner, 109 *U. Pa. L. Rev.*; 27 *Vill. L. Rev.*; and Eisenberg, 83 *Yale L.J.*

82 Ratner, 109 *U. Pa. L. Rev.*, at 171–72.

83 Farrand, *Records of the Federal Convention*, vol. 2, at 425, 431.

84 Ratner, 109 *U. Pa. L. Rev.*, at 171–73.

85 Eisenberg, 83 *Yale L.J.*, at 501, 504–5, 513, 514, 532–33. For a further analysis of the Framers' intentions regarding the Supreme Court's functions, see chapter 2.

86 *Id.*

87 Crosskey, *Politics and the Constitution*, at 609.

88 See Sager, 95 *Harv. L. Rev.*, at 79–80, 82; Wisdom, 21 *Sw. L.J.*, at 421, 422; and Parker, 18 *A.B.A. J.*, at 277, 278. See also *Tarble's Case*, 80 U.S. (13 Wall.) 397, at 403, 404, 407 (1872).

89 Black, *Structure and Relationship*, at 25. However, Black maintains that congressional power over federal jurisdiction is a democratic remedy to judicial decisions that interfere with the legislative function. See Black, *Decision According to Law*, at 17–19. Logically, then, Congress is the ultimate arbiter of national rights.

90 Ratner, 27 *Vill. L. Rev.*, at 929–32, 935–36.

91 320 U.S. 81 (1943).

92 323 U.S. 214 (1944).

93 Sedler, 20 *U. Pitt. L. Rev.*, at 109.

94 Fraenkel, 13 *Law and Contemp. Probs.*, at 137.

95 Sager, 95 *Harv. L. Rev.*, 68, 69, 74–77.

96 Haines, Charles Grove, "Judicial Review of Acts of Congress and the Need for Constitutional Reform," 45 *Yale L.J.* 816–56 (1936), at 849–50; Norris, William A., and Julian Burke, "Congress and the Supreme Court's Appellate Jurisdiction," 35 *L.A. Bar Bul.* 212–15, 229–31 (1960), at 214, 215.

97 The structuralist position does not answer the argument that Congress can employ the exceptions and regulations and ordain and establish clauses to check the federal courts' interference with the authority of the states to make policy within their sphere of constitutional competence.

98 12 *Sargeant and Rawle* (Pa. S.Ct.) 300 (1825).

99 5 U.S. (1 Cranch) 137 (1803).

100 *Eakin*, 12 *Sargeant and Rawle*, at 342–58 (1825) (Gibson, dissenting).

101 See Keynes, *Undeclared War*, at 62–64; and Rostow, Eugene V., "The Democratic Character of Judicial Review," 66 *Harv L. Rev.* 193–224 (1952), at 212, 213, 223–24.

102 See Gunther, 36 *Stan. L. Rev.*, at 900, for a description of the quest for external restraints.

103 Beck, 9 *Hastings Const. L.Q.*, at 775; Braveman, 2 *Cardozo L. Rev.*, at 53; Brilmayer, 69 *Va. L. Rev.*, at 820; Rotunda, 64 *Geo. L.J.*, at 851, 852; Sager, 95 *Harv. L. Rev.*, at 68, 70; "Filling the Void: Judicial Power and Jurisdictional Attacks on Judgments," 87 *Yale L.J.* 164–224 (1977), at 194; and "Removal of Supreme Court Appellate Jurisdiction: A Weapon Against Obscenity?" 1969 *Duke L.J.* 291–325 (1969), at 310–11.

104 Rotunda, 64 *Geo. L.J.*, at 851.

105 See Bator, 27 *Vill. L. Rev.*, at 1034.

106 Rotunda, 64 *Geo. L.J.*, at 851.

107 Bator, 27 *Vill. L. Rev.*, at 1034–35. See also Redish, 27 *Vill. L. Rev.*, at 916–17.

108 Van Alstyne, William W., "A Critical Guide to Ex Parte McCardle," 15 *Ariz. L. Rev.* 229–69 (1973), at 265.

109 Redish, 27 *Vill. L. Rev.*, at 917.

110 In *Hunter* v. *Erickson*, 393 U.S. 385 (1969), and *Washington* v. *Seattle School Dist. No. 1*, 458 U.S. 457 (1982), the majority argued that restricting the governmental process or changing the level of decision making in a racially burdensome manner violates the equal protection concept. But one must demonstrate that the burden is intentional. There is considerable debate about applying these arguments to categories of fundamental rights that do not involve racial or other suspect classifications.

111 Lawrence Sager denies that there is an equal-protection right to access to a federal forum (under the Fifth Amendment's due process clause). However, he does claim that attempts to burden a particular right by selectively denying access raises due process issues. The difference is subtle, but important because litigants must demonstrate in each case that the legislature intends to injure a particular right. See Sager, 95 *Harv L. Rev.*, at 78–80.

112 *Id.*, at 85. As Sager argues, if there is a federally protected right, there must be effective relief. Otherwise, the right to a judicial hearing is meaningless. However, the litigant must show that the remedy is indispensable or, at least, more effective than other remedies in vindicating the relevant constitutional rights.

113 Given the Warren and Burger courts' reliance on the equal protection and due process clauses to secure individual rights, concludes Robert Clinton, it is hardly surprising that scholars have turned to equal protection analysis in the quest for limits on congressional power over the Court. See Clinton, 132 *U. Pa. L. Rev.*, at 916. See also, Tribe, Laurence H., "Jurisdictional Gerrymandering: Zoning Disfavored Rights Out of the Federal Courts," 16 *Harv. C.R. C.L.L. Rev.* 129–56 (1981).

114 U.S. Const. preamble.

115 5 U.S. (1 Cranch) 137, at 177 (1803).

116 See *McCulloch* v. *Maryland*, 17 U.S. (4 Wheat.) 316, at 404 (1819), for a statement of Marshall's view that the Framers intended the Constitution to be a general plan of government rather than a prolix legal code.

117 *Myers* v. *United States*, 272 U.S. 52 (1926), at 292, 293 (Brandeis, dissenting).

2 Jurisdiction and Judicial Review: The Framers' Perspective

1 Elliot, *Debates in the State Conventions*, vol. 1, at 506–7 (Morrisania, December 22, 1814).

2 *Articles of Confederation*, art. 9.

3 *Id.* art. 4.

4 Corwin, Edward S., "The Progress of Constitutional Theory between the Declaration of Independence and the Meeting of the Philadelphia Convention," 30 *Amer. Hist. Review* 511–36 (1925), at 514, 522–23; Wood, Gordon S., *The Creation of the American Republic, 1776–1787* (Chapel Hill: Univ. of North Carolina Press, 1969), at 150–51, 154–55; hereinafter cited as Wood, *Creation*; Sharp, Malcolm, "The

Classical American Doctrine of the Separation of Powers," 2 *Chi. L. Rev.* 385–436 (1935), at 395–96, 397, 399, 402, 417; and Warren, *Making of the Constitution*, at 46.

5 Bishin, William R., "Judicial Review in Democratic Theory," 50 *S. Cal. L. Rev.* 1099–1137 (1977), at 1116–18; and Hayek, F. A., *The Constitution of Liberty* (Chicago: Univ. of Chicago Press, 1960).

6 See Berger, Raoul, *Congress Versus the Supreme Court* (Cambridge, Mass.: Harv. Univ. Press, 1969), at 104; hereinafter cited as Berger, *Congress v. the Supreme Court*. Of the fifty-five delegates, Berger notes that twenty-six favored, six opposed, and the rest did not express any opinion on judicial review.

7 Farrand, *Records of the Federal Convention*, vol. 2, at 76 (Madison's *Notes*, July 21).

8 *Id.*, at 78 (Madison's *Notes*, July 21).

9 *Id.*, at 93 (Madison's *Notes*, July 23).

10 Testifying before the Senate Judiciary Committee on President Roosevelt's Court-packing plan in 1937, Edward Corwin said: "[The] people who say the framers intended [judicial review] are talking nonsense, and the people who say they did not intend it are talking nonsense." *U.S. Congress, Senate, Committee on the Judiciary*, Hearings on Reorganization of the Federal Judiciary, on S. 1392, 75th Congress, 1st Session, Part 2, March 17 to March 20, 1937, at 176.

11 Bator, *The Federal Courts*, at 9.

12 Levy, Leonard, "Judicial Review, History, and Democracy: An Introduction," in Leonard Levy, ed. *Judicial Review and the Supreme Court* (New York: Harper and Row, 1967), at 10–11, hereinafter cited as Levy, *Judicial Review*.

13 Crosskey, *Politics and the Constitution*, at 983, 984–90; and Schmidhauser, *The Supreme Court*, at 25–26.

14 Berger, *Congress v. the Supreme Court*, at 34–36, 78, 117–18; and Abraham, Henry J., *The Judicial Process: An Introductory Analysis of the Courts of the United States, England, and France*, 3rd ed. (London: Oxford Univ. Press, 1975), at 304–6.

15 See Beck, 9 *Hastings Const. L.Q.*, at 781. Beck also argues that the exceptions and regulations clause has no plain meaning. Rather, it should be read in relation to judicial review, the separation of powers, checks and balances, and federalism.

16 Farrand, *Records of the Federal Convention*, vol. 1, at 18 (Madison's *Notes*, May 29).

17 *Id.*, at 19; and Hutson, James H., ed., *Supplement to Max Farrand's The Records of the Federal Convention of 1787* (New Haven, Conn.: Yale Univ. Press, 1987), at 27 (Bedford, May 29). Bedford reports Randolph's criticisms of the Articles and proposed remedies including national judicial power to resolve disputes among the states, with the exception of territorial conflicts, and power to determine the boundaries between state and national authority.

18 Farrand, *Records of the Federal Convention*, vol. 1, at 21–22.

19 One can argue that there is little need to empower Congress to limit the proposed courts' jurisdiction since Randolph's resolution provided for relatively limited jurisdiction. There is no indication of judicial review over the full range of national legislative powers. However, Randolph's nineteen resolutions are a starting point rather than a comprehensive articulation of national power—legislative, executive, or judicial.

20 As Farrand notes, Pinckney's plan was eventually submitted to the Committee of

Detail. But the plan does not appear among the Convention's records. Since there is considerable doubt about whether the copy that Pinckney later sent to John Quincy Adams is the original plan, the author relies upon Farrand's reconstruction of Pinckney's "original" proposal. The draft that Pinckney submitted to Adams in 1818, as Farrand concludes, bears a "striking resemblance to the draft reported by the Committee of Detail on August 6." See Farrand, *Records of the Federal Convention*, vol. 3, at 595, 601–4.

21 *Id.*, at 608.

22 *Id.*, at 600, 608, and 117.

23 *Id.*, vol. 1, at 124 (Madison's *Notes*, June 5).

24 Jensen, *Documentary History*, vol. 1, at 250.

25 *Id.* Jensen remarks that, in addition to Paterson, Roger Sherman and Oliver Ellsworth (Connecticut), John Lansing, Jr., and Robert Yates (New York), John Dickinson (Delaware), and possibly Luther Martin (Maryland) were probably involved in drafting the New Jersey Plan. Whether they were directly involved, they all opposed a highly centralized government.

26 *Id.*, at 252; and Farrand, *Records of the Federal Convention*, vol. 1, at 244 (Madison's Notes and King, June 19).

27 Jensen, *Documentary History*, vol. 1, at 251.

28 *Id.*

29 Farrand, *Records of the Federal Convention*, vol. 3, at 616.

30 *Id.*

31 Jensen, *Documentary History*, vol. 1, at 254, 255; and Farrand, *Records of the Federal Convention*, vol. 3, at 618. The speech was variously recorded by Hamilton, Madison, Robert Yates, Lansing, and Rufus King. See Jensen, at 253.

32 Farrand, *Records of the Federal Convention*, vol. 3, at 626.

33 *Id.*

34 One must remember that Hamilton's draft of a constitution did not appear until the last days of the Convention. Nonetheless, his speech of June 18 provides for a supreme court and lower courts with jurisdiction over revenue and prize cases as well as cases involving foreign citizens. In one copy of his speech, Hamilton is less specific, urging jurisdiction over "all matters of general concern." By comparing various transcriptions, Farrand concludes that the general definition is as plausible as the specific definition reported above. See Farrand, *Records of the Federal Convention*, vol. 3, at 618.

35 See Bator, *The Federal Courts*, at 20; Clinton, 132 *U. Pa. L. Rev.*, at 759–61; and Levy, Jerome T., "Congressional Power Over the Appellate Jurisdiction of the Supreme Court: A Reappraisal," 22 *N.Y.U. Intramural L. Rev.* 178–207 (1967), at 180.

36 Prescott, *Drafting the Federal Constitution*, at 654–55.

37 Farrand, *Records of the Federal Convention*, vol. 1, at 124.

38 *Id.*

39 *Id.*, vol. 3, at 408. On February 25, 1804, as Judge Chase's defense attorney in an impeachment trial before the U.S. Senate, Luther Martin confirmed the Framers' distrust of state judiciaries to enforce federal over state laws. Inasmuch as Martin defended the states' sovereignty throughout the Convention, his later comment adds credibility to the view that the Framers intended the Supreme Court to enforce constitutional supremacy.

40 *Id.*, vol. 1, at 125.

41 *Id.*

42 *Id.*, at 226, 230, 231 (*Journal*, June 13). Although there are minor differences in the several documents that comprise the *Journal* for this date, they corroborate one another on the main points of the debate. Both Madison's *Notes* and Yates' record substantiate the *Journal*.

43 *Id.*, at 232, 238 (Madison's *Notes* and Yates, June 13). Randolph's concern with the rights of foreigners can be traced to Virginia's (as well as several other states') failure to honor the Treaty of Paris (1783), which protected the property rights of British subjects who had remained loyal to the Crown. See Corwin, 30 *Amer. Hist. Rev.*, at 515; Wood, *Creation*, at 150–51, 154–55; and Sharp, 2 *Chi. L. Rev.*, at 417.

44 Farrand, *Records of the Federal Convention*, vol. 1, at 232–33, 237, 238 (Madison's *Notes* and Yates, June 13).

45 *Id.*, at 314–22 (Madison's *Notes*, June 19).

46 *Id.*, at 317, 327 (Madison's *Notes* and Yates, June 19).

47 *Id.*, at 322–23, 328–29, 330–33 (Madison's *Notes*, Yates, and King, June 19).

48 *Id.*, vol. 2, at 37–39 (*Journal*, July 18).

49 *Id.*, at 39, 41, 45, 46 (*Journal* and Madison's *Notes*, July 18).

50 *Id.*, at 41–45 (Madison's *Notes*, July 18).

51 *Id.*, at 45–46.

52 *Id.*, at 46. See note 48, *supra.*, for additional supporting evidence for Randolph's statement.

53 *Id.*

54 Goebel, Julius, Jr., *Antecedents and Beginnings to 1801; History of the Supreme Court of the United States*, edited by Paul A. Freund, vol. 1 (New York: Macmillan Co., 1971), at 232; hereinafter referred to as Goebel, *Antecedents and Beginnings*.

55 Farrand, *Records of the Federal Convention*, vol. 2, at 146 (Committee of Detail, IV).

56 *Id.*, at 146–47. Article II of Randolph's draft also conferred power on the "supreme judiciary" to void state laws in conflict with the Constitution, but this provision was deleted from later drafts. Farrand, at 144. Hutson indicates that Rutledge's emendations included jurisdiction over disputes between a state and a citizen or citizens of other states. Hutson, *Supplement*, at 190.

57 See Goebel, *Antecedents and Beginnings*, at 234. See also Merry, 47 *Minn. L. Rev.*, at 57; Levy, 22 *N.Y.U. Intramural L. Rev.*, at 180; and Bator, *The Federal Courts*, at 13.

58 Farrand, *Records of the Federal Convention*, vol. 2, at 147 (Committee of Detail, IV). Another document in Wilson's handwriting incorporates features of the New Jersey and Pinckney plans. This document establishes a supreme court with original and appellate jurisdiction and grants Congress power to create an admiralty court in each state, but does not confer legislative discretion over federal jurisdiction. Farrand, at 157 (Committee of Detail, No. VII). In Wilson's document, the Supreme Court is an engine of national sovereignty.

59 *Id.* Hutson's *Supplement* includes several commas not in Farrand's version, but these do not change the meaning. Hutson, at 191.

60 See Clinton, 132 *U. Pa. L. Rev.*, at 774–75, 776–78.

61 Farrand, *Records of the Federal Convention*, vol. 2, at 172–73. Following Farrand's notation, the parts in parentheses were crossed out in the original, the italics are Wilson's additions, and the parts marked as follows <> are Rutledge's emendations.

62 *Id.*, at 173.

63 However, Wilson favored the Supreme Court's review of questions of law and fact in admiralty and maritime cases, including factual determinations by juries in prize cases. Since Wilson had been adversely affected by juries' verdicts in prize cases during the Revolutionary War, he believed that the admiralty jurisdiction should be exclusively federal. He also argued for the Supreme Court's review in such cases as a means of protecting ship owners against hostile state courts and juries. See Merry, 47 *Minn. L. Rev.*, at 64–65.

64 *Id.*, at 186–87 (Madison's Notes, August 6). Farrand relies on Madison's copy of the Committee of Detail's report.

65 *Id.*, at 186–87. Madison reported the relevant provision as follows:

> Sect. 3. The Jurisdiction of the Supreme Court shall extend to all cases arising under laws passed by the Legislature of the United States; to all cases affecting Ambassadors, other Public Ministers and Consuls; to the trial of impeachments of Officers of the United States; to all cases of Admiralty and maritime jurisdiction; to controversies between two or more States, (except such as shall regard Territory or Jurisdiction) between a State and Citizens of another State, between Citizens of different States, and between a State or the Citizens thereof and foreign States, citizens or subjects. In cases of impeachment, cases affecting Ambassadors, other Public Ministers and Consuls, and those in which a State shall be party, this jurisdiction shall be original. In all the other cases before mentioned, it shall be appellate, with such exceptions and under such regulations as the Legislature shall make. The Legislature may assign any part of the jurisdiction above mentioned (except the trial of the President of the United States) in the manner, and under the limitations which it shall think proper, to such Inferior Courts, as it shall constitute from time to time.

66 *Id.* at 381–82 (*Journal*, August 23). See also Madison's *Notes*, August 23.

67 *Id.*, at 294–96, 298–301 (*Journal* and Madison's *Notes*, August 15) and 303, 304–5 (*Journal* and Madison's *Notes*, August 16).

68 *Id.*, at 423–24 (*Journal*, August 29). The delegates accepted several other amendments to section 3, but these changes did not appreciably alter the federal courts' jurisdiction.

69 *Id.*, at 430 (Madison's *Notes*, August 29).

70 *Id.*, at 431.

71 A draft resolution (dated August 27) that Mason attributed to John Blair (Va.) supports the thesis that the Supreme Court's appellate jurisdiction extends to questions of law, except in admiralty and maritime cases, where it extends to questions of law and fact. While the draft specifies that the admiralty courts shall have original jurisdiction in such cases, it also provides for appeal to the "Supreme Court of [or?] Congress for any Sum and in such manner as Congress may by law direct." Mason, George, *The Papers of George Mason, 1725–1792*, 3 vols., edited by Robert A. Rutland (Chapel Hill: Univ. of North Carolina Press, 1970), at 970; hereinafter cited as Mason, *Papers*.

72 Merry, 47 *Minn. L. Rev.*, at 58–62.

73 Clinton, *U. Pa. L. Rev.*, at 778–79.

74 Jensen, *Documentary History*, vol. 1, at 251.

75 Justice Owen Roberts argues that Congress has plenary power to abolish the Su-

preme Court's appellate jurisdiction, piecemeal or wholesale, over state court decisions. Roberts, Owen J., "Now Is The Time: Fortifying the Supreme Court's Independence," 35 *A.B.A. J.* 1–4 (1949). But, see Clinton, 132 *U. Pa. L. Rev.*, at 796. Clinton denies that the Framers intended conferring such power on Congress.

76   See Tweed, 31 *B.U.L. Rev.*, at 850; Mickenberg, Ira, "Abusing the Exceptions and Regulations Clause: Legislative Attempts to Divest the Supreme Court of Appellate Jurisdiction," 32 *Am. U.L. Rev.* 497–542 (1983), at 510–11; and Beck, 9 *Hastings Const. L.Q.*, at 781.

77   Farrand, *Records of the Federal Convention*, vol. 2, at 186–87.

78   Mason, *Papers*, at 944, 970.

79   Irving Brant and Henry Merry argue that the Framers could not resolve differences among various states' practices regarding the reviewability of juries' verdicts. Merry, for example, asserts that the Framers could not formulate a uniform rule concerning appeals from jury trials in criminal, civil, equity, and admiralty and maritime cases. Therefore, they gave Congress authority to resolve the problem in the future. Thus the exceptions and regulations clause grants Congress power only to limit the Court's appellate jurisdiction over a jury's determination of fact. See Brant, Irving, "Appellate Jurisdiction: Congressional Abuse of the Exceptions Clause," 53 *Ore. L. Rev.* 3–28 (1973), at 28; and Merry, 47 *Minn. L. Rev.*, at 58–62. But see also Clinton, 132 *U. Pa. L. Rev.*, at 778–79. Clinton does not accept Merry's interpretation since the exceptions and regulations clause was inserted prior to the appearance of the law/fact distinction. Clinton adheres to the argument that the Framers intended the clause as a distributing clause. However, one must emphasize that on August 27 the Framers also removed the specific language permitting Congress to distribute the Court's appellate jurisdiction to the lower federal courts.

80   Mason, *Papers*, at 970–71.

81   Farrand, *Records of the Federal Convention*, vol. 2, at 434, 436–37 (*Journal* and Madison's *Notes*, August 28).

82   *Id.*, at 434, 438.

83   *Id.*, at 435, 438.

84   *Id.*, at 457–59, 463–66 (*Journal* and Madison's *Notes*, August 30).

85   *Id.*, at 493, 497, 503 (*Journal*, Madison's *Notes*, and McHenry).

86   *Id.*, at 547, 553, 554.

87   *Id.*, at 575–76 (Committee of Style).

88   Jensen, *Documentary History*, vol. 1, at 260–84, which contains the Committee of Detail's Draft Constitution (August 6) and the amended draft that the Convention submitted to the Committee of Style (September 10).

89   *Id.*, at 284.

90   *Id.*, at 293–94.

91   *Id.*, at 294.

92   See note 65, *supra*.

93   Wright, Benjamin F., *The Growth of American Constitutional Law* (New York: Reynal and Hitchcock, 1942), at 10; hereinafter cited as Wright, *The Growth of American Constitutional Law*.

94   *Id.*, at 13–14, 14–15; Coxe, Brinton, *An Essay on Judicial Power and Unconstitutional Legislation* (New York: Da Capo Press, 1970), at 178–80, 214–16, 218, 267–69; McLaughlin, Andrew C., *The Courts, the Constitution, and Parties (Studies in Constitutional History and Politics)* (Chicago, Ill.: Univ. of Chicago Press, 1912),

at 84–85, 105–7. However, the state practice of judicial review is disputed. Coxe, for example, denies that *Trevett* v. *Weeden* (R.I., 1786) and *Bayard* v. *Singleton* (N.C., 1787) support the concept of judicial review implicit in a written constitution. See Coxe, *Essays on Judicial Power*, at 267–69.

95 Corwin, Edward S., *The Doctrine of Judicial Review: Its Legal and Historical Basis and Other Essays* (Gloucester, Mass.: Peter Smith, 1963), at 38–41.

96 Levy, *Judicial Review*, at 7, 38–42, 43, 44–45; Corwin, Edward S., *Court Over Constitution: A Study of Judicial Review as an Instrument of Popular Government* (New York: Peter Smith, 1950 [copyright, 1938]), at 24; hereinafter cited as Corwin, *Court Over Constitution*.

97 Madison, James, *The Writings of James Madison*, 9 vols., edited by Gaillard Hunt (New York: G.P. Putnam's Sons, vol. 2, 1901; vol. 5, 1904; vol. 6, 1906; vol. 9, 1910), vol. 2, at 336–40. Madison concluded:

> Let this national supremacy be extended also to the Judiciary department. If the Judges in the last resort depend on the States, and are bound by their oaths to them and not to the Union, the intention of the law and the interests of the nation may be defeated by the obsequiousness of the tribunals to the policy or prejudices of the States. It seems at least essential that an appeal should lie to some national tribunals in all cases which concern foreigners, or inhabitants of other States. The admiralty jurisdiction may be fully submitted to the National Government.

Id., at 338–39.

98 *Id.*, at 346–47.

99 Farrand, *Records of the Federal Convention*, vol. 1, at 94 (*Journal*, June 4), 131 (*Journal*, June 6), vol. 2, at 71 (*Journal*, July 21), and 294–95 (*Journal*, August 15). On June 4, the Committee of the Whole postponed consideration of Randolph's resolution No. 8 (6/4). On June 6 and July 21 the delegates defeated Wilson's motions (3/8 and 3/4/2, respectively), and on August 15 they rejected Madison's motion, seconded by Wilson (3/8), to include a Council of Revision in the Constitution.

100 Jensen, *Documentary History*, vol. 1, at 244.

101 Farrand, *Records of the Federal Convention*, vol. 1, at 97–98 (Madison's *Notes*, June 4).

102 *Id.*, at 98, 109 (Madison's *Notes* and Pierce, June 4).

103 *Id.*, at 94 (Madison's *Notes*, June 4) and 108, 110 (King and Pierce, June 4).

104 *Id.*, at 138 (Madison's *Notes*, June 6).

105 *Id.*

106 *Id.*, at 139, 144 (Madison's *Notes* and King, June 6). Wilson's motion was defeated (3/8). Farrand, at 131.

107 *Id.*, vol. 2, at 73 (Madison's *Notes*, July 21).

108 *Id.*, at 74–75.

109 *Id.*, at 76–77.

110 *Id.*, at 78.

111 *Id.*, at 80.

112 *Id.*, at 298, 294–95 (Madison's *Notes* and *Journal*, August 15).

113 *Id.*, at 298, 300–301 (Madison's *Notes*, August 15).

114 *Id.*, at 298.

115 *Id.*, at 299.

116 *Id.*, at 303, 304–5 (*Journal* and Madison's *Notes*, August 16). The motion was offered by Randolph and agreed to without debate.

117 However, James Madison later denied (October 1788) that the delegates accepted the principle of judicial supremacy. In his "Remarks on Jefferson's Draft of a Constitution," Madison denied judicial supremacy, but he recognized that in the course of deciding cases the judiciary must necessarily determine constitutional issues. Hutson, *Supplement*, at 297.

118 Farrand, *Records of the Federal Convention*, vol. 3, at 516.

119 *Id.*, at 522 (to W.C. Rives, October 21, 1833) and 526 (to John Tylor, dated 1833, but apparently not sent).

120 *Id.*, at 527.

121 *Id.*, vol. 1, at 21 (Madison's *Notes*, May 29).

122 *Id.*

123 *Id.*, vol. 3, at 607.

124 *Id.*, vol. 1, at 293 (Madison's *Notes*, June 18).

125 *Id.*, vol. 3, at 628, and vol. 1, at 245 (Madison's *Notes*, June 15).

126 *Id.*, vol. 3, at 616.

127 *Id.*, vol. 1, at 47, 54, 61 (*Journal*, Madison's *Notes*, and McHenry, May 31), 162, 164–68, 169–71, 172, 173 (*Journal*, Madison's *Notes*, Yates, King, and Hamilton, June 8), and vol. 2, at 21, 27–28 (*Journal* and Madison's *Notes*, July 17).

128 *Id.*, vol. 3, at 56.

129 *Id.*, vol. 2, at 28–29 (Madison's *Notes*, July 17).

130 *Id.*, at 28.

131 *Id.*, at 27.

132 *Id.*, at 27–28.

133 *Id.*, at 382, 390–92 (*Journal* and Madison's *Notes*, August 23).

134 Jensen, *Documentary History*, at 257.

135 *Id.*, at 265.

136 *Id.*, at 277, 296.

137 Farrand, *Records of the Federal Convention*, vol. 2, at 663.

138 Prescott, *Drafting the Federal Constitution*, at 816.

139 Farrand, *Records of the Federal Convention*, vol. 1, at 122 (Madison's *Notes*, June 5).

140 *Id.*, at 194 (*Journal*, June 11).

141 *Id.*, at 203 (Madison's *Notes*, June 11).

142 *Id.*, at 203–4.

143 *Id.*, vol. 2, at 589 (Madison's *Notes*, September 12).

144 Berger, *Congress v. the Supreme Court*, at 49–50.

145 Eisenberg, 83 *Yale L.J.*, at 532–33.

3 The Judicial Function, Jurisdiction, and Congressional Power: The Ratifiers' Intent

1 Farrand, *Records of the Federal Convention*, at 628, 631–32, 635 (Madison's *Notes* and King, September 15).

2 *Id.*, at 638 (Mason, "Objections to This Constitution of Government," September 15). Mason's comments were written on the blank pages of his copy of the September 12 draft, according to Farrand.

3 Indeed, John Locke had criticized the British judiciary in his *Treatise of Civil Government*, arguing that only an independent judiciary could administer justice impartially. An impartial judiciary could also protect the individual's liberty, restrain arbitrary government, and resolve conflicts among political institutions. Political dissatisfaction with the British judiciary's subservience to the Crown eventually resulted in the guarantee of judicial tenure and independence in the Act of Settlement (1701). See Locke, John, *Treatise of Civil Government and a Letter Concerning Toleration*, edited by Charles L. Sherman (New York: Appleton-Century-Crofts, 1965), secs. 131, 136, at 85, 90–91.

4 See Elliot, *Debates in the State Conventions*. There are several important problems in employing Elliot's *Debates* exclusively to determine the Ratifiers' intent. The records of the state ratifying conventions are fragmentary and uneven. However, since the early 1970s Merrill Jensen and, now, John Kaminski have developed a national treasure, the Archive of the Documentary History of the Ratification of the Constitution, at the University of Wisconsin, which contains more than 100,000 items on the ratification of the Constitution. The author is deeply indebted to Dr. John Kaminski, director of the Archive, for granting access to the collection and for his generous assistance during the summer of 1986 in researching, documenting, reproducing, and collating items relevant to the Judiciary Article. The author is also indebted to Dr. Kaminski for permission to use and reproduce items that would not have been otherwise available.

   At this time, the State Historical Society of Wisconsin has published volumes 1–3 and 13–16 of the series. Wherever published items have been used, they are referred to as Jensen, *Documentary History*. All other materials drawn from the Archive are designated as *DH*.

5 As anticipated, the public press was heavily concentrated in Pennsylvania, Massachusetts, New York, Connecticut, and Virginia. While all states had newspapers, the major newspapers were published in Philadelphia, Boston, and New York. For a brief description of the leading newspapers, their editors, and editorial policies, see Jensen, *Documentary History*, vol. 13, at xxx–xxxix.

6 Elliot, *Debates in the State Conventions*, vol. 2, at 489.

7 *Id.*, at 489–90, 492.

8 *Id.*, at 490–92.

9 Timothy Pickering (1745–1829) represented Luzerne County in the Pennsylvania Convention. This defense of the federal courts appears in a letter from Pickering to Charles Tillinghast (Philadelphia, December 24, 1787). See Jensen, *Documentary History*, vol. 14, at 204–5.

10 Tench Coxe was elected to the Confederation Congress in 1788 and served in the national government as assistant secretary of the treasury (1789–92) and commissioner of revenue (1792–97). When President John Adams removed him from office, Coxe became a Jeffersonian Republican, and served as purveyor of public supplies (1803–12). See *DH.*, from the Coxe Papers, Coxe and Frazier's *Foreign Letter Book* (Philadelphia, July 10, 1788).

11 In determining the probable identity of the pseudonyms here and throughout this chapter, the following sources have been employed: Jensen, *Documentary History*; Storing, *The Complete Anti-Federalist*; and *DH*.

   Ellsworth's speeches and writings provide insight into the Framers', Ratifiers', the First Congress's, and the Supreme Court's understanding of the Judiciary Article since he served as a delegate to the Federal Convention, the Connecticut Convention, and, later, as a U.S. Senator and chief justice of the United States (1796–1800). As a U.S. Senator, along with William Paterson (another Framer and, later, associate justice), Ellsworth drafted the Judiciary Act of 1789.

12 Jensen, *Documentary History*, vol. 3, at 337–38.

13 *Id.*, at 483–84.

14 Elliot, *Debates in the State Conventions*, vol. 2, at 185; and Goebel, *Antecedents and Beginnings*, at 338.

15 DH. A.B. to the Hon. E. Gerry, Esq., *Massachusetts Centinel* (Boston, November 14, 1787).

16 Storing, *The Complete Anti-Federalist*, vol. 4, at 129. "Essays by Candidus," *Independent Chronicle* (Boston, December 1787–January 1788).

17 DH. A.B., *Hampshire Gazette* (Northampton, Mass., January 9, 1788).

18 *Id.*, at 6–7, transcription.

19 Elliot, *Debates in the State Conventions*, vol. 4, at 257–58.

20 *Id.*, at 258.

21 *Id.*, vol. 3, at 518.

22 *Id.*, at 517.

23 *Id.*

24 *Id.*, at 531–32.

25 *Id.*, at 532.

26 *Id.*, at 538.

27 *Id.*, at 570.

28 Farrand, *Records of the Federal Convention*, vol. 3, at 117.

29 Hamilton, *The Federalist*, at 143.

30 *Id.*, at 143–44.

31 *Id.*

32 *Id.*, at 144.

33 *Id.*, at 256.

34 *Id.*, at 534–38.

35 Elliot, *Debates in the State Conventions*, vol. 2, at 332–33. Melancton Smith (1744–98) was a lawyer, member of the Continental Congress (1785–88), and member of the New York Convention. In the New York Convention, he was Hamilton's chief protagonist.

36 *Id.*, at 333.

37 *Id.*, at 371–72. John Lansing (born 1754) was a jurist, member of Congress (1784–85), and later chief justice and chancellor of the state of New York. He was chosen as a delegate to the Federal Convention, but withdrew in protest.

38 *Id.*, at 374.

39 *Id.*, vol. 4, at 156–60. Although North Carolina was a Democratic stronghold, Davie favored a strong federal government. In the Federal Convention he supported the Connecticut compromise, and, along with Iredell, he led the fight for ratification in the North Carolina Convention.

40 *Id.*, at 157–58.

41 Clinton, 132 *U. Pa. L. Rev.*, at 806–7, 810–18.

42 Storing, Herbert J., *What the Anti-Federalists Were for: The Political Thought of the Opponents of the Constitution* (Chicago: Univ. of Chicago Press, 1981), at 50, n. 3; hereinafter cited as Storing, *What the Anti-Federalists Were for.*

43 Clinton, 132 *U. Pa. L. Rev.*, at 800.

44 Elliot, *Debates in the State Conventions*, vol. 2, at 481.

45 *Id.*

46 *DH.* Conciliator, "To all Honest Americans," (Philadelphia, *Independent Gazetteer*, February 20, 1788).

47 Storing, *The Complete Anti-Federalist*, vol. 4, at 77–78. Agrippa, "Letters of Agrippa," *Massachusetts Gazette* (Boston, No. 5, December 11, 1787). James Winthrop (1752–1821) was a "rabid Republican."

48 *Id.*, at 88–89 (No. 10, January 1, 1788).

49 *DH.* A Farmer, "To the Town of Boston," *American Herald* (Boston, January 14, 1788).

50 Farrand, *Records of the Federal Convention*, vol. 3, at 204, 220–21.

51 Storing, *The Complete Anti-Federalist*, vol. 5, at 53–54; "Essays By a Farmer," *Maryland Gazette* (Baltimore, No. 6, April 1, 1788). John Francis Mercer (1759–1821) represented Virginia in Congress and later served as governor of Maryland. He studied law at William & Mary under Thomas Jefferson. Mercer represented Maryland in the Federal Convention and was a delegate to the state ratifying convention. He voted against ratification and, subsequently, became a Republican.

52 *Id.*, at 85. Samuel Chase, in the Maryland Convention (April 1788). Samuel Chase (1741–1811) signed the Declaration of Independence, was a delegate to the First Continental Congress, and was a member of the Maryland Convention. He was one of eleven members who voted against ratification. Chase subsequently became a Federalist and served on the U.S. Supreme Court. In 1804 the House of Representatives impeached Chase (73/32), but the Senate failed to remove him, despite a Republican majority.

53 Elliot, *Debates in the State Conventions*, vol. 2, at 550. William Paca (1740–99) signed the Declaration of Independence, served as governor of Maryland, and was a member of the first and second continental congresses. He was also chief judge of the Maryland General Court. Although Paca introduced twenty-eight amendments to the Constitution in the Maryland Convention, eventually he voted for ratification. In 1789 President Washington appointed Paca a district judge.

54 Charles Pinckney, House Proceedings and Debates (Wednesday, January 16, 1788), *South Carolina House and Senate Journals*, in Elliot, *Debates in the State Conventions*, vol. 4, at 257–58.

55 *Id.*, at 340–41. The South Carolina Convention ratified the Constitution on May 24, 1788, by a vote of 140/73.

56 Mason, *Papers*, at 1107. See also Mason's remarks on June 19, 20, and 23, 1788, at 1101–10, 1112–13. Mason reiterated his position several times during the Convention, each time arguing that the Supreme Court's appellate jurisdiction was virtually unlimited.

57 *Id.*, at 1103–5.

58 Another delegate to the Virginia Convention, James Monroe, shared Mason's concerns. In a work entitled "Some Observations on The Constitution," Monroe contended that the Court's appellate jurisdiction "should contemplate national objects only." While Monroe conceded the need to create a supreme court, he doubted the necessity of establishing lower courts, whose jurisdictions would conflict with the states' courts. Furthermore, Monroe questioned the propriety of federal jurisdiction over state, local, and private matters. Neither Mason nor Mon-

roe was satisfied that Congress could or would curb the judiciary's potential abuse of power. See Storing, *The Complete Anti-Federalist*, vol. 5, at 298–99, 303–4.

59   *Id.*, vol. 2, "Essays of Brutus," *New York Journal* (No. 1, October 18, 1787).

60   *Id.*, at 366–67. Robert Yates (1738–1801) was a justice of the New York Supreme Court; he was a leader of the Anti-Federalists and a supporter of Governor Clinton. He represented New York in the Federal Convention, and voted against ratification in the State Convention. Thomas Tre(a)dwell (1743–1832) studied with Chancellor Livingston at Princeton. He was a member of the Continental Congress and the state legislature.

61   *DH.* Richard Henry Lee, "Letters from the Federal Farmer to the Republican" (New York: Thomas Greenleaf, 1788). Richard Henry Lee (1732–94) was the mover of the Declaration of Independence in Congress and the first senator from Virginia.

62   *Id.*, No. 18, at 173, 175–77 (January 25, 1788).

63   *Id.*, at 175–77.

64   Storing, *The Complete Anti-Federalist*, vol. 2, at 426–27. Brutus, No. 12 (February 14, 1788).

65   *Id.*, at 427.

66   *Id.*, at 428. Brutus, No. 13 (February 21, 1788).

67   *Id.*, at 429, 430.

68   Elliot, *Debates in the State Conventions*, vol. 2, at 408–9; *DH.*, New York Convention, *Journal*, July 22, 1788, as reported in the Poughkeepsie, N.Y., *Country Journal* (September 23, 1788). According to West's *Words and Phrases*: "A 'writ of error,' both at the time of the adoption of the Constitution and since, has had a definite meaning, to wit, a writ authorizing an appeal from an inferior court, assigning error in the proceedings as relating only to matters of law arising on the face of the proceedings, so that no evidence is required to substantiate or support it." *Words and Phrases* (St. Paul, Minn.: West Publishing Co., 1970), vol. 46, at 411.

69   Storing, *The Complete Anti-Federalist*, vol. 6, at 184. "Notes of Speeches Given by George Clinton before the New York State Ratifying Convention," probably delivered on June 27, 1788. George Clinton (1739–1812), seven times governor of New York, was a leading Anti-Federalist. He authored a series of letters, under the pseudonym "Cato," opposing ratification of the Constitution.

70   Elliot, *Debates in the State Conventions*, vol. 4, at 136, 138.

71   *Id.*, at 139. Richard D. Spaight (1758–1802) was governor of North Carolina and a member of Congress. An advocate of a stronger federal government, he was chosen to serve in the Federal Convention. He voted for the Constitution.

72   Ford, Paul L., ed., *Pamphlets on the Constitution of the United States* (New York: Da Capo Press, 1968), at 53–54; hereinafter cited as Ford, *Pamphlets on the Constitution*. Noah Webster (1758–1843), a well-known lexicographer, wrote the pamphlet cited above in October 1787, urging ratification of the Constitution.

73   Hamilton, *Federalist*, at 548, 549 (No. 81, May 28, 1788).

74   Ford, *Pamphlets on the Constitution*, at 237. "Remarks on The Proposed Plan of a Federal Government . . . by Aristides," (Annapolis, January 1, 1788). Hanson, who wrote as Aristides, favored ratification of the Constitution. Alexander Contee Hanson (1786–1819) represented Maryland in the U.S. Senate and House of Representatives. He has sometimes been described as an extreme Federalist.

75   Jensen, *Documentary History*, vol. 14, at 388–89. Sherman's essays appeared in the *New Haven Gazette* on December 18 and 25, 1787. They also appeared in the

Connecticut Courant on January 7, 1788, while the Connecticut Convention was in session.

76 Storing, *The Complete Anti-Federalist*, vol. 2, at 143. "Letters of Centinel," *Independent Gazetteer* (Philadelphia, October 1787–April 1788).

77 *Id.*, at 148.

78 *Id.*, at 149.

79 *Id.*, vol. 3, at 60–61; "Essays of a Democratic Federalist, *Pennsylvania Herald* (October 17, 1787). Another anonymous writer, Algernon Sidney, claimed that Article III effectively undermined the right to a jury trial in criminal cases as well as civil cases. See *DH.*, Algernon Sidney, *Independent Gazetteer* (November 21, 1787).

80 *Id.*, at 60.

81 Jensen, *Documentary History*, vol. 2, at 168–69.

82 Elliot, *Debates in the State Conventions*, vol. 2, at 488, 517; *DH.* Webster, *An Examination into the leading principles of the Federal Constitution* (Philadelphia, October 8–9, 1787).

83 *Id.*, at 539–40.

84 Jensen, *Documentary History*, vol. 2, at 633.

85 *DH.* An Honest American, *Independent Gazetteer* (February 15, 1788), and Algernon Sidney, *Independent Gazetteer* (March 4, 1788).

86 *DH.* John Peirce to Henry Knox (October 27, 1787).

87 Jensen, *Documentary History*, vol. 14, at 115.

88 *DH.* Speech to be delivered to the Massachusetts Convention, *Cushing Papers*, Massachusetts Historical Society (Reel 512).

89 Jensen, *Documentary History*, vol. 13, at 552–53.

90 Storing, *The Complete Anti-Federalist*, vol. 4, at 241. "A Friend to The Rights of The People: Anti-Federalist, No. 1," *Freeman's Oracle* (February 8, 1788).

91 *DH.* Alfredus, "Response to a Farmer," *Freeman's Oracle* (June 13, 1788). Samuel Tenney (1748–1816) represented New Hampshire in the U.S. House of Representatives (1800–1807).

92 Ford, *Pamphlets on the Constitution*, at 238; Aristides (Annapolis, January 1, 1788).

93 Farrand, *Records of the Federal Convention*, vol. 3, at 150.

94 The fragment of the Convention debate appears in the *Maryland Journal* (August 5, 1788).

95 *DH.* A Friend to Order, Baltimore *Maryland Gazette* (October 28, 1787).

96 The negative-pregnant doctrine refers to Marshall's opinion that the federal courts can only exercise the jurisdiction that Congress has specifically conferred by statute. If Congress has not granted jurisdiction, the courts cannot assume that such jurisdiction exists for the purpose of deciding a case.

97 *DH.* "Instructions to Delegates to the State Ratifying Convention," Swem Library, the College of William & Mary, *Monroe Papers*, Folder 4 (1788).

98 Madison, *Papers*, vol. 10, at 228. Joseph Jones served in the colonial House of Burgesses, the Continental Congress, and the Confederation Congress. As the *Dictionary of American Biography* states, Jones was a " 'confidential friend' of Washington, correspondent and partisan of Jefferson, and intimate colleague of Madison." Malone, Dumas, ed., *Dictionary of American Biography* (New York: Charles Scribner's Son, 1933), vol. 10, at 192.

99 Lee, Richard Henry, *The Letters of Richard Henry Lee*, vol. 2, edited by James G.

Ballagh (New York: The Macmillan Co., 1914), at 453, 469, 473; hereinafter cited as Lee, *Letters*.

100 *DH*. National Archives, RG 59, Entry No. 836; Printed Sources, Misc. Docs. 1206-1932, Box No. 13.

101 William Grayson (1736?–90), an Anti-Federalist, was a member of the Continental Congress, a U.S. senator, and a member of the Virginia House of Delegates.

102 Farrand, *Records of the Federal Convention*, vol. 3, at 309 (Virginia Convention, June 7, 1788); Elliot, *Debates in the State Conventions*, vol. 3, at 205 (June 10).

103 Farrand, *Records of the Federal Convention*, vol. 3, at 310.

104 Elliot, *Debates in the State Conventions*, vol. 3, at 68–69 (June 16).

105 *Id.*, at 572–73.

106 *Id.*, at 525 (June 24); see also *Id.*, at 525–26, 528–29, 551.

107 *Id.*, at 534.

108 *Id.*, at 540–41. Henry argued:

> But we are told that Congress are to make regulations to remedy this. I may be told that I am bold; but I think myself, and I hope to be able to prove to others, that Congress cannot, by any act of theirs, alter this jurisdiction as established. It appears to me that no law of Congress can alter or arrange it. It is subject to be regulated, but is it subject to be abolished? If Congress alter this part, they will repeal the Constitution. Does it give them power to repeal itself? What is meant by such words in common parlance? If you are obliged to do certain business, you are to do it under such modifications as were originally designed. Can gentlemen support their argument by regular or logical conclusions? When Congress, by virtue of this sweeping clause, will organize these courts, they cannot depart from the Constitution; and their laws in opposition to the Constitution would be void. If Congress, under the specious pretence of pursuing this clause, altered it, and prohibited appeals as to fact, the federal judges, if they spoke the sentiments of independent men, would declare their prohibition nugatory and void.

109 Marshall, John, *The Papers of John Marshall*, 4 vols., edited by Herbert A. Johnson (Chapel Hill: Univ. of North Carolina Press, 1974), vol. 1, at 278–79; hereinafter cited as Marshall, *Papers*.

110 *Id.*, at 283.

111 Elliot, *Debates in the State Conventions*, vol. 4, at 260.

112 *Id.*, at 306–8.

113 Jensen, *Documentary History*, vol. 14, at 442–43.

114 *Id.*, at 442.

115 Elliot, *Debates in the State Conventions*, vol. 5, at 587.

116 Hamilton, *The Federalist*, No. 82 (Hamilton, May 28, 1788), at 556.

117 *Id.*, at 556–57.

118 *Id.*, No. 80, at 541 (Hamilton, May 28, 1788).

119 Farrand, *Records of the Federal Convention*, vol. 3, at 349, 352; Elliot, *Debates in the State Conventions*, vol. 4, at 151–52, 163, 165–66, 167, 170–72.

120 *Id.*, at 246.

121 14 U.S. (1 Wheat.) 304 (1816).

122 U.S. Const. amend VII.

4 Judicial Power, the Judicial Function, and Jurisdiction: The Formative Period (1789–1835)

1 Bator, *The Federal Courts*, at 314, especially n. 2. Bator argues that Story's argument is really an appeal to Congress to vest the entire constitutional jurisdiction in the federal courts and that his opinion should not be read literally.

2 De Pauw, Linda G., ed. *Documentary History of the First Federal Congress of the United States of America, March 4, 1789–March 3, 1791* (Baltimore: Johns Hopkins Univ. Press, 6 vols., 1972), vol. 4, at viii.

3 1 *Annals of Congress* 457 (1789); Wright, *The Growth of American Constitutional Law*, at 26. In introducing his amendments before the House of Representatives, Madison assumed that the judiciary would exercise the power of judicial review to protect individuals from legislative encroachments. For a thorough discussion of the competing theories of judicial review, see Beveridge, Albert J., *The Life of John Marshall*, 4 vols. (Boston, Mass.: Houghton Mifflin Co., 1916–19), vol. 3, at 60–92; hereinafter cited as Beveridge, *The Life of John Marshall*.

   A year before *Marbury v. Madison*, in the debates on the Judiciary Act of 1802, the members of the Senate articulated the major contending views on judicial power. On Jefferson's explanation of the departmental theory of judicial review, see Beveridge, vol. 3, at 605–6. Despite Madison's rejection of the argument for judicial supremacy over Congress, he continued to accept the need for judicial power over the states. See Corwin, *Court Over Constitution*, at 60–61. For a full exposition of Hamilton's advocacy of judicial supremacy, see Hamilton, *The Papers of Alexander Hamilton*, 26 vols., edited by Harold C. Syrett (New York: Columbia Univ. Press, vols. 4–5, 1962; vol. 23, 1976; vol. 25, 1977), vol. 25, at 501, 520–27, 529–35, 539–44, 546–52, 552–58; hereinafter cited as Hamilton, *Papers*.

4 On April 7, 1789, the Senate appointed a committee to draft the Judiciary Act. Oliver Ellsworth and William Paterson actually drafted the bill. The committee was composed of Ellsworth, Paterson, Few, and Bassett, all of whom had attended the Federal Convention. Other members included Strong, R.H. Lee, and C. Carroll, who were elected as delegates to the Convention. The three remaining members of the committee (Izard, Wingate, and Maclay) had not attended the Federal Convention. Of the ten committee members, seven had been delegates to their states' ratifying conventions.

5 Among the members of the First Congress, twenty-four representatives and thirteen senators had participated in the framing and/or ratification of the Constitution.

6 See 1 *Annals of Congress* 457 (1789). Although Madison assumes that the judiciary has the power to enforce constitutional supremacy and protect individual rights, he does not subscribe to Hamilton's theory of judicial review or judicial supremacy.

7 Ch. 20, 1 Stat. 73, at 85–86 (1789). At least one authority, Charles G. Haines, argues that section 25 implies judicial review of congressional acts in the event of a conflict with state actions that have been sustained by a state's highest court. See Haines, Charles G., *The Role of the Supreme Court in American Government and Politics, 1789–1835* (Berkeley, Ca.: Univ. of California Press, 1944), at 144–47; hereinafter cited as Haines, *The Role of the Supreme Court*.

8 Ch. 20, 1 Stat. 73, section 9, at 76–77, and section 11, at 78–79.

9 Berger, *Congress v. the Supreme Court*, at 276–77.

10 Crosskey, *Politics and the Constitution*, at 1032–33.

11 Berger, *Congress v. the Supreme Court*, at 146–47, 149.

12 *Id.*, at 150.

13 Bator, *The Federal Courts*, at 313–14.

14 For an analysis of reaction to the Judiciary Act of 1789, see Charles Warren, *The Supreme Court in United States History*, rev. ed. (Boston: Little, Brown & Co., 2 vols., 1937), especially at 12–15; hereinafter cited as Warren, *The Supreme Court in United States History*.

15 Eisenberg, 83 *Yale L. J.*, at 501, 504–5, 513, 514, 532–33.

16 U.S. Const., art. III. (Italics added).

17 Beginning with *Turner* v. *Bank of North America*, 4 U.S. (4 Dall.) 8 (1799), the Supreme Court has held that the lower federal courts are courts of limited jurisdiction, and that they can exercise only that jurisdiction which Congress confers. See Ellsworth, C.J., in *Turner*, at 11. Thus Congress can withhold jurisdiction to hear a particular controversy. See also *McIntyre* v. *Wood*, 11 U.S. (7 Cranch) 504 (1813), at 506; *Kendall* v. *United States*, 37 U.S. (12 Peters) 524 (1838), at 616, 617; *Cary* v. *Curtis*, 44 U.S. (3 How.) 236 (1845), at 345; *Sheldon* v. *Sill*, 49 U.S. (8 How.) 441 (1850), at 448–49; *Kline* v. *Burke Construction Co.*, 260 U.S. 226 (1922), at 233–34; and *Glidden Co.* v. *Zdanok*, 370 U.S. 530 (1962), at 551. Speaking for the Court, Justice Harlan observed in *Glidden*, "Throughout this period and beyond it up to today, they [the inferior federal courts] remained constantly subject to jurisdictional curtailment." *Glidden*, 370 U.S., at 551.

18 See Friendly, *Federal Jurisdiction*, at 1–2; McGowan, Carl, *The Organization of Judicial Power in the United States* (Evanston, Ill.: Northwestern Univ. Press, 1969), at 25; Wright, Charles, *The Federal Courts*, at 17, 26, 27–28; and Wechsler, Herbert, *Principles, Politics, and Fundamental Law* (Cambridge, Mass.: Harvard Univ. Press, 1961), at 51–52. Friendly, McGowan, Wechsler, and Wright argue that congressional power is plenary.

19 Haines, *The Role of the Supreme Court*, at 144–47; Berger, *Congress v. the Supreme Court*, at 150.

20 Berger, *Congress v. the Supreme Court*, 150–53.

21 *Hayburn's Case*, 2 U.S. (2 Dall.) 409 (1792), at 410. The opinion referred to is from the Circuit Court for the District of New York (1791). In addition, the Circuit Court for the District of Pennsylvania (consisting of justices Wilson and Blair, and District Judge Peters) and the Circuit Court for the District of North Carolina (consisting of Justice Iredell and District Judge Sitgreaves) voiced similar views to Congress and the president. *Id.*, at 410–13.

22 3 U.S. (3 Dall.) 171 (1796), at 175. In a seriatim opinion, Justice Iredell also expressed the view that the act was constitutional. *Id.*, at 181.

23 See Thayer, 7 *Harv. L. Rev.* 129–56.

24 *Ware* v. *Hylton*, 3 U.S. (3 Dall.) 199 (1796), at 237.

25 Indeed, Chase's conduct of the trial became the basis for Article 2 of the Articles of Impeachment that the House of Representatives presented to the Senate.

26 25 *F. Cas.* 239 (C.C.D. Va. 1800) (No. 14,709), at 255.

27 *Id.*, at 256.

28 *Id.*

29 *Id.*, at 256–57.

30 5 U.S. (1 Cranch) 137 (1803).

31 William Van Alstyne argues that the holding in *Marbury* is narrower than most commentators recognize. He reads the decision as a defensive one, namely, that the Court can refuse to give effect to congressional legislation that pertains to the exercise of judicial power. *Marbury* is a defensive use of judicial power to maintain a coequal rather than a superior status to Congress. See Van Alstyne, "A Critical Guide to *Marbury* v. *Madison*," 1969 *Duke L.J.* 1–47 (1969), at 34.

32 See *Cohens* v. *Virginia*, 19 U.S. (6 Wheat.) 264 (1821), at 404.

33 *Marbury*, 5 U.S. (1 Cranch), at 174–76.

34 *Id.*

35 Ch. 20, 1 Stat. 73, at 80–81 (1789). Inasmuch as Oliver Ellsworth and William Paterson (leading Framers, former senators, and former chief justice and associate justice, respectively) had drafted the Judiciary Act, it seems doubtful that they would have drawn a statute so blatantly unconstitutional, as Marshall claimed.

36 *Marbury*, 5 U.S. (1 Cranch), at 162–63.

37 *Id.*, at 179, 180.

38 *McCulloch* v. *Maryland*, 17 U.S. (4 Wheat.) 316 (1819), at 426–27.

39 *Id.*, at 432, 434.

40 *Id.*, at 436.

41 *Cohens* v. *Virginia*, 19 U.S. (6 Wheat.) 264 (1821), at 378.

42 *Id.*, at 379–80.

43 *Id.*, at 383–84.

44 *Id.*, at 385.

45 *Id.*, at 386.

46 *Id.*, at 386–87. Marshall wrote:

> It would be hazarding too much, to assert, that the judicatures of the states will be exempt from the prejudices by which the legislatures and people are influenced, and will constitute perfectly impartial tribunals. In many states, the judges are dependent for office and for salary, on the will of the legislature. The constitution of the United States furnishes no security against the universal adoption of this principle. When we observe the importance which that constitution attaches to the independence of judges, we are the less inclined to suppose, that it can have intended to leave these constitutional questions to tribunals where this independence may not exist, in all cases where a state shall prosecute an individual who claims the protection of an act of congress.

47 *Id.*, at 397.

48 *Id.*, at 415.

49 *Id.*, at 417–18.

50 14 U.S. (1 Wheat.) 304 (1816). The Virginia Court of Appeals had refused to obey an earlier decision, *Fairfax* v. *Hunter* (1813), in which the Supreme Court had sustained the provisions of the treaty protecting Lord Fairfax's property from a Virginia confiscation act passed subsequent to his death. *Id.*, at 305–13.

51 *Id.*, at 329.

52 *Id.*, at 330.

53 *Id.*, at 330–31.

54 *Id.*, at 331.

55 *Id.*, at 334–35.
56 *Id.*, at 335–36.
57 *Id.*, at 336–38.
58 *Id.*, at 340.
59 *Id.*, at 342–46.
60 *Id.*, at 347.
61 *Id.*
62 *Id.*, at 348.
63 *Id.*, at 374–75.
64 Levy, 22 *N.Y.U. Intramural L. Rev.* 178, at 191.
65 *Wiscart* v. *D'Auchy*, 3 U.S. (3 Dall.) 321 (1796), at 321.
66 *Id.*, at 327.
67 *Id.*, at 326–27.
68 Lenoir, James J., "Congressional Control Over the Appellate Jurisdiction of the Supreme Court," 5 *Kan. L. Rev.* 16–41 (1956), at 18–19. Also see Brant, 53 *Or. L. Rev.*, at 16.
69 Anderson, Carl A., "The Power of Congress to Limit the Jurisdiction of the Supreme Court," 1981 *Det. C. L. Rev.* 753–70 (1981), at 754.
70 *Clarke* v. *Bazadone*, 5 U.S. (1 Cranch) 212 (1803), at 214. John Marshall participated for the first time on this point of law. See Lenoir, 5 *Kan. L. Rev.*, at 20.
71 5 U.S. (1 Cranch) 252 (1803).
72 7 U.S. (3 Cranch) 159 (1805).
73 *Id.*, at 173–74.
74 *Id.*, at 172.
75 An act concerning the District of Columbia, Ch. 2, 2 Stat. 103, at 106 (1801). Section 8 of the act regulates appeals on a writ of error to the Supreme Court from the Circuit Court of the District of Columbia.
76 *More*, 7 U.S. (3 Cranch), at 173.
77 Lenoir, 5 *Kan. L. Rev.*, at 22–23.
78 10 U.S. (6 Cranch) 307 (1810).
79 Ch. 36, 2 Stat. 283, at 285–86 (1804). Section 8 of the act establishes a district court and defines its powers and jurisdiction with reference to section 10 of the Judiciary Act of 1789, establishing a district court for the territory of Kentucky.
80 *Durousseau*, 10 U.S. (6 Cranch), at 318.
81 *Id.*, at 318.
82 *Id.*, at 317.
83 *Id.*, at 313–14.
84 *Id.*, at 314.
85 Lenoir, 5 *Kan. L. Rev.*, at 24.
86 11 U.S. (7 Cranch) 108 (1812).
87 *Id.*
88 *Id.*, at 109.
89 22 U.S. (9 Wheat.) 738 (1824).
90 *Id.*, at 739–40.
91 The Eleventh Amendment was a direct response to the Supreme Court's decision in *Chisholm* v. *Georgia*, 2 U.S. (2 Dall.) 419 (1793). As Chief Justice John Jay explained, in *Chisholm*, the Framers intended the Court to exercise original jurisdiction in suits between the citizens of one state against a second state in order to

provide a neutral forum in which individuals could vindicate their rights vis-à-vis the states. *Id.*, at 475–77, 478–79.

92 *Osborn* v. *Bank of the United States*, 22 U.S. (9 Wheat.) 738 (1824), at 818–23, 849–50.

93 *Id.*, at 849–50.

94 *Id.*, at 859.

95 *Id.*, at 817.

96 *Id.*, at 819.

97 *Id.* In a dissenting opinion, Justice Johnson denied that *Osborn* presented a federal question, that Congress had granted the bank the unlimited right to sue in a United States court, or that Congress would have authority to vest original jurisdiction in the lower courts in cases that do not present a federal question. See Johnson's dissenting opinion, at 871–903.

98 *Id.*, at 820–21.

99 Haines, *The Role of the Supreme Court*, at 579–80.

100 *Id.*

101 *Id.*, at 593–94, 595–96, 604, 607.

102 29 U.S. (4 Pet.) 410 (1830).

103 *Id.*, at 425–26, 428–30.

104 *Id.*, at 437–38. Marshall argued that both the Constitution and the statutes imposed a duty on the Court to enforce constitutional supremacy, which he regarded as indispensable to the preservation of the Union as well as the independence and liberty of the states.

105 Haines, *The Role of the Supreme Court*, at 593–96.

106 29 U.S. (4 Pet.) 410 (1830), at 425–26, 430.

107 *Id.*, at 428–29.

108 *Id.*, at 430.

109 *Id.*, at 430–37.

110 *Id.*, at 440.

111 *Id.*, at 445, 449–50.

112 *Id.*, at 451.

113 Haines, *The Role of the Supreme Court*, at 594.

114 *Id.*

115 *Id.*, at 594–95.

5 Congressional Power Over the Supreme Court's Appellate Jurisdiction: From Roger Taney to Earl Warren

1 Haines, *The Role of the Supreme Court*, at 596.

2 46 U.S. (5 How.) 103 (1847).

3 *In re Barry*, 42 F. Cas. 113 (C.C. D. N.Y. 1844). Judge Betts ruled that, under section 14 of the Judiciary Act, the court had power to issue the writ in cases in which persons were in the custody of the United States. Inasmuch as *Barry* involved a question of custody arising out of a domestic relations dispute under the laws of New York, the circuit court lacked jurisdiction and authority to issue the writ of

habeas corpus. Even if this were a case within the court's diversity jurisdiction, Betts reasoned, it would be decided according to the laws of New York. *In re Barry* stands for the proposition that, unlike common-law courts, the circuit courts are not courts of general jurisdiction. They exercise their jurisdiction according to the statutes and can employ the writ of habeas corpus insofar as necessary to vindicate their jurisdiction.

4   *Id.*, at 129–32.

5   *Barry* v. *Mercein*, 46 U.S. (5 How.) 103 (1847), at 119. Unlike appeals from the decisions of state courts, where there is no de minimis dollar requirement, section 22 provides that the Court has power to review and revise "final judgments and decrees in civil actions and suits in equity in a Circuit Court, when the matter in dispute exceeds the sum or value of two thousand dollars, exclusive of costs." *Id.*

6   *Id.*, at 119.

7   47 U.S. (6 How.) 106 (1848).

8   *Id.*

9   *Id.*, at 113.

10 *United States* v. *Boisdoire's Heirs*, 49 U.S. (8 How.) 113 (1850), at 120–21.

11 *Id.*, at 122–23.

12 *Id.*, at 123.

13 *Id.*, at 122. Taney wrote, "In expounding a statute, we must not be guided by a single sentence or member of a sentence, but look to the provisions of the whole law, and to its object and policy."

14 *Id.*, at 121.

15 51 U.S. (10 How.) 72 (1850).

16 *Id.*, at 77, 78–79, 80.

17 *Id.*, at 79. Furthermore, if the Supreme Court accepted jurisdiction and either affirmed or reversed the decision of the lower court, the district court would not have jurisdiction under the Constitution or the laws of the United States to execute the judgment. During the December 1851 term of the Supreme Court, Justice Catron followed the same principle in a fugitive-slave case, *Norris* v. *Crocker*, 54 U.S. (13 How.) 429 (1851). The issue in *Norris* was whether the act of 1850 had repealed the penalties prescribed in the act of 1793 for preventing the owner of a fugitive slave from recovering his property. Since the suit was pending in the circuit court at the time that Congress repealed the relevant provision, the Court no longer had jurisdiction over the subject matter. Two points are relevant to the present argument. First, the plaintiff's right to recover the penalty depended entirely on the statute. Second, Justice Catron's opinion rested on a statutory construction of the acts of 1793 and 1850. There was no constitutional issue present in *Norris*.

18 49 U.S. (8 How.) 441 (1850).

19 *Id.*, at 449–50.

20 *Id.*, at 449.

21 *Id.*, at 450.

22 *Id.*, at 448.

23 69 U.S. (2 Wall.) 561 (1864). Taney's posthumous draft appears at 117 U.S. 697 (1885).

24 117 U.S. 697 (1885), at 697–98.

25 *Id.*, at 698, 699–700.

26 *Id.*, at 700. (citations omitted).

27 *Id.*, at 700–701.

28 *Id.*, at 702, 705.

29 60 U.S. (19 How.) 393 (1857).

30 These case are reported, respectively, at 71 U.S. (4 Wall.) 2 (1866); 71 U.S. (4 Wall.) 277 (1867); 71 U.S. (4 Wall.) 333 (1867); 71 U.S. (4 Wall.) 475 (1867); 75 U.S. (8 Wall.) 85 (1868); and 80 U.S. (13 Wall.) 128 (1872).

31 On Chase's performance in the impeachment trial of Andrew Johnson, see Abraham, Henry J., *Justices and Presidents: A Political History of Appointments to the Supreme Court*, 2d ed. (New York: Oxford Univ. Press, 1985), at 123; hereinafter cited as Abraham, *Justices and Presidents.*

32 Ch. 31, 14 Stat. 27 (1866).

33 See the text of these acts, respectively, in Ch. 28, 14 Stat. 385, sec. 1, at 385–86 (1867); Ch. 114, 16 Stat. 140, sec. 8, at 142, sec. 23, at 146 (1870); and Ch. 114, 18 Stat. 335, sec. 3, at 336, sec. 5, at 337 (1875).

34 Ch. 137, 18 Stat. 470, at 470–73 (1875).

35 70 U.S. (3 Wall.) 250 (1865), at 254.

36 *Id.*, at 256–57.

37 *Id.*, at 254.

38 These cases are reported respectively at 72 U.S. (5 Wall.) 541 (1867); 76 U.S. (9 Wall.) 567 (1870); and 78 U.S. (11 Wall.) 88 (1871).

39 *Merchants Insurance Co.*, 72 U.S. (5 Wall.), at 544.

40 *Id.*, at 545.

41 *The Assessors*, 76 U.S. (9 Wall.), at 573–74.

42 *Id.*, at 575.

43 *Tynen*, 78 U.S. (11 Wall.), at 95.

44 *Id.*, at 92–93.

45 71 U.S. (4 Wall.) 2 (1866).

46 Warren, *The Supreme Court in United States History*, at 446, 448–49.

47 71 U.S. (4 Wall.) 277 (1867); 71 U.S. (4 Wall.) 333 (1867); see also Warren, *The Supreme Court in United States History*, at 449–51.

48 Cushman, Robert F., *Cases in Constitutional Law*, 6th ed. (Englewood Cliffs, N.J.: Prentice-Hall, 1984), at 250.

49 71 U.S. (4 Wall.) 475 (1867).

50 73 U.S. (6 Wall) 318 (1868), denial of motion to dismiss; 74 U.S. (7 Wall.) 506 (1869), decision reported.

51 Van Alstyne, 15 *Ariz. L. Rev.*, at 242.

52 *McCardle*, 74 U.S. (7 Wall.), at 514.

53 Judiciary Act of 1789, Ch. 20, 1 Stat. 73 (1789).

54 *McCardle*, 74 U.S. (7 Wall.), at 515.

55 75 U.S. (8 Wall.) 85 (1869), at 103, 105, 106.

56 *Id.*, at 102–3. Chase wrote:

> It seems to be a necessary consequence that if the appellate jurisdiction of *habeas corpus* extends to any case, it extends to this. It is unimportant in what custody the prisoner may be, if it is a custody to which he has been remanded by the order of an inferior court of the United States. It is proper to add, that we are not aware of anything in any act of Congress, except the act of 1868, which indicates any intention to withhold appellate jurisdiction in *habeas*

corpus cases from this court, or to abridge the jurisdiction derived from the Constitution and defined by the act of 1789. We agree that it is given subject to exception and regulation by Congress; but it is too plain for argument that the denial to this court of appellate jurisdiction in this class of cases must greatly weaken the efficacy of the writ, deprive the citizen in many cases of its benefits, and seriously hinder the establishment of that uniformity in deciding upon questions of personal rights which can only be attained through appellate jurisdiction.

57 U.S. Const. art. I, § 9 states: "The privilege of the writ of habeas corpus shall not be suspended, unless when in cases of rebellion or invasion the public safety may require it." See, for example, Ratner, 27 *Vill. L. Rev.*; Rotunda, 64 *Geo. L.J.*

58 *Yerger*, 75 U.S. (8 Wall.), at 95–97.

59 See, for example, Van Alstyne, 15 *Ariz. L. Rev.* 229. Although Van Alstyne argues that congressional power under Article III, section 2, is plenary, he also argues that other constitutional provisions, including the habeas corpus clause, apply to the exercise of congressional power over the Supreme Court's appellate jurisdiction. *Id.*, at 263–67, 268–69.

60 Indeed, Chase refers to the peculiar, emergency circumstances under which Congress passed the act. 75 U.S. (8 Wall.) 85, at 103–4.

61 80 U.S. (13 Wall.) 128 (1872).

62 *Id.*, at 139.

63 *Id.*, at 139–40.

64 *Id.*, at 132, 140–41, 143. Under the Abandoned Property Act of 1863, the government sold cotton that Wilson had abandoned to Union forces. Between December 1863 and July 1868 presidents Lincoln and Andrew Johnson issued five proclamations providing for a full, unconditional pardon and the restoration of property rights to all who swore allegiance and did not fall under any exceptions, as provided in presidential proclamations. There is no evidence to demonstrate that Wilson was ineligible for an unconditional pardon.

65 Ch. 31, 16 Stat. 230, at 235 (1870).

66 *Id.*

67 *Id.*

68 *Klein*, 80 U.S. (13 Wall.), at 144.

69 *Id.*, at 140, 145.

70 *Id.*, at 147.

71 *Id.*, at 140, 148. Also see *United States* v. *Padelford*, 76 U.S. (9 Wall.) 531 (1870), at 542, in which the Court sustained the president's exercise of a conditional pardon. The effect of the president's pardon was to restore the individual's property rights, with the exception of slaves. Also see *Ex parte Garland*, 71 U.S. (4 Wall.) 333 (1867), at 380, in which the Court held that the effect of a pardon is to treat the offender as innocent.

72 80 U.S. (13 Wall.) 128 (1872), at 144–45.

73 *Id.*, at 145–46.

74 *Id.*, at 147.

75 *Id.*, at 148.

76 For a further analysis of the implications of *United States* v. *Klein* see, e.g., Sager, 95 *Harv. L. Rev.* 17–89 (1981); Norris, *L.A. Bar. Bul.* 212–15, 229–31 (1960); and

Redish, Martin H., "Congressional Power to Regulate Supreme Court Appellate Jurisdiction Under the Exceptions Clause: An Internal and External Examination," 27 *Vill. L. Rev.* 900–928 (1982).

77 Wright, *The Growth of American Constitutional Law*, at 85.

78 Warren, *The Supreme Court in United States History*, vol. 1, at 65, vol. 2, at 625, 626, 642.

79 156 U.S. 1 (1895) and 158 U.S. 601 (1895), respectively.

80 See Warren, *The Supreme Court in United States History*, vol. 2, at 682, 683, 686, 687–88, 703.

81 98 U.S. 398 (1879), 105 U.S. 381 (1882), 208 U.S. 393 (1908), and 210 U.S. 281 (1908), respectively.

82 Ratner, 109 *U. Pa. L. Rev.*, at 182.

83 See 105 U.S. 381 (1882), at 386.

84 *Grant*, 98 U.S., at 401. In *Grant*, the Baltimore & Potomac sought to reverse a judgment of $2,250 against it by the Supreme Court of the District of Columbia. Under section 4 of the Judiciary Act of 1879, however, Congress had limited appeals from the Supreme Court of the district to matters in excess of $2,500. Since the act of 1879 was in conflict with an earlier statute authorizing appeals in cases with a value of more than $1,000, the Court accepted the later act as the most recent expression of the legislative will, even though Congress had not explicitly applied the repealer to pending cases. By looking behind the 1879 act to determine congressional intent, Waite, speaking for the Court, concluded that Congress had intended to apply the jurisdictional limit to pending cases. Despite Waite's remarks on congressional power to regulate and limit the appellate jurisdiction, *Grant* rests entirely on a statutory construction of the Judiciary Act of 1879. Furthermore, there was no substantive constitutional claim present in this case. *Id.*, at 398–99, 401–2, 402–3.

85 105 U.S. 381 (1882), at 384.

86 *Id.*, at 385.

87 *Id.*, at 386.

88 *Id.*, at 386–87.

89 208 U.S. 393 (1908), at 399–400. In *Bitty*, the Supreme Court reversed the decision of the Circuit Court for the Southern District of New York sustaining the defendant's demurrer to an indictment and dismissing the case. The government had charged Bitty with importing a woman from England for an immoral purpose, a criminal violation of the Immigration Act of 1907. The government claimed that the act prohibited importing women and girls for prostitution or any other immoral purpose, including importing a woman to live as a mistress or concubine. Bitty demurred, claiming that Congress had not intended to include bringing a mistress to the United States within the terms of the act. The act also permitted the government to appeal the circuit court's decision in criminal cases in which the lower court had quashed the indictment or sustained the demurrer and in which the circuit court's decision was based on the validity of the statute. However, the act did not permit the defendant to challenge the lower court's decision in cases in which the court overruled the demurrer.

Denying that there was any merit to the argument that the statute was unconstitutional, the Supreme Court reversed the circuit court's judgment. The Court specifically sustained the provision permitting the government to test the validity of the lower court's construction of the statute. Arguing that Congress had an interest in promoting the efficient administration of criminal justice, Harlan sustained the government's right to seek a writ of error. He also denied that the defendant had a constitutional right to appeal the lower court's denial of a demurrer prior to the final determination of a criminal case against him. *Id.*, at 394–95, 395–97, 399, 400, 403.

90 210 U.S. 281 (1908). The Railway Co. challenged the Arkansas courts' interpretation of the Safety Appliance Act of 1893, authorizing the Interstate Commerce Commission to regulate the standard height of draw bars used to couple freight cars on standard gauge railways. The trial court had awarded a judgment to Mrs. Taylor, whose husband had been killed while coupling two freight cars. The Arkansas Supreme Court upheld the judgment for Taylor's estate based on its construction of the 1893 statute. *Id.*, at 282–84, 285–87, 288.

91 *Id.*, at 292.

92 *Id.*, at 293.

93 *Id.*, at 292.

94 *Id.*, at 293.

95 272 U.S. 533 (1926), 281 U.S. 464 (1930), and 285 U.S. 22 (1932), respectively.

96 272 U.S. 533 (1926), at 536. Except as Congress has consented, there is no right to bring these suits against the United States, and therefore the right arising from the consent is subject to such restrictions as Congress has imposed. One of these is that the trial shall be by the court without a jury. Another, in force until changed by the act of February 13, 1925, ch. 229, 43 Stat. 936, forbade an appellate review where the decision was against the claimant and the amount in controversy was not in excess of $3,000. Others, still in force, limit the scope of the review where one is permitted. Apart from the nature of these suits, the well-settled rule applies that an appellate review is not essential to due process of law, but is a matter of grace. *Id.*

97 *Id.*, at 536, 540.

98 281 U.S. 464 (1930) at 465–66, 466, 470. On October 12, 1928, the commission renewed the General Electric Company's license to operate a radio station in Schenectady, New York, under less favorable terms than the previous license had conferred. Under section 16 of the Radio Act of 1927, General Electric appealed the decision to the Court of Appeals for the District of Columbia, which found that the public interest would be served best by renewing the license under the original terms. The commission appealed the lower court's decision to the Supreme Court. *Id.*

99 *Id.*, at 467.

100 *Id.*, at 468.

101 *Id.*, at 469.

102 285 U.S. 22 (1932).

103 *Id.*, at 36–37.

104 *Id.*, at 45–46.

105 *Id.*, at 51–53.

106 *Id.*, at 49–50.

107 *Id.*, at 51–52.

108 *Id.*, at 37.

109 *Id.*, at 62.

110 *Id.*, at 62–64.

111 *Id.*, at 64.

112 See Justice Brandeis's dissenting opinion. Brandeis, with whom Stone and Roberts concurred, attacked the majority's opinion for undermining the administrative process. He denied that the due process clause required a trial de novo to determine the jurisdictional facts. *Id.*, at 65–95.

113 337 U.S. 582 (1949), at 583–84.

114 *Id.*, at 582.

115 6 U.S. (2 Cranch) 445 (1805).

116 *National Mutual Insurance Co.*, 337 U.S. at 600.

117 *Id.*, at 616–17, 621–22.

118 *Id.*, at 619–25.

119 *Id.*, at 627–30, 634–35, 637–38.

120 *Id.*, at 646.

121 *Id.*, at 647.

122 *Id.*, at 655.

123 *Id.*

124 343 U.S. 112 (1952) and 344 U.S. 386 (1953), respectively.

125 *Bruner*, 343 U.S. at 114. Congress had withdrawn the district and circuit courts' jurisdiction over U.S. government employees' actions to recover compensation for services, but the Court of Claims retained jurisdiction to hear and decide Bruner's claim to recover overtime compensation due for his services as civilian fire chief at Camp Wheeler, Georgia. As Vinson remarked, Congress had not altered Bruner's rights; it "simply reduced the number of tribunals authorized to hear and determine such rights and liabilities." *Id.*, at 113, 115, 117.

126 *Id.*, at 116–17.

127 *De La Rama*, 344 U.S., at 386–87.

128 *Id.*, at 388–89.

129 *Id.*, at 389–90. See also *Lynch v. United States*, 292 U.S. 571 (1934).

130 169 F.2d 254 (2nd Cir. 1948) and 174 F.2d 961 (D.C. Cir. 1949), respectively.

131 For a discussion of the background to *Battaglia*, see Silva, Ruth C., Edward Keynes, Hugh Bone, and David Adamany, *American Government: Democracy and Liberty in Balance* (New York: Alfred A. Knopf, 1976), at 427–28.

132 328 U.S. 680 (1945).

133 *Id.*

134 *Battaglia*, 169 F.2d at 262.

135 *Id.*, at 257.

136 *Eisentrager*, 174 F.2d at 961.

137 *Id.*, at 965.

138 *Id.* Prior to May 8, 1945, Eisentrager and others were civilian employees of the German government in China. After Germany surrendered, Eisentrager continued to wage war against the United States in territory that the Japanese Imperial Government controlled. In August 1946, the United States charged Eisentrager with violating the laws of war. A military commission tried and convicted Eisentrager for continuing to wage war against the United States. Subsequently, Eisentrager was incarcerated in Landsberg Prison, a U.S. military prison in occupied Germany. Eisentrager appealed the military proceeding, arguing that the military commission lacked jurisdiction and that his imprisonment violated articles I and III as well as

the Fifth Amendment. He filed a petition for a writ of habeas corpus in the District Court for the District of Columbia, which Eisentrager claimed had jurisdiction over his military custodians. The district court dismissed the petition for want of jurisdiction. *Id.*, at 962–63, 968.

139 *Id.*, at 963–64.
140 *Id.*, at 965, 967.
141 304 U.S. 458 (1938).
142 *Eisentrager*, 174 F.2d, at 967.
143 *Id.*, at 967.
144 Reversed on other grounds, *sub nom.*, *Johnson* v. *Eisentrager*, 339 U.S. 763 (1950).
145 370 U.S. 530 (1962).
146 *Id.*, at 532–33.
147 *Id.*, at 533.
148 *Id.*, at 540.
149 *Id.*, at 551.
150 *Id.*, at 557.
151 *Id.*, at 568.
152 *Id.*
153 *Id.*, at 593–94.
154 *Id.*, at 599, 600–601.
155 *Id.*, at 605.

6 Congressional Power Over the Court: The View from the Capitol

1 Warren, *The Supreme Court in United States History*, vol. 1, at 4–5.
2 Murphy, *Congress and The Court*, at 42–44. Also see *The Legal Tender Cases*, *Julliard* v. *Greenman*, 110 U.S. 42 (1884); *The Civil Rights Cases*, 109 U.S. 3 (1883).
3 The term "mature" policy judgment implies that legislation is the result of a deliberative process that includes Congress and the president. See Murphy, *Congress and The Court*, at 46–52, 53–57; Warren, *The Supreme Court in United States History*, vol. 2, at 703–4; see, generally, Pritchett, C. Herman, *The Roosevelt Court: A Study in Judicial Politics and Values, 1937–1947* (New York: Octagon Books, 1948).
4 See Murphy, *Congress and The Court*; Schmidhauser, *The Supreme Court*; Levy, 22 *N.Y.U. Intramural L. Rev.*, at 193–95; Lytle, Clifford M., "Congressional Response to Supreme Court Decisions in The Aftermath of The School Desegregation Cases," 12 *Pub. L.* 290–312 (1963), at 290–92.
5 Ch. 52, 61 Stat. 84; 29 U.S.C. §§ 201–19 (1947), reversing *Anderson* v. *Mt. Clemens Pottery Co.*, 328 U.S. 680 (1945).
6 *Chisholm* v. *Georgia*, 2 U.S. (2 Dall.) 419 (1793), resulting in the Eleventh Amendment; *Dred Scott* v. *Sanford*, 60 U.S. (19 How.) 393 (1857), resulting in the Thirteenth, Fourteenth, and Fifteenth amendments; *Pollock* v. *Farmers' Loan and Trust Co.*, 158 U.S. 601 (1895), resulting in the Sixteenth Amendment; *Oregon* v. *Mitchell*, 400 U.S. 112 (1970), resulting in the Twenty-sixth Amendment.
7 Witt, Elder, ed., *Guide to The U.S. Supreme Court* (Washington, D.C.: Congressional Quarterly, Inc., 1979), at 664.

8 Ch. 31, 2 Stat., at 156–67 (1802).

9 See Warren, *The Supreme Court in United States History*, vol. 1, at 663–64. In 1823 Senator Richard M. Johnson (D.-Ky.) introduced a bill requiring seven justices to concur in any decision declaring a congressional or state act unconstitutional.

10 29 U.S.C.A. §§ 101–15 (1982).

11 Ch. 676, 52 Stat. 1060 (1938).

12 328 U.S. 680 (1946).

13 Ch. 52, 61 Stat. 84 (1947).

14 "Congressional Reversal of Supreme Court Decisions: 1945-1957," *Harv. L. Rev.* 1324–37 (1958). Also see the Social Security Act, Ch. 531, 49 Stat. 620 (1935); the National Labor Relations Act, Ch. 372, § 2 (3), 49 Stat. 450 (1935); and the Nationality Act of 1940, Ch. 876, § 304, 54 Stat. 1140 (1940).

15 *Id.*, at 1330–32.

16 402 U.S. 1 (1971).

17 The Civil Rights Act of 1964, Pub. L. No. 88-352, § 2003, 78 Stat. 241 (1964).

18 *Id.*, at 248. In *Swann*, the Court interpreted the Civil Rights provision as limiting desegregation efforts under the act to those cases in which de jure segregation can be shown. As Chief Justice Burger's opinion for the Court indicates, the justices ignored section 2003 of the Civil Rights Act of 1964:

> There is no suggestion of an intention to restrict those powers or withdraw from courts their historic equitable remedial powers. . . . [T]here is nothing in the Act that provides us material assistance in answering the question of remedy for state-imposed segregation in violation of *Brown I*. The basis of our decision must be the prohibition of the Fourteenth Amendment that no State shall "deny to any person within its jurisdiction the equal protection of the laws."

Swann, 402 U.S., at 17–18. Indeed, the Court ruled that "affirmative action in the form of remedial altering of attendance zones is proper to achieve truly nondiscriminatory assignments." *Id.*, at 28.

Testifying before the House Judiciary Committee in support of his proposal, H.J. Res. 620, a constitutional amendment forbidding public school assignments based on race, Representative Norman F. Lent (R-N.Y.) stated:

> Congress tried this in the Civil Rights Act of 1964, section 2003 (c), when they spelled out what desegregation would mean and they were very clear in stating that it would not include the assignment of youngsters to schools on the basis of their skin color. In the *Charlotte-Mecklenburg* case the courts said, in effect, our equity jurisdiction to right this wrong is so great that we don't have to pay attention to that section.

U.S. Congress, House of Representatives, Committee on the Judiciary, *School Busing: Hearings on Proposed Amendments Relating to the Constitution and Legislation Relating to the Transportation and Assignment of Public School Pupils*, part 1, 92nd Congress, 2nd Session, February 28–29, March 1–3, 6, 8–9, 13, 15–16; April 12–13, 26–27; May 3–4, 10, 18, and 24, 1972 (Washington D.C.: Government Printing Office, 1972), at 253; hereinafter cited as House Judiciary Committee, *Busing Hearings* (1972).

19   See, e.g., H.J. Res. 620, H.J. Res. 94, H.J. Res. 587, H.J. Res. 628, and H.J. Res. 983, 92d Cong., 2d Sess. (1971). H.J. Res. 620 provides that: "No public school student shall, because of his race, creed, or color, be assigned to or required to attend a particular school."

20   377 U.S. 533 (1964). On the same day, the Court also decided *WMCA* v. *Lomenzo*, 377 U.S. 633 (1964); *Lucas* v. *44th General Assembly of Colorado*, 377 U.S. 713 (1964); *Maryland Committee for Fair Representation* v. *Tawes, Governor*, 377 U.S. 656 (1964); *Davis* v. *Mann*, 377 U.S. 678 (1964); and *Roman* v. *Sincock*, 377 U.S. 695 (1964).

21   S.J. Res. 185, 88th Cong., 2d Sess. (1964); see also Pettit, Lawrence K., and Edward Keynes, eds., *The Legislative Process in The U.S. Senate* (Chicago: Rand McNally & Co., 1969); hereinafter cited as Pettit, *The U.S. Senate.*

22   410 U.S. 113 (1973).

23   See, for example, Senator Orrin G. Hatch's statement in the Senate Judiciary Committee's hearings on the scope of congressional authority to regulate the federal courts' jurisdiction, U.S. Congress, Senate Committee on the Judiciary, *Constitutional Restraints Upon the Judiciary*, 97th Cong., 1st Sess., May 20–21 and June 22, 1981 (Washington, D.C.: Government Printing Office, 1982).

24   *Washington Post*, May 3, 1981, at C.7.

25   376 U.S. 1 (1964), 377 U.S. 533 (1964), and 395 U.S. 486 (1969), respectively.

26   127 Cong. Rec. S3912–14 (daily ed. April 10, 1981) (Remarks of Senator Orrin Hatch); 128 Cong. Rec. S2199–2200 (daily ed. March 16, 1982) (Remarks of Senator Jesse Helms); 127 Cong. Rec. E1801–3 (daily ed. April 10, 1981) (Remarks of Representative Charles F. Dougherty).

27   See Bickel, *The Least Dangerous Branch*, at 16–19, 21–22; Choper, *Judicial Review*, at 4–7, 58–59.

28   247 U.S. 251 (1918).

29   Although Choper admits that Congress incorporates many undemocratic features, he argues that it is fundamentally more democratic than other national political institutions. See Choper, *Judicial Review*, at 10–21, 24–25, 25–28, 29–33, 36.

30   See Senator Slade Gorton's (R.-Wash.) statement before the Senate Judiciary Committee on the fact-finding abilities of Congress and the courts. U.S. Congress, Senate, Committee on the Judiciary, Subcommittee on Separation of Powers, *Court Ordered Busing: Hearings on S. 528, S. 1005, S. 1147, S. 1647, S. 1743, and S. 1760*, 97th Cong., 1st Sess., May 22, September 30, October 1 and 16, 1981 (Washington, D.C.: Government Printing Office, 1982), at 6–7; hereinafter cited as Senate Judiciary Committee, Subcommittee on Separation of Powers, *Busing Hearings* (1981).

31   See Justice Frankfurter's opinion in *Colegrove* v. *Green*, 328 U.S. 549 (1946), at 555; Strum, Philippa, *The Supreme Court and "Political Questions": A Study in Judicial Evasion* (Tuscaloosa: Univ. of Alabama Press, 1974), at 18; Peltason, Jack W., *Federal Courts in The Political Process* (Garden City, N.Y.: Doubleday & Co., 1955), at 10.

32   2 U.S. (2 Dall.) 419 (1793).

33   U.S. Const. amend. XI.

34   Mason, Alpheus T., William M. Beaney, and Donald G. Stephenson, Jr., *American Constitutional Law: Introductory Essays and Selected Cases*, 7th ed. (Englewood Cliffs, N.J.: Prentice-Hall, 1983), at 154–55.

35   Ch. 4, 2 Stat. 89, § 4, at 89–90, § 7, at 90–91, and §§ 10, 11, 12, and 13, at 92–93 (1801).

36 Crosskey, *Politics and The Constitution*, vol. 2, at 759–62.

37 Hamilton, *Papers*, vol. 25, at 501, 520–27, 550–51, 553.

38 Beveridge, *The Life of John Marshall*, vol. 3, at 60–92.

39 *Id.*

40 Hamilton, *Papers*, vol. 25, at 534.

41 Beveridge, *The Life of John Marshall*, vol. 3, at 72, 91–92.

42 Ch. 8, 2 Stat. 132 (1802).

43 Ch. 31, 2 Stat. 156 (1802).

44 5 U.S. (1 Cranch) 137 (1803).

45 5 U.S. (1 Cranch) 299 (1803), at 308.

46 Murphy, *Congress and The Court*, at 11.

47 11 U.S. (7 Cranch) 603 (1813).

48 25 F. Cas. 187 (C.C. D. Va. 1807) (No. 14,694).

49 Murphy, *Congress and The Court*, at 14–15.

50 U.S. (6 Cranch) 87 (1810).

51 11 U.S. (7 Cranch) 603 (1813).

52 *Id.*, at 15–16.

53 14 U.S. (1 Wheat.) 304 (1816).

54 17 U.S. (4 Wheat.) 316 (1819), 17 U.S. (4 Wheat.) 518 (1819), 17 U.S. (4 Wheat.) 122 (1819), 19 U.S. (6 Wheat.) 264 (1821), 21 U.S. (8 Wheat.) 1 (1823), and 22 U.S. (9 Wheat.) 738 (1824), respectively.

55 Haines, Charles G., *The American Doctrine of Judicial Supremacy*, 2nd ed. (Berkeley: Univ. of California Press, 1932), at 428–29.

56 Warren, *The Supreme Court in United States History*, vol. 1, at 663.

57 Murphy, *Congress and The Court*, at 23–24.

58 Haines, *The Role of The Supreme Court*, vol. 1, at 481.

59 Warren, *The Supreme Court in United States History*, at 663–64.

60 Haines, *The Role of The Supreme Court*, vol. 1, at 525.

61 *Id.*, at 511.

62 *Id.*, at 522 (Quoting Madison).

63 *Id.*, at 579–80, 593–94, 595–96, 604, 607.

64 29 U.S. (4 Pet.) 410 (1830).

65 31 U.S. (6 Pet.) 515 (1832).

66 Haines, *The Role of The Supreme Court*, vol. 1, at 497.

67 37 U.S. (12 Pet.) 524 (1838).

68 Baker, Richard C., "Yesterday's Critics of the Federal Judiciary," 47 *Ill. B. J.* 314–22, 394–404, 478–96 564–70 (1958–59), at 478–79.

69 37 U.S. (12 Pet.) 524 (1838), at 616, 617, 639.

70 Haines, *The Role of The Supreme Court*, vol. 1, at 497.

71 60 U.S. (19 How.) 393 (1857) and 62 U.S. (21 How.) 506 (1859), respectively.

72 *Id.*, at 513–14, 515–16.

73 *Id.*, at 517–19, 522, 525, 526.

74 Haines, *The American Doctrine of Judicial Supremacy*, at 428–29.

75 17 F. Cas. 487 (C.C.D. Md. 1861) (No. 9,487).

76 Keynes, *Undeclared War*, at 71, 87, 173.

77 68 U.S. (1 Wall.) 243 (1864).

78 71 U.S. (4 Wall.) 2 (1866); Keynes, *Undeclared War*, at 173.

79 Warren, *The Supreme Court in United States History*, vol. 2, at 496.

80   *Id.*, at 448–49.

81   *Id.*, at 466.

82   *Id.*, at 471.

83   *Id.*, at 491–92.

84   *Id.*, at 492.

85   *Id.*, at 494.

86   Frankfurter, Felix, and James M. Landis, *The Business of The Supreme Court* (Reprint. New York: Johnson Reprint Corp., 1972), at 89; hereinafter cited as Frankfurter, *The Business of The Supreme Court.*

87   *Id.*

88   96 U.S. 369 (1877), at 376–77. Speaking for the majority, Chief Justice Waite applied the removal statutes to extend jurisdiction to the circuit courts over foreign (i.e., nonresident) corporations transacting business through an agent.

89   Frankfurter, *The Business of The Supreme Court*, at 90.

90   *Id.*, at 90–91.

91   *Id.*, at 95–96.

92   *Id.*, at 101; act of March 3, 1891, Ch. 517, 26 Stat. 826 (1891).

93   Warren, *The Supreme Court in United States History*, vol. 2, at 727.

94   Murphy, *Congress and The Court*, at 46.

95   158 U.S. 601 (1895), 156 U.S. 1 (1895), and 158 U.S. 564 (1895), respectively.

96   198 U.S. 45 (1905), 247 U.S. 251 (1918), and 261 U.S. 525 (1923), respectively.

97   See Murphy, *Congress and The Court*, especially at 50–52.

98   Ch. 517, 26 Stat. 826, § 5, at 827–28, § 6, at 828 (1891).

99   Ch. 6, 36 Stat. 105, § 29 (1909).

100 Ch. 2564, 34 Stat. 1246 (1907).

101 Ch. 2, 38 Stat. 790 (1914).

102 For an analysis of congressional expansion and contraction of the Supreme Court's appellate jurisdiction in this period, see Warren, *The Supreme Court in United States History*, at 727–28.

103 Frankfurter, *The Business of The Supreme Court*, at 255.

104 Ch. 448, 39 Stat. 726, § 3, at 726–27 (1916).

105 *Id.*, § 4, at 727.

106 Frankfurter, *The Business of The Supreme Court*, at 255–56.

107 *Id.*, at 257.

108 *Id.*, at 273–80, for an analysis of the legislative history of the Judges Bill.

109 *Id.*, at 285–86.

110 As Walter Murphy notes, during Taft's tenure as chief justice the Supreme Court overturned 141 state statutes. In two-thirds of these cases, the Court found that the statute violated the Fourteenth Amendment's due process clause. Murphy, *Congress and The Court*, at 53.

111 *Id.*, at 47.

112 The Court invalidated the following acts: (1) section 9(c) of the National Industrial Recovery Act, prohibiting the shipment of "hot oil" in interstate commerce, Ch. 90, 48 Stat. 195 (1933), invalidated, *Panama Refining Co.* v. *Ryan*, 293 U.S. 389 (1935); (2) the Railway Pension Act, Ch. 868, 48 Stat. 1283 (1934), invalidated, *Railroad Retirement Bd.* v. *Alton R.R. Co.*, 295 U.S. 330 (1934); (3) the Frazier-Lemke Farm Mortgage Act, Ch. 869, 48 Stat. 1289 (1934), invalidated, *Louisville Joint Stock Land Bank* v. *Radford*, 295 U.S. 555 (1935); (4) section 3(a) of the

National Industrial Recovery Act, Ch. 90, 48 Stat. 195 (1933), invalidated, *Schecter Poultry Co.* v. *United States*, 295 U.S. 495 (1935); (5) the Agricultural Adjustment Act, Ch. 25, 48 Stat. 31 (Title I, §§ 1-21) (1933), invalidated, *United States* v. *Butler*, 297 U.S. 1 (1936); (6) the Guffey Bituminous Coal Act, Ch. 824, 49 Stat. 991 (1935), invalidated, *Carter* v. *Carter Coal Co.*, 298 U.S. 238 (1936); (7) the Municipal Bankruptcy Act, Ch. 345, 48 Stat. 798 (1934), invalidated, *Ashton* v. *Cameron County Dist.*, 298 U.S. 513 (1936); and (8) New York's minimum wage law for women, Laws of New York, Ch. 584 (1933), invalidated, *Morehead* v. *New York ex rel. Tipaldo*, 298 U.S. 587 (1936). However, the Court did sustain several national and state laws that promoted economic recovery: (1) the Gold Repeal Joint Resolution, Ch. 48, 48 Stat. 113 (1933), sustained, *Norman* v. *Baltimore & Ohio R.R. Co.*, 294 U.S. 240 (1935); (2) the Tennessee Valley Authority Act, Ch. 32, 48 Stat. 58 (Title 16, § 831) (1933), sustained, *Ashwander* v. *T.V.A.*, 297 U.S. 288 (1936); (3) Minnesota's mortgage moratorium law, Laws of Minnesota, Ch. 339, at 514 (1933), sustained, *Home Bldg. & Loan Assn.* v. *Blaisdell*, 290 U.S. 398 (1934); and (4) the New York Milk Control Act, establishing a minimum price for milk, Laws of New York, Ch. 158 (1933), sustained, *Nebbia* v. *New York*, 291 U.S. 502 (1934).

113 295 U.S. 602 (1935).

114 295 U.S. 495 (1935).

115 *Louisville Joint Stock Land Bank* v. *Radford*, 295 U.S. 555 (1935).

116 See Abraham, *Justices and Presidents*, at 208–9.

117 Ch. 90, 47 Stat. 70 (1932).

118 Ch. 283, 48 Stat. 775 (1934).

119 Ch. 726, 50 Stat. 738 (1937).

120 Ch. 26, 56 Stat. 23 (1942).

121 Ch. 52, 61 Stat. 84 (1947).

122 McGowan, Carl, "Federal Jurisdiction: Legislative and Judicial Change," 29 *Case W. Res. L. Rev.* 517–55 (1978), at 523. See also Frankfurter, Felix, and Nathan Greene, "Congressional Power Over the Labor Injunction," 31 *Colum. L. Rev.* 385–415 (1931), at 402–3.

123 Ch. 90, 47 Stat. 70, § 4, at 70–71 (1932).

124 *Id.*, § 7(e), at 71–72.

125 *Id.*, at 72.

126 *Id.*, at 72–73.

127 Frankfurter and Greene, 31 *Colum. L. Rev.*, at 408.

128 303 U.S. 323 (1938).

129 *Id.*, at 330.

130 Ch. 283, 48 Stat. 775 (1934).

131 321 U.S. 414 (1944), at 442.

132 Ch. 283, 48 Stat. 775 (1934).

133 Ch. 726, 50 Stat. 738 (1937).

134 319 U.S. 293 (1943), at 299; also see *Hillsborough* v. *Cromwell*, 326 U.S. 620 (1946), at 622–23.

135 Ch. 26, 56 Stat. 23, section 204(a), at 31 (1942).

136 *Id.*, §§ 204(a-d), at 31–33 (1942).

137 *Id.*, § 204(c), at 33.

138 *Id.*, §§ 205 (a) (c), at 33.

139 319 U.S. 182 (1943).

140 *Id.*, at 187.

141 *Id.*, at 189.

142 321 U.S. 414 (1944), at 430–31, 437–38.

143 *Id.*

144 169 F.2d 254 (2nd Cir. 1948).

145 304 U.S. 144 (1938), n. 4, at 152.

146 *Id.* Following Justice Stone's suggestion in *Carolene Products*, the Court later introduced the concept of a standard of heightened scrutiny in cases involving civil rights and civil liberties.

147 *Ex parte Endo*, 323 U.S. 283 (1944).

148 See *Smith* v. *Allwright*, 321 U.S. 649 (1944), in which the Court ruled that a white primary violated the Fifteenth Amendment.

149 334 U.S. 1 (1948).

150 347 U.S. 483 (1954).

151 Aside from *Brown II*, 349 U.S. 294 (1955), in which the Court implemented its original decision, the justices also touched off a storm with *Cooper* v. *Aaron*, 358 U.S. 1 (1958). Until 1969 the Supreme Court relied upon voluntary compliance as the principle means to enforce *Brown I*.

152 See *Peters* v. *Hobby*, 349 U.S. 331 (1955); *Pennsylvania* v. *Nelson*, 350 U.S. 497 (1956); *C.P.U.S.A.* v. *S.A.C.B.*, 351 U.S. 115 (1956); *Jencks* v. *United States*, 353 U.S. 657 (1957); *Service* v. *Dulles*, 354 U.S. 363 (1957); *Kent* v. *Dulles*, 357 U.S. 116 (1958); *Vitarelli* v. *Seaton*, 359 U.S. 535 (1959); *Greene* v. *McElroy*, 360 U.S. 474 (1959); *Taylor* v. *McElroy*, 360 U.S. 709 (1959).

153 *Watkins* v. *United States*, 354 U.S. 178 (1957); *Sweezy* v. *New Hampshire*, 354 U.S. 234 (1957); *Yates* v. *United States*, 355 U.S. 566 (1957).

154 See, for example, *Mallory* v. *United States*, 354 U.S. 449 (1957).

155 *Schware* v. *New Mexico*, 353 U.S. 232 (1957); *Beilan* v. *Philadelphia Bd. of Educ.*, 357 U.S. 399 (1958); *Lerner* v. *Casey*, 357 U.S. 468 (1958); *Konigsberg* v. *California*, 366 U.S. 36 (1961).

156 *Engel* v. *Vitale*, 370 U.S. 421 (1962); *Abington School Dist.* v. *Schempp*, 374 U.S. 203 (1963).

157 *Wesberry* v. *Sanders*, 376 U.S. 1 (1964); *Reynolds* v. *Sims*, 377 U.S. 533 (1964).

158 Schmidhauser, *The Supreme Court*, at 144. Among the 200 bills introduced to reverse specific decisions of the Supreme Court, only two measures were enacted, the Jencks Act, Pub. L. No. 85-269, 71 Stat. 595 (1957), and the Omnibus Crime Control and Safe Streets Act of 1968, Pub. L. No 90-351, 82 Stat. 197 (1968). Although these measures may have resulted in judicial caution and self-restraint, they did not alter the Supreme Court's relationship to Congress or the states. Nor did these measures prevent the Court from deciding constitutional claims.

   For additional analysis of the legislation introduced, see Murphy, *Congress and the Court*, especially 86–96, 193–223; Schmidhauser, *The Supreme Court*, especially 149–63; Lytle, 12 *Pub. L.*, at 290–92, 310–12; Levy, 22 *N.Y.U. Intramural L. Rev.*, at 193–94.

159 Bator, *The Federal Courts*, at 360.

160 *Id.*

161 Strickland, Stephen P., "Congress, The Supreme Court, and Public Policy: Activism, Restraint, and Interplay," 18 *Am. U.L. Rev.* 267–98 (1969), at 274.

162 Murphy, *Congress and The Court*, at 155–56.

163 *Id.*, at 156, 157, 207–8.

164 See Pettit, *The U.S. Senate*, at 115–16.

7 Congress, the Court, and School Prayer

1 370 U.S. 421 (1962) and 374 U.S. 203 (1963), respectively. In *Engel* the Court held that the following prayer, composed by the New York State Board of Regents and adopted by the Union Free School District of New Hyde Park, violated the establishment clause of the First Amendment, as applied to the state through the Fourteenth Amendment's due process clause: "Almighty God, we acknowledge our dependence upon Thee, and we beg Thy blessings upon us, our parents, our teachers and our Country." *Engel*, 370 U.S., at 422. In *Abington* the Court reached a similar result regarding the recitation of passages from the Bible and the Lord's Prayer. *Abington*, 374 U.S., at 225–27.

2 Pub. L. No. 98-377; 98 Stat. 1302; 20 U.S.C. 4071 (1984).

3 In examining congressional intent, the statements and legislative strategies and tactics of a measure's proponents are given greater weight than the position of its opponents. Of course, no individual senator's or representative's statements can reflect the collective intent of 100 senators and 435 representatives who may have diverse motives for supporting and voting on school prayer legislation. Therefore, the analysis in this and the next two chapters focuses largely on the language and the constitutional effects of proposals to curb the federal courts' jurisdiction over school prayer, school busing, and state antiabortion laws.

4 330 U.S. 1 (1947).

5 310 U.S. 296 (1940), at 303, 309.

6 *Everson*, 330 U.S., at 6–7, 17–18.

7 *Id.*, at 14–15.

8 See Justice Stewart's dissenting opinion in *Engel*, 370 U.S. at 446–49.

9 For a summary of this point of view, see Berger, *Government by Judiciary*. But see also Curtis, Michael Kent, *No State Shall Abridge: The Fourteenth Amendment and The Bill of Rights* (Durham, N.C.: Duke Univ. Press, 1986).

10 U.S. Congress, Senate, Committee on the Judiciary, *School Prayer: Hearings on S.J. Res. 148 Before the Subcommittee on Constitutional Amendments*, 89th Congress, 2nd Session, August 1–5 and 8, 1966 (Washington, D.C.: Government Printing Office, 1966), at 4-5; hereinafter cited as Senate Judiciary Committee, Subcommittee on Constitutional Amendments, *School Prayer* (1966).

11 *Everson v. Board of Educ.*, 330 U.S. 1 (1947), at 8–9.

12 *Id.*, at 10–11.

13 Jameson, J. Franklin, *The American Revolution Considered as a Social Movement* (Princeton, N.J.: Princeton Univ. Press, 1926, 1967), at 83–100.

14 *Everson*, 330 U.S., at 15.

15 *Id.*, at 16.

16 *Id.*, at 15–16.

17 See Hamilton, *The Federalist* (No. 10, Madison).

18 See Senator Helms's statement in the 98th Cong., 2d Sess. (1984); 130 Cong. Rec. S2901 (daily ed. March 20, 1984).

19 See Judge Friendly's opinion in *Stein* v. *Oshinsky*, 348 F.2nd 999 (2d Cir. 1965), at 1001.

20 See *Lemon* v. *Kurtzman*, 403 U.S. 602 (1971), at 612–14. Chief Justice Burger summarized the three-prong test that the Court had developed in determining whether an impermissible establishment of religion existed in a particular case. The Court's criteria included a determination of whether a statute or administrative practice (1) had a secular purpose, (2) had a principle effect of either promoting or inhibiting religion, or (3) fostered excessive entanglement with religion. If a statute or administrative practice did not meet all three tests, the Court later concluded, it could not survive the requirements of the establishment clause.

21 *Everson* v. *Board of Educ.* 330 U.S. 1 (1947), at 15–16.

22 *Lemon*, 403 U.S., at 612–13.

23 *Id.*, at 622–23.

24 See, for example, *Committee for Public Educ.* v. *Nyquist*, 413 U.S. 756 (1073), at 820–24 (Rehnquist, dissenting).

25 See *DeSpain* v. *DeKalb County Community School Dist.*, 384 F.2d 836 (7th Cir. 1968), at 839.

26 *Everson*, 330 U.S., at 16.

27 *Abington School District* v. *Schempp* and *Murray* v. *Curlett*, 374 U.S. 203 (1963).

28 *Engel* v. *Vitale*, 370 U.S. 421 (1962).

29 *Tudor* v. *Board of Educ. of Borough of Rutherford*, 100 A. 2d 857 (S.Ct. N.J., 1953), cert. den. 348 U.S. 816 (1954).

30 *Edwards* v. *Aguillard*, No. 85-1513 (S.Ct. June 1987).

31 *Stone* v. *Graham*, 449 U.S. 39 (1980).

32 *Wallace* v. *Jaffree*, 472 U.S. 38 (1985).

33 333 U.S. 203 (1948). In *McCollum* the Court found that a shared-time program of religious instruction conducted in a public school building by private teachers offended the First and Fourteenth amendments. *Id.*, at 207–9; but *cf. Zorach* v. *Clauson*, 343 U.S. 306 (1952), in which the Court sustained a released- or dismissed-time program that was not conducted on school property.

34 *Engel* v. *Vitale*, 370 U.S. 421 (1962), at 424.

35 *Id.*, at 430.

36 *Id.*, at 431.

37 *Id.*

38 131 Cong. Rec. H2499 (daily ed. April 24, 1985).

39 *Engel*, 370 U.S., at 446–49.

40 *Abington School Dist.* v. *Schempp*, 374 U.S. 203 (1963), at 205.

41 *Id.*

42 *Id.*, at 211.

43 *Id.*, at 220.

44 *Id.*, at 222.

45 *Id.*, at 223.

46 *Id.*, at 225.

47 *Id.*

48 See Douglas's opinion for the Court in *Zorach* v. *Clauson*, 343 U.S. 306 (1952), at 313.

49 *Abington*, 374 U.S., at 295 (Brennan, concurring).

50 *Id.*, at 308 (Stewart, dissenting).

51 *Id.*, at 311–12.

52 *Id.*, at 312.

53 *Id.*, at 320.

54 *Chamberlain* v. *Dade County Bd. of Pub. Instruction*, 377 U.S. 402 (1964).

55 160 So. 2d 97 (S.Ct. Fla., 1964).

56 384 F.2d 836 (7th Cir. 1968). Previously, in *Stein* v. *Oshinsky*, 348 F.2d 999 (2nd Cir. 1965), the court of appeals ruled that the First Amendment's free exercise clause does not require the state to permit pupils to recite an equally innocuous prayer.

57 *DeSpain*, 384 F.2d, at 837.

58 *Id.*, at 839.

59 *Cert. den.*, 382 U.S. 957 (1965) and 390 U.S. 906 (1968), respectively.

60 267 N.E. 2d 226 (Mass. S.Ct., 1971).

61 *Id.*, at 228.

62 *Cert. den.*, 404 U.S. 849 (1971).

63 *Wallace* v. *Jaffree*, 472 U.S. 38 (1985).

64 *Id.*, at 56.

65 *Id.*, at 56–57.

66 *Id.*, at 40.

67 *Id.*, at 60.

68 *Id.*, at 77 (O'Connor, concurring).

69 *Id.*, at 76–77.

70 *Id.*, at 68–69; see also *Lemon* v. *Kurtzman*, 403 U.S. 602 (1971), at 612–13.

71 *Wallace*, at 98, 100, 106.

72 *Id.*, at 99 (Rehnquist, dissenting). Also see Lieder, Michael D., "Religious Pluralism and Education in Historical Perspective: A Critique of the Supreme Court's Establishment Clause Jurisprudence," 22 *Wake Forest L. Rev.* 813–89 (1987), at 889. Lieder argues that "the Supreme Court's establishment clause jurisprudence rests on a delusion that government can be neutral in religious matters. It also rests on the mistaken and impossible desire to keep religion out of political affairs. In fact, religious groups have sought to shape education for the last 350 years, including successful efforts to influence governmental policy. The very policies that the Supreme Court now endorses were in large part products of such religious influences."

73 *Wallace*, 472 U.S., at 113–14 (Rehnquist, dissenting).

74 No. 85-1513 (S.Ct. 1987).

75 *Id.*, at 1.

76 *Id.*, at 3.

77 *Edwards*, No. 85-1513, slip op. at 3 (Powell, concurring).

78 *Id.*, at 10–12.

79 *Id.*, at 1, 2, 3, 6, 30–31 (Scalia, dissenting).

80 108 Cong. Rec. 11732 (1962).

81 *Id.*, at 13594.

82 *Id.*

83 109 Cong. Rec. A4692-A4693 (1963).

84 110 Cong. Rec. 6390 (1964).

85 *Id.*, at 6391.

86 130 Cong. Rec. S2901 (daily ed. March 20, 1984).

87   *Id.,* at S2902.

88   *Id.,* at S2901.

89   S.J. Res. 205, 87th Cong., 2d Sess. (1962); 108 Cong. Rec. 11806 (1962). Also see S.J. Res. 206, 207, 87th Cong., 2d Sess. (1962).

90   Also see S.J. Res. 206, 87th Cong., 2d Sess. (1962); U.S. Congress, Senate, Committee on the Judiciary, *Prayer in Public Schools and Other Matters: Hearings on S.J. Res. 205, 206, 207; S. Con. Res. 81; S. Res. 356,* 87th Congress, 2d Session, July 26 and August 2, 1962 (Washington, D.C.: Government Printing Office, 1963), at 1–2; hereinafter cited as Senate Judiciary Committee, *Prayer in Public Schools* (1963). Similar to Senator Beall's resolution, S.J. Res. 206 also permitted the "invocation of the blessing of God" as well as other nondenominational religious observances. Also see S.J. Res. 207, 87th Cong., 2d Sess. (1962); Senate Judiciary Committee, *Prayer in Public Schools* (1963), at 2.

91   See, for example, H.J. Res. 343, 88th Cong., 1st Sess. (1963); U.S. Congress, House of Representatives, Committee on the Judiciary, *School Prayers: Proposed Amendments to the Constitution Relating to Prayers and Bible Reading in the Public Schools,* parts 1–3, 88th Congress, 2d Session, April 22–24, 28–30; May 1, 6–8, 13–15, 20–21, 27–28; and June 3, 1964 (Washington, D.C.: Government Printing Office, 1964), part 1, at 6–7; hereinafter cited as House Judiciary Committee, *School Prayers* (1964); and H.J. Res. 553, 88th Cong., 1st Sess. (1963); House Judiciary Committee, *School Prayers* (1963), at 18.

92   Also see H.J. Res. 488, 88th Cong., 1st Sess. (1963); House Judiciary Committee, *School Prayers* (1963), at 9. Also see H.J. Res. 771, 88th Cong., 1st Sess. (1963); *id.,* at 41; and H.J. Res. 603, 88th Cong., 1st Sess. (1963); House Judiciary Committee, *School Prayers* (1963), at 19–21.

93   S.J. Res. 148, 89th Cong., 2d Sess. (1966); Senate Judiciary Committee, Subcommittee on Constitutional Amendments, *School Prayer* (1966), at 1.

94   *Id.,* at 602, testimony of Professor Paul Kauper.

95   112 Cong. Rec. 23556 (1966).

96   S.J. Res. 1, 90th Cong., 1st Sess. (1967); 113 Cong. Rec. 263 (1967).

97   S.J. Res. 6, 91st Cong., 1st Sess. (1969); 115 Cong. Rec. 25528 (1969).

98   115 Cong. Rec. 18822–46 (1969).

99   116 Cong. Rec. 36479 (1970).

100   *Id.*

101   *Id.,* at 36505. The vote here is on the substitution of Senator Baker's language rather than on final passage of the joint resolution, which requires a two-thirds majority.

102   *Id.,* at 39885.

103   *Id.,* at 39926.

104   *Id.,* at 39889.

105   *Id.,* at 39957.

106   H.J. Res. 981, 92d Cong., 2d Sess. (1972).

107   118 Cong. Rec. 318–19 (1972). Also see S.J. Res. 7, 84, 89, 122, 92d Cong., 2d Sess. (1972).

108   120 Cong. Rec. 30720, 30721 (1974).

109   S. 3981, 93d Cong., 2d Sess. (1974); 120 Cong. Rec. 30721 (1974).

110   *Id.*

111   *Id.*

112   S. 283, 94th Cong., 1st Sess. (1975); 121 Cong. Rec. 872 (1975). Mr. Ashbrook offered

a similar measure in the House, remarking:

> The action I am proposing is both constitutional and effective. The Constitution grants Congress the right to restrict the Supreme Court in those areas where the Court does not have original jurisdiction. For passage, such legislation would be treated as any other piece of legislation and would require a simple majority vote of Congress to be enacted. The two-thirds vote roadblock will be avoided.
>
> I urge the 94th Congress to move immediately toward restoring voluntary school prayer. Our Nation has already waited long enough for Congress to act.

Id., at 1954.

113 *Id.*, at 870, 870–71.

114 *Id.*, at 872.

115 S. 1467, 95th Cong., 1st Sess. (1977); 123 Cong. Rec. 13729–30 (1977); H.R. 154, 391, 1159, 5703, 95th Cong., 1st Sess. (1977).

116 S. 1467, S.J. Res. 49, 95th Cong., 1st Sess. (1977); 123 Cong. Rec. 13729 (1977).

117 *Id.*, at 13730.

118 124 Cong. Rec. 4342 (1978).

119 *Id.*, at 4343–44.

120 S. 438, 96th Cong., 1st Sess. (1979); 125 Cong. Rec. 2868 (1979). Also see S. 2070, H.R. 466, 1082, 1173, 96th Cong., 1st Sess. (1979).

121 125 Cong. Rec. 2868 (1979).

122 *Id.*, at 7631–33, 7634–36.

123 *Id.*, at 7638.

124 *Id.*, at 7644, 7648.

125 S. 2070, S.J. Res. 121, 96th Cong., 1st Sess. (1979); 125 Cong. Rec. 34295 (1979).

126 *Id.*, at 34296.

127 Discharge Petition No. 7, 96th Cong., 2d Sess. (1980); 126 Cong. Rec. E138 (daily ed. Jan. 28, 1980).

128 127 Cong. Rec. S1284 (daily ed. Feb. 16, 1981).

129 H.R. 72, 97th Cong., 1st Sess. (1981); H.R. 73, 97th Cong., 1st Sess. (1981).

130 127 Cong. Rec. S1284 (daily ed. Feb. 16, 1981).

131 *Id.*, at S9119 (daily ed. July 31, 1981).

132 *Id.*

133 *Id.*, at H6050 (daily ed. Sept. 9, 1981).

134 *Id.*, at S13515 (daily ed. Nov. 17, 1981).

135 See S. 1742; also see S. 2231, 481, 97th Cong., 2d Sess. (1982); 128 Cong. Rec. S4726–S4730 (daily ed. May 6, 1982).

136 128 Cong. Rec. S12022 (daily ed. Sept. 23, 1982).

137 *Id.*, at S13291 (daily ed. Oct. 1, 1982).

138 *Id.*

139 S. 47, 99th Cong., 1st Sess. (1985).

140 131 Cong. Rec. S20 (daily ed. Jan. 3, 1985).

141 *Id.*

142 *Id.*

143 *Id.*, at S11183 (daily ed. Sept. 10, 1985).

144 129 Cong. Rec. S994 (daily ed. Feb. 3, 1983).

145 Pub. L. No. 98-377; 98 Stat. 1302; 20 U.S.C. 4071 (1984).

146   475 U.S. 534 (1986).

147   *Id.*, at 549.

148   *Id.*, at 537–39.

149   *Id.*, at 551–55, 555–56.

150   See *Shapiro* v. *Thompson*, 394 U.S. 618 (1969), ruling that a statute burdening a previously recognized constitutional right may deny equal protection.

151   See *Washington* v. *Seattle School Dist. No. 1*, 458 U.S. 457 (1982), and *Hunter* v. *Erickson*, 393 U.S. 385 (1969).

152   See *Bolling* v. *Sharp*, 347 U.S. 497 (1954), in which the Court read the Fourteenth Amendment's requirement of equal protection into the Fifth Amendment's due process clause. Also see *Hurd* v. *Hodge*, 334 U.S. 24 (1948).

8   School Desegregation and Court-Ordered Busing: Where There Is a Right, Is There a Remedy?

1   402 U.S. 1 (1971).

2   See, e.g., the testimony of Senator J. Bennett Johnston (D-La.) in U.S. Congress, House, Committee on the Judiciary, Subcommittee on Courts, Civil Liberties, and the Administration of Justice, *Limitations on Court-Ordered Busing—The Neighborhood School Act*, 97th Congress, 2nd Session, June 17, July 15 and 22, and August 5, 1982 (Washington D.C.: Government Printing Office, 1983), at 54; hereinafter cited as House Judiciary Committee, Subcommittee on Courts, etc., *Neighborhood School Act Hearings* (1983).

3   *Plessy* v. *Ferguson*, 163 U.S. 537 (1896).

4   *Id.*, at 551–52.

5   347 U.S. 483 (1954).

6   *Id.*, at 492.

7   *Id.*, at 494, n. 11.

8   *Id.*, at 495.

9   De jure segregation is defined as segregation resulting from intentional state action. In *Brown* the Court found that unconstitutional state action resulted from state statutory or constitutional provisions authorizing segregative practices. In *Keyes* v. *School Dist. No. 1*, 413 U.S. 189 (1973), the Court found that de jure segregation could arise from intentional school board policies in school districts without prior, statutorily mandated dual schools. De jure segregation is distinguished from de facto segregation, which is generally defined as segregation arising independently of any action by state or local officials. In *Swann* v. *Charlotte-Mecklenburg Bd. of Educ.*, 402 U.S. 1 (1971), the Supreme Court held that federal courts may only remedy de jure segregation. For a detailed discussion of the ambiguous distinction between de jure and de facto segregation and a history of the differing and shifting burden of proof required to demonstrate constitutional violations in desegregation cases, see Gutermann, Paul E., "School Desegregation Doctrine: The Interaction Between Violation and Remedy," 30 *Case Western Reserve L. Rev.* 780–815 (1980).

10   *Brown* v. *Board of Education*, 349 U.S. 294, 298 (1955) [hereinafter cited as *Brown II*]; see also *Brown I*, 347 U.S., at 495, n. 12; In *Bolling* v. *Sharpe*, 347 U.S. 497 (1954),

the Court read the Fourteenth Amendment's requirement of equal protection into the Fifth Amendment's due process clause.

11 *Brown II*, 349 U.S., at 299, 300, 301.

12 *Id.*, at 299.

13 *Id.*, at 300.

14 *Id.*, at 294.

15 358 U.S. 1 (1958).

16 *Id.*, at 16, 17.

17 373 U.S. 683 (1963).

18 *Id.*, at 686.

19 377 U.S. 218 (1964).

20 *Id.*, at 229.

21 See Kluger, Richard, *Simple Justice: The History of Brown v. Board of Education and Black America's Struggle for Equality* (New York: Alfred A. Knopf, 1976), at 751–66.

22 391 U.S. 430 (1968).

23 *Id.*, at 437–38.

24 Many districts adopted "freedom of choice" desegregation plans, under which any student could attend the school of her or his choice. As the Court observed in *Green*, after three years such a plan had made absolutely no progress in eliminating the dual school system. The Court found that "[r]ather than further the dismantling of the dual system, the plan has operated simply to burden children and their parents with a responsibility which *Brown II* placed squarely on the School Board." *Green*, 391 U.S., at 441–42.

25 *Id.*, at 438.

26 *Green*, at 439. See also *Alexander* v. *Holmes County Board of Education*, 396 U.S. 19 (1969), at 20.

27 See *Keyes* v. *School Dist. No. 1*, 413 U.S. 189 (1973), at 200, n. 11.

28 402 U.S. 1 (1971).

29 *Id.*, at 16.

30 *Id.*

31 *Id.*

32 *Id.*, at 28.

33 *Id.*, at 27.

34 *Id.*, at 28.

35 *Id.*, at 29–30.

36 *Id.*, at 30.

37 *Id.*, at 31.

38 *Id.*, at 30–31.

39 *Id.*, at 27.

40 *Id.*, at 31–32.

41 *Davis* v. *Board of School Commissioners*, 402 U.S. 33 (1971); *McDaniel* v. *Barresi*, 402 U.S. 39 (1971); *North Carolina Bd. of Educ.* v. *Swann*, 402 U.S. 42 (1971).

42 *Davis*, 402 U.S., at 38.

43 *Id.*, at 37.

44 *North Carolina*, 402 U.S., at 46.

45 *Id.*, at 44.

46   *Id.*, at 45. See also *Washington* v. *Seattle School Dist. No. 1*, 458 U.S. 457 (1982), discussed *infra* at notes 202–5 and accompanying text.

47   *North Carolina*, 402 U.S., at 46.

48   See *Swann*, 402 U.S., at 17–18.

49   *Keyes* v. *School Dist. No. 1*, 413 U.S. 189 (1973), at 220 (Opinion of Justice Powell).

50   *Id.*, at 191.

51   *Id.*, at 200.

52   *Id.*, at 201.

53   *Id.*, at 208. In *Keyes*, purposeful discrimination was only identified in the Park Hill section of Denver, a section in which over 37% of Denver's blacks attended public schools. *Id.*, at 198–99.

54   In separate opinions, justices Douglas and Powell called upon the Court to abolish the de jure/de facto distinction and "formulate constitutional principles of national rather than merely regional application." *Id.*, at 219 (Opinion of Justice Powell). According to Powell, in light of the "evolution of the holding in *Brown I* into the affirmative duty doctrine [e.g., *Green*], the distinction no longer can be justified on a principled basis." *Id.*, at 224. See also Justice Douglas's opinion at 215–17.

55   418 U.S. 717 (1974).

56   *Id.*, at 739–40.

57   *Id.*, at 744–45.

58   *Id.*, at 745.

59   *Id.*, at 746.

60   *Id.*

61   429 U.S. 990 (1976).

62   433 U.S. 406 (1977).

63   426 U.S. 229 (1976).

64   *Id.*, at 239–45. However, the Court in *Davis* qualified its holding by stating "in proper circumstances, the racial impact of a law, rather than its discriminatory purpose is the critical factor." *Id.*, at 243.

65   *Dayton I*, 433 U.S., at 420.

66   427 U.S. 424 (1976).

67   *Id.*, at 435.

68   *Id.*, at 434.

69   443 U.S. 526 (1979).

70   443 U.S. 449 (1979).

71   *Dayton II*, 443 U.S., at 538–39; *Columbus*, 443 U.S., at 461.

72   *Dayton II*, 443 U.S., at 537. See also *Columbus*, 443 U.S., at 455, 458–59.

73   *Columbus*, 443 U.S., at 464; see also *Dayton II*, 443 U.S., at 538.

74   Ducey, Michael F., "The Unitary Finding and the Threat of School Resegregation: *Riddick* v. *School Board*," 65 *N.C. L. Rev.* 617–44 (1987), at 630.

75   *Columbus*, 443 U.S. at 465; see also *Dayton II*, 443 U.S., at 541.

76   784 F.2d 521 (4th Cir. 1986), *cert. den.* 107 S. Ct. 420 (1986).

77   795 F.2d 1516 (10th Cir. 1986), *cert. den.* 107 S. Ct. 420 (1986).

78   *Riddick*, 784 F.2d at 534.

79   While the Court has never adopted a rigid definition of unitariness, many district courts have followed the suggestion in *Green* that a school system is unitary if there is evidence of racial integration in a "system's faculty, staff, transportation

practices, extracurricular activities, facilities and pupil assignments." *Riddick*, 784 F.2d, at 533. See *Green*, 391 U.S., at 435. The district court's judgment in this respect should not be questioned by an appellate court unless it is "clearly erroneous." *Riddick*, 784 F.2d, at 533.

80 *Riddick*, 784 F.2d, at 524–29.

81 *Id.*, at 538.

82 *Dowell*, 795 F.2d, at 1517–19.

83 In a footnote, the Court explicitly rejected the Fourth Circuit's reasoning in *Riddick*:

> The Fourth Circuit has taken a different view with which we cannot agree. In *Riddick* . . . the court seems to treat a district court order terminating supervision as an order dissolving a mandated integration plan, despite the absence of a specific order to that effect. The court makes a bridge between a finding of unitariness and voluntary compliance with an injunction. We find no foundation for that bridge. . . . A finding of unitariness may lead to many other reasonable conclusions, but it cannot divest a court of its jurisdiction, nor can it convert a mandatory injunction into voluntary compliance.

Id., at 1520, n. 3.

84 The Fourth Circuit believed that a finding of unitariness would allow a school board to modify or terminate a district court's desegregation order. The Tenth Circuit maintained that a district court must explicitly vacate its desegregation decree in order to return full discretion to the school board regarding public school assignments. Emphasizing that the case "in reality is a petition for a contempt citation," the Tenth Circuit flatly rejected any suggestion that it was ruling on the constitutional merits of the school board's proposed assignment plan. *Id.*, at 1523.

85 See *Swann* v. *Charlotte-Mecklenburg Bd. of Educ.*, 402 U.S. 1 (1971), at 31–32, and *Green* v. *New Kent County School Board*, 391 U.S. 430 (1968), at 439.

86 See Note, "Allocating the Burden of Proof After a Finding of Unitariness in School Desegregation Litigation," 100 *Harv. L. Rev.* 653–71 (1987), at 653.

87 *Austin Indep. School Dist.* v. *United States*, 429 U.S. 990 (1976), at 995 (Powell, concurring). The Court has also recognized that district courts "must take into account the interests of state and local authorities in managing their own affairs" when devising desegregation remedies. *Milliken* v. *Bradley*, 433 U.S. 267 (1977) (*Milliken II*), at 280–81. Additionally, several justices have recognized that a court should consider the social and educational consequences of a busing order to avoid resegregative effects, e.g., white flight, which are counterproductive to the goal that the remedy addresses. See Justice Powell's dissenting opinion (joined by justices Stewart and Rehnquist) in *Estes* v. *Metropolitan Branches of the Dallas NAACP*, 444 U.S. 437 (1980).

88 *Swann* v. *Charlotte-Mecklenburg Bd. of Educ.*, 402 U.S. 1 (1971), at 25.

89 96th Cong., 1st Sess., 125 Cong. Rec. 1348 (1979).

90 *Id.*

91 The Civil Rights Act of 1964, Pub. L. No. 88-352, § 2003, 78 Stat. 241 (1964).

92 See chapter 6, note 18.

93 See, e.g., Senator William V. Roth's (R.-Del.) testimony, U.S. Congress, Senate, Committee on the Judiciary, *Busing of School Children: Hearings on S. 1651*,

95th Congress, 1st Session, June 15–16 and July 21–22, 1977 (Washington, D.C.: Government Printing Office, 1977), at 7; hereinafter cited as Senate Judiciary Committee, *Hearings on S. 1651* (1977).

94 A 1973 Gallup Poll indicated that only 5 percent (4 percent—whites; 9 percent— blacks) of those surveyed believed that cross-district busing was the best way to achieve integration in public schools. In 1975 the number decreased to 4 percent (3 percent—whites; 6 percent—nonwhites). Gallup, George H., *The Gallup Poll: Public Opinion 1972–1977* (Wilmington, Del.: Scholarly Resources, Inc., 1978), at 178–80, 266–67. A 1982 survey revealed that 72 percent of those surveyed opposed busing to achieve a better racial balance in the public schools. See Gallup, George H., *The Gallup Poll: Public Opinion 1982* (Wilmington, Del.: Scholarly Resources, Inc., 1983).

95 See, e.g., Representative Ronald M. Mottl's (D.-Ohio) statement on offering a discharge petition on H.J. Res. 74, a neighborhood school amendment. 125 Cong. Rec. 20588 (1979).

96 See Senator J. Bennett Johnston's (D.-La.) statement in introducing the Neighborhood School Act of 1981, a bill to limit the federal courts' authority to order desegregative busing. 127 Cong. Rec. S142 (daily ed. Feb. 4, 1981).

97 "Nixon's School Desegregation Policies Remain Unclear," 1969 *Congressional Quarterly* 255, at 257–59, February 14, 1969.

98 Pub. L. No. 90-557; 82 Stat. 969, 995 (1968).

99 Pub. L. No. 91-204, 84 Stat. 23, 48 (1970); Pub. L. No. 93-192; 87 Stat. 746, 761–62 (1973); Pub. L. No. 93-517; 88 Stat. 1634, 1648–49 (1974).

100 Pub. L. No. 94-206; 90 Stat. 3, 21–22 (1976).

101 Pub. L. No. 95-480; 92 Stat. 1567, 1585–86 (1978). This restriction was upheld in *Brown* v. *Califano*, 627 F.2d 1221 (D.C. Cir. 1980).

102 Pub. L. No. 97-377, 96 Stat. 1830, 1900–1901 (1982); Pub. L. No. 98-139, 97 Stat. 871, 894–95 (1983); and Pub. L. No. 98-619, 98 Stat. 3305, 3328–29 (1984).

103 1980 government data indicated that the Justice Department was responsible for court-ordered busing in 544 out of 711 school districts under such orders. *Congressional Quarterly*, December 13, 1980, at 3542.

104 On September 26, 1978, the House adopted the "Collins amendment" 235/158, 124 Cong. Rec. 31714 (1978), but the compromise version of the bill (S. 3151) did not include the amendment. The "Collins amendment" was similarly added to the House version of the 1980 Justice Department Appropriations bill (H.R. 4292), 209/ 190, July 12, 1979, 125 Cong. Rec. 18368–69 (1979). However, the Senate rejected an identical amendment that Senator Jesse Helms (R.-N.C.) introduced, 37/60, July 24, 1979, 125 Cong. Rec. 20296 (1979). The Collins amendment was dropped in conference.

105 President Carter's veto message is reprinted in *Congressional Quarterly*, December 20, 1980, at 3633.

106 *Id.*

107 Senate roll-call vote No.39 (52/37), 128 Cong. Rec. S1336 (daily ed. March 2, 1982); House Judiciary Committee, Subcommittee on Courts, etc., *Neighborhood School Act Hearings* (1983).

108 See, e.g., S. 2336, 93rd Cong., 1st Sess. (1973); S. 2937, S. 1743, S. 1647, S. 1760, 97th Cong., 1st Sess. (1981); and S. 139, 98th Cong., 1st Sess. (1983). S. 139 and S. 1760 would remove lower federal-court jurisdiction to make any public school

assignments on the basis of race, while S. 2937, S. 1647, S. 2336, and S. 1743 would extend the jurisdictional limitation to decisions that would require school closings and teacher transfers.

109 See, e.g., H.R. 12827, 92nd Cong., 2nd Sess. (1972); and S. 287, 93rd Cong., 1st Sess. (1973).

110 H.R. 1211, 99th Cong., 1st Sess. (1985). See also H.R. 13024, 92nd Cong., 2nd Sess. (1972), H.R. 1180, H.R. 1801, 96th Cong., 1st Sess. (1979); H.R. 340, H.R. 1079, H.R. 3332, H.R. 1180, 97th Cong., 1st Sess. (1981); H.R. 798 and H.R. 158, 98th Cong., 1st Sess. (1983).

111 H.R. 556, 96th Cong., 1st Sess. (1979). See also H.R. 761, 97th Cong., 1st Sess. (1981).

112 H.R. 81, 99th Cong., 1st Sess. (1985). See also H.R. 10614, 92nd Cong., 1st Sess. (1971); H.R. 992, 96th Cong., 1st Sess. (1979); H.R. 867, H.R. 869, and 97th Cong., 1st Sess. (1981).

113 S. 1005, 97th Cong., 1st Sess. (1981), Senate Judiciary Committee, Subcommittee on Separation of Powers, *Busing Hearings* (1981), at 682.

114 *Id.*, at 682–83. See also H.R. 159, 92nd Cong., 1st Sess. (1971); S. 1737, 93rd Cong., 1st Sess. (1973).

115 S. 179, 93rd Cong., 1st Sess. (1973). See also H.R. 693, 92nd Cong., 1st Sess. (1971).

116 H.R. 11401, 92nd Cong., 1st Sess. (1971), House Judiciary Committee, *Busing Hearings*, part 3 (1972), at 1916–17. See also H.R. 65, 92nd Cong., 1st Sess. (1971); S. 619, 93rd Cong., 1st Sess. (1973); H.R. 468, 96th Cong., 1st Sess. (1979); S. 1147, H.R. 327, 97th Cong., 1st Sess. (1981). See also H.R. 13916, 92nd Cong., 2nd Sess. (1972), proposing a moratorium on all new busing orders until a specified date, or until Congress could enact legislation on the subject, whichever came first; and S. 619, 93rd Cong., 1st. Sess. (1973), prohibiting any federal court from ordering a student to be bused beyond the closest, or next-closest, school to his or her place of residence.

117 See, e.g., H.R. 11312, 92nd Cong., 1st Sess. (1971), and S. 1651, 95th Cong., 1st Sess. (1977).

118 H.R. 13534, 92nd Cong., 2nd Sess. (1972), House Judiciary Committee, *Busing Hearings*, part 3 (1972), at 1922.

119 *Id.*, at 1922–23.

120 Amendment No. 69 to S.951, 97th Cong., 1st Sess. (1981), 127 Cong. Rec. S6645 (daily ed. June 22, 1981). See also S. 528 and H.R. 2047, 97th Cong., 1st Sess. (1981), earlier versions of the Neighborhood School Act. See also H.R. 5200, 97th Cong., 1st Sess. (1981).

121 Pub. L. No. 92-318, Title VIII, 86 Stat. 235, 372, § 803 (1972).

122 Pub. L. No. 93-380, 88 Stat. 484, 514–21, Title II (1974).

123 Pub. L. No. 92-318, 86 Stat. 235, 372, § 803 (1972).

124 409 U.S. 1228 (1972).

125 Powell stated: "In light of this Court's holding in *Swann* . . . it could hardly be contended that Congress was unaware of the legal significance of its "racial balance" language. . . . At most, Congress may have intended to postpone the effectiveness of transportation orders in "de facto" cases." *Id.*, at 1229–30.

126 Pub. L. No. 93-380, 88 Stat. 484, 571, Title II, § 215(a) (1974).

127 *Id.*, at 515, § 203(b).

128 See *Brinkman* v. *Gilligan*, 518 F. 2d 853 (6th Cir. 1975): "We construe the 1974

Act, read as a whole, as not limiting either the nature or scope of the remedy for constitutional violations." *Id.*, at 856, *cert. denied, Dayton* v. *Brinkman*, 423 U.S. 1000 (1976).

129 H.R. 13915, S. 3395, 92nd Cong., 2nd Sess. (1972).

130 H.R. 13916, S. 3388, 92nd Cong., 2nd Sess (1972).

131 See, e.g., the testimony of Acting Attorney General Richard G. Kleindienst, House Judiciary Committee, *Busing Hearings*, part 3 (1972), at 1141–46.

132 In the House, H.R. 13915 was passed August 17, 1972, 283/182. 118 Cong. Rec. 28915–16 (1972). On October 12, the Senate failed for the third and final time to invoke cloture, 49/38, 9 votes short of the 58 votes required. 118 Cong. Rec. 35330 (1972).

133 S. 1651, § 1, 95th Cong., 1st Sess. (1977), U.S. Congress, Senate, Committee on the Judiciary, *Transportation as a Remedy in School Desegregation: Report to Accompany S. 1651*, 95th Congress, 1st Session, September 21, 1977 (Washington D.C.: Government Printing Office, 1977), at 4; hereinafter cited as Senate Judiciary Committee, *Report on S. 1651* (1977).

134 See Senate Judiciary Committee, *Hearings on S. 1651* (1977) and Senate Judiciary Committee, *Report on S. 1651* (1977). Roll call vote No. 352 to table amendment No. 1721 to the ESEA extension bill (49/47) is reprinted at 124 Cong. Rec. 27358 (1978).

135 Senate roll call vote No. 39 on the final passage of S. 951 is reprinted at 128 Cong. Rec. S1336 (daily ed. March 2, 1982).

136 House Judiciary Committee, Subcommittee on Courts, etc., *Neighborhood School Act Hearings* (1983).

137 See, e.g., H.J. Res. 855, 92nd Cong., 1st Sess. (1971); H.J. Res. 623, 96th Cong., 2nd Sess. (1980); H.J. Res. 56, 91, and 95, 97th Cong., 1st Sess. (1981); H.J. Res. 28, 98th Cong., 1st Sess. (1983); and H.J. Res. 651, 98th Cong., 2nd Sess. (1984).

138 See, e.g., H.J. Res. 94, 561, 579, 587, 620, 628, 636, 983, 92nd Cong., 1st Sess. (1971); H.J. Res. 1076, 92nd Cong., 2nd Sess. (1972); S.J. Res. 9, 14, 28, 35, 36, 47, 93rd Cong., 1st Sess. (1973); S.J. Res. 29 and 60, 94th Cong., 1st Sess. (1975); H.J. Res. 293, 96th Cong., 1st Sess. (1979); and H.J. Res. 16 and 46, 97th Cong., 1st Sess. (1981).

139 See, e.g., H.J. Res. 43, 92nd Cong., 1st Sess. (1971); H.J. Res. 600, 92nd Cong., 1st Sess. (1971); S.J. Res. 137, 94th Cong., 1st Sess. (1975); H.J. Res. 384, 96th Cong., 1st Sess. (1979); and H.J. Res. 210, 97th Cong., 1st Sess. (1981).

140 See, e.g., H.J. Res. 30, 92nd Cong., 1st Sess. (1971); H.J. Res. 1073, 92nd Cong., 2nd Sess. (1972); S.J. Res. 62, 93rd Cong., 1st Sess. (1973); H.J. Res. 12, 20, 173, 192, 226, 264, 96th Cong., 1st Sess. (1979); H.J. Res. 22, 28, 86, 312, 329, 97th Cong., 1st Sess. (1981); and H.J. Res. 9, 14, 287, 98th Cong., 1st Sess. (1983).

141 See, e.g., H.J. Res. 66, 75, 179, 607, and 854, 92nd Cong., 1st Sess. (1971).

142 H.J. Res. 620, 92nd Cong., 1st Sess. (1971), House Judiciary Committee, *Busing Hearings*, part 3 (1972), at 1877–78.

143 H. Res 610; H. Rept. No. 92-1274, 92nd Cong., 2nd Sess., (1972).

144 These hearings were not published, but were made available to the author by the National Archives, Washington D.C., with the assistance of Mr. Phil Shippman (Documents Clerk, Senate Judiciary Committee), and Mr. Reginald Washington, of the National Archives. The author is indebted to both gentleman for their assistance.

145 125 Cong. Rec. 20412–13 (1979).

146 H.J. Res. 74, 96th Cong., 1st Sess. (1979), 125 Cong. Rec. 20362 (1979).

147 H.J. Res. 56, 97th Cong., 1st Sess. (1981).

148 *Congressional Quarterly*, August 22, 1982, at 1580.

149 See Note, "The Nixon Busing Bills and Congressional Power," 81 *Yale L. J.* 1542–73, at 1545 (1972). See also Sagar, 95 *Harv. L. Rev.* 17–89 (1981), at 85–89.

150 U.S. Const. art. XIV, § 5. See, e.g., statements of Senator J. Bennett Johnston (D.-La.) in House Judiciary Committee, Subcommittee on Courts, etc., *Neighborhood School Act Hearings* (1983), at 31–34. For a scholarly examination of Congress's power under section 5, see, e.g., Cox, Archibald, "The Role of Congress in Constitutional Determinations," 40 *U. Cinn. L. Rev.* 199–261 (1971); Burt, Robert A., "Miranda and Title II: A Morganatic Marriage," 1969 *S.Ct. Rev.* 81–134 (1969); and Gordon, Irving A., "The Nature and Uses of Congressional Power Under Section Five of the Fourteenth Amendment to Overcome Decisions of the Court," 72 *Nw. L. Rev.* 656–705 (1977).

151 384 U.S. 641 (1966).

152 *Lassiter* v. *Northampton Election Board*, 360 U.S. 45 (1959).

153 *Morgan*, 384 U.S., at 651.

154 *Id.*, at 656.

155 *Id.*

156 *Id.*, at 668 (Harlan, dissenting).

157 *Id.*

158 *Id.*, at 651–52, n. 10 (Opinion of the Court). Some antibusing proponents have questioned the binding authority of this limitation. See, e.g., statements of Senator J. Bennett Johnston (D.-La.), House Judiciary Committee, Subcommittee on Courts, etc., *Neighborhood School Act Hearings* (1983), at 33.

159 Sharon Susser Harzenski argues that the Court owes Congress less deference in evaluating antibusing proposals than the deference given in evaluating the Voting Rights Act amendment in *Morgan*. While Congress has demonstrated its continuing desire to extend voting rights to minorities, Harzenski concludes, congressional efforts to desegregate the nation's public schools "are noticeable only for their absence." Sharon Susser Harzenski, "Jurisdictional Limitations and Suspicious Motives: Why Congress Cannot Forbid Court-Ordered Busing," 50 *Temple L.Q.* 14–57, at 55.

160 460 U.S. 226 (1983).

161 *Id.*, at 262.

162 *Id.* Also see *Oregon* v. *Mitchell*, 400 U.S. 112 (1970), in which the Court considered congressional power under section 5 to enable any citizen, eighteen years or older, to vote in all state and federal elections. The Court sustained the statute with respect to federal elections, but struck it down with respect to state elections in an ambiguous opinion in which no five justices agreed on the extent to which Congress can expand Fourteenth Amendment guarantees under section 5. Also see *South Carolina* v. *Katzenbach*, 383 U.S. 301 (1966).

163 458 U.S. 718 (1982).

164 *Id.*, at 732–33 (quoting *Morgan*).

165 Rotunda, 64 *Geo. L. J.*, at 860–61. (1976).

166 *Marbury* v. *Madison*, 5 U.S. (1 Cranch) 137 (1803), at 177.

167 347 U.S. 497 (1954).

168 *Id.*, at 499.

169 *Id.*, at 500.

170 *Id.*

171 394 U.S. 618 (1969).

172 405 U.S. 330 (1972).

173 *Shapiro*, 394 U.S., at 634.

174 *Id.*, at 629–30.

175 *Dunn*, 405 U.S., at 342.

176 See Van Alstyne, 15 *Ariz. L. Rev.*, at 265.

177 U.S. Const. art. VI, cl. 2.

178 122 Cong. Rec. 2509 (1976).

179 U.S. Const. art. III, § 1.

180 See *Cohens* v. *Virginia*, 19 U.S. (6 Wheat.) 264 (1821), at 386–87.

181 See *Washington* v. *Davis*, 426 U.S. 229, 242–45 (1976).

182 442 U.S. 256 (1979).

183 *Id.*, at 272.

184 See, e.g., statements of Senator Jesse Helms (R.-N.C.) at 132 Cong. Rec. S6551 (daily ed. June 3, 1986).

185 458 U.S. 457 (1982).

186 *Id.*, at 471–72.

187 *Id.*, at 470.

188 *Id.*, at 471.

189 393 U.S. 385 (1969).

190 318 F. Supp. 710 (1970).

191 *Hunter*, 393 U.S., at 389.

192 *Id.*, at 391.

193 *Nyquist*, 318 F. Supp., at 718.

194 *Id.*

195 *Seattle*, 458 U.S., at 485.

196 Harzenski, 50 *Temple L.Q.*, at 24.

197 *Hunter*, 393 U.S., at 393.

198 80 U.S. (13 Wall.) 128 (1872).

199 *Id.*, at 146.

200 *Id.*, at 145.

201 House Judiciary Committee, *Busing Hearings*, part 1 (1972), at 502.

202 *Id.*

203 Senate Judiciary Committee, Subcommittee on Separation of Powers, *Busing Hearings* (1981), at 9.

204 S. 1651, 95th Cong., 1st Sess. (1977) [emphasis added].

205 429 U.S. 252 (1977).

206 *Id.*, at 265–66. See also *Wright* v. *Council of City of Emporia*, 407 U.S. 451, 462 (1972).

207 House, Judiciary, *Busing Hearings*, part 2, 1972, at 1195.

208 *Id.*, at 1137–38. As one commentator has noted, "[t]o permit Congress to prohibit court-ordered busing places the Supreme Court in the uncomfortable position of being forced to 'validate' or 'legitimize' the continuing existence of at least some dual school systems." Harzenski, 50 *Temple L.Q.*, at 34 [footnotes omitted].

209 Senate Judiciary Committee, Subcommittee on Separation of Powers, *Busing Hearings* (1981), at 6–7.

210 House Judiciary Committee, *Busing Hearings*, part 2, (1972), at 1148–49.

211 *Swann* v. *Charlotte-Mecklenburg Bd. of Educ.*, 402 U.S. 1, at 29.

212 See, e.g., *Milliken* v. *Bradley*, 418 U.S. 717 (1974); *Dayton Board of Education* v. *Brinkman*, 433 U.S. 406 (1977).

213 See *Milliken* v. *Bradley* (1974). Also see Sawyer's testimony in House Judiciary Committee, Subcommittee on Courts, etc., *Neighborhood School Act Hearings*, (1983), at 163–65; 167–70; 211–13.

214 See Olson's statement, *id.*, at 160.

215 Senate Judiciary Committee, Subcommittee on Constitutional Rights, *Busing Hearings* (1974), at 35–36.

216 *Id.*, at 31. See also the testimony of Senator Jesse Helms (R.-N.C.), *id.*, at 111, and the testimony of Representative John D. Dingell (D.-Mich.), House Judiciary Committee, *Busing Hearings*, part 1 (1972), at 501.

217 House Judiciary Committee, Subcommittee on Courts, etc., *Neighborhood School Act Hearings* (1983), at 69. See also testimony of Senator John P. East (R.-N.C.), Senate Judiciary Committee, Subcommittee on Separation of Powers, *Busing Hearings* (1981), at 10.

218 Senate Judiciary Committee, Subcommittee on Constitutional Rights, *Busing Hearings* (1974), at 237.

219 S.J. Res. 29, 94th Cong., 1st Sess. (1975).

220 122 Cong. Rec. 2509 (1976).

221 Senate Judiciary Committee, *Hearings on S. 1651* (1977), at 11.

222 Senate Judiciary Committee, Subcommittee on Constitutional Rights, *Busing Hearings* (1974), at 27.

223 *Id.*

224 House Judiciary Committee, Subcommittee on Courts, etc., *Neighborhood School Act Hearings*, (1983), at 64, 69.

225 *Id.*, at 89.

226 Also, by implicitly discouraging various state courts from fashioning desegregation orders, including busing, in cases where the remedy is necessary, antibusing proposals arguably encourage state courts to disregard their duty under the supremacy clause, Article VI, section 2.

227 House Judiciary Committee, *Busing Hearings*, part 2 (1972), at 1087.

228 *Id.*, part 1, at 60.

9 The Undying Issue: Congress, the Court, and Abortion Rights

1 410 U.S. 113 (1973).

2 *Id.*, at 154.

3 See the statement of Senator Orrin Hatch (R.-Utah), chairman of the Senate Judiciary Subcommittee on the Constitution, in U.S. Congress, Senate, Committee on the Judiciary, Subcommittee on the Constitution, *Constitutional Amendments Relating to Abortion: Hearings on S.J. Res. 17, 18, 19, and 110*, vol. 1., 97th Congress, 1st Session, October 5, 14, 19; November 4–5, 12, 16; December 7 and 16, 1981 (Washington D.C.: Government Printing Office, 1983), at 2; hereinafter

cited as Senate Judiciary Committee, Subcommittee on the Constitution, *Abortion Amendments* (1983).

4   In fact, there is nothing in the record of the Thirty-ninth Congress or in the Report of the Joint Committee on Reconstruction to indicate that Congress considered the abortion question in framing the Fourteenth Amendment's language. See generally James, Joseph B., *The Framing of the Fourteenth Amendment* (Urbana, Ill.: Univ. of Illinois Press, 1965); and Kendrick, Benjamin B., *The Journal of the Joint Committee of Fifteen on Reconstruction, 39th Congress, 1865–1867; Columbia University Studies in History, Economics and Public Law*, vol. 62 (New York: Columbia University Press, 1914). See also Congressional Globe, 39th Cong., 1st Sess., parts 1–4, February 13–June 13, 1866.

5   198 U.S. 45 (1905). Although *Roe* and *Lochner* obviously raise quite different substantive due process questions, critics of both decisions argue that the Court's opinions rest on the same logic and incorporate the same mistaken judicial rationale. Namely, the framers of the Fifth and Fourteenth amendments intended to protect procedural rights. They did not intend the justices to insinuate their own or contemporary social values into the due process clauses or to create new substantive rights under the umbrella of due process. Some scholars argue that *Roe* and other recent due process cases protect personal liberties, rather than property rights, but they fail to demonstrate why property rights are not personal liberties. Recent scholarship and judicial opinions reject Justice Stone's distinction between the presumptive validity of economic regulatory legislation and the application of strict scrutiny and searching judicial inquiry into legislation that affects other personal liberties or "discrete and insular minorities." See *United States* v. *Carolene Products Co.*, 304 U.S. 144 (1938).

6   384 U.S. 641 (1966).

7   *Id.*, at 651–52, n. 10.

8   410 U.S. 197 (1973).

9   *Roe* v. *Wade*, 410 U.S. 113 (1973), at 139.

10 American Law Institute's Model Penal Code, § 230.3, cited in *Doe* v. *Bolton*, 410 U.S. 179 (1973), at 205–6 (Appendix B to Opinion of the Court).

11 *Roe*, 410 U.S. at 118–19.

12 *Id.*

13 *Roe*, 410 U.S., at 117–18.

14 *Id.*, at 120.

15 The Supreme Court has recognized privacy rights that are implicit in the First, Fourth, and Fifth amendments. Speaking for a unanimous Court in *NAACP* v. *Alabama*, 357 U.S. 449 (1958), Justice Harlan argued that the First Amendment freedoms of speech and assembly presume a privacy right of "group association" that "is an inseparable aspect of the 'liberty'" that the Fourteenth Amendment guarantees. *Id.*, at 460. Also, in 1886, the Court recognized that the Fourth Amendment's freedom from unreasonable searches and seizures and the Fifth Amendment's freedom from self-incrimination "apply to all invasions on the part of the government and its employs of the sanctity of a man's home and the privacies of life." *Boyd* v. *United States*, 116 U.S. 616, 630 (1886). The Court has applied these Fourth and Fifth Amendment guarantees to the states through the due process clause of the Fourteenth Amendment. See *Mapp* v. *Ohio*, 367 U.S. 643 (1961) and *Malloy* v. *Hogan*, 378 U.S. 1 (1964).

16 277 U.S. 438 (1928).

17 *Id.*, at 478.

18 *Id.*

19 262 U.S. 390 (1923).

20 *Id.*, at 399.

21 *Loving* v. *Virginia*, 388 U.S. 1 (1967).

22 *Pierce* v. *Society of Sisters*, 268 U.S. 510 (1925); *Wisconsin* v. *Yoder*, 406 U.S. 205 (1972).

23 *Prince* v. *Massachusetts*, 321 U.S. 158 (1944).

24 *Skinner* v. *Oklahoma*, 361 U.S. 535 (1942).

25 *Poe* v. *Ullman*, 367 U.S. 497 (1961) (Harlan dissenting); *Griswold* v. *Connecticut*, 381 U.S. 479 (1965) (Goldberg concurring).

26 405 U.S. 438 (1972).

27 *Id.*, at 453.

28 Subsequent to *Roe* v. *Wade*, the Court has continued to recognize individual, marital, and familial rights of privacy rooted in the Fourteenth Amendment's due process clause. See, e.g., *Paul* v. *Davis*, 424 U.S. 693 (1976); *Carey* v. *Population Services International*, 431 U.S. 678 (1977); *Whalen* v. *Roe*, 429 U.S. 589 (1977); *Smith* v. *Organization of Foster Families*, 431 U.S. 816 (1977); *Zablocki* v. *Redhail*, 434 U.S. 374 (1978); *Mobile* v. *Bolden*, 446 U.S. 55 (1980).

    However, the Court has denied that these cases support the contention that "any kind of sexual conduct between consenting adults is constitutionally insulated from state proscription." *Bowers* v. *Hardwick*, 106 S. Ct. 2841 (1986), at 2844. In *Bowers*, the Court ruled that there is no Fourteenth Amendment right to privacy for consenting adults to engage in homosexual sodomy in the privacy of their homes.

29 *Roe* v. *Wade*, 410 U.S. 113 (1973), at 153. For an analysis of the Supreme Court's decisions in *Roe* and subsequent cases see Byrn, Robert M., "An American Tragedy: The Supreme Court on Abortion," 41 *Fordham L. Rev.* 807–62 (1973); Ely, John Hart, "The Wages of Crying Wolf: A Comment on *Roe* v. *Wade*," 82 *Yale L.J.* 920–49 (April 1973); Tribe, Laurence H., "The Supreme Court, 1972 Term Foreword: Toward a Model of Roles in the Due Process of Life and Law," 87 *Harv. L. Rev.* 1–53 (1973); Heymann, Philip B., and Douglas E. Barzelay, "The Forest and the Trees: *Roe* v. *Wade* and its Critics," 53 *B.U. L. Rev.* 765–84 (1973); Destro, Robert A., "Abortion and the Constitution: The Need for a Life-Protective Amendment," 63 *Cal. L. Rev.* 1250–1351 (1975); Regan, Donald H., "Rewriting *Roe* v. *Wade*," 77 *Mich L. Rev.* 1569–1646 (1979).

30 *Roe*, 410 U.S., at 154.

31 *Id.*

32 *Id.*

33 *Id.*, at 155.

34 *Id.*, at 173 (Rehnquist, dissenting).

35 *Id.*, at 163 (Opinion of the Court).

36 *Id.*, at 159.

37 *Id.*, at 160–61.

38 *Id.*, at 162–63.

39 *Id.*, at 155.

40 *Id.*, at 163.

41 *Id.*
42 *Id.*
43 *Id.*
44 *Id.*, at 163–64.
45 *Id.*, at 165.
46 *Id.*
47 *Id.*, at 164.
48 410 U.S. 179 (1973).
49 *Id.*, at 202 (Appendix A to Opinion of the Court).
50 *Id.*, at 202–4.
51 *Id.*, at 195.
52 *Id.*, at 197, 198.
53 *Id.*, at 199.
54 *Id.*, at 200. Relying on its decision in *Shapiro* v. *Thompson* (1969), the majority concluded that the residency requirement interfered with the right to travel freely. "Just as the Privileges and Immunities Clause, Const. Art. IV, § 2, protects persons who enter other States to ply their trade . . . so must it protect persons who enter Georgia seeking the medical services that are available there." *Id.*
55 *Gerstein* v. *Coe*, 417 U.S. 279 (1974).
56 *Coe* v. *Gerstein*, 376 F. Supp. 695 (1973), at 698; see F.S.A. § 458.22(3).
57 *Coe*, 376 F. Supp., at 697.
58 *Gerstein* v. *Coe*, 417 U.S. 279 (1974).
59 *Poe* v. *Gerstein*, 517 F.2d 787 (1975).
60 *Id.*, at 796.
61 428 U.S. 52 (1976).
62 *Id.*, at 67.
63 *Id.*
64 *Id.*, at 90 (Stewart, concurring). Justices Stewart and Powell agreed that Missouri had a legitimate interest in "ensuring that the abortion decision is made in a knowing, intelligent, and voluntary fashion." *Id.*
65 *Id.*, at 69 (Opinion of the Court).
66 *Id.*, at 90 (Stewart, concurring). Once again, Stewart and Powell agreed with Blackmun, arguing that, since the woman bears the child, "the balance weighs in her favor." *Id.*, at 101 (Opinion of Justice Stevens). Although he did not comment specifically on the spousal-consent procedure, Stevens joined this part of the majority's opinion.
67 *Id.*, at 93 (Opinion of Justice White).
68 *Id.*, at 75 (Opinion of the Court).
69 *Id.*
70 *Id.*
71 *Id.*, at 90 (Stewart, concurring).
72 *Id.*, at 95 (Opinion of Justice White).
73 *Id.*, at 102 (Opinion of Justice Stevens).
74 *Bellotti* v. *Baird*, 428 U.S. 132 (1976).
75 *Id.*, at 151–52.
76 *Id.*, at 146.
77 *Id.*, at 143–45.
78 *Id.*, at 145.

79 *Id.*, at 151–52. Although Justice Blackmun emphasized the importance of resolving the case quickly, *Bellotti* v. *Baird* (*Bellotti II*) did not reach the Supreme Court until 1979. In the interim, the district court certified nine questions to the Supreme Judicial Court, which the Massachusetts court answered in 1977. As the Supreme Judicial Court interpreted the statute, the law (1) required "parental notice in virtually every case where the parent is available," (2) permitted "a judge to veto the abortion decision of a minor found to be capable of giving informed consent," and (3) "failed explicitly to inform parents that they must consider only the minor's best interests in deciding whether to grant consent." The district court concluded that the statute had a chilling effect on a minor's decision to seek an abortion. 443 U.S. 622 (1979); 371 Mass. 741; 360 N.E. 2d 288 (1977).

80 371 Mass. 741; 360 N.E. 2d 288 (1977).

81 *Baird* v. *Bellotti*, 428 F. Supp. 854 (1977).

82 *Bellotti II*, 443 U.S., at 634.

83 *Id.*, at 635.

84 *Id.*, at 637.

85 *Id.*

86 *Id.*, at 643–44.

87 *Id.*, at 644.

88 *Id.*, at 645, 647, 647–48.

89 *Id.*, at 651. Dissenting from the majority opinion, Justice White commented, "Until now, I would have thought inconceivable a holding that the United States Constitution forbids even notice to parents when their minor child who seeks surgery objects to such notice and is able to convince a judge that the parents should be denied participation in the decision." *Id.*, at 657 (White, dissenting). Neither Rehnquist's nor Steven's concurring opinion disagreed with Powell's conclusion that the Massachusetts statute was unconstitutional. See *id.*, at 651–52 (Rehnquist, concurring) and 652–56 (Stevens, concurring).

90 450 U.S. 398 (1981).

91 *Id.*, at 400 (emphasis supplied by the Court); Utah Code Ann. § 76-7-304 (1974).

92 *Bellotti II*, 443 U.S., at 407.

93 *Id.*, at 409.

94 *Id.*, at 411, 410.

95 *Id.* In a concurring opinion, Powell agreed that Utah's law did not unconstitutionally burden the young, unemancipated woman's rights. Stevens also concurred with the majority that the state's interest in protecting a dependent minor's health is sufficiently compelling to justify the parental-notice requirement. *Id.*, at 418 (Powell, concurring), 425 (Stevens, concurring).

96 *Id.*, at 454 (Marshall, dissenting).

97 462 U.S. 416 (1983).

98 *Id.*, at 422, n. 4, Akron Codified Ordinances, §1870.05 (1978).

99 *Akron*, 462 U.S., at 423–24.

100 *Id.*, at 440.

101 *Id.*, at 444.

102 *Id.*, at 443.

103 *Id.*, at 443–44.

104 *Id.*, at 444–45.

105 *Id.*, at 452–53 (O'Connor, dissenting).

106   *Id.*, at 462.

107   *Id.*, at 465.

108   *Id.*, at 466–75.

109   462 U.S. 476 (1983).

110   *Id.*, at 490–91.

111   *Id.*, at 491. Concurring in part with Powell's opinion, justices O'Connor, White, and Rehnquist found the parental-consent provision constitutional because it "imposes no undue burden on any right that a minor may have to undergo an abortion." *Id.*, at 505 (Opinion of Justice O'Connor).

112   *Id.*, at 503–4 (Opinion of Justice Blackmun).

113   476 U.S. 747 (1986).

114   *Id.*, at 762. The statutory requirements that the physician must inform the woman of:

> "[D]etrimental physical and psychological effects" and of all "particular medical risks" compound the problem of medical attendance, increase the patient's anxiety, and intrude upon the physician's exercise of proper professional judgment. This type of compelled information is the antithesis of informed consent. That the Commonwealth does not, and surely would not, compel similar disclosure of every possible peril of necessary surgery or of simple vaccination, reveals the anti-abortion character of the statute and its real purpose.

Id., at 764.

115   *Id.*, at 783–84 (Burger, dissenting).

116   *Id.*, at 784.

117   *Id.*, at 800–801 (White, dissenting).

118   *Id.*, at 831 (O'Connor, dissenting).

119   *Id.*, at 788–89 (White, dissenting).

120   *Id.*, at 789.

121   No. 88-605, cert. granted, 57 U.S.L.W. 3441 (Jan. 10, 1989).

122   *Reproductive Health Serv.* v. *Webster*, 851 F.2d 1071 (8th Cir. 1988) at 1075.

123   *Id.* at 1076–77 and 662 F. Supp. 407 (W.D. Mo. 1987) at 413.

124   851 F.2d at 1077.

125   *Id.* at 1081–82.

126   448 U.S. 298. For a discussion of *Harris* see *infra.*, at 276–78.

127   432 U.S. 464. For a discussion of *Maher* see *infra.*, at 274–76.

128   851 F.2d at 1081.

129   *Id.*, at 1073–75 and 1079–80.

130   *Id.*

131   *Id.*, at 1083.

132   *Rosen* v. *Louisiana State Board of Medical Examiners*, 419 U.S. 1098 (1975).

133   380 F. Supp. 875 (1974).

134   *Id.*, at 877.

135   *Id.*

136   *Id.* Later in 1975, in *Connecticut* v. *Menillo*, the Supreme Court sustained the application of Connecticut's criminal abortion law to an unlicensed person. The Court concluded that even in the first trimester, the state has a reasonable interest

in requiring that an abortion be performed under conditions that make terminating a pregnancy safer than normal childbirth.

137 *Akron* v. *Akron Center for Reproductive Health*, 462 U.S. 416 (1983), at 427.

138 *Id.* See also *Collautti* v. *Franklin*, 439 U.S. 379, at 387 (1979).

139 *Akron*, 462 U.S., at 430.

140 *Id.*, at 444–45. Similarly, in *Thornburgh*, the Court held that Pennsylvania's informed-consent procedure intruded into the physician-patient relationship, interfered with the physicians' exercise of his professional medical judgment, and, therefore, infringed on the woman's right to privacy. "Under the guise of informed consent," Blackmun wrote, the law required the physician to provide "information that is not relevant to such consent, and, thus, it advances no legitimate state interest." *Thornburgh* v. *American Coll. of Obst. & Gyn.*, 476 U.S. 747 (1986), at 763.

141 *Id.*, at 447–49.

142 *Planned Parenthood of Mo.* v. *Danforth*, 428 U.S. 52 (1976), at 76.

143 *Id.*, at 75–76, 77. The law mandated the use of other abortion procedures, including hysterotomy and hysterectomy, that posed greater risks than saline amniocentesis, which was safer than normal childbirth. Although a safer abortifacient, prostaglandin injection, existed, apparently, it was not available in Missouri. *Id.*, at 76–77, 77–78.

144 *Id.*, at 78.

145 *Id.*, at 79.

146 *Id.*, at 99 (White, dissenting).

147 439 U.S. 379 (1979).

148 The act also required the physician to:

> [E]xercise that degree of professional skill, care and diligence to preserve the life and health of the fetus which such person would be required to exercise in order to preserve the life and health of any fetus intended to be born and not aborted and the abortion technique employed shall be that which would provide the best opportunity for the fetus to be aborted alive so long as a different technique would not be necessary in order to preserve the life or health of the mother.

> *Id.*, at 380–81, n. 1; Pa. Abortion Control Act § 5(a), 1974 Pa. Laws.

149 *Collautti*, 439 U.S., at 400.

150 *Id.*, at 394.

151 *Id.*, at 396.

152 *Id.*, at 395.

153 *Id.*, at 397–401.

154 *Id.*, at 400.

155 *Planned Parenthood Association* v. *Ashcroft*, 462 U.S. 476 (1983).

156 *Id.*

157 *Id.*, at 485–86.

158 *Id.*, at 499–500 (Opinion of Justice Blackmun).

159 *Thornburgh* v. *American Coll. of Obst. & Gyn.*, 476 U.S. 747 (1986).

160 *Id.*, at 768.

161 *Id.*

162 *Id.*, at 770.

163 *Id.*

164 *Id.,* at 771.

165 *Id.,* at 772.

166 429 U.S. 968 (1976).

167 *Akron v. Akron Center for Reproductive Health,* 462 U.S. 416 (1983), at 432–34; *Planned Parenthood Association. v. Ashcroft,* 462 U.S. 476 (1983), at 481–82.

168 462 U.S. 506 (1983).

169 *Id.,* at 516.

170 *Id.,* at 519.

171 *Akron,* 462 U.S., at 450.

172 *Id.,* at 449–51.

173 *Ashcroft,* 462 U.S., at 487.

174 *Id.,* at 486.

175 *Id.,* at 489.

176 *Id.,* at 490.

177 428 U.S. 106 (1976).

178 *Id.,* at 108.

179 432 U.S. 438 (1977).

180 *Id.,* at 444–45.

181 *Id.,* at 445.

182 *Id.,* at 446.

183 *Id.,* at 447.

184 Dissenting from the majority's opinion, Justice Brennan, with whom justices Marshall and Blackmun concurred, concluded that the state's refusal to fund nontherapeutic abortions burdened the indigent woman's constitutional right to terminate her pregnancy. *Id.,* at 449, 454 (Brennan, dissenting), 461 (Marshall, dissenting).

185 432 U.S. 519 (1977).

186 *Id.,* at 519, 521.

187 *Id.,* at 520.

188 *Id.,* at 522 (Brennan, dissenting).

189 432 U.S. 464 (1977).

190 *Id.,* at 465–66.

191 411 U.S. 1 (1973), at 17.

192 *Maher,* 432 U.S., at 471.

193 *Id.,* at 470–71.

194 *Id.,* at 473.

195 *Id.,* at 474, 475.

196 *Id.,* at 478–79.

197 *Id.,* at 480. Once again, justices Brennan, Marshall, and Blackmun dissented from the majority's opinion. Speaking for the dissenters, Brennan argued that the Court's decision retreated from *Roe* v. *Wade,* created special hardships for indigent women, and coerced poor women into bearing unwanted children. *Id.,* at 483, 484 (Brennan, dissenting).

198 *Harris* v. *McRae,* 448 U.S. 297 (1980); see also *Williams* v. *Zbaraz,* 442 U.S. 1309 (1979), where Justice Stevens (sitting as circuit justice) denied "a stay of the district court's order in enjoining the state of Illinois from refusing to fund under its medical assistance programs 'medically necessary' abortions performed prior to the viability if the fetus." *Id.,* at 1309, 1316.

199 *Id.*, at 302; Pub. L. No. 96-123, § 109, 93 Stat. 1926 (1979).

200 *Harris*, 448 U.S. at 307–11.

201 *Id.*, at 308.

202 *Id.*, at 309.

203 *Id.*, at 315.

204 *Id.*, at 316–17.

205 The Court rejected McRae's claim that the Hyde Amendment violates the establishment clause because it incorporates the Roman Catholic Church's doctrine concerning the commencement of human life and "the sinfulness of abortion." *Id.*, at 319.

206 *Id.*, at 322–23.

207 *Id.*, at 324–25.

208 *Id.*, at 334 (Brennan, dissenting).

209 *Id.*, at 338 (Marshall, dissenting).

210 *Id.*

211 *Id.*

212 *Id.*, at 343.

213 *Id.*, at 354 (Stevens, dissenting).

214 See *Maher* v. *Roe*, 432 U.S. 464 (1977), at 483 (Brennan, dissenting); *Griffin* v. *Illinois*, 351 U.S. 12 (1956), at 23 (Frankfurter, concurring); Anatole France, *Le Lys Rouge* (Paris: Calmann-Levy, Editeurs, 1894), at 117–18.

215 448 U.S. 297 (1980).

216 U.S. Congress, Senate, Committee on the Judiciary, Subcommittee on Constitutional Amendments, *Abortion—Part 4: Hearings on S.J. Res. 6, 10, 11, 91*, 94th Congress, 1st Session, March 10; April 11; May 9; June 19; and July 8, 1975 (Washington D.C.: Government Printing Office, 1976), at viii.; hereinafter cited as Senate Judiciary Committee, Subcommittee on Constitutional Amendments, *Abortion Hearings, Part IV* (1976). See also H.J. Res. 61, 94th Cong, 1st Sess. (1975), introduced by Representative Richard Ichord (D.-Mo.), which provided that "[t]he States shall have the power to regulate or forbid the voluntary termination of human pregnancy." U.S. Congress, House of Representatives, Committee on the Judiciary, Subcommittee on Civil and Constitutional Rights, *Proposed Constitutional Amendments on Abortion*, part 2, 94th Congress, 2nd Session, February 4–5; March 22–26, 1976 (Washington D.C.: Government Printing Office, 1976), at 519.

217 Senate Judiciary Committee, Subcommittee on Constitutional Amendments, *Abortion Hearings, Part IV* (1976), at 697.

218 Senate Judiciary Committee, Subcommittee on the Constitution, *Abortion Amendments*, vol. 1 (1983), at 13. See also H.J. Res. 372, 97th Cong, 1st Sess. (1981), and H.J. Res. 504, 97th Cong., 2d Sess. (1982).

219 See testimony of Professor Donald H. Regan, *id.*, at 561.

220 1982 *Congressional Quarterly Almanac*, at 403; S. Rept. 97-465 (1982).

221 S. Rept. 97-465 (1982), minority views, at 67–68.

222 Text in U.S. Congress, Senate, Committee on the Judiciary, Subcommittee on the Constitution, *Legal Ramifications of the Human Life Amendment*, 98th Congress, 1st Sess., February 28 and March 7, 1983 (Washington D.C.: Government Printing Office, 1983), at 10–11.

223 *Id.*, at 9.

224 See *id.*, at 10–11 and 16–17.

225 *Id.*, at 16–17.

226 See the prepared statement of Victor G. Rosenblum of the Americans United for Life, *id.*, at 115–24.

227 129 Cong. Rec. S9082 (daily ed. June 27, 1983).

228 *Id.*, at S9083.

229 129 Cong. Rec. 9310 (daily ed. June 28, 1983).

230 In 1975, Representative Sullivan proposed H.J. Res. 681 to the House of Representatives, which provided that "[t]he Congress within Federal jurisdiction and the several states within their jurisdictions shall have power to protect life including the unborn at every stage of biological development irrespective of age, health, or condition of physical dependency." H.J. Res. 681, 94th Cong., 1st Sess. (1975).

During the same Congress (94th Congress, 1975–76), representatives George M. O'Brien (R.-Ill.), James G. O'Hara (D.-Mich.), and Charles M. Price (D.-Ill.) introduced similar resolutions, which differed slightly in detail and language. H.J. Res. 180, 94th Cong., 1st Sess. (1975), H.J. Res. 681 and 783, 94th Cong., 2d Sess. (1976), respectively.

231 S.J. Res. 130, 93d, Cong., 1st Sess. (1973); S.J. Res. 6, H.J. Res 246, 405, 485, 94th Cong, 1st Sess. (1975); H.J. Res. 773, 775, 796, 94th Cong., 2d Sess. (1976); S.J. Res. 19, H.R. 392, H.J. Res. 13, 104, 97th Cong., 1st Sess. (1981); S.J. Res. 8, 13, H.J. Res. 82, 84, 98th Cong., 1st Sess. (1983); S.J. Res. 19, 21, 91, H.J. Res. 138, 99th Cong., 1st Sess. (1985); S.J. Res. 292, 99th Cong., 2d Sess. (1986).

232 S.J. Res. 6, 94th Cong., 1st Sess. (1975); Senate Judiciary Committee, Subcommittee on Constitutional Amendments, *Abortion Hearings, Part IV* (1976), at vii.

233 U.S. Congress, Senate, Committee on the Judiciary, Subcommittee on Constitutional Amendments, *Abortion—Part 1: Hearings on S.J. Res 119 and 130*, 93rd Congress, 2nd Session, March 6–7, and April 10, 1974 (Washington D.C.: Government Printing Office, 1974), at 2.

234 S.J. Res. 119, 93d Cong., 1st Sess. (1973); H.J. Res. 41, 99, 121, 132, 170, 187, 189, 197, 221, 238, 248, 259, 275, 279, 311, 317, 337, 383, 397, 403, 419, 422, 447, 451, 467, 520, 566, 567, 568, 658, 675, 602, 632, 741, 753, S.J. Res. 11, 94th Cong, 1st Sess. (1975); H.J. Res. 774, 779, 790, 834, 841, 842, 872, 942, 94th Cong., 2d Sess. (1976); H.J. Res. 27, 125, 127, 133, 198, 249, 380, S.J. Res. 11, 17, 18, 97th Cong., 1st Sess. (1981); H. J. Res. 15, 26, 73, 92, 114, 223, S.J. Res. 4, 9, 14, 24, 98th Cong., 1st Sess. (1983); H.J. Res. 641, 98th Cong., 2d Sess. (1983); H.J. Res. 94, 147, 165, 99th Cong., 1st Sess. (1985). S.J. Res. 291, 99th Cong., 2d Sess. (1986).

235 Immediately following *Roe* v. *Wade*, Senator James Buckley (R.-N.Y.) introduced S.J. Res. 11, which simply defined the fetus as a person deserving the protection of the Fifth and Fourteenth amendments. Senate Judiciary Committee, Subcommittee on Constitutional Amendments, *Abortion Hearings, Part IV* (1976), at vii.

236 *Id.*

237 Pub. L. No. 93-189, 87 Stat. 714, 716 (1973); Pub. L. No. 95-424, 92 Stat. 937, 946 (1978), respectively.

238 432 U.S. 464 (1977).

239 448 U.S. 297 (1980).

240 Pub. L. No. 94-439, 90 Stat. 1418, 1434 (1976).

241 See Pub. L. No. 97-12, 95 Stat. 14, 96, Title IV, § 109 (1981); Pub. L. No. 97-114, 95 Stat. 1565, 1588 (1981); Pub. L. No. 97-377, 96 Stat. 1830, 1860, Title VII, § 755

(1982); Pub. L. No. 98-139, 97 Stat. 871, 887, Title II, § 204 (1983); and Pub. L. No. 98-212, 97 Stat. 1421, 1447, Title VII, § 751 (1983).

242 See *San Antonio* v. *Rodriguez*, 411 U.S. 1 (1973), at 17; and *Maher* v. *Roe*, 432 U.S. 464 (1977), at 471.

243 The Continuing Appropriations Act for fiscal year 1980, for example, provides for three exceptions to the general prohibition: (1) in cases where carrying the fetus to term would endanger the woman's life, (2) in cases of rape or incest, and (3) in cases of ectopic pregnancy.

244 Pub. L. No. 95-205, 91 Stat. 1460 (1977); Pub. L. No. 95-457, 92 Stat. 1231, 1254, Title VIII, § 863 (1978); and Pub. L. No. 95-480, 92 Stat. 1567, 1586, Title II, § 210 (1978), respectively.

245 Pub. L. No. 95-205, 91 Stat. 1460 (1977).

246 S. 272, 273, 100th Cong., 1st Sess. (1987). S. 273 is an identical measure that applies to the Department of Defense.

247 S. 272, at 3.

248 *Id.*, at 3–4.

249 *Id.*, at 4–5.

250 See *Thornburgh* v. *American Coll. of Obst. & Gyn.*, 476 U.S. 747 (1986).

251 *Planned Parenthood of Mo.* v. *Danforth*, 428 U.S. 52 (1976).

252 *Bellotti* v. *Baird*, 443 U.S. 622 (1979).

253 *Akron* v. *Akron Center for Reproductive Health*, 462 U.S. 416 (1983).

254 S. 272, at 6–7, § 7(a).

255 See *Akron*, 462 U.S. 416 (1983), and *Thornburgh* v. *American Coll. of Obst. & Gyn.*, 476 U.S. 747 (1986).

256 Pub. L. No. 93-45, 87 Stat. 91, 95-96, Title IV (1973); Pub. L. No. 93-355, 88 Stat. 378, 385 (1974); Pub. L. No. 95-215, 91 Stat. 1503, 1507 (1977); and S. 557, 100th Cong., 2d Sess. (1988), respectively.

257 134 Cong. Rec. S163 (daily ed. Jan. 27, 1988).

258 S. 2372, 97th Cong., 2d Sess. (1982). See also H.R. 5862, 6455, S. 2148, 97th Cong., 2d Sess. (1982); H.R. 618, S. 467, 98th Cong., 1st Sess. (1983); H.R. 555, 2287, S. 26, 99th Cong., 1st Sess. (1985).

259 *Roe* v. *Wade*, 410 U.S. 113 (1973), at 162.

260 S. 2148, 97th Cong., 2d Sess. (1982), at 3.

261 S. 46, 131 Cong. Rec. S19-S20 (daily ed. Jan. 3, 1985).

262 *Id.*, at S20.

263 *Id.*

264 *Id.*

265 See 121 Cong. Rec. 11982 (1975).

266 H.R. 16118, 15636, 14760, 14337, 93d Cong., 2d Sess. (1974); H.R. 1133, 1515, 5658, 94th Cong., 1st Sess. (1975); H.R. 1914, 4273, 4274, 7422, 95th Cong., 1st Sess. (1977); H.R. 993, 96th Cong., 1st Sess. (1979); H.R. 867, 97th Cong., 1st Sess. (1981); H.R. 523, 98th Cong., 1st Sess. (1983); H.R. 80, 99th Cong., 1st Sess. (1985).

In 1976 Representative Paul introduced a bill (H.R. 15169) that would abolish the Supreme Court's appellate jurisdiction over state antiabortion cases. In addition to impairing the Court's function of promoting constitutional supremacy and providing a uniform construction of national law, the bill would promote serious conflicts between the state and federal courts. In some states, federal and state courts might rule differently on the constitutionality of antiabortion laws. Without recourse to the Supreme Court, these conflicting rulings would leave fundamental rights in doubt, create friction between the state and federal judiciaries, and undermine the comity between the two judiciaries that is essential in a federal system.

267 H.R. 5440, S. 2138, 96th Cong., 1st Sess. (1979); H.R. 7307, 96th Cong., 2d Sess. (1980); H.R. 73, S. 583, 97th Cong., 1st. Sess. (1981).

268 H.R. 8682, 93d Cong., 1st Sess. (1973); H.R. 900, H.R. 3225, S. 158, 97th Cong., 1st Sess. (1981); S. 26, 98th Cong., 1st Sess. (1983).

269 H.R. 993, 96th Cong., 1st Sess. (1979).

270 121 Cong. Rec. 11983 (1975).

271 *Id.*

272 127 Cong. Rec. E2263 (daily ed. May 12, 1981).

273 128 Cong. Rec. S399 (daily ed. Feb. 4, 1982).

274 *Id.*

275 128 Cong. Rec. S1040 (daily ed. Feb. 24, 1982).

276 *Id.*

277 *Id.*

278 *Id.*, at S1040–S1041.

279 *Id.*, at S1041.

280 S. 2138, 96th Cong., 1st Sess. (1979).

281 62 U.S. (21 How.) 506 (1859).

282 80 U.S. (13 Wall.) 397 (1872).

283 This analysis suggests that Senator Hatch's bill would raise serious equal protection questions. See *Shapiro* v. *Thompson*, 394 U.S. 618 (1969).

284 See chapter 6, note 162.

285 See U.S. Congress, Senate, Committee on the Judiciary, Subcommittee on Separation of Powers, *Human Life Bill: Hearings on S. 158*, 97th Congress, 1st Session, April 23–24, May 20–21, June 1, 10, 12, 18, 1982 (Washington D.C.: Government Printing Office: 1982); hereinafter cited as Senate Judiciary Committee, Subcommittee on Separation of Powers, *Hearings on S. 158* (1982).

286 127 Cong. Rec. S8420 (daily ed. July 24, 1981).

287 *Id.*

288 *Id.*

289 For a legal analysis of the pros and cons of S. 158, see, generally, Senate Judiciary Committee, Subcommittee on Separation of Powers, *Hearings on S. 158* (1982), especially the testimony of Laurence H. Tribe, at 248–56, John T. Noonan, Jr., at 261–75, Victor G. Rosenblum, at 469–91, Craig J. Blakely et. al., at 527–75, and Theodore Eisenberg, at 580–606. Also see the following articles reprinted in the hearings: Galebach, Stephen H., "A Human Life Statute," at 205–83, and Uddo, Basile J., "A Wink From the Bench: The Federal Courts and Abortion," at 356–422.

290 384 U.S. 641 (1966).

291 *Id.*, at 651–52, note 10.

292 See *Mississippi University for Women* v. *Hogan*, 458 U.S. 718 (1982), at 732–33; and *EEOC* v. *Wyoming*, 460 U.S. 226 (1983), at 262 (Burger, dissenting).

293 Rotunda, 64 *Geo. L. J.*, at 860–61 (1976).

Epilogue

1 Choper, *Judicial Review*, at 4.

2 Bickel, *Least Dangerous Branch*, at 16.

3 369 U.S. 186, at 267 (Frankfurter, dissenting).

4 347 F. Supp. 689 (E.D. Pa. 1972), at 707.

5 Fellman, David, "Original Intent—A Footnote," 49 *Rev. of Politics* 574–78 (1987), at 575.

6 *Id.*, at 578.

7 *Id.*

8 Ely, *Democracy and Distrust*, at 102.

9 Quoted in Silva, *American Government*, at 183.

Table of Cases Cited

....

Index

....